Humanistic Foundations
of Education

John Martin Rich
University of Texas

Charles A. Jones Publishing Company
Worthington, Ohio

1 2 3 4 5 6 7 8 9 10 / 75 74 73 72 71

Library of Congress Catalog
Card Number: 73-130867

Printed in the United States of America

TO MY PARENTS

Preface

This book addresses itself to some present great issues. It is organized in such a way that educational concerns, as conceived in the broader sense, provide the framework, as well as the problems, issues, and content, for discussion. Different modes of inquiry—philosophical, sociological, psychological—constitute the basis for treating these concerns. A problems approach is used whenever appropriate because inquiry is more likely to be generated by problem situations than by finished conceptual systems. Learning is better facilitated when one is faced with conflicting positions and problematic situations rather than authoritative answers. Such an approach helps the individual to examine his own assumptions and to develop warranted grounds for his beliefs.

The pursuit of the question "What does it mean to be fully human?" constitutes the underlying theme of the book. Educational institutions concern themselves with this question, or a modified form of it, in various ways, and problems arise over conflicting interpretations. Clarification of basic issues in the teaching-learning process, knowledge and the curriculum, and the purpose of education in the larger society may be gained by an investigation of this theme, and a number of philosophical concerns in education can be illuminated by this process.

Humanistic Foundations of Education is divided into three parts. The first part focuses on "Educators and Learners" by examining the question of man, the student as a person, the teaching process, and the educated man. The second part centers on "The Content of Instruction" by first studying the problems of knowledge and education, and then relating these to the sciences and humanities. The final part centers on "The Role of Education in Society" by examining the New Left and conflicting roles in higher education, equal opportunities and the control of education, and future prospects for education and human development.

I wish to thank Thomas Gregory, Indiana University, Everett Kircher, Ohio State University, Harry S. Broudy, University of Illinois, Joseph Wetmore, Ohio Wesleyan University, James W. Merritt, Northern Illinois University, Martin Levit, University of Missouri at Kansas City, Ayers Bagley, University of Minnesota, Charles Galloway, Ohio State University, and Prudence Dyer, Drake University for their helpful comments and suggestions. I also wish to thank Joyce, my wife, with whom I discussed many of the ideas that later took shape in the book, and Mrs. Myrna Schoenfeld and Miss Barbara Stivers for their efficient typing. I am, of course, responsible for any of the book's shortcomings.

John Martin Rich

Contents

Preface   v

Part One   **Educators and Learners   1**

Chapter One   **The Question of Man   3**

Introduction   3
Biological and Cultural
   Bases of Life   7
Psychological Views of Man   11
Marxist Philosophy of Man   23
Religious Perspectives   30
Existentialist Perspectives   47
Perspectives of the Drama   52
A Reassessment of Man   56
Questions for Discussion   57
For Further Reading   58

Chapter Two   **The Student as a Person   63**

Study as Work:
    The Process of Alienation   63
Identity and Alienation   68
Dehumanization in the Classroom   74
The Concept of a Person   80
Questions for Discussion   87
For Further Reading   88

Chapter Three   **The Teaching Process   93**

The Need to Study Teaching   93
An Analysis of Teaching   95
A Theory of Instruction   102
Empirical Studies of Teaching   105
Questions for Discussion   115
For Further Reading   115

Chapter Four   **The Educated Man   119**

Introduction   119
Misconceptions About the
    Educated Man   120
Criteria for Assessing the
    Educated Man   129
Questions for Discussion   139
For Further Reading   140

Part Two   **The Content of
                                    Instruction   143**

Chapter Five   **Knowledge and Education   145**

Students' Questions About
    Knowledge   145
The Search for Certitude   147
Knowledge and Belief   154
Knowing Oneself   160

Chapter Five (continued)

Relevant Knowledge   170
Questions for Discussion   175
For Further Reading   176

Chapter Six   **The Sciences   179**

Scientific Approaches to
    Knowledge   179
Science and Human Affairs   189
Science and the Curriculum   196
Questions for Discussion   201
For Further Reading   202

Chapter Seven   **The Humanities   205**

The Meaning of the Humanities   205
Dimensions of the Humanities   216
The Humanities and the
    Sciences   225
Questions for Discussion   236
For Further Reading   236

Part Three   **The Role of
                                         Education in Society   239**

Chapter Eight   **The New Left and Conflicting
                                         Roles of Higher Education   241**

Role Conflict in the Development
    of the American University   242
The Impact of Student
    Movements   255
Humanistic Roles for Higher
    Education   265
Questions for Discussion   268
For Further Reading   270

Chapter Nine   **Equal Opportunities and the**
                                    Control of Education   275

                                    Misconceptions Over the
                                        Control of Education   276
                                    The Basis of Social Control   277
                                    Bureaucratic Educational
                                        Systems   283
                                    The Concept of Equal
                                        Educational Opportunity   285
                                    Problems of Desegregation   296
                                    Questions for Discussion   302
                                    For Further Reading   302

Chapter Ten   **Future Prospects for Education**
                                    and Human Development   307

                                    Imminent Perils to Man's Future   309
                                    Education, Productivity,
                                        and the Meritocracy   319
                                    Autonomy and Full Humanness   324
                                    Questions for Discussion   329
                                    For Further Reading   329

                                    Index   333

Part One
Educators and Learners

Chapter One
The Question of Man

Introduction

Man does not know what he wants his life to be because he does not know who he is and where he wants to go. Modern man is the confused child of his age, a reflection of the confusions of the times in which he lives. Living as he is in a period of unprecedented rapidity of change when sacrosanct values of the past are eroding before his eyes, he searches frenetically for some basis of certainty as a grounding for his beliefs and a haven of security. It then seems natural for those who fail to find this sense of certainty in the present to turn their gaze to the past to recapture, even though fleetingly, nostalgic visions of a glorious bygone age, whether imaginary or real. Others seek through the political process to resurrect past conditions and practices. Except for a temporary but false sense of psychological security that these tendencies may provide, they ultimately are self-defeating in a time when clear perception and a vision of a socially meaningful future, as well as the will to do the work and to plan such a future, are urgently needed.

3

Part of the task of envisioning and planning such a future is to make some assessment of man himself in order to find out who he is and what he can become. The basic limitations upon the creation of a better future is man, and before plans for future arrangements can be made, an assessment of man and his capabilities is needed.

Many of us, particularly youth, are concerned about the future. How, one may wonder, does this concern relate to education? Education must not only prepare youth to live effectively today and during the immediate years following graduation, but it also must equip youth with the types of skills needed to plan a more distant future intelligently. And as already indicated, a clearer understanding of man can aid in this process.

Education is concerned with man, not things, and to know whether educational programs and practices are sound, one must consider the person to be educated. An understanding of man provides us also with an understanding of his creations, particularly the type of world that he has created and the types of worlds he may likely create in the future. The purpose of our inquiry is not to make education and its aims conform to man's nature, but rather, to take into account the many factors that can be compatibly related to the educational process. Various perspectives on human nature provide imaginative frameworks to view the possibilities that one may find in different designs of the educational process.

In attempting to fulfill the above objectives a basic theme is found in the question, "What does it mean to be fully human?" Our assumption is that many persons do not become fully human, which does not mean they are "inhuman," although sometimes their acts are characterized by that label. Many people do not get all they can out of life; their present life is ineffectual and frustrating in many ways; their future is poorly conceived and inadequately planned. They are only half alive. What may come to mind now is Charles Atlas' ad or a circular extolling the merits of the Great Books. One of them tells us that we are only half alive because our bodies remain underdeveloped, while the other warns that our minds are becoming flabby from disuse. What would we say about one who needs to enroll in both courses?

To be fully human will equip man with all of the ability and creativity to live meaningfully and fruitfully at a high level in today's complex world. This surely is a big order. There are certain assumptions in advancing this claim. Man need not call on superhuman, divine, magical, or mystical powers to advance his estate in the world. He has within himself the ability to secure the Good Life, and if world civilization

Education is concerned
with man. . . .

is to survive and advance, it lies with man himself to use his abilities creatively to assure such ends. Education can be harnessed to whatever ideals society chooses; but if education is to secure human betterment, it ignores at its own peril the provision of educative situations that help make man more fully human.

Whether or not we realize it, all of us operate in our social relations with concepts of human nature. How often have we heard, "People are basically selfish," or, "Everyone is interested in himself," or "Most people really want to do good." These statements could be multiplied many times, but, undoubtedly, others will come to mind from one's own experience that further illustrate the point. Some people tend to judge others by gross, stereotyped views, while still others are more flexible in their response by attempting to evaluate persons on more of an individual basis. In any case, people operate with some rough and ready theory of human nature, even though their concepts may vary from unitary and consistent to multiple and conflicting. Sooner or later one draws on his conceptions of human nature when relating to others. It would be better, then, if these conceptions had some basis in fact and were reasonable and realistic.

Our knowledge of human nature, however, is not as exact and as extensive as our knowledge of the physical world. This discrepancy is due in part to the fact that historically speaking man first turned his attention to those things farthest removed from himself, such as questions concerning the heavens and the solar system. With the rise of modern science in the early sixteenth century, great progress began to be made in the physical sciences while the social sciences did not become independent disciplines until the nineteenth century. True, some valuable insights about man were provided by philosophers in ancient Greece and the late Middle Ages even though the masses usually were guided by custom, myth, superstition, and folklore.

The social and behavioral sciences have advanced rapidly in spite of their late beginnings, but the natural sciences are still more sophisticated and have a larger store of cumulative knowledge. The natural sciences have also received a larger proportion of the subsidies for basic research from the federal government and private foundations. Nonetheless, a substantial body of knowledge presently exists in the social and behavioral sciences; yet the findings are often atomized and fractionated among the separate disciplines. We will attempt to bring together some of these findings and relate them to our purposes.

A simple, unequivocal response such as to the question "5 + 7 = ?" will not answer the question, "What does it mean to be fully human?"

Neither does the question take the form of "What was the date of Lincoln's birth?" or "How much does Smith weigh?" Such questions are mathematical, historical, and empirical questions; and, although historical and empirical findings may be needed in dealing with the original question, these findings do not supply "answers" in a straightforward, simple, and unequivocal way. Different interpretations of the theme will turn up, and these interpretations may be evaluated on their respective merits with reference to the illumination they provide and the social and educational consequences that accrue from acting on the basis of a particular interpretation. There are social, educational, political, philosophical, and personal factors that will warrant consideration as the various positions are examined, and these factors become more intelligible as the pursuit of the original question in light of several major perspectives progresses.

Biological and Cultural Bases of Life

Scientific work within the past hundred years has established that all living things — men, animals, plants, microbes — have many physiochemical processes in common. All living things must maintain a supply of energy by synthesizing protein compounds which have approximately the same amino acid composition for enzyme activity(1).* Life itself is interdependent; no single structure or process defines life. Rather, life is characterized by complex structures in which a cluster of mutually dependent processes are integrated into a unique and orderly pattern(2).

All men, by the very fact that they are *Homo sapiens,* have certain basic drives which cause tensions until gratified. The drives of breathing, thirst, hunger, rest and sleep, elimination, and sex are those commonly mentioned. Potency of drives usually is indicated by their urgency in galvanizing an organism to action and the length of time that may elapse without gratification before serious damage results in the organism. Thus, it would appear that the drive for oxygen is the most potent and the sex drive the least, since in the case of denied gratification of the latter drive — frustrating as it may be — no deaths have been reported.

Drives result from the basic physiological needs of man, but culture determines how these needs will be expressed. The culture determines

---

*Notes appear in numbered sequence at the end of each chapter.

which drives will be gratified and which ones will be suppressed or sublimated; and among those to be satisfied, the culture determines the mode by which they may be expressed in a socially acceptable manner. For example, man does not satisfy the hunger drive in any way he chooses, but in socially approved ways if he does not wish to be ridiculed or socially ostracized. Whether he will cultivate the soil or purchase his food is determined by prevailing economic conditions of his society. The culture, and particularly the group from which he acquires many of his values, the reference group, defines what is edible, what is a delicacy, and the manners and customs surrounding group dining. Not all foods in one culture are thought edible, even though in another culture they may be considered delicacies. Whether one eats with his hands, knife and fork, chopsticks, or other utensil is culturally determined. Biological factors surrounding the need for good nutrition may be observed by one culture and ignored by another. Biological factors set up the outer limits (that man must provide nutritive materials for his system in order to survive), while culture determines the content and expression within the broad and expansive outer limits.

Similarly, the sexual drive has been restricted by cultural norms. Among Puritans, Victorians, Medievalists, and others, the sex drive was deemed sinful, wicked, and the work of the Devil. These attitudes became imbedded in the Western culture during certain historical periods and were enforced by a system of rewards and punishments (either in the form of laws, norms, or a combination of both). The fundamental biological problem ensnaring persons of this outlook was that their suppression and denial of sex, if carried to its logical conclusion, would extinguish the race. In order to avoid this outcome, certain socially approved forms of sexual intercourse were decreed within the institution of marriage, namely, for procreation but not for pleasure.

One may believe that there are no cultural factors intruding upon the oxygen drive, but this assumption would be a mistaken one, for some believe that it is all right for people to breathe polluted air, while others call attention to the dangers of pollution.

Culture, as important as it is, needs a precise interpretation at this point. Numerous definitions of culture can be found(3). The definition presented here will be a working one to be used for discussion and analysis. Culture could be thought of as the nonbiological aspects of human life, consisting of artifacts and technology (material aspects) and the customs, traditions, values, and way of life of a society (nonmaterial aspects). Persons are born into an established culture and acquire the distinctive traits and patterns of behavior that are socially acceptable. This process, known as "acculturation," is one that all human beings, irrespective of what part of the world or what strata of society they are born in, go through in order to learn their expected social roles and become an accepted member of the group. But the forms and content of the acculturation process vary from one culture to another due to different traditions and value systems. Thus, one learns how he is expected to behave, how to make necessary distinctions in relating to others holding positions of differing degrees of influence, and how to interpret his acts with reference to a system of socially imposed rewards and punishments so that his behavior will be essentially gratifying rather than frustrating. Culture, then, is learned behavior; it is a learning process that begins at birth, continues in concentrated form through the use of formal schooling, and takes various informal arrangements throughout the life span of the individual. Culture is invested with considerable emotion because the process begins early in the life of the individual and is conducted by authority figures — such as parents, teachers, ministers — whom the individual is taught to respect and obey. As he continues to practice what has been taught, he usually comes to accept it as being natural, right, and good, and may look upon differing cultural patterns as bizarre, foolish, or immoral. This outlook places schools in a difficult position, because not only are they expected to foster acculturation, but also to develop the abilities of reflective thinking and broaden the cultural background of the individual as he learns to entertain views regarding ways of life that differ from his own. All societies place restrictions upon schools as to how far they may carry the latter function. Arguments about this issue center on whether the school is too restrictive or overly permissive in handling these important decisions.

In looking at the interaction of biological and cultural factors, it may seem that the basic drives of man are those features he shares with the animal kingdom and that the drives are shared in their own peculiar form by the higher vertebrates. Yet, it should be noted that the expression of human drives is culturally determined in such a manner that various culturally approved elaborations transform their manifestations from their original unrestricted expression. They have acquired an elaborate symbolization and a network of cultural meanings that they did not possess in their original state.

Man has various distinguishing traits that demarcate him from the animal kingdom. There is not merely one trait, such as reason as Aristotle would have us believe, that distinguishes man, but he has a highly developed cerebral cortex, walks upright, and has an opposable thumb for tool making. He not only is conscious but is aware that he possesses consciousness. He has a comic sense and can laugh at the inscrutability of the world and his fate. He also has complex emotions and feelings that lead frequently to the development of imposing ethical systems. Every other species but man has met the problem of survival by body differentiation and specialization of structure and function in order to adapt to and utilize the environment effectively. These specialized body forms restrict animals to certain types of environment and further changes and adaptations are slow to develop. Man's greater adaptability is related to the traits previously enumerated. Since man is a more complex, highly developed organism, the period of dependency lengthened for the development of these traits, and with his greater brain capacity and ability to develop linguistic systems for communication purposes, man has relied less and less on instinctive patterns of behavior. Man's behavior, therefore, is largely learned because he is not controlled primarily by instincts. These traits have made possible the development of human culture.

Whether these traits are distinct and unique or are only more highly developed forms continuous with the less developed forms of the primates is not as important for our purposes as it has been for some writers. Our contention would be that man's biological drives in their great complexity and variety of cultural expression are every bit as human as his other traits, though some people believe that the desires to which the drives give rise have too often led men to sin and degradation and are nothing more than animal characteristics. Animal behavior, spoken of here, is not viewed with a sneering condescension due to the belief that all human traits invariably are superior. Just knowing what human traits and animal traits are does not reveal that one set is good and the other bad. To make such distinctions is to assume a set of values which would need to be examined separately. Neither is it logically justified to infer from human traits the type of educational system some believe uniquely appropriate to them. Our study of these traits only gives us an idea of what man is like and provides a rough understanding of what he may be capable of becoming. But this understanding is important because it may provide us with different perspectives on human existence and enlarge the range of conceptual possibilities previously entertained. In order to broaden these perspectives one can look at certain significant views of human nature(4).

Psychological Views of Man

Freudianism

Sigmund Freud's psychoanalysis was brought by his disciples to the United States, and it soon spread rapidly, taking deep root in our culture and offering one of the most influential theories of human nature for the twentieth century. Many of his views, particularly those on sex, struck deeply at the Victorian morality of the time and aroused considerable opposition. In spite of this reaction, the Freudian system continued to gain converts and practitioners until more recent years when the efficacy of psychoanalysis has sharply been questioned and competing systems have gained strength.

Freud postulated driving forces inherent in human nature. He held that not all impulses are based on the seeking of pleasure, for some, as he found in treating traumatic neuroses, are satisfied by the reinstatement of painful traumatic experiences. Organic matter has the tendency toward the reinstatement of an earlier condition, to return to its primeval inorganic state(5). There would be a regressive tendency in organic life, the goal of which is death. This force he referred to as Thantos.

But by postulating Thantos, Freud was faced with the dilemma of accounting for reproductive cells and the sexual instinct for the perpetuation of the race and was, therefore, led to the acceptance of instincts for the sustaining and enhancing of life processes(6). These instincts he called Eros.

Freud's dualism centered around the sexual instincts, Eros, and the aggressive instincts, Thantos, whose aim is destruction(7). The opposition of these two forces creates the phenomenon of life, and these two instincts are inherent in all living substances. Eros and Thantos instinct are "fused, blended, and mingled with each other . . ."(8) The death instinct of the single cell is neutralized by the combination of unicellular into multicellular organisms, and the death instinct expresses itself destructively toward the external world and other organisms. But it may also be directed against itself. In the Freudian system man is faced with the intractable dilemma of either turning the aggressive instincts against others or turning them against himself. Thus, Freud developed a theoretical position to support his belief in the inherent evilness of man.

From this conception follows the explanation for sadism and masochism. Sadism represents a fusion of the erotic and aggressive instincts turned outward toward others, while masochism represents the fusion of these instincts turned against oneself for the purposes of self-destruction(9).

Eros and Thantos relate to the fundamental drives but do not explain how these drives are organized in the personality. This personality organization can be understood more clearly by examining the conceptions of id, ego, and super ego.

The id is the first dimension of personality which develops; it lies wholly in the unconscious and is, thus, beyond conscious awareness. The id is mentioned figuratively as a "cauldron full of seething excitations."(10) The id cannot reveal what it desires, but is constituted by contradictory impulses existing side by side without neutralizing one another or separating. These impulses combine in formations under overpowering pressure to discharge their energy. The id is impulsive, blind, and irrational.

The ego represents a portion of the id that has been modified by proximity and influence of the external world(11). It represents the external world to the id and thereby keeps the id's blind, impulsive efforts from leading to its own destruction. The id operates on the basis of the pleasure principle, a psychological apparatus that pursues pleasurable excitement and attempts to avoid pain. Pleasurable excitement has the effect of decreasing the amount of stimuli present in the psychic apparatus, while pain increases the amount of stimuli.

The ego represents a gradual development in the history of the race and the individual. The ego represents everything to an infant, and only later does he make a distinction between himself and the external world. Pain and unpleasant sensations help bring about recognition of the external world. Gradually he learns to protect himself from unpleasant external sensations and, by so doing, begins to adopt the "reality principle," which competes with the pleasure principle. While the ego remains addicted to pleasure, it learns that some pleasures must be postponed and pains must be borne. It must take the facts of life, the requirements for existence into account, and this can be facilitated by work, which is of utmost importance in bringing the person more closely to reality(12).

The super ego is the last development in the individual. Part of the ego can be split off when it assumes a self-observing, self-critical function. This mental realm, while also a function of the ego, has a degree of independence to pursue its own ends. It tends to dominate the ego in a severe and cruel manner by exacting stringent moral standards. The super ego is associated with morality, religion, and a social sense(13). Small children do not exhibit restraints in seeking pleasure; inhibitions are first instilled by parents by threat of punishment and the child's fear of the loss of their love. The child begins to develop a super ego by adopting the moral codes and restrictions advocated by parents or their surrogates. The super ego becomes a parental substitute and threatens the ego with punishment for transgressions just as the parents did. The ego has three severe masters: the external world, the super ego, and the id. The claims they make upon the ego differ widely and frequently appear incompatible. One must gain knowledge of the external world and consider the necessities it imposes. The ego is under the demands of the super ego to adhere to moral codes and social traditions. And finally, the ego is in the service of the id and tries to respond to its insatiable impulses for pleasure(14).

For Freud, repression is the basic idea on which psychoanalysis rests. The purpose of repression is to avoid pain, and its basis lies in rejecting something and keeping it out of consciousness(15). Repression goes on continually unless it is denied by the self. All of this activity takes a great deal of energy unless the repressive forces can be abrogated. Repressed ideas move toward consciousness but must be repressed if their awareness would bring too much pain. The conflict between one's desires, particularly sexual ones, and the moral codes of society constitutes repression. Instincts do not become part of consciousness, only the ideas and feelings which instincts represent; thus, repression prevents the ideational aspects of instincts from becoming conscious. The affects or feelings and emotions frequently become detached from the ideational factors which created them causing the affect to displace itself, such as in the case of displaced aggression. Repression, Freud believed, inhibits the expression of affect.

The repressed ideation and affect become part of what Freud called the unconscious. But the unconscious is more than that which is repressed: it is the driving force in psychic life. Unconscious impulses are dynamic and are forever pressing for expression and, as in the case of sexual impulses forbidden expression by taboos and codes, manifest themselves in devious forms such as mental illness.

The problem for psychoanalysis is to get at the root of the symptoms (mental illness) which lies in the unconscious. The ideational factors surrounding sex become repressed in early childhood as the child goes through stages of infantile sexuality — oral, anal, and genital eroticism — through which the individual must move successfully, avoiding fixating at any one stage, in order to avoid neurotic behavior. Freud was the first to develop a theory of infantile sexuality and show its importance for the treatment of psychoneurosis. Most of his colleagues repudiated it and championed the older notion that sexual awakening and its concomitant problems began at the onset of pubescence.

Freud presents several psychological types of individuals based on their life styles: the erotic, the narcissistic, and the obsessional(16). The erotic type centers his existence on love and, above all, on being loved. These individuals dread the loss of love and are dominated by the id. The obsessional type is controlled primarily by the super ego, and rather than fearing the loss of love, is governed by the anxiety of conscience. This type manifests independence, self-reliance, and are the "true upholders of civilization." The ego is dominant in the narcissistic individual and his concern is primarily one of self-preservation. This type is active, assumes leadership, and tends to stimulate cultural developments and changes.

Freud also notes that there are mixed types which are found more frequently than the pure types discussed above. However, he only makes a limited presentation of these types.

A Reassessment of Freudian Psychology.   Freud's contribution to psychology, psychotherapy, and modern man's views of himself has been very great. Psychoanalysis provided for the first time a perspective on the inner workings of psychic processes by analyzing the subterranean dynamics of the unconscious and thereby providing an understanding of the causes of neurotic behavior. The psychoanalytic approach also offered a lengthy and complex mode of treatment for psychoneurosis and, in the hands of thousands of clinicians, served as a testing ground for Freud's theories. Freud also brought to light the role of infantile sexuality in the life of the individual and the pervasiveness of the sex drive in human life as well as the distortions in its expression, due to the impress of society and the super ego, which sometimes leads to neurotic behavior. This approach was a healthy corrective to the Victorian attitudes of the day and helped bring about more recent open discussions and research into human sexual life.

Some of his followers, such as Carl Jung and Alfred Adler, who later broke from Freud to form their own systems, disagreed as to the importance of the sexual drive in human behavior (but their disagreement was not on puritanical grounds). They constructed systems, with varying degrees of success, that delineated and explored the dynamics of man's inner life.

Freud considered man as a total individual who had to be examined piecemeal, partitioned off for scientific study. His work does not convey a view of man as a complete person; psychology is not viewed holistically or organically. Freud's treatment of man is thoroughly mechanistic in the best of the nineteenth century tradition of science. Events and entities are related to one another externally rather than organically. The self, personality, consciousness are mere epiphenomena or by-products of the pleasure-principle. The processes of the psyche are considered to be following laws or are law-like, but without purpose. The notion of man as a purposive, goal seeking organism who frequently strives for less mundane goals than that of pleasure fulfillment has no place in Freud's system. The explanation of one's present behavior in terms of early modes of adjustment is mechanically based on laws of association, which explain the behavior of the whole in terms of the parts without attempting to show how the parts come together to make the whole. How the parts affect other parts through mechanical laws is never clearly explained. The parts are viewed as antecedent to the whole which somehow constitutes a derived product. Biological research does not support the position that parts are antecedent to structures and are primary in relation to the whole. In fact, the opposite is held to be the case.

Relation in Freud's mechanistic position is a causal determinism that proceeds in a lineal fashion by relating every present act to antecedent acts beginning in infancy. Man, in this scheme of things, is not free to act; a hard determinism causes his present behavior, and what man is results from early childhood influences. Freud erroneously believed that a causal determinism was necessary in order to make prediction possible. Physical science has relinquished its earlier views of mechanism and causal determinism; but the newer conceptions are only slowly making their way into the social and behavioral sciences, which in a concern to be considered "scientific" have aped nineteenth century science. Freud never really handled the dilemma of trying to cure patients whose lives were heavily determined and lacking in the needed freedom of choice to make decisions and perform actions that would promote therapy and lead to a successful treatment.

Man is caught up in infantile strivings to serve the pleasure principle. The workings of human life are reduced to the pursuit of pleasurable excitement and the avoidance of pain. That man is no more than a pleasure seeking animal who inevitably will be frustrated in this pursuit overlooks the countless persons throughout human history who have followed a course of action in pursuit of a goal that has lead, frequently with their prior awareness, to pain and suffering. Nowhere in Freud's system do we find man the purposive, organically viewed being who creates ideals, lofty goals, and noble values and pursues them in the face of hardships and suffering.

The problem with Freud is that he built a theory of human nature by studying man at his worst. What we know about personality and motivation has all too often been gleaned from the study of neurotics and other sick people rather than man at his best(17).

Freud conceived the test of his theory in the psychoanalysis-patient relationship. The success of psychoanalysis, in spite of its popular acceptance particularly in the United States, is scarcely impressive(18) and would lead us to seriously question the worth of such lengthy and expensive treatment.

Behaviorism

In the efforts of psychology to become a science, it detached itself from the speculations of philosophy and attempted to emulate the rigor found in the scientific methods used by the natural sciences. Structuralism, a development during the nineteenth century, was the earliest school of psychology which attempted to apply a scientific approach. However, behaviorists during the early part of the twentieth century objected strenuously to the methodology of the structuralists and their attempt to study consciousness and interior life. The early behaviorists believed that if psychology is to become a science, it must focus its attention on overt behavior rather than the mysterious inner workings of mind and consciousness.

John B. Watson is generally considered the father of behaviorism, and in his writings(19) can be found the new approach that promised to make psychology a full-fledged science.

Watson's system, based on a stimulus-response model, was deterministic. He believed that given the stimulus, psychology could predict the response; and, on the other hand, if given the response, the nature of the effective stimulus could be specified(20).

Behaviorism, as he saw it, should become empirical in approach and discard all references to consciousness and mental states. Instead, the study of the human organism was to concentrate on overt and observable forms of behavior generated from the muscles, tissues, and glands. Watson was reductionistic in his claim that all behavior can be interpreted in physical-chemical terms. The workings of the nervous system and glands could be observed in their manifestations in overt behavior. Human behavior, he held, can actually be reduced to a sensory-central-motor reaction. It involves a chain of incoming stimuli along the sensory nerves to the central nervous system and then outward over neural pathways to the muscular system for overt response. Memory, too, was explained reductionistically as created by residues of sensory stimulation combined with kinesthetic elements of the mouth muscles in implicit speech processes.

Watson was an environmentalist in the nature-nurture controversy. Humans, he held, have only the instincts of fear, rage, and love, and these were limited in comparison with the importance of experience. He declared that if he were given a dozen healthy infants he could take one at random and make of him any type of specialist — doctor, lawyer, thief, etc(21). This development would take place through education, which for Watson is nothing more than conditioning. The emotions as well, derived as they are from the basic instincts of fear, rage, and love, are developed by means of conditioning. Personality, in this scheme of things, is considered the end-product of habit systems.

All behavior can be divided into explicit and implicit forms. Explicit behavior includes all observable activities performed by the muscular system; whereas implicit behavior includes glandular, visceral, and nerve functions as well as some muscle contractions. Watson wished to avoid the introspective accounts used by the structuralist in studying consciousness, so he defined speech as a verbal report and a form of explicit behavior and thinking as subvocal behavior of the implicit variety. Thus, there would be no need to deal with unobservable data.

In spite of the worthwhile attempt and some pioneering work to place psychology on firmer scientific footing, Watson's approach is vulnerable on several counts. The reduction of thinking, feeling, and perceiving to certain implicit physiological states is a gross oversimplification of these complex processes. Man becomes nothing more than a stimulus-response organism built primarily by a process of conditioning. Behaviorism as a theory of behavior becomes highly mechanistic, failing to account for purposive behavior and unable to provide a satisfactory explanation for the higher processes of learning in the form of cognitive and affective processes. Psychology must also deal with unobservable data. Watson, in admitting the verbal report, left the door open for introspection — which he strove to avoid. Yet he continued to believe that unobservable data was not a domain for psychological investigation. With the stimulus-response model, based as it is on mechanistic cause and effect assumptions, all novel behavior is impossible; present behavior is primarily conceived as the recapitulation of past behavior established through the conditioning process.

B. F. Skinner.   Skinner is an influential contemporary behaviorist who avoids deductive theories and relies on an inductive approach in his experimentation. His investigations start with empirical data and proceed tentatively to limit range generalizations. His positivistic approach is reminiscent of the tenor of Auguste Comte's positivism, and his inductive method falls within the grand tradition of Francis Bacon and John Stuart Mill.

Skinner rejects any method of inquiry that does not depend upon sensory observation. His method proceeds by first clearly identifying the observed data. Then the data are placed in classes, and laws are established to indicate their interrelationships. Finally, a higher and more abstract order of general concepts is developed.

He differs with Watson in limiting the function of his system to description rather than the more customary goal of explanation. His position attempts to avoid Watson's reductionism by defining concepts in terms of observables rather than reducing them to physiological states. Although private events are not accessible to research, there is no reason to believe that the stimulus from an infected tooth is different from a hot stove. The former can be treated as an inference rather than an observable fact(22). With the advancement of research techniques, private events will one day become accessible to scientific investigation. The task of psychology is to find out what the relationship is between the stimulus controlled by the researcher, the other experimental variables, and the response of the subject.

The simple unit of behavior is the reflex, which Skinner stipulates as being "any observed correlation of stimulus and response." Scientific inquiry must discover the laws regulating reflexes because they are the basic unit of observable behavior. Skinner provides a considerable number of laws(23).

There are two types of behavior: respondent and operant. Behavior is called 'respondent'* when it is correlated to "specific eliciting stimuli;" behavior is 'operant' when no stimuli are present. 'Stimulus' means any modification of the environment, and a 'response' is a correlated part of the behavior. And, as mentioned previously, a reflex is "any observed correlation between stimulus and response."

Conditioning in the form of respondent behavior was used by Skinner in his experiments with pigeons. Reinforcement (reward) was dependent upon the response. Whenever the pigeon exhibited the desired behavior as a result of stimuli, the response was reinforced by providing food. On the other hand, with operant conditioning the response comes first and then it becomes reinforced. It is through operant conditioning that the efficiency of behavior is improved. This form of conditioning builds a repertoire by which we handle such processes as walking, playing games, using tools, and other activities(24).

Skinner conscientiously tried to avoid reductionism and mentalistic terms in his behavioral studies. In treating the concept of reinforcement, Skinner avoided the pleasure pain notions of Edward L. Thorndike as well as Ivan Pavlov's interpretation of reinforcement as the amount of energy discharged by the stimulating factor. Skinner could not discover why reinforcement actually reinforced behavior, so instead he offered a precise description of the reinforcement process without resorting to reductionism or mentalistic concepts.

He thought that 'deprivation' could be operationally defined and measured, but that there was a tendency of psychologists to treat the term 'drive' by going beyond empirical data. The notion of drive provides a way of referring to observables of deprivation and satiation. Skinner also rejected the idea of will power and an "inner self" because all behavior should be open to public observation in order to be treated by the psychologist.

Skinner has been an influential figure in psychology and in his leadership role in the development of programmed materials for the schools. His method is based on a consistent and persistent inductive empiricism applied rigorously in observation and experimentation, and his approach marks a considerable advance over Watson in sophistication, rigor, and the avoidance of reductionism and mentalistic elements.

---

*The convention of single quotation marks whenever a term is referred to instead of being used will be employed throughout.

Yet, one may still charge Skinner with adopting scientific methods of the past, for if we wish to be as scientific as possible — as Skinner surely does — one could not imagine the great progress made in the physical sciences during this century if scientists had been content to limit their methodology to description and observation.

Skinner is unable to deal with problems of motivation because of the unobservables and mentalistic concepts that may be needed in such a treatment. The range of experimentation on drives and emotions is restricted by the nature of psychological laboratory procedures. Rather than neglect these areas, it would seem to be better to change the procedures and framework of inquiry. Furthermore, work in psychotherapy indicates that some type of theoretical explanation of inner behavior is needed in order to successfully treat patients. Our understanding of man is severely limited when interior life is avoided, when the organism is broken into bits and pieces for their amenability to certain forms of investigation, leaving human purposes, values, and ideals with no place in the study of human behavior.

Humanistic Psychology

A loose and not altogether clearly defined movement has developed in recent years that refers to itself as humanistic psychology or the "third force" in psychology. The proponents do not represent a unitary view or hold to a single position, but work from a number of different theories and approaches in the study of man. In spite of this fact, they do share certain common characterictics. Thus, our approach will be to search for the common characteristics rather than singling out particular individuals whose approach may not be representative of the whole group.

Humanistic psychology differs from behaviorism and psychoanalysis by taking an organismic and holistic approach to the study of man. Such studies are designed to view man as a whole person who formulates goals and purposes for which he strives to attain. This approach is not to be found in the other two schools. Other psychologies believed that man could be understood by careful examination and cataloging of the parts. The parts approach is a structural rather than a process approach; but man being as dynamic as he is, a process approach is needed in order to capture his complexity, individuality, and striving for goals of his own choosing.

Man cannot be understood by making the pleasure-principle the fundamental basis of behavior. Such a principle leaves out the most important aspects of man's existence: his willingness to sacrifice pleasure and undergo pain and suffering to achieve his goals; his ability to choose ideals and devote his life to their fulfillment; his strivings for self-realization and actualization; his ability to work and play, love and create. The older psychologies are unable to account for these features of man that even common sense has long recognized.

In some forms of behaviorism the model is that of tension building (from drives) and tension reduction (gratification of drives). The organism seeks to maintain homeostasis — an inner balance or equilibrium. But the equilibrium is transitory, for deficiencies in physiological states are always arising, leading to tension building and the subsequent propulsion of the organism to relieve the tension and regain homeostasis. Humanistic psychologists cannot accept this homeostatic model for human strivings. Man is more than a homeostatic mechanism. Goal-seeking activities create some tensions which have a salutary effect on the processes of planning, organizing, testing alternatives, and exerting effort for the attainment of ends deemed desirable. A person without tensions would soon fall asleep; he scarcely would be able to do or to create anything worthwhile. Of course not all tensions are necessarily healthy. Some inhibit and divert one's effort to create a meaningful life. Man, by nature a social being, finds these unhealthy tensions usually springing from incapacities in interpersonal relations. But other tensions create growth-fulfilling tendencies and, rather than be discouraged or extinguished, should be channeled in directions that best promote the individual's development. Thus, the variety, complexity, and richness of human life cannot be explained by reductions to homeostatic mechanisms.

Related to homeostasis is the notion in the older psychologies of adjustment as the goal of the individual's life. Humanistic psychology does not accept adjustment as a goal because one can adjust to a gang of thieves, a life of crime, an unjust government, or to bigoted and intolerant groups. Coupled with adjustment is the concept of normalcy; when one is adjusted he is a normal individual. The model for normalcy is drawn from how most people, who are not in mental or penal institutions, act in their daily lives. The model is developed from the life of a society at a particular time and place. This theory is repudiated by the humanistic psychologists on several counts. The society from which the model is drawn may be basically corrupt, manipulative, discriminatory in its policies, and led by persons with totalitarian mentalities. What would be the virtue of being considered normal in such a society? But even if a society does not have most of these characteristics, normality still would not be the goal of human life. When it is realized that most people do not use their potentials effectively, hence, are not very creative, original, or self-actualizing, then merely to be normal is the acceptance of stunted growth. The problem with Freud is that he studied man at his worst and then constructed his conception of human nature from these observations. A conception of human nature worthy of the efforts of man's aspirations should be developed from observations of man at his best. It should be drawn from those individuals who are creative, inventive, original, humane, those who more closely approach the utilization of their full potentials. Anything less will be unworthy of man. In keeping with this ideal, the goal of psychotherapy should no longer be merely the elimination of illness and the promotion of adjustment; rather, its aim is to encourage growth and creativity.

Man, then, should no longer be considered a reactive organism which the environment shapes, molds, and conditions as if he were little more than a puppet. Man is not a mental robot; neither is he a helpless pawn driven to commit acts by his childhood reactions or by massive forces of conditioning in society. Humanistic psychology attempts to reestablish the dignity and worth of man and his ability to choose to live creatively.

Humanistic psychology focuses on the experiencing person as primary in the study of man. This focus leads to a research interest in the study of problems that are humanly meaningful and significant rather than those which fit neatly into prior canons of objectivity and limited, but precise, laboratory procedures.

The strengths of humanistic psychology lie in its willingness to view man as a whole, his choices, goal seeking, creativity, and attempts to utilize his full potential. Man is seen in a more optimistic, promising light by also studying the best specimens of the human race. The general tenor of this psychology is one of hope and encouragement that a more complete understanding of man can be gained, reaching from his heights to his depths, and out of such studies new insights can be offered for the improvement of interpersonal relations through the development of more fully-functioning persons.

On the other hand, humanistic psychology can be criticized by other schools as being overly ambitious and unrealistic. Behavioral science, it is claimed, has not been developed to the point where man can be

studied wholly and at his best. To attempt to do so would be to for-
sake the canons of rigorous scientific inquiry resulting in findings of
questionable validity. The precision and rigor of laboratory and clinical
procedures established by the older, more recognized schools should
be adhered to if psychology is to advance as a science. Furthermore,
humanistic psychology has introduced into the lexicon such terms as
values, purposes, ideals, self-realization, and others. These terms are
best left to philosophy and literature, for they have no place in a scientific discipline. They cannot be treated objectively or made accessible
to testing and verification. At best, it may be possible to redefine them
operationally so that the behavior to which they refer can be open to
measurement.

Humanistic psychologists would generally admit that their framework
does not possess the rigor of older laboratory procedures. But rigor and
precision, unfortunately, have too often been purchased at the cost of
triviality of findings. Aspects of man that did not fit into established
procedures were either ignored or distorted for purposes of treatment
into an oversimplified theoretical framework based on a pleasure-pain
or a homeostatic model. Humanistic psychologists can point out that
their approach is still young, and in due time their methods of inquiry
will gain greater sophistication and rigor; however, since humanistic
psychology treats of man as a total person in all his complexity, it would
be misleading to believe that the complete rigor of more limited laboratory studies will likely be obtained.

Marxist Philosophy of Man

The influence of Karl Marx (1818-83), German philosopher and radical leader, is felt today in Asia, Africa, Europe, and Latin America.
Whatever one may think about his teachings, his vast influence over the
lives of hundreds of millions of people and the events of our time cannot
be ignored.

Our concern lies with the Marxist philosophy of man; however, in
order better to understand it and grasp its full import, it will need to be
related to the other principal facets of his philosophy. Labor is the
touchstone for self-realization in Marx's philosophy of man. Labor
represents the efforts of men to create and satisfy their desires and
to achieve happiness. Man labors to create, to transform the world,
and make himself at home in it. Man, then, relates himself to his

world and makes it a hospitable and worthy place to live through his labors. As Marx's literary collaborator, Frederick Engels has said it is man who is "the sole animal capable of working his way out of the merely animal state—his normal state is one appropriate to his consciousness, *one to be created by himself.*"(25) Man creates himself by dint of his own productive labors. But Marx would caution us to be on guard against considering man as if he was isolated from others. One should speak of "men" and the relations of men in their concrete behavior, so that rather than talking about an abstraction of man inherent in each individual, Marx speaks of men always within a context of "the *ensemble* of social relations."(26)

The problems of men arise in their labor when the growing complexity of the division of labor and the advancement and application of technological knowledge alienate them from their work and serve as an increasingly dehumanizing force. The theory was more fully developed in Marx's early manuscripts. The workers in capitalistic societies feel free when they are not at their work and apart from themselves when they are working. Work becomes compulsion — not the satisfaction of genuine needs to create and relate oneself to the world, but merely a means to the satisfaction of wants external to oneself. Hence, for Marx, one can only act freely in what he considers man's animal functions — eating, drinking, reproducing, etc., while in the functions that make man human—his work—he is nothing more than a work animal. The worker becomes a unit of labor cost, a saleable commodity, a thing. The alienation of the workers from labor and the dehumanization brought about by this process is due to the means of production. The means of production has established a division of labor that has the effect of isolating man from the community, separating men and jobs from one another; and through specialization work narrows until it becomes inherently monotonous.

Since alienation stems from the means of production, it will be necessary to sketch briefly Marx's philosophy of history and his theory of surplus value in order to show how he arrives at this position. It may be recalled that Marx did not wish to speak of an essence for individual man, but only what men are in the ensemble of their social relations. This theory may seem to lead to the view that it is possible to talk about different sets of social relations and their respective characteristics but not to make generalizations about man because social relations are characterized by wide differences and variations. Marx avoids this problem (although he creates more serious ones to replace it) by developing a philosophy of history that can be used to denote regularities and derive generalizations according to the particular period of economic development in which social relations are being assessed.

Marx borrowed from Hegel the dialectic, which attempted to account for the unfolding of events in nature as a result of the conflicts of opposites and the development of negations leading to a new synthesis. For Hegel, every state, condition or proposition calls forths its own negation, which provokes the negation of the negation leading to a new synthesis. Early in his career, Marx joined the "Left Hegelians" at Berlin University and subscribed to Hegel's logic while criticizing the political and religious implications of Hegel's philosophy. The Left Hegelians were concerned that Hegel's philosophy, leading as it does to higher and higher levels of self-consciousness culminating in an absolute self-consciousness, offered a metaphysical justification for Prussian absolutism. Marx then turned to the works of Feuerbach, and while keeping the Hegelian dialectic, reversed it by eliminating the idealistic content of Spirit and self-consciousness by substituting a "materialistic" content, the basis of which he borrowed from Feuerbach. Thus, by keeping the dialectic and substituting a materialistic content, he developed the functional structure for his philosophy of history that he called "dialectical materialism."

Marx probably developed his key concept of "class war" from his contact with the French socialists of his time. Class war had usually symbolized to earlier socialists the conflict between rich and poor, but in the hands of Marx it denoted the conflict between employer and employee, with the former referred to as the bourgeoisie and the latter the proletariat. This terminology applies to the relationship that obtains in capitalistic economies.

It is rather odd that Marx's philosophy of history, which some observers regard as his most original contribution, is not developed systematically but is scattered throughout his writings. Marx contends that the mode of production of the material means of existence affects and conditions the whole of social, intellectual, and political life. Religion, art, and morality do not develop first with the mode of production emerging from these factors; instead, religion, art, and morality are determined by the material mode of production. Man's social existence determines his consciousness rather than the other way around(27).

Thus, the mode of production conditions all the other factors in a society and becomes the key for understanding societies at different historical periods. Engels provides a sketch of historical evolution by using Marx's thesis as an explanatory principle(28). He finds production on a small scale in Medieval society. The fruits of production are used for immediate consumption by the producer or feudal lord, and it is only when production exceeds consumption that the excess is offered for sale. However, the seed of "anarchy in the production of society at large" may already be found.

Capitalism emerges, without affecting the form of exchange, when the development of manufacturing replaces scattered workshops. The capitalist makes his entrance upon the historical stage and promptly sets out to control the means of production and transform it from individual to social acts. The capitalist appropriates the products and turns them into commodities for his personal profit. Unrestrained competition develops in the market and antagonism arises between the proletariat and the bourgeoisie. As men change the way they earn their living, they change their social relations. Thus, a sense of alienation from labor and from one's fellows develops.

To summarize, the development of capitalistic controls over the mode of production leads to class conflict, alienation from labor, and dehumanization. Class conflict stands in the center of Marx's conception of history, because other than class conflict history is a record of insignificant trivialities. One must still look at the theory of surplus value to comprehend Marx's view of capitalistic exploitation.

Borrowing from the British economist David Ricardo, Marx held in *Das Kapital* that the value of the commodities consumed by a worker is less than the value of the commodities he produces; the difference, called "surplus value," represents the profit of the capitalist. It is labor-power rather than labor that the capitalist purchases. The natural price to pay for labor is that which allows the worker to subsist and continue his existence. But when labor-power is used it produces more value than it costs, because even though the worker may make enough for his maintenance in six hours, he has sold his labor-power and thereby may be forced to work ten or twelve hours each day.

Marx explains further by differentiating capital into constant and variable, which corresponds generally to the distinction between machinery and wages. But since machines transfer their value, neither more nor less, to the product, machines yield no surplus value. This thrusts on labor the burden of providing surplus value. The capitalist could provide additional surplus value by introducing more machinery or improving the technical processes of production. He also could require wives and children to work, for if the family wage should be no more than that needed for maintenance, then wives and children would offer their services gratuitously.

There is something strange, however, in Marx's suggestion that by introducing more machinery greater surplus value could be produced, since we have already been told that it does not yield surplus value. Presumably it does not yield surplus value in the long run but only averages out from one industry to another over a period of time. If, as Marx suggested, surplus value derives from labor alone and the ratio of constant to variable capital varies greatly from one industry to another, it should follow that those industries with a high percentage of variable capital (labor) should secure the highest rate of profits. This outcome is not the case in actual practice, however. The capitalist does not get an unusually high rate of profit in those industries where a large amount of labor is exploited. Thus, it would seem that Marx's theory of surplus value is not corroborated by the actual workings of capitalistic systems.

A belief related to surplus value was Marx's interpretation of the capitalist. He held that a capitalist was one who lived off the surplus value produced by the workers while he himself remained idle. To be a capitalist one must secure sufficient surplus value so that work no longer is necessary. Following this line of thinking, if surplus value is a form of theft, the act is reprehensible so long as the manager is a capitalist, but once he does work of his own he no longer is a capitalist, and though he may be extracting surplus value, his acts no longer can be labelled reprehensible.

Additionally, Marx's system applies to an economy based upon vendible commodities; whereas for many years we have been living in an economy where services play an increasingly large role. It would be difficult for service personnel to have legitimate grievances within the Marxian framework because they are ignored in his schema. Yet we know that service personnel as well as workers may have legitimate grievances.

What we have seen so far with reference to Marx's philosophy of man is that as history moves to more advanced stages shifting from a feudal to a capitalistic society, exploitation increases and alienation from labor, the source of creative relations with others and the world, becomes more acute. The seeds of its own destruction can be found in the capitalistic system with its overproduction, crises every ten years, and its unemployed workers. The capitalist waits to turn his products into capital before circulating them. But circulation is limited due to overproduction. The bourgeoisie are indicted for their incapacity to manage the productive forces of society.

The next historical stage is represented by socialism wherein the proletariat revolt against and overthrow the bourgeoisie, leading to the "dictatorship of the proletariat," in which the agencies of production would be organized first by joint-stock companies, later by trusts, and then finally by the state. Socialized production, which has eliminated the abuses of capitalism, constitutes an interim stage which will give way to communism, the final historical stage. The state will "wither away" and classes will no longer be necessary. Thus, whereas the capitalistic state sought to perpetuate itself and maintain its power structure, the dictatorship of the proletariat deliberately prepares for its own demise by striving to abolish the class system. The alienation of labor endemic in capitalism will cease to exist when communism is reached. And the division of labor, which is the ultimate reason for the existence of classes, will be eliminated. Productive labor will become a creative and pleasurable activity by giving the individual the opportunity to develop his abilities, both physical and mental. Since no division of labor exists in a communist society, there is no one sphere of activity to which an individual will be limited, for he can perform one activity today and another tomorrow, hunting in the morning, fishing in the afternoon, and raising cattle in the evening, if he so chooses(29).

It should be noted that communism, not religion, removes the basic source of alienation and dehumanization. For Marx, religion is the emotional outcry of real misery and a protest against human misery. But at the same time it deflects men's minds away from the actions necessary to rectify these conditions. Religion is the "opium of the people." Religion, then, is an illusory happiness. "The demand to give up the illusions about its condition is *the demand to give up a condition which needs illusions*."(30)

Marxism Today

Early Marxist writings on alienation had been neglected until more recent years, and Marxist scholars have been intent on showing their relevance for today's social and political problems by developing interpretations in light of preceding historical developments. And as cracks appeared in the allegedly impregnable wall of the philosophy of history and the theory of surplus value, Marxists become more interested in the earlier writings. Another reason, no doubt, is that some observers found alienation endemic in highly industrial societies of our times and turned to Marx for guidance out of the morass.

Adam Schaff is a prominent Polish philosopher who operates intellectually from a Marxist framework and has attempted to reassess Marxist philosophy of man for our time(31). Schaff sees Marxism as a form of socialistic humanism whose objectives are to view the individual as "the totality of social relations" on the basis of an historical materialist conception of social relations. This conception leads to the realization that ideals can be attained only with reference to the concrete social relations to which they refer rather than by the establishment of abstract ideals apart from specific relations (utopianism). Man is both the product and the creator of the social conditions under which he lives. The Marxist is interested not in an abstraction of man's essence; rather, his concern lies with man's social existence from the point of view of its objective, material dimension. Likewise, questions of freedom are social questions which cannot be considered in the abstract but only in reference to their social and political implications.

Socialist humanism, according to Schaff, is not only concerned with the full development of man, but it is also a militant humanism that believes in fighting to make such goals an actuality. There is only a seeming paradox in the expression, "Hatred for the sake of love," for it is necessary that those who love people must hate the enemies of the people's welfare and engage vigorously in the struggle to liberate man from the yoke of enslavement.

It was no oversight that Marx seldom used the terms 'freedom,' 'justice,' 'equality,' and others that so frequently are bandied about in democratic countries. Those countries still laboring under the abuses of capitalism adopted these terms to cloak their tyrannical machinations against the workers. Lately, Marxists have claimed that these terms are used as a subterfuge for the imperialistic designs of democratic capitalistic nations. Schaff recognizes that differences exist between democracies and dictatorships, but democracies are limited by using the freedom of one social class to deny the freedom of another class. No doubt historical evidence can be adduced to illustrate his point. Surely in the United States the American Indian, Oriental Americans, Mexican Americans, and Negroes have been oppressed classes. But Schaff, on the other hand, does not seem to recognize that the grand design of Marx did not halt and solidify prematurely with the "dictatorship of the proletariat," but instead, in most communist countries, has been subverted to the dictatorship of the Communist Party.

One may still wonder what, other than the fear of armed might, keeps the peoples of communist countries from revolting. It was believed by some in the Eisenhower administration that sooner or later—and more likely sooner—uprisings would become widespread behind the Iron Curtain. In spite of Hungary and Czechoslovakia, this has turned out to be a forlorn hope. What, then, is the magnetic power of Marxism that mesmerizes hundreds of millions sufficiently that they become averse to generating widespread insurrections?

Arthur P. Mendel provides one explanation by showing that Marxism draws upon and appeals to other respected values and ideals present in Western cultures(32). Marx appeals, first of all, to the rational ideals of the Enlightenment with its beliefs in the use of reason, empiricism, and the idea of human progress. The Enlightenment, rather than attributing the evils of social life to innate depravity (as some religious views were inclined to do), attributed human afflictions to the wrong social arrangements. Here Marx enters the picture by presenting to the world a comprehensive and compelling perspective that delineates the exploitative relations of material life. He then further indicates (in keeping with the Enlightenment faith in science) that his "scientific socialism" provides a blueprint for the abolishment of these evils.

Another source of appeal in Marxism is his demand for social justice, which relates to the Judaic-Christian ethic. Marx, then, not only had a scientific dimension to his program but an ethical one as well. Many writers, both before and after Marx, had pointed out the shortcomings of industrial nations, but none synthesized as well as Marx the twin appeals of science and ethics as the approach to the solution of the problems. The ethics of the day did not carry their appeal because it smacked too much of moralisms, preachments, and religion in the eyes of the sophisticated men of reason. Yet social reformers wanted a program grounded in high ideals and ethical values, and science was too bloodless, antiseptic, and "objective" to brook any such sentiments. Marx's triumph did not lie so much with originality as his ability to draw upon, reconstruct, and implant the dominant ideals of his time into a compelling new synthesis that not only explained to many the causes of their suffering but provided as well a plan of action by which human misery could be overcome. And the real risks to life and limb faced by those in the revolutionary cause no longer were so frightful when one had the assurance that history was on his side.

Religious Perspectives

Religion has been a pervasive force, for good and ill, in human cultures. Anthropologists report that religion has been found in some form in all cultures: that is, if religion is defined not just as a belief in a transcendent deity, but including as well the deification of inanimate objects and the investiture of the state with religious symbols and significance. The universality of this phenomenon has lead some to conclude with the *non sequitur* that religion is good or true or right; otherwise, it would not be found in all cultures. Merely because beliefs or practices are widespread does not corroborate their worth or value. Slavery, the burning of heretics, and religious pogroms have at one time or another been widespread in some countries. Belief in witchcraft, that the earth is the center of the universe, that some races are superior to others, that bloodletting cures disease, and other beliefs have been vigorously upheld and defended.

What can be concluded is that many people have found a need for some form of religious belief. If one concludes that all needs are healthy, then the problem is solved; however, this is not the case, because it is known that many "needs" of individuals are unhealthy. Whether religious needs are healthy or unhealthy cannot be answered in the abstract. It would be necessary to examine the religious functions within their cultural context and the way in which they enter into and influence the lives of persons of that culture. Such an evaluation would presuppose choosing some psychological theory of personality and needs in order to arrive at an evaluation. Our purpose here is not that of pursuing this line of investigation, but only to mention it as a guide to the reader who does wish to pursue it.

Two questions must be raised: the issue of needs and the truth-claims of religious beliefs. The former is a psychological question; the latter an epistemological one. Religions, naturally, do not fare too well when narrow positivistic criteria are adopted for their assessment, namely, because religious statements cannot be operationally defined and made accessible to scientific verification. A more sympathetic approach is that adopted by ordinary language philosophers who seek to trace the rich metaphorical character of religious statements within the context of the language game used by the religion under investigation. One problem that has been identified is the usual inability to falsify religious statements(33). In science, one can imagine the conditions necessary to falsify an experiment to show that the claims were ill-founded; this, however, cannot be done with religious statements. No matter how definitive the evidence produced to the contrary, religionists deny that it in any way falsifies their knowledge-claims. Religion is not an open system. Nonetheless, the influence of organized religion has been great and the religious perspectives of man are worthy of careful attention.

Too often people in our culture are limited to an understanding of their own religion rather than holding a broad understanding of religions around the world. One reason for this is the belief that their own religion is absolutely right and true, while other religions, as they see them, fail to grasp the truth—or may even be pernicious and dangerous. The other reason, when the former does not dominate, is sheer intellectual laziness.

The religions of the East, while sharing certain affinities and common outlooks with those of the West, differ in certain significant ways. Their divergent views of man and the purpose of life warrant an examination in some detail.

In contrast to Christianity but not Judaism, Hinduism and Jainism do not proselyte. Hinduism, however, deters the conversion to another religion by the remarkable process of offering a place as a lesser divinity for the saints and leaders of their religions. Rama, Krishna, Buddha, Christ, and others are regarded as Divine Incarnations. God can be worshipped through them. In Indian philosophy the whole truth, great and complex as it is, is difficult to attain; therefore, a number of divergent perspective systems are admitted to secure some portion of the truth. Other positions are not merely "tolerated" as in the West but are actually encouraged and embraced as different pathways to truth.

What is considered to be a religion is much broader in its criteria in the East than in the West. The common conviction in the West is that religion is identified, if not wholly at least largely, by beliefs in supernaturalism and a transcendent Deity who is eternal, immutable, and possesses absolute truth, beauty and goodness. Buddhism, Jainism, and Confucianism, however, are not supernaturalistic but naturalistic. This perplexes the Western observer and causes him to wonder how they can be called religions. Yet, these systems have all the outward symbols generally associated with religion, and evoke from their members the acts of observance, piety, supplication, and devotion found in Western religions. In light of these manifestations and the way in which their observance enters the lives of the people, one's criteria are too limited if they rule out these systems as religions.

Since space does not permit a consideration of the beliefs of the many religions of the East, let us survey some of the teachings of Buddhism as a way to provide a sharp contrast with the religions of the West and to gain another perspective on man.

Buddhism

The exact number of Buddhists in the world today is not known due to lack of uniformity in methods of counting and the divergence of criteria

as to what constitutes a Buddhist. It has been variously estimated that
the number of Buddhists range anywhere from 150 to 200 million.
Buddhism is found in Ceylon, Burma, southeast Asia, China, Korea,
Japan, and Tibet.

A number of points are generally accepted about the life of Buddha
(c 563-483 B.C.). He was born into the family of a minor ruler of one
of India's principalities and was given the name "Siddharta." The name
"Gautama" comes from the clan to which the father belonged, a name
that Buddha took in later life. Growing dissatisfied with palace life,
Buddha's thoughts turned toward religion. At the age of 29, he left
the palace, his wife and newborn son to find what he was seeking. He
first studied with two noted religious leaders without securing any degree of satisfaction; then, for the next six years he turned to extreme
asceticism, but failed to find peace and tranquility. Finally, while practicing his own form of meditation under a tree, he vowed that he would
not rise or leave the spot until he solved his problem. Thus, he finally
succeeded, and the tree became known as the *bo* tree or tree of enlightenment. His followers increased, he founded a monastic community, and
provided instructions for laymen. He became known as the Buddha,
which is not a proper name but a descriptive one, meaning "the en-
lighted one."

There is neither a cosmic self or eternal soul in Buddhism. Neither
do we find sacrifices to nature deities as in the Vedic tradition, or a
changeless self-essence as found among the Brahmanism of the Upanishads. It will seem strange to Westerners who think in terms of self-
concepts and individualism that Buddhists believe that permanent states
and selves are illusions fostered by language. There is no permanent
self and no rebirth from one life to the next. Everything is transitory
and impermanent.

All phenomena are parts of a beginningless causal series, and whatever has a beginning must also have an ending. Thus death is a certainty
for all born beings. The misery and suffering *(dukkha)* of existence has
a cause found in a state of ignorance. But by diagnosing this cause,
changes can be made; for all life is a process capable of improvement
through right thoughts and right deeds. Every act *(Karman)* has its
consequences, and by recognizing "the law of Karma" the impulses
which bring suffering can be eliminated.

The characteristics of life are misery, transience, and the absence of
any persistent individuality. However, it does not follow that the Buddhist would wish never to be born or desire to commit suicide. Birth is
the supreme opportunity to escape from ever being born again.

Since causes bring about events which have their own results, every individual, it is believed, reaps what he sows. The Buddhist is expected to conduct his life by following "four noble truths":

1) The Noble Truth of Suffering: suffering is inherent in all existence: birth, old age, sickness, and death
2) The Noble Truth of the Cause of Suffering: lies in craving or grasping, which leads to rebirth
3) The Noble Truth of the Cessation of Suffering: cessation of suffering is brought about by the cessation of craving
4) The Noble Truth of the Path that Leads to the Cessation of Suffering: consists of an eightfold path: right view, right thought, right speech, right action, right livelihood, right effort, right mindfulness, and right concentration. The first two pertain to the early development of a proper frame of mind; the next three are ethical requirements; and the last three concern the training for contemplative knowledge and serenity

Deliverance from suffering is brought about by practice of the Eightfold Path which ultimately finds release in Nirvana. Nirvana is absence of craving and release from selfish desires. Nirvana implies death of some sort, but this should not be considered annihilation and nothingness. It is not expressible in existence or nonexistence as ordinarily understood. Nirvana is the end of becoming and beyond all states of being. The destructive work on the craving self has been completed. The heavy burden of existence has dropped away and no more will there be a return to a conditioned existence. The limitations of our ordinary language structure makes Nirvana ineffable. At best, it can only be approached through analogies such as, "the way of a bird in the air, leaving no tract."

Buddhism is not easy for the Westerner to grasp, not merely because it is naturalistic rather than supernaturalistic, but because of the abolition of the self-concept, which is a cornerstone of the Western outlook. Yet, for the Buddhist suffering is bound up with the self-concept, with the belief that "I am this or that." Other than the traditional manner of rejecting this view because it clashes with Judaic-Christian basic preconceptions, there exists a fundamental philosophical difficulty in that of personal identity and agenthood. To whom should good and evil acts be attributed if the individual is composed of changing states? Furthermore, if all substances are transient, how could one thing or event bring another into existence, since by the time the new thing or state has come into existence the first has disappeared.

A serious problem with Buddhism—although one that it has in common with some other religions—is its fundamental tendency to be life-negating rather than life-affirming, which is summed up well by a leading scholar of Buddhist thought. "To a person who is thoroughly disillusioned with the contemporary world, and with himself, Buddhism may offer many points of attraction . . ."(34) Buddhism, in its attempt to abolish the existential self-concept, provides a sharp and conflicting contrast to other views of human nature.

The Death of God Movement

The "Death of God" movement can first be found outside the Christian church in the writings of the German philosopher Friedrich Nietzsche, and is found again slightly less than a century later among a small minority of churchmen, sometimes referred to as "radicals" by their colleagues.

The movement is probably presaged by the theologians Dietrich Bonhoeffer and Rudolf Bultmann. Bonhoeffer believed that hitherto the church has based its preaching of the Gospel on the appeal of religious experience and that each man had a deep need for such experiences. But suppose man believed that he could carry on his life without religion? Does this leave Christianity, then, only with those remaining who still have this need? Bonhoeffer's answer for twentieth century man is that God is calling us to a form of Christianity that does not depend upon religion.

Rudolf Bultmann spoke of the mythological element in the New Testament that goes beyond actual history. This element, he contended, is unintelligible jargon for modern man. The mythological elements related to an anachronistic and antiquated world view, which Bultmann sought to "demythologize" for twentieth century man.

Probably the Death of God moved into high gear with the writings of the Anglican bishop John A. T. Robinson(35). Robinson prefers, rather than wrestling with traditional proofs for the existence of God, to turn to Paul Tillich's approach. Here a transcendent Deity is dismissed and the centrality of focus becomes one of centering on man's ultimate concern, which expresses itself as "the ground of our being."(36) From this perspective theological statements are not statements about God, but those that point to the depth of experience—those questions which engender ultimate concern.

Other theologians of the movement are divided as to how one would talk about God. Some would declare a moratorium on such discourse when it is likely to confuse modern man; whereas, others believe that God is actually dead. Today we live in a post-Christian secularized era in which mythological views of Christianity have been exchanged for a scientific view. Christianity no longer dominates Western life but has been synthesized into the secular culture and is found in popular beliefs surrounding nationalism and capitalism.

Some may find a viable theology without God whereby Christian life may derive from a faith in Christ. Thomas J. J. Altizer declares that the Christian must accept the death of God as an irrevocable event(37). God no longer is present in human history. God is only present by his absence, by the void that is filled with despair and rebellion. For Altizer, God negated himself by becoming flesh in Jesus and ceased to exist in his original form. However, for Gabriel Vahanian, God's death came when man began to comprise the beliefs in God's transcendence by merging the conception with human identity(38).

There is a shift of emphasis from God to Jesus. For Altizer, it is Jesus who sets man free to give himself to the present. Thus, Christian religion becomes a Christology without God. Jesus becomes progressively incarnate in the body of humanity—wherever there is energy and life.

In order to place the Death of God movement in a more complete perspective, we may profit by turning our attention to Friedrich Nietzsche's original statement and divination of the death of God. Nietzsche lived at a time when science and technology were beginning to dominate secular life, a crossroads in human thought when the speculative philosophies, he believed, had exhausted themselves. It was incomprehensible to him that mankind could not see that they had lost God. Mankind will go mad when they find they have lost God, because this will leave them only with nihilism and a void. Nietzsche was able to experience and comprehend the misery of a godless world more than a generation before the Death of God movement.

God is dead, Nietzsche asserted, because we have killed him. What people have revered as God is not godlike. He recognizes that the way Christians claim to express faith in God and the acts which they believe their faith entails, diminishes man; yet, when people realize the consequences of what they have done resulting in the death of God, these consequences will threaten life by diminishing its purpose and significance. Nietzsche saw that his role was that of questioning rather than rationalizing the values of society, which is why he believed that he could see more clearly the death of God.

The problem with the death of God was to escape nihilism by developing naturalistic values that would not resort to invoking God for explanations. Thus, his purpose was to find a way (a way at least for him since a general way or "the way" does not exist) of affirming life, saying "yes" to life. To affirm one must not rationalize the values of his own society. There is too much hypocrisy, delusion, and comfortableness hidden behind the moralities of society. One must question our accepted moralities in order to bring about a reevaluation of values. In this process we will find how many idols of our age and of the past have a hollow sound when questions are posed with a hammer. The striking illumination that follows will be more than traditional values can withstand. By his triumph over dogma and the false virtues and religious beliefs of his time, Nietzsche felt that he could attain a new openness, a free and unlimited view.

One may wonder why the time gap exists between Nietzsche's original formulation and the Death of God movement. This gap should not be surprising in view of the conservatism in organized religion. Whether or not we agree with the movement, a surprising aspect is that some religious leaders finally had the audacity to break out of the traditional mold and be willing to weather the wrath of their colleagues and superiors in the hierarchy. Unfortunately, if those in the movement had been attentive students of the past criticisms and observations of philosophers and other writers, their analysis would be more penetrating and far-reaching. This criticism is even more true of "situation ethics," a new approach to ethics among a few theologians, which proposes that individuals should make relative value decisions in light of social situations rather than rely, as past theologians had advocated, on absolute moral standards. The situation ethicists could profit by studies made by philosophers and social scientists from a situationist perspective; these studies would assist them in formulating a firmer theoretical base without demanding in any way the relinquishment of their religious convictions.

That the church—an even greater center of authority and conservatism than the schools—is not merely the recipient of criticisms from without but is slowly yielding to fundamental changes from within, is evidence that certain far-reaching changes are taking place in our and other postindustrial societies. Our own civilization is presently in the throes of a series of great transformations equally or even more profound than those experienced during the Renaissance, Reformation, or the Industrial Revolution. In keeping with this new age men will one day call for religious perspectives more consonant with the time. One perspective already available that may fulfill this criterion can be found in the writings of Teilhard de Chardin.

Pierre Teilhard de Chardin

Teilhard de Chardin (1881-1955), a French Jesuit priest and paleontologist, held important academic positions in Paris, traveled widely in pursuing paleontology field studies, and wrote a number of important books, which were not published until after his death due to church prohibitions. An approach to his system of thought can be made through his most important book, *The Phenomenon of Man*(39).

Teilhard has attempted to show the intimate relationship between consciousness and the material world through his original interpretation of the evolutionary process. Within this process one finds an effort to delineate and maintain a continuity between past, present, and future within the framework of a unifying perspective that recognizes diversity in the universe.

The procedure that Teilhard follows is to view the earth in evolutionary fashion by tracing in detail each successive stage of development and its interconnections. He begins with the earliest stages after the origin of the earth and its subsequent transformations (this can be called "geogenesis"). From that point he turns to the evolution of life on earth ("biogenesis") and, in turn, treats of the rise of thought ("psychogenesis") and the higher development of thought as it envelops the earth ("noogenesis"). Finally, he envisions a future point in the higher evolution of man ("Omega").

In the "geosphere" and in the process of geogenesis, we find that matter can be characterized by its plurality, unity, and energy. Unity exists in plurality when we consider the atom to be potentially co-extensive with every other atom; a collective develops, since matter is not a result of simple aggregation. Energy passes from one atom to another in the course of interaction and movement. This interdependence and unity of the universe means that we must study it as a whole rather than looking at it in terms of separate parts and unconnected processes. The universe, according to Teilhard, is woven into a single piece, which can best be explained by the Law of Consciousness and Complexity. Moving from the atom to the molecular level, a growing complexity is exhibited. The earth assumes greater levels of complexity as it evolves. As for consciousness, Teilhard has in mind any kind of psychism from rudimentary inner perception to thought processes. Everything in the universe has a "without" or exterior and a "within" which are co-extensive with one another. The "within" constitutes consciousness. Life has a prelife as far as we can see; therefore, everything in nature is a form of life or prelife. The simpler elements have a weak "within"; then we pass in evolution to complex groupings which have a richer "within." For Teilhard, the story of the universe is understood by applying the Law of Consciousness and Complexity (40).

So far Teilhard's position diverges most sharply from the traditional evolutionary view by positing the inner as well as the outer dimension to all things. This provides a continuity between inorganic and organic realms; both these realms are controlled by a movement of growing complexity of form and the growth toward a psychic consciousness. Teilhard attempts to avoid a dualism by postulating that all energy is psychical in nature. There are energy tangents that connect with other forms of energy of the same order, and there is a radial form of energy that draws the universe forward toward complexity and centricity.

There is a prelife as far as we can see, because nothing could come forth in evolution which did not already exist in "an obscure and primordial way." The organic would not have begun later in evolution; it existed from the very first. This prelife had a simple inner consciousness or "within," which releases a spiritual energy that grows in complexity without determinable limits. The "within" tends to react as it coils upon itself in a closed volume. There is a double coiling or involution involved, since the planet itself folds upon itself within a closed surface.

A jump or metamorphosis occurs in the evolutionary process from prelife to life ("biogenesis"). The "within" may at first be an irregular closed surface which in time becomes centered; therefore, either by rearrangement of parts or acquisition of a new dimension, an element can change to the point that it gives rise to another level. As the arrangement of the elements occurs, a change in consciousness develops. The beginnings of cellular life emerge. Cells multiply and live in a state of interdependence with one another. Teilhard recognizes a continuity of all living creatures from bacteria to man in light of the fact that they all have the same complicated enzymes and proteins.

Teilhard's position emphasizes the continuity of life, its interdependence, and its total organic nature. With respect to the latter, he points out that every organism can be studied in terms of its parts, but the sum of its parts, however, is not the same as the whole. In fact, in this whole some new value may very well emerge.

Teilhard assumes a teleological view of nature (in contrast to most of his fellow biologists) by contending that evolution is directed toward a precise orientation, to certain ends. The process of evolution in man is not over: it is moving to higher forms in the future.

We can better understand what this higher evolution is all about by comprehending more clearly what precedes it, and the processes and stages out of which it emerges. In the biosphere one finds among the chordates the development of brains of varying size. The brain is the measure of consciousness; nervous tissue differentiates itself and begins to mark out a direction for evolution.

From the biosphere to the psychosphere is a movement of great ramifications where psychism seeks to express itself through different forms. Man is the being who is the object of his own reflection; he is not only conscious, but aware that he is conscious. The greater brain power and intelligence mark off the emergence of the psycho-sphere. In this sphere we find that life has transformed itself in depth. Man, in reaching the level of reflection, constitutes one of the many modalities tried out in the animal kingdom. Yet this modality is a trans-formation that points to the direction in which our earth is evolving.

This argument again raises an interesting question: namely, whether man is continuous or discontinuous with the animal kingdom. Some biologists take the former position in order to provide a continuous and coherent view of evolution, while individuals representing diverse fields may hold to the latter position in order to emphasize man's uniqueness. Theologians, in particular, claim that man is discontinuous with the animal kingdom in order that they may find a place for his distinctive spirituality. Teilhard's position is that there is a discontinuity in the continuity. He attempts to provide a new synthesis by first recog-nizing a continual process from cell to psychism as one movement toward greater complexity and concentration of consciousness. This process continues without interruption in the same direction. Secondly, there were certain leaps that transformed this process (discontinuity).

Psychogenesis has led to the development of man and his distinctive type of consciousness. As the mind develops and thoughts are com-municated in different parts of the earth, this leads to "noogenesis" and the rise of the "noosphere" or the thinking sphere, which today is the active and progressive sphere of the earth.

Modern man's great transformation in thought is that he no longer thinks of the universe in terms of space and time; he also views it in terms of duration. He is now capable of looking back to envisage the entire process of evolution, seeing from where we have come and the direction we may be going. Man now recognizes that he is not the center of the universe; however, rather than make this fact the occasion for despair as some theologians once believed, it is seen in an entirely different light by Teilhard. It is man who points the way toward the final unification of the universe. Man, becoming conscious of himself, can, within evolutionary time, transform himself. Consciousness, among all the energies of the universe, has no limits. Teilhard's theme is that man will not only survive but there will be a form of superlife in the future. But he repudiates the notion that it may be necessary to sacrifice one group for the development of a supergroup. In light of the interdependence of man, all must grow to assure a superlife in the future. There is a compression of elements on earth and the energy of the noosphere is inexorably increasing, which leads to the recognition that evolution is still in process; that man, as presently constituted, is not the highest development. Yet we must remember that evolution is a fantastically slow process in comparison with the way humans measure time in terms of their own life-span. Thus we should not expect to observe evolution taking place under our very eyes.

Superlife culminates in a future point that Teilhard calls Omega. This future point is not a pantheistic state that absorbs the individual into an encompassing whole; rather, it is a hyper-personal state of supreme consciousness in which personality is the chief ingredient and maintains its integrity by its center of consciousness while uniting with all other forms of superconsciousness. At Omega, consciousness has greatly increased its depth and distinctiveness. Omega is the distinct center of hyper-personality, a core of radiating system of subcenters.

The energy forms at Omega point can also be explained in terms of Teilhard's conception of love. Love is a form of energy that is found in the uniting of things. An inchoate form of love exists in all things that unite. Teilhard conceives this uniting process as extending to all persons on earth. Love provides the cohesiveness of Omega while spirituality, selfhood, personality, and superconsciousness constitute its core(41).

In assessing Teilhard's contribution, it can be observed that he has attempted to provide an evolutionary continuity between past, present, and future, and has sought to effect a synthesis between the diversity of things and their inherent unity, and finally, he offers a workable reconciliation between matter and spirit or consciousness. He uses a broad canvas and paints with bold and compelling strokes. He combines the firm grasp and systematization of his subject in keeping with his scientific self with the prophetic vision of the seer.

His scientific colleagues are not likely to accept his notion of an "interior" form of consciousness, even of a prelife level, in all things; neither will they assent to his vision of a future point of human evolution, or that the law of entropy is being reversed by the noosphere. Theologians will probably take exception to his notions of spirituality and man's relation to the universe.

The hypothesis that the universe is still evolving is not entirely new. Nietzsche earlier had viewed man not as an end but as a bridge to the higher or overman who has yet to come. Bernard Shaw, in his play *Back to Methuselah,* traces man's evolution to a future state of pure thought and cognition devoid of corporeal existence. And in more recent times in the book and motion picture, *2001: A Space Odyssey,* a much higher form of life than man is depicted, already evolved, living in man's universe.

That Teilhard has integrated a world view combining the spiritual and scientific dimensions of life into a coherent, although at times mystical, view should give pause to the thought that here may be a compelling philosophical perspective for this secular, scientific, post-industrial age that still exhibits some concern for various religious values. Certainly this view does integrate the spiritual and scientific dimensions. But could it serve as a new religion for man? Teilhard's position would probably not be comprehensible or entirely satisfying for the average man. It probably could be popularized to render it more intelligible; but just as Shakespeare has been translated into other idioms for mass consumption rendering the end product something quite less than the original, the same fate would likely await such transformations of Teilhard's works. On the other hand, as larger percentages of the population receive a more advanced education, it is more likely that Teilhard's works will increasingly be studied during the next twenty years. Finally, the emotional elements which offer security and sustenance in organized religion seem to be lacking in Teilhard's writings — at least in terms of what is found in religions today. However, organized religion is changing and may likely at a not-too-distant date attempt to provide a more comprehensive and integrative view of the world and man as Teilhard has done, especially if it hopes to maintain its followers.

Paul Tillich

The point of view of the liberal Christian theological perspective marks
a sharp contrast with Teilhard's scientific-spiritual vision of evolution.
The Christian theological perspective of Paul Tillich has been exceedingly influential among Anglo-American theologians. Tillich, a German
by birth, emigrated to the United States to escape what he considered
to be intolerable conditions in his native land; he taught during his
illustrious career at Union Theological Seminary and the Divinity
School at the University of Chicago.

Tillich's position moves forward in the liberal tradition of
Schleirmacher, Otto, and Bergson; it utilizes, from time to time, several
existential themes which are related to Tillich's own way of engaging
in theological inquiry. His aim is not that of examining the religion of
the churches, but rather, to focus on the moving of Christian faith in
the larger culture. Theology exists for Tillich in the tension of reve-
lational truth and the questions man faces in his daily existence.
Theology responds to man's self-interpretation during various historical
periods. The conception of community found in St. Augustine under-
lies Tillich's thinking. Whereas where Augustine speaks of supreme
love as an orientation for man, Tillich speaks of an "ultimate concern."
Communities are formed by an ultimate loyalty to some common object
of love. Each culture has its own ultimate concern giving it its unique
style of life. Out of anxiety man generates his need for ultimate concern, and God is the name given to this ultimate concern that answers
the meaning of existence. It is out of ultimate concern and the tension
it generates that different conceptions of God are created in history.

Tillich, in sharp contrast to traditional religious positions, rejects
supernaturalism and the notion of a divine being outside and above the
naturalistic world. Following Kant, he conceives reason as the structure
of the mind which enables it to grasp reality. Reason, however, is
finite: that which is ultimately significant — "being-itself" — cannot be
known by reason. God is "being-itself" and is manifested inexhaustibly
in everything. One's finiteness is temporarily overcome not by reason
but by revelation, which is an ecstatic, mystical experience whereby
one is related in an immediate sense with the very "ground of being" —
one's ultimate concern.

Religion traditionally has presented truth-claims about man, the universe, and God which in some sense are held to be true or warranted,
that provide a perspective that transcends the world of scientific phenomena. Believers accept a particular religious stance not only because

it is emotionally satisfying, but also because it is thought to be the true position among the multitude of different religious systems. This, however, is not Tillich's position. Christianity would not be changed even if the historical Jesus had never lived, for Christian revelation is not based on an historic figure but on Jesus as the Christ. Religious symbols, in other words, need not be true; they need to be existentially effective so that they evoke the power of being. All religious symbols have this power.

Tillich's approach to theological concerns leads him to a treatment of existential themes. This approach is of interest because it affords an amplification of his view of man as well as provides a connection with other theories of human nature.

The principal existential concern for Tillich is that of the courage of self-affirmation in the face of nonbeing. Courage has both an ethical and an ontological dimension which must be united for a proper interpretation of this phenomenon. The ethical dimension expresses concrete action and signifies that one cares enough to decide to pursue a course of action despite opposition. The ontological dimension consists of affirming oneself in spite of the threat of nonbeing. Courage can best be understood, according to Tillich, when the ethical is rooted in the ontological dimension of one's being. Man is aware of the threat of nonbeing through anxiety. Anxiety, in contrast to fear, has no specific object or situation to focus upon. There is the human tendency to attempt to transform anxiety into fear in order to have a situation to confront and overcome. But the basic anxiety of man is his awareness of nonbeing, his finitude. One's finitude is an irremovable part of one's being; thus, existential anxiety cannot be removed. It must be courageously faced so that it does not become a form of pathological anxiety.

Anxiety becomes pathological when one no longer fully affirms himself in the face of nonbeing. The neurotic can only affirm himself on a limited scale resulting from his refusal to accept his finitude. Therefore, for Tillich, a neurosis is "the way of avoiding nonbeing by avoiding being." (42) The actualization of being implies the acceptance of finitude and existential anxiety; therefore, due to his inability to accept nonbeing, the neurotic's response is limited to a weak self-affirmation.

Tillich delineates three types of anxiety: 1) ontic anxiety or the anxiety of fate and death, 2) moral anxiety or the anxiety of guilt and condemnation, 3) spiritual anxiety or the anxiety of emptiness and meaninglessness. Although these three forms of anxiety are present in every age, each form tends to be predominant during a particular cultural period. Ontic anxiety was predominant during the terminal stages of ancient civilization, moral anxiety at the end of the Middle Ages, and spiritual anxiety at the end of the contemporary period.

The neurotic is caught up in his inability to handle these three types of anxiety. In facing the anxiety of fate and death, he tries to build security by insulating himself from the threats of existence. He expresses an unrealistic perfectionism when confronted with the anxiety of guilt and condemnation. These defense mechanisms limit his range of moral experience and restrict his ability to affirm himself. Finally, in the face of anxiety of emptiness and meaninglessness, he seeks certitude in beliefs by immersing himself in an absolute authority in the form of a social or religious institution or a fanatical leader. This leads to a refusal to entertain doubt, engage in independent thinking, and face courageously the existential dimension of meaningless.

There is a basic polarity of being consisting of participation and individualization. The danger of the first is the loss of the self in the collective; whereas the danger of the second is the loss of oneself from the world. Tillich believes that these polarities can be united by transcending them through absolute faith. This absolute faith can also conquer the three forms of anxiety. The courage to be must be rooted in being-itself which transcends the self and the world and unites the polarities of participation and individualization. Tillich rejects the traditional theological notion contained in the subject-object view whereby God is an object to man. Such a God, Tillich believes, would become a tyrant who destroys man's freedom. Nietzsche already pronounced the death of this God of traditional theology. Tillich's being-itself or the ground of being manifests itself inexhaustibly in everything and unites and transcends the courage to be as oneself (individualization) and the courage to be a part (participation). Being-itself can best be understood through man's ultimate concern. Thus, God is being-itself, the structure of all being but not determined by the structure itself. The important point to remember is that the two polarities and the three forms of anxiety can be transcended through absolute faith. (Absolute faith is erected by Tillich even though he is critical of collective absolutes and God viewed as an absolute in an object form.)

Tillich, as we have seen, has afforded insight into the stages and causes of anxiety and the type of courage needed to transcend it; he has also provided a conception of God that is not the traditional God of theology. His important works have enjoyed great influence, particularly in the English-speaking world.

Obvious criticisms from traditional theologians come to mind with Tillich's every departure from orthodoxy. In light of the many assessments of Tillich's thought, we will limit ourselves to one philosophical critique. Paul Edwards has offered a searching examination of Tillich's position(43).

Edwards believes that, apart from certain empirical and descriptive statements, some of Tillich's theological statements are compatible with anything whatsoever. For example, Brown claims that Smith will make his appearance at a party in brown leather boots. Others notice after Smith's arrival that he is barefoot. Now suppose Brown continues to insist Smith is wearing brown leather boots, holding to this position even when Smith puts on a pair of socks to warm his feet. What would we say about Brown's observations? Obviously his reference to the brown leather boots is not a reference to anything, for he has deprived the alleged boots of meaning. He has excluded no conceivable state of affairs, in spite of evidence to the contrary, that would refute his claim that Smith is wearing brown leather boots. This is similar, Edwards contends, to Tillich's statements about God, which are compatible with anything whatsoever. For Tillich, God is not all-powerful or all-good in the literal sense. The world could be incredibly wicked, one where concentration camps, mass torture and extermination could exist in every community throughout the world and Tillich's view of God would still not be falsified. The same would be true if any other worldly development imaginable would occur. The arguments about evil in the world have no effect on being-itself: it is compatible with any possible state of affairs.

Tillich admits that many statements in his system are metaphorical statements. The problem with any system that depends to a high degree on metaphorical statements is whether their meaning can be comprehended when they are translated or reduced to other statements. If, for example, someone asserts, "Get down to brass tacks!" we know that he means that it is time to focus on the matter at hand and cease wasting time. Likewise, if someone says, "Bottlenecks must be ironed out," one knows that the speaker does not mean that an iron should be run back and forth over the neck of a bottle until it is smooth or flat, but rather, that obstacles or stoppages in some process should be corrected. Thus, metaphors frequently may be translatable or reducible to other terms in order that they may be rendered understandable. However, a number of Tillich's key metaphors are not reducible in this way. Being-itself is beyond our ability to translate. God is neither object nor subject; one cannot say that God exists because existence is a finite characteristic. The structures of the mind by means of which we represent the world are finite; therefore, God can be spoken of only metaphorically. These metaphors cannot be reduced to other, more understandable terms; hence, are primarily unintelligible. At best, one metaphorical statement is substituted for another, leading to circularity.

Tillich's treatment of the courage for self-affirmation in the face of anxiety is an important theme in existentialism and serves as an introduction for the reader to this philosophy.

Existentialist Perspectives

There are other possible views of human nature that deserve greater exploration. These views can be found within a diverse group of thinkers beginning with the late nineteenth century Danish philosopher, Sören Kierkegaard, expressed again by Tillich, and highlighted in their chief European forms by the French philosophers and writers, Jean-Paul Sartre, Gabriel Marcel, and Albert Camus, and among the German philosophers, Martin Heidegger and Karl Jaspers. Existentialism came of age during the horrors and brutalities experienced by Western European nations during the second world war; it was during this period, and in the years following the war, that existentialism became a prominent philosophical movement in Europe. Its influence has proven to be considerably greater in novels and the drama in the United States and in books, popular with college youth, than in philosophy itself.

It may be difficult at first to understand why the philosophers mentioned above are called "existentialists" in light of the fact that some are theists and others are atheists. Usually distinctions of this nature tend to align individuals with different philosophies. However, these philosophers have sufficient affinities that would not make it unreasonable to speak of them, for purposes of discussion, as existentialists, even thought some of them have publicly repudiated this label.

One theme found in existential writing is a distrust of reason itself; although not a distrust of all reason — since the existentialists also use reason — but a denial that the systems of rationalism, erected by the philosophers since Descartes and the Enlightenment, applied to social and natural life will lead to higher and higher levels of human progress. As for their disenchantment with rationalistic systems, it stems from a skepticism that any metaphysical system is adequate to encompass, and account for, the variety and richness of human existence. These systems, they contend, are remote, abstract, and academic in dealing with actual experiences, thus, have failed to confront the problems of existence that should be central to philosophy. On the other hand, they claim the claims of the Enlightenment are ill-founded, for reason has been used to destroy as well as create. It was reason that devised our technology of destruction as well as the vast bureaucratic systems that dehumanize man and turn him into an automaton. To use reason, to be rational, is not the same as saying that one is reasonable or sensible or humane.

Whenever stable social institutions exist and rather widespread normative consensus obtains, the questions raised by existentialists do not appear, at first glance, to be highly significant. It is only in the more extreme situations of war, terror and brutality, the conviction that God is dead, and the disruption of the normative fabric of society that existential issues move to the forefront. Man becomes more acutely aware of his existence, his inability to find a grounding for his beliefs, and begins to recognize that he must choose his own life without certitude in his decisions. Man begins thinking not in terms of abstract philosophical ideas but his own existence and what it entails. Awareness of existence leads to an awareness of nonexistence. For Sartre, human consciousness is spoken of as "being-for-itself," which contrasts to "being-in-itself," which is relatively fixed and complete, devoid of potency and becoming, and prior to being-for-itself. The latter is derived from being-in-itself. Being-for-itself is incomplete and in a state of becoming, and it is through man, human consciousness, that nonexistence or nonbeing is recognized or comes into the world. Nothingness is dependent upon being for its ontological status. The category of nonbeing is existentially real. Sartre finds that in freedom man finds nothingness in the world. It is through anxiety, according to Heidegger, that man encounters nothingness and develops awareness of his finitude.

Through the interconnecting strands of these themes we move to an understanding of human nature. There is, for Sartre, no difference in being free and being human. Man's anxiety reveals his total freedom. This opens great possibilities to man; yet it also brings with it feelings of dread and nausea, for one recognizes the reality of nonbeing and death and the great responsibilities for shaping oneself out of one's choices that comes from such a radical freedom. Man is condemned to be free; he is responsible for everything he chooses.

It could be noted that with complete free will each person is completely responsible for his own actions, what he is, and what he will become. Most people really do not want this much freedom; it places too much responsibility on their own shoulders and leaves little room for rationalization and shifting of responsibility. They prefer a rigorous determinism when matters go badly so they can ascribe responsibility to their parents, teachers, foreman, and other authority figures; and generally when they achieve success, they revert to the doctrine of free will in order to take credit for it. But it cannot be both ways. Existentialists are basically agreed that the nature of man is freedom. But this can prove to be a dreadful freedom in the recognition that man and man alone must choose and make his own life. That is to say, there is both exhilaration and anxiety in the existential belief that one's nature is not preformed for him — each person must make his own nature. Each person has this awesome and terrifying responsibility to choose and assume responsibility for his choices without recourse to shifting the blame to others or to institutions by claiming that he could not do otherwise due to a vast array of unseen forces causing him to act. Freedom prevents one from attributing his behavior to childhood experiences over which he had no control. It also rules out the ascription of responsibility for decisions to authority figures, organizations, institutions, or the cultural milieu of the times. It is through existential choices that man makes his nature. Even an attempt to evade or flee the situation is a choice for which one must assume responsibility. Choice is ubiquitious with radical freedom. Deliberation is governed by criteria which the individual chooses, but there is no rational ground for such choices. The criteria may be related to a way of life, but the way of life cannot be justified by reason or logic. One cannot provide a sufficient reason for his choice and in that sense it is baseless.

Out of anxiety over choice and the dread of nonbeing, there are traps to ensnare man and diminish his ability to be an authentic person. Sartre mentions "bad faith" as a tendency when man is making use of freedom; he also denies it. It is a form of lying — not to others but to oneself. Heidegger finds another danger to authenticity in "fallness." This is a universal tendency of man to lose himself in present possibilities, and thereby alienating himself from his future possibilities. Man retreats from his genuine self, from his past and future through gossip, curiosity, and ambiguity. Gossip, filled with clichés and repetitions of the conventional, represents a restricted view. Curiosity, when engaged for novelty rather than understanding, turns away from authenticity. Ambiguity constitutes a lack of comprehension and singleness of purpose that sacrifices the self for a preoccupation with the present. In the face of these ensnarements, man must affirm himself by seeking an authentic existence. But what he can become is limited by nonbeing which is imminent from the time of birth. One frequently tries to cope with the recognition of death by objectifying and externalizing it, speaking of it as if it were something that befalls man in general. To become authentic one has to recognize his own death, something one can only face by himself. Many responsibilities can be carried out by proxy, but not death.

Another theme found particularly among the French existentialists is the notion of the absurd. Sartre uses the term nausea while Camus speaks of the absurd. For Sartre everything is contingent; there is no sufficient reason for things being what they are rather than something else. Man lives in a senseless world which he continually tries to make sensible without finding any ultimate reason for the way things are.

Camus, on the other hand, considers the absurd a confrontation between man and the world in which neither man nor the world is absurd, but rather, the lack of correspondence between the two is. Man seeks a meaningful existence; the world, however, lacks coherence and unity. It is the strain created between man and the world that estranges the two. There are a number of situations that provide an awareness of the absurd: the recognition that one is aging, even though, if possible, one would will to remain young; the discovery that the world is not beneficient but, rather, is indifferent to our desires; or the sudden awareness of one's alienation from others. There is no unity between the individual and the world and no ultimate reason can be given for the way things are. But rather than abject resignation in the face of these distressing features, life can be made worth living by living in revolt against the absurd by asserting oneself and creating values in spite of a world that is indifferent and, at times, threatening to the values man creates.

In conclusion, existentialism has clearly articulated many concerns of twentieth century man caught in an alien and indifferent world in which the older values that formerly afforded direction for his life appear to be crumbling before his very eyes. But the existentialist interpretation of several philosophical issues has been open to a number of criticisms.

One could find some existentialists using the terms 'being' and 'nothing' as if they were subjects to which predicates could be abscribed. One finds that nothing or nonbeing has an ontological status; being, also, is a name of a realm which we try to comprehend. The problem here is one of assuming that there is such a world as nonbeing or nothingness, that it is named by the word 'nothing' as the word ordinarily is used. 'Nothing' does not function as a name of a special realm; rather it functions as a sign of denial. It does not name or describe anything. But those existentialists who try to use words such as 'nothing' and 'nonbeing' in this fashion embroil themselves in all sorts of unnecessary philosophical difficulties.

In their attempt to repudiate nineteenth century materialism that rules out freedom and responsibility for action, the existentialists deny that there were causal explanations for action, for they believe that causal explanations (which they associate with the materialists) would rule out human freedom. However, by adopting this position, they also rule out the possibility for the social and behavioral sciences, which utilize explanations of this type. What the existentialists overlook in their concern that determinism renders freedom impossible is the fact that freedom is not necessarily annulled by causal explanations. One needs to distinguish here between the notion of being compelled and being determined. Causal determinism states that there are no causally contingent events — either they are causally necessary or causally impossible. At one time it was believed that the statement, "Every event has a cause," entailed fatalism; this belief stemmed from the belief that for man to be free there must be uncaused events. However, there can be future events in which one's decisions and actions are part of the cause. Thus, as G.E. Moore claimed, the opposite of 'free' is not 'caused' but 'compelled' or some similar word. It appears, then, that the animus of the existentialists toward causal explanations is misdirected. By making these amendments the existentialists could then recognize more realistically than they have done the diverse factors influencing human choice while still maintaining a modicum of human freedom.

There is also a rather odd ambiguity in extolling the notion that freedom is the nature of man while lamenting the absurdity of existence that this freedom entails. This discrepancy can probably be explained by the implied use of the principle of sufficient reason and the conclusions drawn by the existentialists when the principle is found inadequate. German philosopher Gottfried Leibniz defines the principle of sufficient reason as a claim that no facts or judgments can be true unless there is a sufficient reason why it should be so and not otherwise, even though we often may not know the reasons. Additionally, nothing happens without it being possible for one who should know these things to give a reason why it should be so and not otherwise. For Leibniz, God can know these things. But the existentialists, perhaps because of their attitude toward rationalism and theism, cannot accept the principle of sufficient reason. There is no sufficient reason, they believe, as to why things are as they are and not otherwise. This leads some to take the view that we live in a senseless world, that we unremittingly try to make sense out of. Yet, it would seem that existentialists should delight in their belief that Leibniz is not right, for if he is right, his form of determinism would deny the freedom that the existentialist claims for man. What the existentialist should do is to question the rationalists' use of sufficient reason; instead, he loads himself down with the weight of rationalistic systems and, after finally rejecting some of it, erects another rationalist system. The existentialist lament that no ultimate justification exists for our value system and way of life does not become an acute problem except under the more extreme situations of the ravages of war, concentration camps, and totalitarian abuses. Under everyday situations most people do not give much consideration to an ultimate justification for their value system. The existentialists have been accused of concentrating on extreme situations. Their retort is that these situations confront man with the most critical problems of choice in life in which his decisions make him what he is to become.

The various modalities of existence cannot be contained within being and nonbeing or any conceptual terms. Descriptions of existence are inadequate; all statements about existence, according to Jaspers, can only be clarified by reference to concrete situations. These concrete situations can be illustrated well in the drama where existential themes are characterized in all their particularity and concreteness. Changing perspectives on man in the world can be seen by the contrasting views of classical and contemporary drama.

Perspectives of the Drama

In the history of the drama we find the reflection of a shifting *Weltanschauung* (world view) and a changing perspective of man. The ancient Greek dramas of Sophocles paraded the myths and ethos of the time against a backdrop of a reasonable coherent view of the world. The tragedy originated at this time, first with Aeschylus. It treats the growth of thought and the ability to perceive evil, injustice and consequent suffering in the world. Each of the tragedians approached evil in their own way. Aeschylus saw an inexorable curse of the sins of the fathers visited upon the children; while Sophocles depicted men as helpless to change their fate or destiny except to align themselves with good and to suffer and die nobly.

Tragedy itself is not essentially cruel or violent; neither does it necessarily appear during historical periods when nations are subjected to subjugation and servitude. Tragedy reached its height in Periclean Athens and Elizabethan England, two periods of vigor and optimism. The pallid middle-range emotions, boredom, indifference, and hopelessness, did not dominate. Rather, these periods were ones of great heights and depths when joy and tragedy were deeply felt, and the grays of middle-range emotions are dissipated. Tragedy grows from the conviction of the dignity and significance of human life, the exaltation in the heights man can achieve and his potential for great suffering. It becomes for some tragedians, such as Aeschylus, a reaffirmation of the will to live in the face of suffering and death. The backdrop of the tragedy was usually that of an accepted and familiar cultural view of man in the world. This led to a reasonable degree of predictability, a sense of direction and culmination, and permitted the audience to identify, in some sense, with the characters and gain, as Aristotle believed, a purging and purification of the emotions. Shakespeare's own artistic development was a gradual progression toward a more negative view of life wherein a recompense for human suffering is less likely to be found than in some Greek tragedies. Shakespeare did not believe in the idea of progress or original sin; he thought that most men merited contempt and only a few rise above the rest of mankind. The prerogative of this few is tragedy. Shakespeare usually relies upon a radical distinction between the hero and other characters in the play, and the hero invariably is not understood by the other characters. The hero possesses a high degree of grandeur because he does not bemoan the fact that others do not understand him. Shakespeare's heroes live in a world of their own, a world where inexorable fate signals the disaster that will befall. The inevitability of the tragedy is less evident and obvious in Shakespeare's plays than it is with Aeschylus and Sophocles.

The ostensible unity and coherence of the classical tragedy is missing from the modern theatre. The intent of the modern theatre is vastly different because many historical events and developments have changed man's view of himself in the world. The destruction of political liberties, the horror of two world wars, and the unleashing of the atomic bomb have left in their wake disillusionment with the old answers and panaceas. The cries of "liberty" and "equality" have been used to mask the hypocrisy of the exploiters and rapacious power seekers. Science, which held out promise to dispel superstition and intolerance and transform the world, has increasingly led to a more mechanized and bureaucratized society while providing the means to destroy the world. Industrialism and urbanization have created many problems leaving post-industrial man with an atomised and mechanical society run by a computerized network. Naturalism and secularism have replaced supernaturalism although conventional pieties of religious orthodoxy still may be found.

With these developments and the Death of God movement, the fixed world order that would provide an ultimate justification for human values and man's place in the world has disappeared. Rather than the coherent and unified world view placing each aspect in relation with everything else in the system, we are left with a senseless world, one that is indifferent to human purposes and strivings, a world where no ultimate explanation can be given.

The reaction of the playwrights is not one of passive acceptance or resignation but of open revolt. The revolt, according to Robert Brustein, takes three forms(44). The first form is *messianic revolt* where the playwright rebels against God and attempts to take His place. This can be found in the plays of Strindberg, Ibsen, Shaw, O'Neill, and Genet. The second form, also revealed in the plays of Shaw, Ibsen, Strindberg, as well as Chekhov, Brecht, and Pirandello, is *social revolt* in which the dramatist rebels against the conventions and values of society. Finally, *existential revolt* takes the form of rebellion against one's existence; it is the same as Camus' "metaphysical rebellion" against the human condition, and can be found again in the plays of O'Neill, Strindberg, in addition to Williams, Albee, and Pinter.

Rejecting established institutions, the dramatist attempts to vindicate the individual against the claims of government and morality. He no longer seeks popularity and a large audience, but is more likely to indict the bourgeois for his lack of culture and his sham morality. In fact, the spectator is likely to find himself and his class under attack in the play itself. This revolution has caused grief and estrangement for some dramatists who have found their plays censored and pillored. They have experienced the anguish of rejection leading to a feeling of banishment. The dramatist is caught in the dilemma between his tendency to reject the world and the need to be acutely aware of the life and events of his time.

The stage, it seems, is a better medium for the exemplification of existential themes than the ponderous works of existential philosophers. Existentialism is concerned with the issues faced by the individual in his own existence; and by the use of discursive thought and the systematization of ideas the existentialist is more remote from the individual than the playwright who can dispense with rational categories in the play itself. The use of language as a logical mode of structuring the universe can be radically devalued or annihilated in the hands of a playwright such as Samuel Beckett. Often what occurs on the stage conflicts with or transcends the words actually spoken. We have long overestimated the ability of language and conceptual systems to provide us with truth. Some youth, for example, discover early the discrepancy between what their parents say and what they actually do. Freud points out the gap between what is said and its real meaning in the unconscious psychological life of the individual. And Marx brought to awareness the discrepancy between the entrepreneur's claims of interest in the welfare of the proletariat and the reality of the conditions themselves. The propaganda of nation-states and political campaigns and the hard-sell of advertisers generate skepticism that language is primarily used to pursue and communicate truth. Furthermore, the infinite manifestations of human existence as it is being lived in its multiple forms, spills over the boundaries of language and rushes chaotically, untrammelled, in seemingly limitless directions.

Rather than ideological debates, the representation of events, or the narration of the lives of characters, dramatists are concerned with the individual's confrontation of a situation in terms of the concrete images that this situation evokes. Dramatists often treat of themes of truth and illusion, intent on eliciting a more acute awareness of the precariousness and purposelessness of life. This treatment is done by bringing the vague anxieties surrounding illusion to consciousness so that they may be faced in their stark reality. The immersion in the absurd, one may surmise, may only lead to madness, for one needs his illusions in order to live in this world. On the other hand, many persons have too many protective and distortive illusions to live authentically, and once unnecessary illusions are relinquished their loss leads to a new sense of freedom and exhilaration.

That man can live courageously in an absurd universe is also possible by his comic spirit. Man is the only animal who can laugh and laugh at himself, at his own frailties and the absurdity of life and the world. Laughter serves a therapeutic function; it keeps us from taking our own selves too seriously, our own plans, projects, and aspirations. It strips away the falseness and hypocrisy of our institutions and moralities, allowing us to see them as they are, free from illusions. And it enables us to live courageously in the face of the absurd. When man can no longer laugh, his world will crumble. Closed societies will not tolerate public laughter at its institutions and political policies, for laughter can indict and become subversive. Man can live in spite of the absurdity of existence and by laughter overcome it. "For," as Martin Esslin says, "the dignity of man lies in his ability to face reality in all its senselessness; to accept it freely, without fear, without illusions — and to laugh at it."(45)*

A Reassessment of Man

What does it mean to be fully human? In response to this question, it is imperative that those positions discussed above, which are life-affirming rather than life-negating, be given primary consideration as reference points in the forthcoming chapters. Life is caught between the tensions of the perils of nihilism and a closed system of absolute truths. The danger in the latter "solution" is that thinking ceases; one only needs to apply the ready-made "truths" of a predetermined system to each situation in order to know what to believe and how to act. When the solution is not clear one goes to a shaman for direction. One's education is over (assuming it ever began), for there is no reason to inquire, to be open-minded when the truths have been handed down from a high authority. If the world is unjust and the faithful believer is oppressed, the promise is held out that if one lives by a rigid code in the mundane world to resist iniquity, he will be rewarded in the hereafter. He will have the satisfaction of seeing those who make life wretched for him spending an eternity in suffering and torment. This view is life-negating because it turns away from this world for the hope of another. It also is based upon a position of weakness and impotence by refusing the attempt to change one's condition in the world. Hence, one does not affirm oneself out of weakness and impo-

---

*Excerpt from *The Theatre of the Absurd* by Martin Esslin. Copyright © 1961 by Martin Esslin. Reprinted by permission of Doubleday and Co., Inc.

tence. In keeping with a predetermined code of conduct, one principle may be the belief that the body is basically evil and the spirit divine. Today, the actual mortification of the body is seldom seen, but beliefs about the wickedness of desires and the need to shamefully suppress them is not uncommon. However, to affirm oneself is to take body and mind as an organic unity, to make oneself whole by cultivating a creative expression of this unity. Neither is Buddhism a way to affirm life, since desires and cravings are capitalized upon to propel man to live more creatively and abundantly rather than extinguished. Desires are sources of energy that can be directed into channels that help to ennoble life.

Man has to plan intelligently, but in the course of his planning he sometimes, in his anxiety over future events, sacrifices the quality of his life in the present for an uncertain future. And at times out of the loss of ideals and a sense of direction, he reverts to living in an imaginary more golden age of the past. Both of these tendencies are life-negating. The present is the focal point of temporal continuity where past and future meet in the human mind and in the thread of ongoing experience.

That which leads to the emergence and growth of creative thought, self-expression and life style, and which does not deny the same rights for others, is life-affirming. That which enables man to live courageously in the face of the growing artificiality and mechanization of culture and the threat of nonbeing and the absurd is creative and life-affirming. Here one's task is to face the realities of existence and laugh at their absurdities. To have the courage to make oneself whole in an uncertain universe is the height of the life-affirming spirit.

Questions for Discussion

1. What are the views of man held by laymen in your home community? What evidence or arguments do they offer in support of their views? What inferences do they draw from these views about education?

2. As you read in the educational literature, try to detect what assumptions the authors make about man. How are these assumptions used to advance their line of thinking? In what way could these assumptions be made more explicit and provided with greater support?

3. Do your college or university officials take a position with respect to the question of man? If their views are not explicit, see if you can detect from their policies what they believe about students. Assuming the university had a diametrically different set of beliefs, in what manner and direction would this alter its policies? Make a similar analysis of public school systems with which you are familiar.

4. In what way will the holding of different and even conflicting views about man affect teaching practices and the way in which the teacher relates to students. For example, think about two teachers you have had who expressed contrasting and conflicting views about man (as you compare them to one other). To what extent did these views enter into their teaching practice and influence their relations with students? What significant differences exist between the two teachers?

5. It is tempting when reassessing the perspectives on man presented in the chapter to seek out one position which could possibly objectively embrace the strength of each of the other positions and unify them into a compelling outlook. This may be difficult to do in light of man's complexity, diversity, and cultural differences. If Nietzsche is correct, there can be no objectively grounded perspective of all perspectives. Nevertheless, some positions will seem to be more sound than others. Which ones appear sounder, and why?

6. Do you believe that some of the more acute problems of education could be ameliorated to some significant extent if educators and those who hold political power changed their conception of man? If so, what are the views they should espouse? If not, why would such changes fail to make a significant difference?

7. Make a list of your beliefs about man; then try to support your beliefs by adducing evidence and arguments in their behalf. How do your beliefs affect your actions? Are the two consistent? How will your beliefs about man affect the way you fulfill your tasks as an educator?

For Further Reading

On the biological basis of life, the reader should see some of the following works: René Dubos, *The Torch of Life*, New York: Pocket Books, Inc., 1963; Lawrence K. Frank, *Nature and Human Nature*, New Brunswick, N.J.: Rutgers University Press, 1951; Th. Dobzhansky, *Mankind Evolving*, New Haven: Yale University Press, 1962; Ashley Montagu, *On Being Human*, New York: Hawthorn Books, Inc., 1966. Man's biological nature is presented from different perspectives. The authors represent the following disciplines respectively: bacteriology, psychology, genetics, and anthropology.

One of the best introductions to cultural anthropology is Clyde Kluckholn's *Mirror for Man*, Greenwich, Conn.: Premier Books, 1959. For the relationship between education and anthropology see George F. Kneller, *Educational Anthropology*, New York: John Wiley & Sons, 1965. A comprehensive review of anthropology may be found in A. L. Kroeber, ed., *Anthropology Today*, Chicago: University of Chicago Press, 1953.

As for psychological views of man discussed in the chapter, a good library will have *The Standard Edition of the Complete Works of Sigmund Freud*, London: The Hogarth Press, 1955. Numerous paperback editions of Freud's works are also available. John B. Watson's behaviorism can be found in *Psychology from the Standpoint of a Behaviorist*, Philadelphia: J. B. Lippincott, 1919. For B. F. Skinner, see his *Science and Human Behavior,* New York: Macmillan, 1953. Among the writings of the humanistic psychologists: Erich Fromm, *Man for Himself*, New York: Rinehart, 1947; Abraham H. Maslow, *Motivation and Personality*, New York: Harper and Bros., 1954; Carl Rogers, *On Becoming A Person*, Boston: Houghton Mifflin, 1961; and Viktor Frankl, *Man's Search for Meaning*, Boston: Beacon Press, 1962.

For readings on Marx and Marxists see: Lewis S. Feuer, ed., *Marx and Engels: Basic Writings on Politics and Philosophy*, Garden City, N.Y.: Doubleday, Anchor Books, 1959; and Arthur P. Mendel, ed., *Essential Works of Marxism*, New York: Bantam Books, 1965. George Lichtheim's *Marxism: An Historical and Critical Study*, New York: Frederick A. Praeger, 1961, is a sophisticated survey of the development of Marxism within the backdrop of the larger socialist movement.

Works on religion, starting first with the section on Buddhism: Lin Yutang, ed., *The Wisdom of China and India:* New York: Random House, The Modern Library, 1955; Abraham Kaplan, *The New World of Philosophy*, New York: Random House, Vintage Books, 1961; Edward Conze, *Buddhism: Its Essence and Development,* New York: Harper, Torchbooks, 1965. The Death of God movement can be found in John A. T. Robinson's *Honest to God*, Philadelphia: Westminister Press, 1963; Gabriel Vahanian, *The Death of God*, New York: George Braziller, 1961; and Thomas J. J. Altizer and William Hamilton, *Radical Theology and the Death of God*, Indianapolis: Bobbs-Merrill Co., Inc., 1966. For an introduction to Nietzsche's thought see Walter Kaufmann, ed., *The Portable Nietzsche*, New York: Viking Press, 1954. Teilhard de Chardin's leading work is *The Phenomenon of Man*, New York: Harper, Torchbooks, 1965. Lucid and thoughtful presentations by Paul Tillich are found in his *The Courage to Be*, New Haven, Conn.: Yale University Press, 1952, and *Dynamics of Faith,* New York: Harper and Row, 1957.

Among the many works on the drama and its perspectives of man, the following relate to the themes treated in this chapter: Edith Hamilton, *The Greek Way to Western Civilization*, New York: New American Library, Mentor Books, 1948; Robert Brustein, *The Theatre of Revolt,* Boston: Little, Brown and Co., 1964; and Martin Esslin, *The Theatre of the Absurd,* Garden City, N.Y.: Doubleday, Anchor Books, 1961.

Notes

1. René Dubos, *The Torch of Life* (New York: Pocket Books, Inc., 1962), p. 34.

2. *Ibid.,* p. 38.

3. A. L. Kroeber and Clyde Kluckhohn analyzed 164 definitions of culture in "Culture: A Critical Review of Concepts and Definitions," *Papers of the Peabody Museum,* 47, no. la, 1952.

4. The interested reader will find in the bibliography references for further reading on man's biological and cultural characteristics.

5. Sigmund Freud, *Beyond the Pleasure Principle* (London: The Hogarth Press, Ltd. and The Institute of Psycho-Analysis, 1942), pp. 44-45.

6. Sigmund Freud, *New Introductory Lectures on Psychoanalysis,* trans. J. H. Sprott (New York: W. W. Norton and Co., Inc., 1933), p. 147.

7. *Ibid.,* p. 141.

8. Sigmund Freud, *The Ego and Id* (London: The Hogarth Press, Ltd. and The Institute of Psycho-Analysis, 1935), p. 56.

9. For further implications of the death instinct, see: Sigmund Freud, *Civilization and Its Discontents,* trans., Joan Riviere (London: The Hogarth Press, Ltd. and The Institute of Psycho-Analysis, 1939).

10. Freud, *New Introductory Lectures,* p. 73.

11. *Ibid.,* p. 75

12. Freud, *Civilization and Its Discontents,* p. 34n.

13. Freud, *The Ego and the Id.* p. 23.

14. Freud, *New Introductory Lectures,* p. 77.

15. Sigmund Freud, *Collected Papers,* vol. IV (London: The Hogarth Press, Ltd. and The Institute of Psycho-Analysis, 1924), p. 86.

16. Sigmund Freud, *Character and Culture* (New York: Crowell-Collier Publishing Co., 1963), p. 211-212.

17. Abraham Maslow, *Motivation and Personality* (New York: Harper and Row, Publishers, 1954), chapter 18.

18. See: H. J. Eysneck, *The Uses and Abuses of Psychology* (Baltimore: Penguin Books, 1953), chapters 10-12.

19. John B. Watson, *Psychology from the Standpoint of a Behaviorist* (Philadelphia: J. B. Lippincott, 1919).

20. *Ibid.,* p. 10.

21. John B. Watson, *Behaviorism* (London: Kegan Paul, 1925), p. 82.

22. B. F. Skinner, *Science and Human Behavior* (New York: Macmillan, 1953), p. 258.

23. B. F. Skinner, *The Behavior of Organisms* (New York: D. Appleton-Century Co., 1938), pp. 12-13.

24. *Ibid.,* p. 66.

25. Frederick Engels, *Dialectics of Nature* (New York: International Publishers Co., 1939), p. 187.

26. Karl Marx, *Theses on Feuerbach,* VI (New York: International Publishers Co., 1939), p. 148.

27. Karl Marx, Preface to *A Contribution to the Critique of Political Economy* (Chicago: Charles H. Kerr and Co., 1904).

28. Arthur P. Mendel, ed., "Socialism: Utopian and Scientific", *Essential Works of Marxism* (New York: Bantam Books, 1961), pp. 81-82.

29. Lewis S. Feuer, ed., *The German Ideology in Marx and Engels: Basic Writings on Politics and Philosophy* (Garden City, N.Y.: Doubleday, 1959), p. 254.

30. *Ibid.,* p. 263.

31. Adam Schaff, *A Philosophy of Man* (New York: Dell Publishing Co., 1968).

32. Mendel, ed., *Essential Works of Marxism,* pp. 1-10.

33. See: Antony Flew and Alasdair MacIntyre, eds., *New Essays in Philosophical Theology* (New York: Macmillan, 1964), pp. 96-130.

34. Edward Conze, *Buddhism: Its Essence and Development* (New York: Harper, Torchbooks, 1965), p. 13.

35. John A. T. Robinson, *Honest to God* (Philadelphia: The Westminister Press), 1963.

36. This idea will be developed when Tillich is discussed.

37. Thomas J. J. Altizer and William Hamilton, *Radical Theology and the Death of God* (Indianapolis: Bobbs Merrill Co., 1966), p. 126.

38. Gabriel Vahanian, *The Death of God* (New York: George Braziller, Inc., 1961), chapter 8.

39. Pierre Teilhard de Chardin, *The Phenomenon of Man* (New York: Harper, Torchbooks, 1965).

40. *Ibid.,* chapters 1 and 2.

41. Teilhard's growing mysticism at this point makes it difficult to provide a more precise explanation.

42. Paul Tillich, *The Courage to Be* (New Haven, Conn.: Yale University Press, 1967), p. 66.

43. Paul Edwards, "Professor Tillich's Confusions," *Mind,* vol. 74, no. 294 (April 1965), 192-214.

44. Robert Brustein, *The Theatre of Revolt* (Boston: Little, Brown and Co., 1964), pp. 16-33.

45. Martin Esslin, *The Theatre of the Absurd* (Garden City, N.Y.: Doubleday, Anchor Books, 1961), p. 316.

Chapter Two
The Student as a Person

A widespread reassessment is now being made of the student's role in the educational process, and a number of policy changes have already resulted. Education can be made more meaningful and relevant to the pressing concerns and aspirations of students. In order to pursue the question, "What does it mean to be human?" in a new context significant criticisms of educational systems in terms of the way they define the student's role in the educational process must be examined.

Study as Work:
The Process of Alienation

Is study actually work? Most students agree that it is hard work. But is it actually work in the sense of an occupation enlisting one's efforts to produce a product or perform a service, a regular process where one is governed by rules and performance standards and is paid for his services?

It would seem at first glance that study is not exactly the same thing. But let us look more closely at the similarities to see whether an analogy can be drawn between study and work.

Obviously, study can be laborious, just as some forms of work are. In college, one follows a schedule of classes and pursues assignments; one is not free to do at all times what he would really like to do. Sanctions are applied whenever students refuse to follow schedules: low grades, probation, dismissal. The worker, too, must follow a schedule (which varies with the occupation and even within an occupation) and sanctions are applied when he does not follow it properly or refuses to follow it. The student produces a product in the form of papers, exams, laboratory work, and various objects in art classes. Pay is usually missing, although there are scholarships, fellowships, assistantships, and instructorships. Just as in the occupational world, there is "moonlighting" by some students after their classes in order to help pay for their education. The analogy can be carried further by noting that students, held as they are to time schedules and appointments, must fulfill quotas (assignments) and have their products evaluated (the grading system). The activities of students are important to the future welfare of society because this society, more than ever before in its history, needs highly-trained specialists. It is also true that some workers in the occupational structure are presently performing tasks essential to the future welfare of society. However, one should notice that the labor of students in their studies and assignments is more closely related to those in the occupational structure whose work is primarily intellectual in nature rather than those whose tasks demand physical skills, dexterity, or stamina. Thus, the tasks of students resemble the intellectual requirements demanded of professionals and semi-professionals in the occupational force (and these basically are the occupational levels toward which college students aspire).

There are sufficient analogous elements in study to call it — at least for purposes of analysis — a form of work. Therefore, the student can be alienated from his studies just as the worker, according to Marx, is alienated from what he produces.

You may recall that for Marx man gains self-realization through his work, his sense of creativity and the satisfaction of his desires. It is through his labors that man transforms his world, makes himself at home in it, and creates himself and his essential nature. But with a growing division of labor and the application of technological processes to industry, man has become increasingly alienated from his work. Work becomes compulsive, a process to satisfy external wants. It no longer satisfies genuine needs or helps the worker relate himself to the world. Thus, with the growth of capitalism dehumanization became more widespread and intensified.

The student also feels increasingly alienated from his studies and his educational program for similar reasons. Higher education, as well as industry, has undergone great changes. Burgeoning enrollments, resulting from the high birth rates following the second world war coupled with greater educational aspirations of the younger generation and the more specialized requirements for gainful employment, have transformed the university into what Clark Kerr calls "the multiversity." The multiversity is a city within itself held together rather loosely through a central administration that attempts to coordinate diverse colleges, schools, and departments, with a faculty, representing incredibly diverse interests, moving off in all directions — sometimes at once. Unfortunately, in all the activities of research, service, consulting work, and committee meetings, the student has too often been forgotten. In order to operate the vast bureaucratic machinery that keeps the university running the student has become a number on an I.B.M. card. He has become an indistinct force in the mass, whose identity and personal desires and aspirations seem to be blotted out while those in authority frenetically strive to keep the vast organizational machinery from breaking down. The student many times feels that he no longer is treated like a person but more like a number in a mass, a name on a chart, a body that occupies classroom seating space. He has become depersonalized and dehumanized and, as a result, his studies seem more onerous and vapid and his college experience begins more and more to lack a sense of direction and afford genuine satisfaction and personal fulfillment.

In addition to the sheer size, confusion and conflicts in the multiversity, students complain that the curriculum and the quality of instruction seem distant, mechanical, unrelated to their interests, and lacking a tangential relation to the significant social and political issues of the times. The curriculum, some students contend, is undergirded by a rigid set of rules that make for lock-step procedures based upon hours, grades, and the accumulation of credits toward graduation. This form of organization leaves the impression that knowledge is purveyed in an atomized fashion by being sliced up into bits and pieces in the form of courses. Since many of the most pressing problems facing youth transcend the boundaries of most existing course structures, the pursuit of these problems cannot be very well undertaken within actual course organization. And since professors increasingly are finding their professional status directly related to greater degrees of specialization within subareas of their specialty, most instructors not only lack the ability to offer interdisciplinary explorations of the great social issues of our time but are also adverse to acquiring it. The student is left with the formidable task of integrating into a meaningful and workable perspective the bits and pieces of knowledge and skills acquired in diverse courses. Yet students today, probably more attuned and sensitive to the problems of their age than any previous generation, generally believe it their responsibility to concern themselves with the relevance and uses of knowledge gained in their college experience. For those students who do not accept existing arrangements as relevant, the present organization of the curriculum in many institutions is a source of alienation from one's college experiences. As a result, students have, in many cases, sought to devise ways in which the curriculum can be effectively reorganized.

Alienation also is in part a function of expectation, so that those who come to college expecting their experiences to prove intellectually exciting and challenging to their active curiosities are likely to be more disappointed and, in time, experience a greater degree of alienation than those who come seeking a degree in the shortest possible time in order to obtain a secure position. Alienation towards academic life is a more characteristic feature of the intellectually superior, rather than the average, student because the intellectually superior student has higher expectations and is more able to envision possibilities for the integration and application of knowledge to the pressing social issues of the times. But his academic experiences do not usually bear out the possibilities, for he finds the curriculum atomized and the instructors staking out their privileged domains and equipping themselves with arcane methodologies devoted to plunging deeper and deeper into a minuscule area. The professor's enthusiasm for such tasks cannot be genuinely shared with students because they are tied up with the former's professional status, promotion, and sometimes government contracts.

The entire responsibility, however, cannot be placed upon the colleges and their faculty and administration. At times when students chastise a curriculum pattern for its lack of "relevance," they have in mind not relevance to the great social issues of our time, but an indictment for its failure to be immediately applicable to narrow personal concerns. It is doubtful that a curriculum designed to address itself to such concerns would be in the best interests of students, for students are more likely to profit by the development of broad and flexible skills and integrative approaches to knowledge.

Some students, as well as some who teach them and administer educational programs, are engrossed in some of the less desirable features of our culture such as quantification and externality. Quantification pervades American culture in the fascination with size and bigness: the size of the latest commercial airliner, the area of a state, the height of a skyscraper, the bigness of cars; and in a fixation on quantity: the enrollment of a university, the amount of income a person has, the concern over bodyweight, the number of calories consumed each day, the longevity of the adult male or female, the number of American men fighting in foreign wars. Numbers have become instrumental in running our society: Social Security, employment, driver's license, charge accounts, telephone, insurance, and bank account. All of this leads to a conviction that we know more about things and people than we really do, for if we can quantify the characteristics of our lives, we have introduced accuracy, orderliness, coherence and convenience into a complex world. Or so it seems. The first pitfall is to believe that one really knows a great deal about something by quantifying it. The second misconception is to believe that the end product of all this quantification makes life more reasonable and eventually more satisfying due to its orderliness and manageability. We only know things externally by quantifying them, and suffusing our lives with numbers and quantities depersonalizes the individual while offering greater orderliness. This process of depersonalization is often subtle and diffused. Therefore, one may likely argue that it is not taking place. He is not likely to be aware of it unless he develops keener perception and greater sensitivity to the significance of the events occurring all around him.

Externality is another factor that contributes to dehumanization and alienation. Many social relations are based upon superficial and fleeting appearances. Too many of us are prone to judge others quickly and impressionistically after being introduced for the first time and talking for only a few minutes. Categories and compartments are immediately at our command for classification and stereotyping. Race, religion, nationality, political affiliation, and parental background are ready categories for the convenience of stereotyping. With an alarming number of dossiers, credit ratings, and personnel files available we are armed with material about the private lives of people, even though the information may be false or misleading. The breakdown of primary group relations and the multiplication of secondary relations and impersonality has led to the development of mistrust of others not well-known. Tendencies exist to view others in terms of their usefulness in helping one occupationally and socially to get ahead. Less frequently do we really want to get to know others as persons, because it takes time, is demanding, and emotional attachments are built up that later can be damaged or destroyed. It involves risk and a willingness to sacrifice one's feelings for others' welfare. It is safer and easier to see and treat people with a sense of externality, forgetting that they have an inner life of thought and feeling. This attitude of externality facilitates the treatment of persons as things or objects to be manipulated in getting ahead. However, as more people adopt the attitude of externality in social relations, greater depersonalization and alienation result. The type of society we live in discourages the development of deeper interpersonal relations, not only in bureaucratic organizations, but in clubs, voluntary groups, the school, and the family. The forces contributing to depersonalization in Western societies have engendered a loss of personal identity and a sense of direction in life. The quest for identity is not a new problem, but its peculiar form, as expressed today, seems to be a product of an advanced industrial civilization.

Identity and Alienation

The search for identity is exemplified in the question, "Who am I?" It is a search that is cumulative in terms of one's life experiences and interpersonal relations. It is a conception that is modifiable in light of new experiences; and one's sense of well-being, individuality, and belonging is directly related to one's ability to cope with the search for identity. Education, hopefully, is a process whereby the individual can establish a sense of identity and a direction for his life.

One's sense of identity is shaped by cumulative life experiences in a particular culture. It is shaped, first of all, in childhood when the individual's life centers primarily in the home wherein interaction is limited to parents, siblings, nurses, and friends of the family. Later, one's peers begin to assume more importance, particularly after the onset of puberty. Teachers, administrators, ministers, and other authority figures also enter into the lives of youth. The individual's tendency to identify with the values of his social class, religion, nationality, and the dominant values of his community leads to the internalization of certain attitudes and standards. A very large factor today in the lives of youth is the

Who am I?

mass media. Whether or not we ascribe to Marshall McLuhan's position, it is scarely deniable that the new media have had far-reaching effect on youth.

The problems of identity are acute in our times due to widespread transformations and dislocations in social, political, and economic life. These changes have also wrought in their wake the gradual erosion of traditional value systems and formerly accepted modes of behavior. Some of the cultural ideals have become increasingly worn, if not entirely tattered, and far less credible, particularly with the younger generation that has grown up in a culture no longer fully imbued with them. Many ideals, among them the venerable Horatio Alger tales, hard work and diligence leading to success, no longer seem believable in light of existing economic conditions. In fact, William Whyte found that many young Americans preferred to settle for the security and fringe benefits of a large, established organization rather than taking risks in the pursuit of one's future(1). Modern man looks primarily to others for support and assurance to gain a sense of identity and a feeling of worth. Man has become, in our own age, more other-directed(2).

An ideal that has deep roots in the past but now appears more illusory and less compelling is that of continuous progress. This ideal essentially grew out of the Enlightenment faith that through the use of "Reason" in all aspects of life, superstition, myth, dogma and all the shackles on men's minds would soon fall away, and the highest stage of civilization in human history would be ushered in. This same faith, although at times less connected with the use of reason and science, was found in nineteenth century America in the drive of intrepid settlers to conquer a new frontier and tame a wilderness. America, many believed, was the land of opportunity, of vast untapped resources and unlimited possibilities for personal advancement, where even the most impoverished immigrant could hope to rise from his socio-economic level. But the enormous social and technological changes during the twentieth century as well as two world wars, concentration camps, the threat of atomic warfare, and constant international conflicts throughout the world, have caused many people to realize that Science and Reason did not usher in the millennium. Instead, mankind dangles precariously on the precipice of imminent annihilation. People seek to escape such realities by engaging in a ceaseless round of frenetic activity whereby no time will remain to think about pressing world-wide problems. They immerse themselves in group and organizational life to gain a feeling of security by following the dictates of the group. Others seek some system of certitude by identifying with an absolutistic system of a religious, or political nature which promises security and certainty through participation in routine and orderliness. The problem of identity can become acute. The problem of identity does not disappear merely because one attempts to remain too busy to think about it. Neither can one discover his authentic sense of self by having it prescribed by others or through the framework of a rigid social, religious, political system. True, one's sense of identity is not grasped in isolation from others. Actually there are two dimensions to the process. Tillich speaks of them as "individualization" and "participation."(3)

Individualization and participation could be thought of as correlated. Individualization is the affirmation of self without regard to participation in the world. The person determines his own direction in life. As Nietzsche would state it, the will to power wills itself by preserving and transcending itself; it becomes a self-affirmation that overcomes that which would negate life. Participation is the act of affirming oneself as part of a larger whole, to be oneself while being a part of community. Dangers arise, according to Tillich, when the two dimensions become disassociated from one another. When this occurs, the courage to be as oneself (individualization) results in a loss of the world or community as an aspect of selfhood, while the courage to be a part (participation) leads to a loss of the self in the collective. The latter seems to be the greater danger today. Social movements of the times ostensibly ascribe collective arrangements with having more worth or embodying a greater sense of reality than the individual. A collective identity emerges based upon successful role playing, while the roles themselves are imposed upon the individual by groups and organizations. The individual, in his anxiousness to be accepted, liked, respected, and his yearning for success, wealth or fame, will usually succumb to whatever roles society demands he play in order to achieve his personal goals. People become obsessive in role playing. Sometimes they respond unthinkingly to rewards and punishments. They are eager for approval and dread rebuke or rejection. Their selves become little more than the totality of roles they have adopted. They become, after a period of time, a mirror image of the accepted norms of a particular social class or occupational group. Apart from such groups they lack any sense of identity, and they experience a general feeling of dread at the thought of being alone. It may be necessary in such cases, as Sidney Jourard says, "to inculcate the value of being oneself, over and above our role-responsibilities."(4)

Another way to view the problem is in terms of the genesis of identity in the life of the individual. George Herbert Mead's explanation of the process is from the standpoint of a social behaviorist(5). Man uses what Mead calls "significant symbols" which are linguistic in form and evolve from roles played in social life in response to others. Communication makes it possible to consciously take the role of the other in a social context. Communication involves the presence of meaning in social experience which enables others to respond to symbols, and their responses serve as stimuli to the user in such a manner that future action of others can be anticipated.

The self emerges in childhood from this early pattern of communication whereby the social group serves as "the generalized other." Two dimensions of the self emerge at this time: "me" and "I." The "me" is formed by the attitudes and roles acquired from the "generalized other." The "I" is the response the individual makes to the attitudes of others. As the "me" serves to organize the attitudes and roles adopted from others, the "I" responds to "me" in certain novel ways. The "I" appears in the memory of what the individual has done, what reactions and responses the individual has made in terms of others. The "I" can retrospectively call upon memory to devise novel ways of acting in situations, and the individual is not compelled to act in the same way once a self-concept is developed. As a result of the "I," the individual's belief in himself and his sense of importance is not entirely determined by others.

Mead's analysis, then, provides an explanation of the development of a self-concept by showing how it develops through the process of social interaction, communication, and the adoption of attitudes acquired from others. At the same time, the "I" provides the unique, novel, and idiosyncratic element in human behavior by enabling the individual to perform his social roles without entirely succumbing to them. Each person is more than the totality of his social roles; he is capable of responding in unique and unpredictable ways and is able to chart a life for himself over and above the press of social role. Unfortunately, such direction is less the case today. Although persons seeking security and status increasingly are willing conformists to social roles and frequently regard others who do not do likewise with disdain, there are social conditions which contribute strongly to such behavior over and above a middle-class tendency of supineness.

The vast changes that have occurred in society have generated a feeling of powerlessness among the middle class in terms of politics, organizational bureaucracy, and the economy. Whereas powerlessness is endemic in the lower class, more recently it has become a pervasive feeling in the middle class, that is, largely the lower-middle class. The feeling arises from the belief that one is incapable of influencing the course of events, that events and persons in power are shaping one's life, and there is not much one can do about it. This leads to a feeling of insignificance as though unknown forces were shaping one's life into a preconceived, desired mold. Powerlessness, coupled with an existential sense of isolation and meaninglessness, creates great anxiety and alienation.

Emile Durkheim's concept of "anomie," which refers to a condition of normlessness in industrial societies, has been analyzed by Robert Merton in terms of American society(6). In Durkheim's original statement of the problem, he found national suicide rates generally increase with a rise in prosperity and are lowest in the poorest countries. This trend may be interpreted as a result of industrialization. As prosperity increases, the sanctions of culture weaken and normlessness appears, thereby generating societal disorganization or disintegration of the individual in society(7). Merton analyzes anomie in an attempt to account for different frequencies of deviant behavior according to social structures and why the forms of deviancy vary according to social structure. Merton sees a discrepancy between the cultural good of success in economic competition and the institutionalized means used in reaching the goal. He finds a stronger emphasis upon the goals than upon the means, thereby leading individuals to think in terms of expediency. The preferred procedure, irrespective of its legitimacy or approval value, is the one which provides the greatest personal advantage and is likely to avoid punishment. A greater degree of normlessness develops with the attenuation of institutional means, and higher expectations exist that socially disapproved behavior is required to achieve cultural goals.

Thus, as anomie increases, role behavior becomes less clear-cut, and the sense of stability that role-playing engenders is undermined when one knows what he can and cannot do. The permissable and acceptable is beclouded by emphasis upon the goals at the expense of institutional means. Both goals and means are in a state of flux during periods when societies, such as our own, are undergoing rapid transformations. One's identity in mass society becomes more unstable as ambiguities increase in one's multiple roles such as student, son or daughter, brother or sister, comrade, lover, wage-earner. Both Tillich and Mead provide insight into the problem of cultivating and regaining a sense of identity. Other approaches and possible solutions will be presented later in the chapter. At this time certain processes of dehumanization in schools which, in turn, exacerbate the problem of identity should be examined.

Dehumanization in the Classroom

What is dehumanization? The concept is rather difficult to deal with because it has an inward as well as an outward dimension. The outward dimension is the interpersonal relationships by which people relate themselves to one another. The inward dimension is the way a relationship makes a person feel and how it affects his self-concept and sense of personal dignity. The latter dimension can be observed in facial expressions, body posture, and other outward manifestations of feelings. There are various interpretations of dehumanization. Observers may be relying on outward criteria to evaluate dehumanization that do not fully take into account individual variations in response or the personal background of the individual. However, there are certain cases or paradigms that can be used to determine a dehumanizing situation. A situation interpreted as dehumanizing to the vast majority of persons in Western culture might be interpreted differently in another culture. It would be necessary to study the culture and its traditions carefully before any paradigms could be developed. This discussion is limited to our own culture. Anthropologists and other specialists are left with the task of developing paradigms for other cultures.

Any interpersonal relationship that has one or more of the following effects on the individual is dehumanizing: (1) brutalization, (2) humiliation in terms of one's sense of dignity, (3) a situation that causes a partial loss or aggravation of one's sense of identity, (4) a situation wherein one perceives himself as treated as a thing, object, or piece of property to be manipulated rather than a person to be respected and nurtured, and (5) a situation that causes one to feel that he is not in control of his own actions, but that they are caused by known or unseen forces which he cannot resist.

A closer look will reveal that dehumanizing situations are not limited to the schools but may be found in all institutions. One of the most extreme situations is that of the brutalizing type. Trauma is a primary factor in determining a brutalizing situation. During the situation, but particularly after its termination, when the individual has had time to comprehend it, he experiences profound feelings of shock, mortification, dismay, incredulity, shame, guilt, resentment, worthlessness, or other emotion. The distinguishing feature is the profoundness of the emotions that causes a temporary psychical paralysis and sends shock waves through the system. Brutalizing experiences, although less frequent in occurrence in the life of the individual than the other types, are still so highly damaging that they may leave permanent psychical scars.

A second form of dehumanization that is damaging but less traumatic than brutalization is humiliation in terms of one's sense of dignity. In some respects humiliation is the antithesis of dignity. One's sense of dignity is invariably destroyed, even if only temporarily, whenever he is genuinely humiliated. Humiliation is not merely a cause of embarrassment and shame; it also constitutes a blow to one's dignity and his self-respect. Whenever humiliation becomes severe enough to cause trauma, it then becomes brutalization. A sense of dignity is essential for every person in order to maintain self-respect and a feeling of personal worth, and self-respect and personal worth are damaged by each humiliating situation.

Situations which cause a partial loss or aggravation of one's sense of identity are a third type of dehumanizing. This is brought about when others, intentionally or unintentionally, strike at, erode, and undermine what and who one believes himself to be. There are, however, therapeutic situations wherein the therapist helps the individual to reshape his thoughts and feelings about himself, so that his sense of identity is restructured. These situations can generate a temporary state of disequilibrium and confusion, but they are designed to help, not injure, the person. However, they may, at times, have untoward dehumanizing effects. Our concern is not the therapeutic sessions but everyday relationships which dehumanize by endangering one's sense of identity. The effects of these situations arouse a sense of personal loss, a feeling that one no longer is clear who he is and what he is about. Whatever the factors that precipitate the situation, whether the intent of the other party is malicious or not, the focal point is always on the end result within the inner life of the individual and its effect on his future social relations. Thus, disturbances that shake one's sense of identity are to be judged in terms of whether they eventually enable the person to be more self-fulfilling or whether they prove to be chronically injurious.

A fourth type of dehumanization occurs when one perceives himself treated as an object to be manipulated rather than a person to be respected and nurtured. It is found in several different types of social relationships. One form is the "slave relationship" which occurs when the individual is treated like a piece of property to be bought and sold, used and manipulated as the "owner" sees fit. Another form that this type of dehumanization takes is the "robot relationship" in which the individual is treated much like a machine. He is thought of in terms of efficiency. He is little more than a physical body that performs work and responds to orders promptly and without question. Machines do not have feelings and emotions, so the desires and purposes of the individual are never considered. The individual becomes a cog in the organization; he is evaluated by his ability to do work, to keep his minute sub-section of the organization running smoothly, and to obey orders unquestioningly and with dispatch. Both the slave and the robot relationship are found today, but whereas the slave relationship was the dominant type in the nineteenth century, the robot relationship has become a predominant form in our own age.

Finally, a fifth type of dehumanization is found in those situations when the individual is made to feel that he is not the author or source of his actions, but that his actions are caused by known or unseen forces over which he has no control. Whenever a social relationship engenders a feeling of personal impoverishment wherein one no longer experiences himself as the bearer of his own powers and abilities and the source of his own actions, then a form of dehumanization and alienation from self has begun. One no longer feels himself the subject and author of his thoughts, experiences, and actions, but feels that his own actions in the world are of a foreign quality that he is powerless to oppose. We see this attitude developing in the conviction of many citizens that they have no voice in government, but the activities of government influence their actions immeasurably. We also see this attitude toward the occupational structure and large organizations whereby the worker believes that his actions are not only subjected to but are increasingly controlled by unseen authorities in the hierarchy.

A qualification should be made at this point. Each type of dehumanizing relationship mentioned above may possess some overlapping characteristics with those of other types, so that in making observations of actual situations, a pure type may not necessarily be found. The purpose of dividing them in this manner is for the sake of clarity and for purposes of analysis.

Each of these types, whenever carried to their logical extremes in the life and feelings of the individual, can lead to a serious breakdown of interpersonal relations and result in mental illness. The problem for modern man is to find a way to live in the world, to seek in his own way, and within his own limitations to transform its undesirable features without succumbing to the dehumanizing forces to the extent that he loses a productive and fulfilling relationship with life.

Obviously these types of dehumanizing situations may be found in varying degrees in all social institutions, but since our concerns are educational in nature, we shall limit our attention to certain cases in the educational literature that illustrates dehumanizing relationships in the schools. Singling out these cases does not imply that all teachers and schools are indicted. But the cases to be presented are far too serious and the conditions too widespread to be ignored or passed off as extreme and isolated instances.

In his autobiography, Malcolm X relates his experiences as a youth and recalls how white people would often talk in his presence to other whites about Negroes in the most derogatory terms without seeming to care how it affected him. It was as if he were invisible (a phenomenon that Ralph Ellison has treated at length in his novel) (8). Malcolm noted, ". . . even though we might be *with* them, we weren't considered *of* them . . . Thus they never did really see *me*."(9) This pattern of behavior also was found among his teachers in the Michigan community in which he was reared. Malcolm liked history but soon developed an aversion to his history teacher who sometimes sang songs to the class which placed the Negro in a degraded and foolish position and, on other occasions, made Negroes the butt of jokes(10). Another such situation arose in the junior high school when Malcolm discussed his career plans with his English teacher. Malcolm had been one of the best students in the class and had always felt that his teacher liked him. When Malcolm confided one day that he would like to be a lawyer, his teacher registered an expression of surprise and stated candidly that because of his race (the teacher used the term "nigger," which all the teachers used) he should be realistic and not aspire to such goals. Rather, because Malcolm had demonstrated skill in the carpentry shop, he should set his sights upon a career in carpentry(11).

Alexander Moore reports in *Realities of the Urban Classroom* a number of dehumanizing situations based on observations in elementary schools(12). Many separate instances are recorded where children heard or saw the teacher attack their sense of worth and dignity in some way. This took several different forms. As observations were made in different classrooms, teachers occasionally came over to the observer and made audible remarks within hearing-range of the children about how slow, dull, or stupid particular children were. The children were singled out by name. Memos were written to the parents in a child's notebook bluntly stating the child's problem, which when read by the child, caused chagrin, a loss of self-esteem, and a growing conviction that he was not really capable and productive. A child's belief in himself is shaken when an authority figure conveys that he, the child, is less than he really thinks himself to be. Dehumanization also took the form of ridiculing a child's art work, letting him know that he was incompetent because he would not stay within the lines or follow the stereotyped materials and preconceptions of the teacher. There were instances where the teacher audibly told the observer, "This is a class of low intelligence." Imagine the effects upon children who overheard it! At best it becomes a self-fulfilling prophecy so that as the children's self-esteem is eroded, they begin to take on the characteristics the teacher ascribes to them and no longer think of themselves as capable and productive. The teachers observed in the study rarely considered the fact that poor teaching and lack of humaneness may be at the root of the problem. The observer also overheard a teacher telling a boy that maybe he should be put in the zoo "like the other animals." Classroom observers also witnessed many instances where teachers pulled and jerked children around by their hair and ears in attempts to discipline them(13).

There are other studies that show the dehumanizing effects of classroom practices. Jonathan Kozol's *Death at an Early Age* offers a vivid portrayal of the dehumanization of Negro children in Boston public schools (14). The account of his teaching experiences portrays how he felt some school officials dissemble conditions existing in the inner-city schools. These conditions are shown by Kozol as depriving children, particularly Negro children, of quality education and as engendering a cumulative effect on the hearts and minds of these young people. Kozol depicts some officials as responsible for rationalizing and ignoring these conditions while funneling new funds into large increases in administrators' salaries. Kozol also analyzes the attitudes of some Bostonians who support these officials.

The dehumanization takes many forms over and above school building and facilities. Situations regularly developed where children were made to confess to acts they did not commit and, in turn, received vigorous corporal punishment. A contrived collaboration of teachers, Kozol reports, shielded them from complaints and possible law suits from parents.

Kozol feels that the outright racists on the teaching staff were easier to handle than those who considered themselves liberals because those who discriminated openly could be confronted openly. The liberals discriminated in their attitudes and treatment of Negroes in comparison to their relationship with the white children according to Kozol. Among them was a "liberal" white teacher who had been a long-standing member of the N.A.A.C.P. Throughout his book, Kozol relates situations and conversations that serve to demonstrate his charge of discrimination. The difficulty with this type of discrimination is the failure to admit prejudice — in fact, to deny it — while continuing to discriminate in multiple and subtle ways. This is the type of behavior Kozol found in several fellow teachers.

It is, for some, a source of dismay and indignation that these conditions may be found in school systems throughout the nation. Professionally outstanding educators with strong humanistic qualities have always been highly prized. Such outstanding talent is critical for youth and the future of the country.

Perhaps the problem rests in part with certain erroneous assumptions about the manner in which the educational process should be conducted. According to Jules Henry, the schools have not functioned to develop creative intelligence, but rather, they strive "to prevent the truly creative intellect from getting out of hand."(15) He contends that the school has served to bind the mind and spirit of children by "praise, ridicule, admonition, accusation, mutilation, and even torture to chain them to the culture pattern."(16) The schools have sought obedience and docility rather than originality. Moreover, schools make the failure of one child the success of another, all to the chagrin of the former and the elation of the latter. This is illustrated by what Henry considers a typical situation that occurs in classrooms throughout the country — and, for that matter, in many other countries as well. In the classroom situation, Boris is standing at the chalkboard and is struggling desperately without success to reduce a fraction to the lowest terms while a number of children at their seats are waving their hands to be recognized. The teacher, for a minute or two, offers clues, which Boris is unable to comprehend. The teacher then turns back to the sea of faces and the frenetic flurry of raised hands and selects Peggy to tell Boris how to solve the problem. Peggy solves the problem quickly and receives the teacher's praise; Boris walks back, head bowed, along the row of desks where his friends and classmates are seated, and slumps down heavily in his chair.

Such situations are the result of a system where success is the ultimate and the means to that success is often at someone else's expense. Students, Henry tells us, are willing to believe anything their instructors tell them, whether true or not, in order to avoid failure. Not all systems, however, operate in this fashion. Among noncompetitive cultures, such as the Zuni, Hopi, or Dakota Indians, Boris' classroom scene would seem cruel beyond belief. But in our own culture, precepts about every person's opportunity for success notwithstanding, we learn to hate the success of others and would like to prevent it. Henry believes that the school is a preparation for later life, not because it attempts to teach the 3 R's, "but because it instills the essential cultural nightmare fear of failure, envy of success, and absurdity."(17) Whether or not one agrees with Henry or believes that his case is overstated, there is too much truth in his analysis for it to be taken lightly. In fact, the future of our schools may very well be transformed by those who take it seriously.

In retrospect, examining the five types of dehumanization and comparing them to the case studies helps one to analyze actually what was taking place and the significance it may have in the lives of youth. To understand the student as a person one should examine the concept of a person and trace its meanings and implications.

The Concept of a Person

Analysis of the Concept

The term 'person' comes from the Latin word *persòna* meaning masks and/or actor. It refers to the individual's roles and his relation to other men. A number of philosophers have attempted to analyze the notion of a person. John Locke held that the term person stands for a thinking intelligent being who through consciousness is able to consider itself as itself in different times and places. When we feel, think, will, use our senses, we are conscious then that we are doing so. Locke believed that it is through consciousness, which accompanies thinking, that self or personal identity is constituted. Consciousness enables us to identify the thoughts held in the past with the same self that holds such thoughts today. Consciousness provides the self with an identity in time. For Locke, the identity of self was equated with an identity with consciousness, but not an identity with the body(18). What we do with the body is not altogether clear in Locke's system.

Other philosophers have addressed themselves to the concept of person. Thomas Reid, an eighteenth century Scottish philosopher, considered the idea of a person as indivisible(19). Reid's theory was that memory provides us with the notion of our existence in the past. The question arises whether one may have existed prior to his remembrance of it. But Reid held that whatever may have happened prior to one's memory, one cannot impute such occurrences or acts to oneself. It is through "identity" that existence has continuity. Identity is the relation between a thing known to exist at one time with that known to exist at another time. The use of memory in developing the notion of identity leads Reid to the idea that the person is indivisible, for to speak of a part of a person is an absurdity. A man can lose an arm, his strength or health, or his estate but he still is the same person. Reid illustrates this by noting that in a court of law an amputated arm cannot claim part of an estate. However, what sense does it make, we may ask, to speak this way? The loss of the limb is real, it may be sufficiently traumatic to change one's way of life. One's self-concept prior to the operation included a body image where the limb was part of his being. What Reid is asserting is the indivisibility of the person in the same way the elemental units that Leibniz called "monads" are indivisible. Thoughts and feelings change but the self is permanent, Reid says, and the self has the same relation to all succeeding thoughts. This permanent self is known through memory. However, he does not explain how one determines if memory is reliable.

There are two major problems in our knowledge of self as persons. One is that of determining the nature of *my* self, and the other is to determine how we know *other* selves and ascribe characteristics to them. Reid handles the *myself* problem by arguing for the indivisibility of self and postulating an identity through memory. The *other self* is handled by the factor of similarity, so that the similarities between a person one month ago and what he appears to be today are taken to account for identity of other persons. It seems, however, that Reid's explanation is unsatisfactory in the sense that if we know our self through memory, others know their selves in the same manner. Yet, we do not have their memories, although there are ways to elicit memory so that it can be known to others. In any case, Reid has moved us to a point where we have a clearer idea what it means to use the concept of person. However, it may be helpful to turn to a contemporary commentary on the problem to overcome some of the difficulties with which Reid has left us.

P. F. Strawson attempts to overcome some of the problems mentioned above, and others, by developing a theory of persons(20). Strawson notes that the nonphilosopher has no trouble in referring to someone or to oneself as being "in pain." The dictionary does not provide different meanings depending upon whether one is referring to himself or to someone else. The philosopher encounters difficulty because one verifies his own pain differently than he would verify another person's pain. One has direct knowledge of his own sensations. 'Person,'

for Strawson, is a primitive concept that is an axiom, i.e., it is not derived. Predications ascribed to states of consciousness and to corporeal
characteristics can be applied to the entity known as a person. The concept of a person, being primitive, is prior to consciousness, therefore,
should not be thought of as a body housing consciousness or an ani-
mated body. Whenever we predicate consciousness to our self, we should
be willing to ascribe such characteristics to others. Strawson divides
predications referring to persons into M-predicates which refer to
bodies, and P-predicates which refer to persons. The M-predicate would
be represented by such expression as he "weighs 160 lbs," and the
P-predicates would be such expressions as he "is thinking hard." P-
predicates imply the possession of consciousness. We have to ascribe
these predicates before one is identifiable as a person. By using P-
predicates one is able to ascribe states of consciousness to himself and
others. One ascribes P-predicates to others on the basis of observations
of their behavior. It would appear to be the case that before we could
speak of x as a person, we would have to be able to ascribe one P-
predicate. Strawson should have added that one M-predicate also would
be needed, else we have disembodied persons. In conclusion, a person
has conscious states and physical attributes, but we cannot reduce the
concept of person to one or the other.

Normative Issues

In light of the pernicious effects of dehumanization, the problem arises
as to what values and norms one should adopt in interpersonal relations
in order to overcome these conditions? How should one relate to other
persons so that the relationship will not prove alienating and dehumanizing, and the integrity of the involved persons is respected? Among the
many possible perspectives three philosophers' writings contribute to an
understanding and possible resolution of the problem.

Immanuel Kant approaches the problem by noting that imperative
statements command either hypothetically or categorically(21). Hypothetical imperatives relate to action which is willed as a means to a
particular end; whereas the categorial imperative represents action
"necessary of itself" without referring to another end. There are numerous hypothetical imperatives. One usually values the products of our
technological culture for the ease and convenience they bring into our
daily lives, but they are not usually valued as an ends in themselves.

People are usually courteous because they wish others to be courteous in turn and believe that courtesy enables individuals to work together without undue friction. Courteousness is not usually valued for its own sake alone. A business man may observe honest practices, not necessarily because honesty is good in itself, but because it enables him to keep his customers.

Kant's primary concern is to state a categorical imperative or practical law that holds in all social and moral relations. Thus, Kant says that "man and generally any rational being *exists* as an end in himself, *not merely as a means* to be arbitrarily used by this or that will, but in all his actions, whether they concern himself or other rational beings, must be always regarded at the same time as an end."(22) Rational beings, according to Kant, are persons and must not be treated merely as means but also as ends in themselves. Moreover, a rational being is an end in himself and no other person can be substituted for him as an end, for if this was the case no person would have absolute worth. By permitting substitution the categorical imperative would become conditional and no longer would serve as a practical law of human relations. Therefore, the categorical imperative can be succinctly stated as follows: "So act as to treat humanity, whether in thine own person or in that of any other, in every case as an end withal, never as a means only."(23)

Kant believes that compliance with the categorical imperative would involve several forms of moral action. It would involve ruling out suicide as a form of moral action because it would show that one treats himself as a means to maintaining a merely tolerable condition until he takes his life. A person has value only as a means to make life tolerable. It also follows that one should not take another's life. Kant, however, does not clarify what to do in matters of self-defense or the occasional need to expose oneself to danger and possible death in order to preserve life. Apparently, one could not sacrifice himself for the sake of an allegedly "higher good" because only persons are ends in themselves. It is not altogether clear whether a parent could sacrifice his own life to save his children. These are examples of situations where the categorical imperative is not clear as to how one would determine the conflict. This is not a problem that is peculiar to Kant but is found in other imperatives of the same form. To take the Ten Commandments as an illustration, what does one do if his father asks him to help in repairing the roof of the house on Sunday? And what about the virtue of honesty when it is held that one always should be honest? If one's friend's physician tells him that his friend has only six months to live and that his heart is so weak that any shock will kill him, what does one say, assuming that one must always tell the truth, when his friend (who has not heard the news) asks how long he has to live? How would this case relate to Kant's belief that those who make promises to others should not lie because it would be using the other person merely as a means? Kant also believes that one should promote duties to oneself and to others as long as they involve ends in themselves. However, he does not tell us what to do whenever these ends are mutually incompatible.

Another approach to persons and the way they should relate to one another is found in the writings of Martin Buber. For Buber, there is no independent "I," which first establishes its own existence and then moves outward to God and the world. Instead, there is no "I" in itself but only in relation. The two primary relations are "I-It" and "I-Thou." The "It" and "Thou" do not represent different things, but two different possible relations between the self and an "object."(24)

The "I-It" is the typical subject-object relationship. "I-It" symbolizes experiencing and using; it depends upon an "object," a thing. It is a unilateral experience in which the "I" is active and does not treat the "object" or "other" as capable of entering into a relationship bound by mutuality. The "It" becomes a thing. It is true that man can live securely in the world of the "It," but if he only lives in that world he is not a man.

The relation of "I-Thou" is a direct and intense mutual relation in which one meets the "other" as genuinely different than oneself but as someone with whom one can enter into an active relation. One becomes an "I" by virtue of a "Thou"; in other words, self is a social and relational concept. We can study things in terms of their components in an objective manner ("I-It"), but when they are encountered with "the power of exclusiveness," the components become united in a relational event. Buber maintains that art is of the "I-Thou" relationship. One can study music in terms of bars, chords, and notes; this is the realm of the "I-It." But the same music can be encountered as an "I-Thou" relation in which the components become an inseparable unity. The "I-Thou" relation combines subjectivity and objectivity in a totality that transcends the "I-It" relation.

The relation of "I-Thou" is a relation of love. It also is the instinct for communion(25). The educative relationship is one of inclusion; it is a "true inclusion of one another by human souls."(26) The educator's concern is the person as a whole, in his present actualities and future possibilities(27).

The educator's concern is the person as a whole, in his present actualities and future possibilities.

We can now see that in Buber's philosophy the treatment of persons should take the form of an "I-Thou." This has a rough similarity with Kant's imperative to treat persons as ends and never merely as means. Undoubtedly such action would diminish dehumanization and alienation.

Whenever one is humiliated, his sense of dignity is shattered, if only temporarily. Humiliation occurs frequently in societies where persons are not treated as ends and where the "I-Thou" relationship is not predominant among its members. André Malraux has concerned himself with the meaning of human dignity in his novels and other writings. Malraux, a man of action and of letters, has led a life that has a legendary quality: he has undertaken archaeological expeditions in Cambodia and the Sahara, participated in revolutions in China and Southeast Asia, fought in the Spanish Civil War, served in the tank corps and was a leader in the French Resistance in World War II; he also is an art historian and aesthetician, revolutionary novelist, and was Minister for Cultural Affairs in Charles DeGaulle's cabinet.

The theme of human dignity pervades Malraux's novels. It is a dimension of a larger concern with man and destiny and the forces of death that seek to crush him. Man's response to the challenge of death can bring out what is most exalted in him. Death wears many guises, whether in the form of torture, fear, torpor, nature, or time. It is destiny that provides an awareness of man's fate. By inflicting humiliation and suffering, man brings into awareness his destiny and death and extends to life a sense of absurdity and nothingness. It is through the strivings to promote dignity and fraternity that life can be made worthwhile. But the forces that confront man with his fate are everywhere. These forces are omnipresent in Malraux's novels, all of which contain episodes of imprisonment and death. Nature, too, confronts man with his destiny, for the forces of nature and time obliterate man's works — his art, artifacts, and creations — and engender a struggle between man, nature and death. Nature is not viewed as beneficient or as a force to propitiate. Man must struggle against nature in its role as a despoiler.

The state should serve man rather than the converse; it is through the action of men united through shared feelings and a common cause to wrest human dignity from the forces of enslavement that fraternity acquires its significance. Manuel, in the novel *Man's Hope,* in discussing his ideas with his comrade Garcia, remembered the words of old Barca, "The opposite of humiliation, my lad, is not equality; it's fraternity."(28) Men combine their efforts to fight the forces which would crush them and make their existence absurd. This concept is illustrated in *Man's Hope* by Scali's remark to Alvear: "Well, men who are joined together in a common hope, a common quest, have, like men whom love unites, access to regions they could never reach left to themselves."(29)

Man has "a will to dignity,"(30) a will to triumph over the forces of humiliation. The relation of dignity and humiliation can be seen in the dialogue between König and Kyo in *Man's Fate* when König asked Kyo, "What do you call dignity?" and Kyo responds: "The opposite of humiliation."(31) Man strives for dignity against the conditions of life that would crush him and render his existence senseless. Concerted action is needed in the struggle, and Malraux's characters advocate time and again that man is not just what he thinks, believes, or claims to be: man is what he does(32). Ideas, for Malraux, are not merely to be thought, pondered, speculated about: ideas are to be lived. Malraux's emphasis is upon action, participation, and fraternity in man's struggle against destiny and death, a conviction that "A man is the sum of his actions, of what he has *done,* of what he can do. Nothing else."(33) Coupled with action and fraternity in man's struggle against humiliation, one may still share the puzzlement and concern in Scali's question to Garcia, "Tell me, Major, how can one make the best of one's life, in your opinion?" Garcia pondered and then responded, "By converting as wide a range of experience as possible into conscious thought, my friend."(34)

It is possible for man to think about death, not with a view to dying, but with a new attitude toward living. This is illustrated by the Baron in *Man's Fate* who asks Kama-San that if he knew he was going to die in three months would he still paint? "The master says that if he was going to die, he thinks he would paint better, but not differently."(35) In one sense, man counts for little: he and his planet are just a speck among the millions of galaxies in the universe. Yet, man can, within his own existence, count for much and is capable of achieving considerable grandeur. Malraux says about man in *The Walnut Trees of Altenburg:* "The greatest mystery is not that we have been flung at random between the profusion of matter and of the stars, but that within this prison we can draw from ourselves images powerful enough to deny our nothingness."(36)

Questions for Discussion

1. Enumerate the chief factors in education that contribute to the alienation of students from their studies. What factors contribute to dehumanization

within the process of schooling? What suggestions do you have for reorganizing the educational system so that alienation and dehumanization will be sharply reduced?

2. From your observations, how does "quantification" and "externality" lead to the treatment of persons as things to be manipulated, as means to an end? To what extent do these tendencies exist in our educational systems? What can be done about them?

3. What are the primary identity problems of today's society? To what extent and in what ways do our social institutions exacerbate the problem? How can one achieve a healthy sense of identity in today's world? Does this involve a transformation of one's self-concept?

4. Five forms of dehumanization were discussed in the chapter. Think of occasions when you observed these forms of dehumanization within school systems. What actually generated these situations? How could they have been avoided? Can dehumanization be sharply reduced by gradual, piecemeal reforms, or will revolutionary changes be necessary in the sense of transforming the basic structure, content, and purposes of education?

5. Why is a concept of a person important for education? What is your concept? How, do you believe, should persons be treated, both in education and the larger society? Can you offer a sound justification for your position?

For Further Reading

A number of studies have revealed the problems of youth in our culture and the educational conditions which alienate them. These include Edgar Z. Friedenberg, *The Vanishing Adolescent*, Boston: Beacon Press, 1964; Paul Goodman, *Compulsory Mis-Education* and *The Community of Scholars*, New York: Vintage Books, 1966; and Carl Nordstrom, *et al.*, *Society's Children*, New York: Random House, 1967.

Carl Rogers has shown how classrooms can be more facilitating for student learning and fulfilling in *Freedom to Learn*, Columbus, Ohio: Charles E. Merrill Publishing Co., 1969. A collection of essays concerned with recapturing individuality may be found in *The Individual and Education*, Frederick M. Raubinger and Harold G. Rowe, eds., New York: Macmillan, 1968.

As for student protest and faculty action against bureaucratic restrictions on college campuses see *Beyond Berkeley*, Christopher G. Kapote and Paul G. Zolbrod, eds., Cleveland: World Publishing Co., 1966; and *The Dissenting Academy*, Theodore Rozak, ed., New York: Random House, 1967.

Problems of alienation and the quest for identity are treated in a number of books. An approach to alienation through the writings of Marx and Tonnies may be found in Fritz Pappenheim's *The Alienation of Modern Man*, New York: Monthly Review Press, 1959; from the viewpoint of social psychology in Anselm Strauss' *Mirrors and Masks*, New York: The Free Press, 1959; and from the approach of a psychiatrist in Allen Wheelis' *The Quest for Identity*, New York: W. W. Norton, 1958. For a collection of essays see Maurice R. Stein, *et al.*, eds., *Identity and Anxiety*, New York: The Free Press, 1960. One will not want to miss the novels of Franz Kafka, which reveal a world of guilt, isolation, and anxiety, particularly *The Trial*, New York: Alfred A. Knopf, 1955; and *The Castle*, New York: Alfred A. Knopf, 1956.

Treatments of dehumanization in the classroom may be found in Jonathon Kozol's, *Death at an Early Age*, New York: Bantam Books, 1968; Jules Henry, *Culture Against Man*, New York: Vintage Books, 1965; and Alexander Moore, *Realities of the Urban Classroom*, Garden City, N.Y.: Doubleday, Anchor Books, 1967. For a broad treatment of dehumanization by a humanistic psychologist and psychiatrist, see Erich Fromm's *The Sane Society*, Greenwich, Conn.: Fawcett Premier Book, 1965.

Those seeking certain normative conceptions of the treatment of persons may turn to Martin Buber, *I and Thou*, New York: Charles Scribner's Sons, 1958; and Andre Malraux, *Anti-Memoirs,* New York: Holt, Rinehart and Winston, 1968.

Notes

1. William H. Whyte, Jr., *The Organization Man* (New York: Simon and Schuster, 1956).

2. David R. Riesman, Nathan O. Glazer, and R. O. Denney, *The Lonely Crowd* (New Haven, Conn., Yale University Press, 1950).

3. Paul Tillich, *The Courage to Be* (New Haven, Conn.: Yale University Press, 1952).

4. Sidney M. Jourard, *The Transparent Self* (Princeton, N. J.: D. Van Nostrand, 1964), p. 105.

5. George H. Mead, *Mind, Self, and Society* (Chicago: University of Chicago Press, 1934).

6. Robert K. Merton, *Social Theory and Social Structure*, rev. ed. (New York: The Free Press, 1957), chapters 4-5.

7. Emile Durkheim, *Suicide* (New York: The Free Press, 1951).

8. Ralph Ellison, *Invisible Man* (New York: Random House, 1947).

9. *The Autobiography of Malcolm X* (New York: Grove Press, 1966), p. 27. Copyright © 1964 by Alex Holey and Malcolm X. Copyright © 1965 by Alex Holey and Betty Shabazz. Published by Grove Press, Inc.

10. *Ibid.*, p. 29.

11. *Ibid.*, p. 36.

12. Alexander Moore, *Realities of the Urban Classroom* (Garden City, N.Y.: Doubleday, Anchor Books, 1967).

13. *Ibid.*, pp. 60, 63, 66, 67.

14. Jonathan Kozol, *Death at an Early Age* (New York: Bantam Books, 1968).

15. Jules Henry, *Culture Against Man* (New York: Vintage Books, 1965), p. 286. Published by Random House, Inc.

16. *Ibid.*

17. *Ibid.*, p. 305.

18. John Locke, *Essay Concerning Human Understanding,* Book II, chapter 21.

19. Thomas Reid, *Intellectual Powers of Man*, Essay III, chapter 4.

20. P. F. Strawson, *Individuals* (Garden City, N. Y.: Doubleday, Anchor Books, 1963), pp. 81-113.

21. Immanuel Kant, *Fundamental Principles of the Metaphysic of Morals* (New York: The Liberal Arts Press, 1949).

22. *Ibid.*, p. 45.

23. *Ibid.*, p. 46.

24. Martin Buber, *I and Thou* Part I (New York: Charles Scribner's Sons, 1958).

25. Martin Buber, *Between Man and Man* (Boston: Beacon Press, 1955), pp. 87-88.

26. *Ibid.*, p. 98.

27. *Ibid.*, p. 104.

28. André Malraux, *Man's Hope* (New York: Bantam Books, 1968), p. 170. Published by Random House, Inc.

29. *Ibid.*, p. 267.

30. André Malraux, *Man's Fate* (New York: The Modern Library, 1961), p. 282. Published by Random House, Inc.

31. *Ibid.*, p. 306.

32. Malraux, *Man's Hope*, p. 33; *Man's Fate*, pp. 59, 69; *Anti-Memoirs* (New York: Holt, Rinehart, and Winston, 1968), p. 20.

33. Malraux, *Man's Fate*, p. 242.

34. Malraux, *Man's Hope*, p. 327.

35. Malraux, *Man's Fate*, p. 201.

36. Malraux, *Anti-Memoirs*, p. 24.

Chapter Three
The Teaching Process

The Need to Study Teaching

It has become increasingly evident to a number of educational researchers that a need exists to focus their energies directly upon a study of
the teaching process rather than, as in the past, on learning and learning theories. Several researchers have pointed out the limitations of
learning theory for classroom practice. William K. Estes noted that a
gap exists between the activities of the educator and those of the laboratory scientist, and little progress has been made in bridging the gap(1).
Ernest Hilgard recognized the lack of relevance between learning theory
and classroom practice and suggested that the problem lies, first, in the
general problem, shared by all disciplines, of applying theory. Secondly,
educators have not sufficiently specified the tasks of classroom learning
and criteria of success for them in order that learning theorists could
develop theories which would prove useful and relevant(2).

There are other possible reasons why learning theory has not proved
more relevant. Hugh G. Petrie argues that there is no neutral observa-

tional language, and experience cannot be described independently of theory, even though some learning theorists have apparently believed the converse(3). If Petrie is correct, our interpretation of experience is dependent upon a theory used to explain it, and since researchers may have different theories, they will arrive at different interpretations of experience. If this is the case, observational categories may be logically incompatible and this incompatibility cannot be removed by appealing to experience nor can it be adjudicated on empirical grounds. Rather, the difference seems to be a philosophical one between the educator who uses teleological explanations based upon goals, actions, and purposes and the behavioristic learning theorist who structures inquiry in terms of stimulus and response concepts. If Petrie's analysis is correct, these differences explain, at least in part, why learning theory has failed to prove very useful to the teacher.

Other reasons have been given why learning theory is not adequate to our task. Jerome Bruner suggests that societies need ways to "pace and structure" the experiences of children(4). To construct most effectively, a theory of instruction is needed. We cannot substitute learning theory because it is not a theory of instruction. He believes that one of the essential differences between the two types of theory is that a theory of instruction is *prescriptive;* it brings about certain ends or objectives in an optimal way, prior to the teaching act. Learning theory *describes* what is taking place during the learning process and after the process ends. There is no way, he contends, that a curriculum can be derived from learning theory; but a theory of instruction does afford ways to structure knowledge for the purpose of attaining certain ends.

N. L. Gage also believes that learning theories are inadequate for performing some of the tasks to which they have been assigned(5). Learning theories deal with the way organisms learn, while teaching theories relate to ways "a person influences an organism to learn."(6) Since much of what is known about learning can be applied only by teachers and since the effectiveness of learning depends considerably upon teachers, theories of teaching are needed. Gage sees a place for theories of learning in the classroom once theories of teaching are more fully developed. These two types of theory can be closely connected once sophisticated theories of teaching are constructed. Thus learning theories alone are inadequate to provide the understanding needed in teaching practice.

Two approaches have been paramount in the study of teaching. One approach is to analyze teaching philosophically and to clarify its relation to indoctrination, conditioning, the learning of skills, and the types of acts involved in the teaching process. The other approach is an empirical one in which different aspects of teaching, such as the logic of teacher discourse on the forms of teacher-pupil interaction, are studied by various procedures ranging from direct observation to audio-visual transcriptions. Theories of instruction may be developed from empirical studies to explain various dimensions of the teaching process. The possibilities and promise of these two approaches can be seen by a closer examination of them.

An Analysis of Teaching

A teacher's day is consumed by many tasks: collecting money for milk, monitoring the lunchroom, supervising children on the playground, preparing bulletin-board displays, attending faculty meetings, disciplining pupils for misdeeds, etc. We are aware of these and other functions, although their full significance may not be grasped until we have had the teaching experience. Then these tasks are no longer viewed from the perspective of the pupil. Few would confuse the tasks enumerated with the process of teaching. Yet, if these tasks do not constitute teaching it will be necessary to inquire as to exactly what does. A teacher performs various roles. Teachers informally counsel students, keep records, engage in activities connected with the socialization process, make assignments, evaluate, help plan curricula, and serve on faculty committees. Which of these activities can accurately be referred to as teaching? Obviously, just because someone is employed as a teacher does not mean that all of his expected roles in fulfilling his position will constitute teaching. In fact, some of the roles (as the more vocal and dissatisfied teachers have asserted) may actually interfere with good teaching. But that is another problem.

What, then, exactly is teaching if the activity cannot be equated with the teacher's roles? One may wonder whether the socialization process — in which students learn the basic beliefs and modes of behavior of their culture — is actually part of the teaching process. It is well known that some forms of socialization are conducted through the use of indoctrinating procedures. Should the process be called "teaching" when indoctrination is used? Is indoctrination one species of the genus known as teaching, and, if so, would there not be other species, such as drill, conditioning, demonstrations to impart the learning of skills, as well as others? Or is teaching one activity and indoctrination another? How could this question be settled? One could, first of all, observe what teachers do, classify the activities, and determine whether indoctrination was one of them. If so, then indoctrination must be a form of teaching. But this approach is not sufficient for it has already been indicated that teachers are expected to engage in many diverse activities in school, and many of these activities are not teaching. Thus, observations alone will not settle the issue. One must observe on the basis of a theory that provides operational definitions of terms, constructs, and behaviors; otherwise, it would merely be an accumulation of a random conglomeration of sense data devoid of ordering principles(7).

Perhaps the issue is really a conceptual problem that has its roots in the uses of language. Puzzles may be resolved once one recognizes the ambiguity of language or concepts. How do we use such terms as "teaching" and "indoctrination" in ordinary discourse? Is there a standard use of these terms? What functions do the terms serve in our language? Can they be used to report, describe, prescribe, or command? One approach is that taken by Thomas F. Green(8). Green places simple conditioning, indoctrination, training, and instruction on a continuum. There is a region of vagueness in which indoctrination and conditioning lie vis à vis teaching so that their inclusion as a feature of teaching is called for whenever they display characteristics of training and instruction. They would be excluded whenever these characteristics are not displayed(9). Green believes that our concepts in use — such as "teaching," "indoctrination, " "training" — should not be dispensed with because these concepts will exist even if we invent new concepts. If we understand more fully the concepts that are currently in use, we can better achieve consistent goals.

Undoubtedly it is worthwhile to gain a clearer understanding of our concepts in use. By so doing we can chart the logic-in-use or contextual logic of their linguistic functions and dissolve some of the puzzles surrounding them. This is an important task that should not be slighted. Inquiry should not end there, for it may be found that the ordinary use of these concepts does not dissolve the puzzles that arise due to our lack of understanding of the full range of such use. Rather, the puzzles may be generated by ordinary use itself, and, if such is the case, we need new and more fruitful definitions and conceptualizations rather than rest with the range of ordinary use or seek a paradigm case somewhere within this range. There are times, in other words, when the ordinary use of concepts fails to prove adequate for the tasks

established, and it is necessary at that point to undertake other forms
of inquiry in order to resolve the original puzzle.

Indoctrination and Teaching

The task, then, is to make some distinctions that may prove functionally
valuable in the analysis of teaching. One way that teaching may be
clarified is to examine other activities — indoctrination, for instance —
in order to determine if they overlap with teaching, constitute a dimension of it, or whether they are separate and fairly distinct. Examining
indoctrination in this manner may illuminate teaching.

Some liberal American educators earlier in this century conceived
indoctrination as more closely related to authoritarian forms of life,
while teaching, they thought, was closely related to democracy and
democratic principles. They may have oversimplified the issue by
sharply distinguishing "the good guys from the bad guys," but at least
their position was clear. What may not have always been evident to
them was the pervasiveness of indoctrination in American public education: they much preferred to consider it to be an insidious tool of
totalitarian states.

Some writers believe that indoctrination presents a problem of truth
and evidence for belief. Teachers who present ideas that are false or
which cannot be supported by adequate, publicly-accepted evidence,
are considered to be engaged in indoctrination(10). Thus, there are
two criteria in the interpretation: truth and evidence. If the teacher
presents ideas he knows to be false, but presents them because these
ideas are consistent with his ideology or because they fit into some larger
purpose he has in mind, his activities constitute indoctrination but only
if his intent is to convince students that the ideas are true. This latter
point is important, for it is part of teaching — and even part of what
some would consider good teaching — to present false ideas (which may
represent the way a group of people think or thought about some concept) in order to compare them to a set of true ideas, to note their
difference and possibly show how thinking and research can be or have
changed. For instance, a teacher can present the ideas, at one time
considered true, that the earth is the center of our solar system, or that
the earth is flat. Or, he could present the phlogiston theory(11). In
each case the teacher recognizes the present truth-value of the beliefs,
introduces them to illustrate certain changes in thinking in the physical
sciences in order to show the evolution of these disciplines. Thus we

could not say that in this case the teacher was indoctrinating. Indoctrination cannot be determined merely by the fact that false ideas are introduced; it is necessary, first of all, to know what the objectives are. Before it can be said that indoctrination is taking place, false ideas have to be introduced for the purpose of encouraging pupils to believe them as true. However, if the teacher states that the ideas are true but permits pupils to examine other ideas, then the fullness or completeness of indoctrination would not be as great. Yet, because the teacher is generally regarded as an authority figure and because he says that the ideas are true while permitting the examination of contradictory ideas many pupils are discouraged from believing the contradictory ones. This problem is primarily a psycho-social one. The case remains one of indoctrination because the intent of the teacher is to present false ideas with the aim of getting pupils to accept and adopt them. The degree of success achieved does not change the matter; such action and intent still constitutes indoctrination. If the attempt fails, it is still considered to be indoctrination(12).

It may be helpful to distinguish not only between intent and success, but also intent and results. Antony Flew believes that some cases thought to be indoctrination could be a matter of teacher incompetence, and even if the ideas are false, should not necessarily be considered an instance of indoctrination(13). In other words, an incompetent teacher may believe that what he is teaching is true when it is actually false. Would this be indoctrination? A distinction should be made between intent and results: the intent is not that of indoctrination, but it may result in indoctrination. The effect on pupils is the same, even though an impartial observer would distinguish between this act and one in which the intent is to knowingly introduce false ideas. Indoctrination occurs. What we say is that the teacher was careless or incompetent in a particular performance. Of course, if the pupils reject or do not learn or accept what is being presented, indoctrination does not occur. But it can still be said that certain inherent possibilities could be found, that under other conditons, could result in indoctrination. However, we judge the teacher differently if his intent is to indoctrinate as opposed to his carelessness or incompetence in teaching function.

Flew furthermore points out that one of the basic meanings of indoctrination is that of implanting doctrines(14). Flew is not clear on this point, but if by a doctrine he means a principle accepted by a body of believers or adherents to a school or philosophy, then whether the presentation of doctrines could be called indoctrination is inconclusive. There are several factors that first must be examined before a conclusion can be reached. It is necessary, first of all, to know the intent of the teacher. Secondly, one must know if the doctrine is true or false. Finally, one must examine the learning outcomes. If the intent of the teacher is to gain pupil acceptance of a false doctrine and if the teacher precludes the examination of alternate and opposed doctrines, then the process is one of indoctrination even if there is only a limited degree of acceptance of the doctrine. Perhaps it would be a clearer case if Flew had used the word "dogma" rather than doctrine, for a dogma implies a doctrine that is laid down as true and beyond dispute. If the teacher presents ideas as dogma, the case would be an obvious one of indoctrination.

John Wilson's notion of indoctrination raises an additional question. For an educational practice to be indoctrination inadequate evidence or false ideas must be involved(15). True ideas can be indoctrinated as a result of the teacher's intent and mode of presentation. For instance, the teacher can present true ideas as though they were forever incontrovertible and eternally true. Furthermore, the teacher can discourage inquiry into the grounds for their acceptance and can attempt to thwart investigation of alternative positions. As in all areas of knowledge, we cannot know that presently accepted ideas will remain true. If the development of the various disciplines is any indication, concepts are always subject to change. There are, of course, true statements or propositions within a system which hold true so long as one is operating within that system, such as "all bachelors are men" and "$2+2=4$." However, this situation does not hold true for empirical forms of knowledge. One cannot teach true ideas or knowledge of this type as incontrovertible, for not only is it a misleading method, but it discourages pupils from investigating the grounds for such propositions and disinclines them from the task of exploring alternate or opposed ideas. Therefore, we conclude that the truth or falsity alone of an idea is an insufficient condition for determining whether a presentation could be construed as indoctrination.

Ideas which rest on inadequate evidence require examination of the teacher's intent. Did he make it clear to the class that the evidence was inadequate? Did the teacher encourage an exploration of the grounds for accepting or rejecting the ideas along with an open-ended analysis of other ideas?

A concept of teaching (as opposed to indoctrination) has been emerging throughout this discussion. Teaching may be considered "an activity aimed at the achievement of learning, and practiced in such manner as to respect the student's intellectual integrity and capacity for independent judgment."(16) This concept clarifies to a certain extent the analysis of indoctrination. The definition may also help distinguish teaching from conditioning and the inculcation of skills.

Conditioning and Inculcation of Skills

These two processes usually do not draw upon "independent judgment," but to the extent they do, they overlap with teaching. But how could they draw upon independent judgment when, by their very nature, they are generally thought to circumvent this process? Hypothetically speaking, one could exercise his own choice in determining how, if at all, he wishes to be conditioned, knowing full well the significance and educational consequences of the process. One also, even after undergoing conditioning, could maintain awareness of the basis for the actions stemming from the process and utilize his intelligence to determine whether the conditioning has proved to be desirable or whether it should be modified, eradicated, or supplanted by other behavior patterns. The inculcation of skills could overlap with teaching (although many times it does not) if it is conducted so that one could assess the reasons for developing skills, the learning mechanisms that are operative in their behalf, their desirability, and the individual and social consequences of employing them.

The teacher's intent is important in a consideration of indoctrination and is of concern in an analysis of teaching because the intent in teaching differs by its focus on the promotion of learning in such a manner that "the student's intellectual integrity and capacity for independent judgment" is preserved and fostered. In teaching a particular form of learning is advanced. In other words, there are various types of learning — from learning nonsense syllables, learning by rote the capitols of the different states, or learning to work advance mathematical problems. Whether such learning is desirable or not is another question. The learning that results from teaching is usually more desirable because it preserves the student's intellectual integrity and promotes his capacity for independent judgment. However, as long as societies desire other forms of learning and the different attitudes and behavior patterns that accompany these forms, there is little likelihood that what we previously defined as teaching will become more dominant as a mode of promoting learning. Neither the history of education nor existing practices indicate that these other practices will be sufficiently modified to at least overlap with teaching. And surely much of what goes by the rubric "socialization" is largely imparted by processes other than teaching.

Intention in Teaching

To discuss the issue of intent involves an analysis of "intent." A teacher may say: "I shall teach the class about the westward movement in American history this Tuesday afternoon following the geography lesson." There are several allusions to intention in this statement. It is an expression of what the teacher intends to do at a certain time; it is not only an avowal by the teacher, but it also refers to a general objective to be obtained in the particular teaching episode. And it is a dispositional statement insofar as observers could assess whether the expression of intent was actually performed and whether the objectives were attained. In the former case, one would observe the teacher's actions under the specified time and conditions expressed. In the latter case, one would need some evaluation device to determine whether the objectives were realized. But even if they were not successfully achieved, the teacher's intention to attempt to do so cannot be ruled out.

However, there are cases where a teacher expresses an intent to teach a particular lesson at a specified time to a certain group of students, and, from the point of view of an outside observer, the teacher does not fulfill the intent. What is claimed in the statement of intent does not occur. In that case, did the teacher really intend to do what was claimed? Obviously this cannot be known apart from the actual situation itself. Nonetheless, there are several general distinctions that could be made which may provide clues for purposes of clarifying what occurred. The teacher may have forgotten his intention or seen that he was unprepared or may have changed his mind with regard to the appropriateness of the lesson. In each of these cases the teacher had the intent of performing the tasks necessary to carry out the intent. Only if the teacher, for whatever reason, lied about his intentions would we say that there was never such an intent in the particular case. But suppose a teacher claims that he will teach a certain lesson or concept to a particular group of students and persists in making the claim in spite of the fact that he makes no move to do what he claims? We would have to conclude that this really was not the teacher's intent unless some untoward circumstances or disability on the part of the teacher prevented him from acting as intended. And this could not be known without examining the particular situation and the circumstances surrounding it.

There are times when intentions go awry. The teacher may intend to teach something about the westward movement in American history but end up teaching something about the family in rural America during the nineteenth century. Did the teacher actually intend to teach the former or the latter? If intentions are conceived as statements of preferences which are related to a potential disposition to act in a certain setting in order to realize these preferences, then we could consider intentions as plans of action and, by knowing these plans, determine what exactly the original intention was.

Teaching can be thought of as a triadic relation in which A teaches B to C(17). In other words, A does not merely teach C, but he teaches him a certain content, B. These are the three variables involved, although we could inject another one to be more exact in our formulation. It could be stated that A teaches B to C in order that C may do X. Thus C is not merely taught something, but is taught in order that he may be able to perform certain actions better or to make more intelligent decisions. Even when educators claim that the content is intrinsically worthwhile, or that it has no immediate or vocational usefulness, they still would admit that certain changed dispositions, whether of tastes, appreciation or judgment, would result from its being taught.

A Theory of Instruction

Bruner outlines a prescriptive theory of instruction: it is designed to establish optimal instructional approaches prior to the teaching act(18). The theory does not treat ends or objectives, but it does prescribe means. Whatever ends the teacher establishes, the theory, ideally, would be able to prescribe in a general way the means to attain them: what sorts of instructional behaviors and patterns of organization ought to be used to achieve the desired ends.

Bruner's theory consists of four dimensions: 1) predispositions to learning, 2) optimal structuring of knowledge, 3) optimal sequence required for learning, and 4) reinforcement. The first aspect is concerned with factors that predispose a child to learn more effectively. These factors include knowledge of the types of stimulation and learning experiences needed in his preschool environment. There are certain mini mum social and intellectual skills that a child needs in order to profit from his early school experiences. There also are differing attitudes based on sex, social class, and ethnic background which influence and predispose a child to learn. Children have differing tendencies to explore alternatives. Curiosity provokes exploration; therefore, it is important that situations not be so routine as to stifle curiosity. Nor should they be so ambiguous and uncertain that anxiety and confusion are generated. Bruner believes that encouraging exploration of alternatives is done best with a teacher than done alone. The teacher's presence is beneficial whenever the student makes errors, for the teacher can help arrive at the source of the difficulty. But there is a tendency to treat teachers as authority figures in matters of knowledge and in other areas of competency, which may sometimes discourage the pursuit of alternatives.

The second aspect of Bruner's theory of instruction is that of the structure of knowledge. Bruner stated in one of his earlier studies of the educational process that "any subject can be taught effectively in some intellectually honest form to any child at any stage of development."(19) His theory of instruction is an attempt to follow this up by designing a general plan of instructional features which must be given consideration before the task can be successfully conducted.

The structure of knowledge is one critical dimension in this plan, for it is necessary to understand basic structures of whatever discipline is being studied in order to gain intellectual power and some degree of mastery in the field. Bruner states that a structure of knowledge can be characterized by 1) mode of representation, 2) its economy, and 3) its effective power(20). A body of knowledge can be represented in three ways: enactive representations, ikonic representations, and logical or symbolic propositions(21). Enactive representations refer to knowledge necessary in order to gain certain results, such as knowing how to ride a bicycle, fly a kite, or make a dress. A student may have the knowledge to do these things without actually being able to explain the underlying principles.

An ikonic representation is a pictorial representation, although Bruner does not consider it to be a strict imitation of nature. Rather, it is an image that helps us gain a better understanding of some aspect of knowledge. Suppose one asked a student "What is a parallelogram?" He may not be able to provide a definition, but he may be able to represent his understanding by drawing one.

A third way to represent knowledge is symbolically or logically. One does this by framing knowledge with linguistic statements or by mathematical symbols. In this representation we give the definition of a parallelogram, state physical laws, interpret essays or poems, and develop theories. The child is not able to handle the symbolic stage well during his early school years. Bruner recognizes that the child first works best with enactive representations, and as he matures, he can, in turn, handle ikonic representations and then symbolic knowledge. The structure of the curriculum should take this development into account.

A structure of knowledge can be characterized not only by its mode of representation but also by its economy. Economy stems from the ability to simplify, to arrive at valid conclusions in the least amount. The more information one must possess in order to understand a concept, the more steps needed to process the information, and the longer it will take to do so. Knowledge can be organized for its economy. Economy also is a function of the sequence in which knowledge is presented. But in order to determine organization, it is necessary to understand the structure of a discipline and the way it can best be presented to students at various levels of their development.

A third way that knowledge may be characterized is by its power. By using symbolic systems, theories and principles, one has the ability to manipulate knowledge and offer explanations for phenomena. The power of a particular domain of the structure of knowledge depends upon the ability of the structure to generate propositions that possess a high degree of explanatory value. Economy and power are related negatively in the sense that although one may be able to reach a conclusion by attending to a minimum number of steps, it may not be the most powerful explanation because it may omit, oversimplify, or fail to explain. However, they are related positively by the fact that a powerful explanation usually has a high degree of economy, for it usually brings a host of related phenomena under some law-like propositions and renders the complex simpler and more understandable without unnecessary steps in thinking or in processing information.

Sequence is the third dimension of Bruner's theory of instruction. There is not merely one ideal sequence by which a body of knowledge can be presented because much depends on the level of development of the learner and the types of learning desired. The best sequence for the presentation of material depends a great deal upon what the teacher is trying to do. Does the teacher desire to promote speed, economy, or power of learning? Or perhaps the teacher is more interested in transferability of learning or resistance to forgetting. Whatever the learning outcomes desired, they will greatly influence the best sequence needed to bring them about. If one is teaching students about poetry, the sequence that may discourage forgetting would not necessarily be the sequence to be used for transferring understandings to related materials.

The fourth dimension of Bruner's theory of instruction is that of re-inforcement. This dimension is divided into 1) success and failure, and 2) rewards and punishments. The teacher needs to provide the student with knowledge of the results of his efforts to learn in a given episode of a learning task. Instruction should be so organized that the learner receives the corrective information at the proper time and under the conditions that the learner can best use it. The information should be presented in a form that is most amenable to use by providing knowledge as to whether one's activities are leading to the attainment not only of immediate goals but through what Bruner calls a "hierarchy of goals." The learner should be encouraged to assume the rewarding role rather than having the teacher reward in terms of grades and other devices. That is, the learner should eventually move to the point where problem-solving is intrinsically rewarding. This role may be encouraged by rewarding students for fruitful errors. Errors should be analyzed to discover the student's interpretation of the question, for the student may misconstrue the question and, in fact, be answering another question.

Bruner has offered an interesting and provocative outline for a theory of instruction. His belief that a subject or body of knowledge can be taught to a student in some intellectually respectable manner at any stage of development rests upon the conviction that symbolic representations can be translated back into ikonic and enactive representations so that the elementary student can grasp them. This approach may be true for geometry and set theory, but it is a questionable one with material from physics, biology, philosophy, social sciences, and the humanities. Much of this material presupposes a certain amount of life experience, sophistication in the subject, and cognitive maturity.

Bruner's theory of instruction provides a means for explaining how certain aspects of instruction can attain goals more effectively in the sense of delimiting the types of behaviors, structures, and functions which enter into the process. However, his theory constitutes only one possible aspect of the much larger process of instructional behaviors. A number of important variables are not adequately accounted for: the cognitive maturity of the learner, matters of pacing and practice, social variables in peer relations, and teacher personality and instructional style.

Empirical Studies of Teaching

Empirical studies have been undertaken that seek to classify, analyze, and explain a dimension of teaching, such as logical and linguistic discourse, social interaction among students or between teacher and students, strategies in teaching, the emotional climate of the classroom, and other types of behavior. They differ from Bruner's theory of instruction of attempting to explain all major variables in instructional behaviors by choosing to limit their study to one domain. The procedures for developing empirical studies is that of classroom observations or audio and video tapings of instructional and student behaviors. A classification schema is used initially and later modified in light of evidence of its adequacy. Further observations are then interpreted on the basis of a refined schema. The teacher, hopefully, can use the research findings for evaluating his own instruction.

The Logic of Teaching

Among studies pertaining to various aspects of the teaching process, the research conducted by B. Othanel Smith and Milton Meux on the logic of teaching has greatly increased knowledge of the logical operations found in teacher discourse(22). Their approach and procedures, their principal findings, and possible applications to the improvement of teaching as well as those of other studies are outlined below(23).

Smith and Meux distinguish logical operations from teaching strategies. Strategies are large-scale maneuvers in teaching consisting of a cluster of acts designed to secure certain learning outcomes. Strategies may consist of inducing students to exchange ideas on a topic, attempting to minimize wrong responses in the learning of concepts, and organizing instruction so that particular learnings can be acquired in the shortest time period. Within these large-scale maneuvers the logical operations of teaching can be located. These are the operations to which their research was directed.

Through the analysis of tapes of classroom discourse, it was possible to observe the uses made of certain logical categories and to refine the categories in light of further evidence. The wide variety and complexity of the logical and symbolic operations used in classrooms made it impossible to cover these operations merely by adopting the classifications found in the usual text in logic.

Two types of units of classroom discourse were established: episode and monolog. An episode involves one or more verbal exchanges between two or more persons. A monolog is a solo performance by one person addressing the group. Smith and Meux found two patterns among episodes: reciprocating and coordinating. In reciprocating episodes there is a discourse transaction between two speakers. Coordinate episodes are characterized by successive speakers responding to an initiating remark or question usually made by the teacher, rather than responding to the previous speaker (student). Judges were used to determine the logical operations found in each episode and the decisions of the judges were compared in order to secure higher reliability.

The researchers arrived at the following categories as constituting the logical operations of the classroom: 1) defining, 2) describing, 3) designating, 4) stating, 5) reporting, 6) substituting, 7) evaluating, 8) opining, 9) classifying, 10) comparing and contrasting, 11) conditional inferring, 12) explaining, 13) directing and managing classroom. It should be noted that the last category has no logical importance but would consist of teacher activities that keep the proceedings of the classroom moving when no logical discourse is taking place. The twelfth category consists of several different types of explaining: a) mechanical explaining, b) causal explaining, c) sequent explaining, d) procedural explaining, e) teleological explaining, f) normative explaining. It was found in the high school classrooms studied that describing, designating, and explaining were the operations that occurred most frequently, while substituting, reporting, and classifying occurred least frequently.

The Smith and Meux study indicates the logical operations found in classroom discourse and shows how these operations were handled by teachers and students. In light of the prominence that logical operations have in instructional behavior, it would prove valuable to know how the use of such operations could be improved and how improvements by teachers affect student learning(24). Smith has concluded that the logical operations of both teachers and students are generally of low quality as judged by logical standards(25). Unfortunately, there is no more logical rigor in the classroom than could be found in casual discussion in other areas of life. Methods courses, for the most part, have done little to correct this condition. Teacher preparation programs have heavily emphasized methods courses and the psychology of learning and problem solving, but seldom have directed sufficient attention to the logical operations of the teaching process. And the fact that the logical abilities of students were no better in the classroom behooves teachers to improve their own abilities and understanding of these processes so that, in turn, they may help students to do likewise. Preservice education has used, in more recent years, tapes of students teaching a concept from their specialty to other students. From such tapes the logical operations involved in the presentation, as well as other characteristics, can be analyzed and used for improvement of instructional activities. Courses in method should use the twelve logical operations and indicate the most effective ways that they may be employed in teaching. This can best be done, Smith suggests, in relation to the subject matter, for the operations tend to vary with the discipline(26).

A study which included some features of the logical operations in the Smith and Meux research but also attempted to encompass all major forms of classroom discourse, was conducted by Arno A. Bellack and associates(27). Bellack adopts several basic ideas of the philosopher Ludwig Wittgenstein, namely, that the meaning of a word is determined by its use in language(28). Language, for Wittgenstein, consisted of more than words whose meanings represented objects or activities which the words stood for or named. Although previous philosophers have tended to reduce language to this function, there are, according to Wittgenstein, many other language games which have their own rules of use. To understand language is to understand how to operate with the rules of various language games (naming, reporting, describing an object, telling a joke, testing an hypothesis, etc.). It is this very conception of language and language games that Bellack claims he is following in his study.

Although Bellack states that his study deals with the range of language and communication in the classroom, it would appear that it consists of three primary factors: 1) strategies, 2) cognitive operations and content, and 3) feeling, tone, or emotional climate of the classroom.

Strategies consists of four pedagogical moves by which the operations of the classroom are facilitated. These moves are called structuring, soliciting, responding, and reacting. A structuring move is made when the teacher focuses student attention on the subject to be discussed at the opening of a class period. It sets the stage for what is to follow. Soliciting moves are in the form of commands or requests designed to elicit verbal or physical responses from the students. Responding moves occur in relation to soliciting moves, such as the students' answers to the teacher's questions. Finally, reacting moves may be occasioned by any of the four types of strategy moves but are not directly elicited by them. These moves shape classroom language by modifying, rejecting, or responding to previous activities. They differ from responding moves in that they do not fulfill the expectation of soliciting moves. Reacting moves, depending upon context, occur when the teacher reacts positively or negatively to a student's response. They may also be occasioned whenever there are pauses in classroom discourse. Reacting moves are a larger part of teacher discourse than the discourse of students. Various combinations of these moves set up teaching cycles that can be studied(29).

The second major area in the study of classroom discourse consists of the analysis of content, which is basically a cognitive operation. There are four different categories for classroom discourse: 1) substantive with associated, 2) substantive-logical meanings, 3) instructional with associated, 4) instructional-logical meanings. "Substantive with associated" meanings are the concepts found in the subject matter being presented. "Substantive-logical" meanings are the logical operations in the class. Here Bellack has borrowed heavily from the logical categories of Smith and Meux. "Instructional with associated" consists of such matters as assignments and routine class procedures involved in the instructional process. "Instructional-logical" meanings are didactic verbal processes in which procedures are explained, directions are given, and ratings are made(30).

Bellack's study consists of strategies, concepts in subject matter, logical operations in discourse, classroom routines, and teacher directives. These are all brought together for use in a framework for the analysis of the language of the classroom. It is a comprehensive framework for studying classroom discourse; however, in order to be comprehensive, it must ostensibly mix logically unrelated categories and modes of analysis. Bellack's study, besides providing a relatively precise methodology for the transcription and analysis of classroom discourse, has confirmed what has long been suspected—teacher dominance of classroom discourse.

Teacher Influence and Classroom Climate

Most students notice, after several weeks in a class, that a certain atmosphere or climate prevails, which may vary from or have certain similarities with that found in other classes. There is such a sufficiently distinctive atmosphere in some classes that one tends to associate the atmosphere with the substantive content and activities of the course. The climate tends to color and give a certain perceptible feeling tone to the course (whether one can articulate what this means or not) so that, in retrospect, when one thinks of the course, he not only may review the events that transpired and the learning outcomes achieved, but will also hold certain attitudes and feelings toward these activities.

Ned Flanders has sought through his research studies to assess certain critical variables of classroom climate and teacher influence(31). His approach is called "Interaction Analysis" and is based upon studies of verbal interaction in the classroom in order to ascertain teacher influence and the overall classroom climate. The study was conducted by having trained observers categorize teacher and student talk in roughly three second intervals during an activity period. An hour of class was divided into different sequences of activities, such as student reports, teacher exposition of material, and class discussion so that the tally of classroom discourse would relate to the particular activity. Ten categories were used: 1) accepting student feelings, 2) giving praise, 3) accepting, clarifying, or making use of a student's ideas, 4) asking a question, 5) lecturing, giving facts or opinions, 6) giving directions, 7) giving criticism, 8) student response, 9) student initiation, and 10) confusion or silence. One through seven pertain to teacher talk, and eight and nine relate to student talk. Teacher influence is conceived as either direct or indirect. The first four categories represent indirect influence, and five, six and seven are considered direct influence. Direct influence is thought of as restricting student action, while indirect influence enlarges the student's freedom of action. In tallying instances of classroom discourse within an activity sequence, the tallies by each category were so arranged that they could be placed within a matrix. The teacher could quickly visualize the results and determine the amount of teacher talk that would fall respectively into direct or indirect influence categories.

Hypotheses were formulated and pre- and posttests were used with a two-week unit of study to ascertain whether the hypotheses were warranted. Two positive hypotheses formulated were: 1) learning would increase under indirect teacher influence whenever a student's perceptions of goals were ambiguous and confused, and 2) learning would increase under direct influence when perceptions are clear and acceptable. The negative hypothesis stated that direct influence will tend to decrease learning when perceptions of goals are ambiguous. The results of the tests corroborated these hypotheses. According to Flanders, the explanation for these results is that direct influence increased the student's dependency upon the teacher while less disabling dependency ensues from indirect influence. But positive results obtain under direct influence when goals are clear because the student knows whether to accept or reject teacher influence and can assess and evaluate alternate possibilities for himself. When goals are ambiguous, the student must rely heavily on the teacher for direction that has not been clearly defined. Students who made significantly higher tests scores were in those classes where teacher influence was flexible. Teacher verbal behavior considered flexible was characterized by its ability to vary from one activity to another, whenever the occasion demanded, in terms of direct and indirect influence.

The reliability of the information obtained in studies of teacher influence depends upon the skill of the observer, and there appears to be a problem of training adequate observers(32). Flanders' system enables us to understand verbal forms of influence, but it does not provide us with an understanding of cognitive aspects of classroom interaction. The study focuses on verbal behavior because it can be treated with a higher degree of reliability than nonverbal behavior. On the other hand, an assumption made in the study that teachers' verbal behavior is an adequate sample of total behavior(33), is open to question, for surely the old cliche, "Actions speak louder than words," cannot be summarily dismissed. Facial expression, eye movements and fixations, smiles, grimaces, bodily carriage, and other outward signs may often reveal more about a person (if we know how to interpret them) than words. Often one can notice a discrepancy between verbal behavior and these nonverbal cues—if one is observant. Some type of reevaluation of the person must be made in order to accurately reinterpret the person's intentions. Even though the nonverbal level is difficult to appraise with precision, its significance for teaching is too important to be overlooked.

Nonverbal Behavior

Nonverbal behavior constitutes the movements, behaviors, and physical expressions that "communicate" to others but do not make use of linguistic systems for exchanging meanings. The term "communication," as used here, is broader than language systems. A language can be considered a mode of communication.

For example, how often has someone been thanked or praised and had the feeling that the person speaking really did not mean it? It may be that the person's statements are inconsistent with past statements and no ostensible reason exists for the sudden change. This is verbal behavior. But let us suppose that the person's statements are consistent with past statements, but one still feels a lack of sincerity. The nonverbal behavior reveals how the person really thinks and feels. How exactly would one arrive at this conclusion? Observations of what the person does, how he acts in the situation when making statements and the tone and inflection of the voice may reveal discrepancies. By taking the totality of these outward responses and assessing them within the context of the situation one is able to supplement or overrule previous conclusions derived from the exchange of meanings in linguistic behavior.

How does this relate to the classroom? Teachers continually are evaluating students not only by their verbal behavior but by their actions and expressions as well. Yet teachers are not always aware of the extent and precision with which youths evaluate their teachers. Just as some blacks know and understand whites far better than whites understand blacks (for the survival of blacks depends upon it), so, too, the student must understand the wishes and will of the teacher better than the teacher understands him (for the student's academic and psychological survival depend upon it). Emerson, in commenting on the teacher's relation to students, perceptibly observed in his essay on education that students "detect weakness in your eye and behavior a week before you open your mouth . . ."

Cultural differences complicate the teacher's problems, for what is fraught with a certain set of meanings for one cultural group is accorded a different interpretation and significance by another group. And since it has long been known that teachers generally understand and relate best to white, middle-class children from a similar socio-economic background as their own, there is strong likelihood that teachers may misconstrue nonverbal behavior of youth from social classes and subcultures that differ from their own unless considerable effort is made to acquire such understanding. Not only do most middle-class teachers fail to understand and know how to cope with the more aggressive behavior of lower-class youth, they also do not comprehend many of their indigenous customs. The white middle class believes that "looking the other fellow in the eye" shows that one is honest and has nothing to hide. However, this is not part of the cultural background of Negroes and Navajo Indians, and the teacher's misconstrual of their behavior is likely to lead to needless chagrin and recriminations. Or, as noted by Edward Hall, Americans prided themselves on their candid and forthright behavior in negotiating with Greeks, only to find negotiations constantly at an impasse(34). The Greeks considered these qualities liabilities and indicative of a lack of finesse. The failure to understand the customs regulating the nonverbal behavior of the representatives from the two countries occluded the reaching of viable agreements.

What sort of "static" does one give off? How often do our mouths say one thing and our nonverbal cues another? How often do we witness persons expressing love or affection for someone in formal verbal solemnities while their nonverbal cues give the message that they are really irritated, impatient, disappointed, or even feel domineering and contemptuous in their attitudes and emotions. It is much easier to fabricate verbally than nonverbally—unless one is a professional actor. For some persons at least, verbal fabrication becomes an avocation. Greater awareness among teachers can be generated by studying classroom interaction for nonverbal behavior, even though the precision and reliability of such findings are unequal to verbal behavior studies.

A study by Basil Bernstein showed that lower class youth depend more on nonverbal behavior of the teacher than other youth due to the inability to grasp abstract symbols and to handle academic language with facility. The teacher communicates through language in culturally restricted symbols because the teacher represents middle-class cultures(35).

In a study by Charles M. Galloway, nonverbal communication was divided into those behaviors which encourage communication and those which inhibit it(36). Seven observational categories were used by observers to record the teacher's nonverbal behavior, with four categories representing encouragement and three inhibiting encouragement. Such behavior as facial expressions, actions and voice qualities which reinforce or inhibit behavior were studied. Teachers who encouraged students displayed this characteristic by the way they listened, the emotional support they offered, and their responsiveness. Teachers who discouraged pupils by their nonverbal behavior acted disinterested in what students said, seemed more often to express disapproval by their behavior and did not act consistently in their responses to pupils.

Thus, it is possible to study nonverbal activities of the classroom in order to help teachers understand influences which frequently remain at a subconscious level. Verbal behavior is only one aspect of teacher behavior and must be brought in line with the attitudes and feelings exhibited in nonverbal behavior if teachers hope to bring about significant classroom learning.

Greater awareness among teachers can be generated by studying classroom interaction for nonverbal behavior.

Questions for Discussion

1. Is it necessary for an educator to develop a concept of teaching?

2. Do such concepts have any bearing upon actual teaching practice?

3. How would you distinguish teaching from indoctrination, simple conditioning, and the acquisition of skills? In what way do these concepts overlap?

4. Should one's concept of teaching be based upon considerations of the student as a person? Are some concepts of teaching inimical to such considerations?

5. Do you think it possible to develop a theory of instruction that would embrace and explain all major variables in teaching, or would it be more reasonable and feasible to take only one major aspect of teaching and develop an explanatory system which would promote greater understanding?

6. What dimensions of teaching are worthy of consideration? Cognitive only? Social interaction and effective learnings? Nonverbal as well as verbal behavior? On what criteria would you base your decision?

7. Do you believe that your own observations of instruction can be improved by using one of the systems discussed in the chapter?

8. If you were asked to develop your own empirical system for studying instructional behavior, how would you go about it?

For Further Reading

Those interested in further study of philosophical analyses of teaching should see Israel Scheffler's *The Language of Education*, Springfield, Ill.: Charles C. Thomas Publisher, 1960. Valuable essays can be found in the following: T.H.B. Hollins, ed., *Aims in Education*, Manchester: Manchester University Press, 1964, chapters 2, 3; R. S. Peters, ed., *The Concept of Education*, London: Routledge & Kegan Paul, 1967; Bertram Bandman and Robert S. Guttchen, eds., *Philosophical Essays on Teaching*, Philadelphia: J. B. Lippincott, 1969; B. Othanel Smith and Robert H. Ennis, eds., *Language and Concepts in Education,* Chicago: Rand McNally, 1961. Valuable sources also include the *Annual Proceedings of The Philosophy of Education Society* and back issues of the journals *Studies in Philosophy and Education* and *Educational Theory.*

Jerome Bruner's theory can be found in his book *Toward A Theory of Instruction*, Cambridge, Mass.: Harvard University Press, 1967. For a series of essays which seek to provide several theoretical positions and methodological models upon which to base empirical studies, consult Lawrence Siegel, ed., *Instruction: Some Contemporary Viewpoints*, San Francisco: Chandler Publishing Co., 1967. Various empirical studies of teaching may be found in the following collected essays: Ronald T. Hyman, ed., *Teaching: Vantage Points for Study*, Philadelphia: J. B. Lippincott, 1968; James B. McDonald and Ronald R. Leeper, eds., *Theories of Instruction*, Washington, D.C., Association for Supervision and Curriculum Development, 1965; and John R. Verudin, Jr., *Conceptual Models in Teacher Education*, Washington, D.C.: American Association of Colleges for Teacher Education, 1967.

Notes

1. William K. Estes, "Learning," *Encyclopedia of Educational Research*, 3rd ed. (New York: Macmillan, 1960), p. 767.

2. Ernest R. Hilgard and Gordon H. Bower, *Theories of Learning*, 3rd ed. (New York: Appleton-Century-Crofts, 1966), chapter 16.

3. Hugh G. Petrie, "Why Has Learning Theory Failed to Teach Us How to Learn?" *Philosophy of Education* 1968, Society Proceedings, George L. Newsome, Jr., ed. (Edwardsville, Ill.: Studies in Philosophy and Education, 1968), pp. 163-170.

4. Jerome S. Bruner, "Needed: A Theory of Instruction," *Educational Leadership* 20 (May 1963): 523-532.

5. N. L. Gage, "Theories of Teaching," *Theories of Learning and Instruction*, 63rd Yearbook, Part I, National Society for the Study of Education (Chicago: University of Chicago Press, 1964), pp. 268-285.

6. *Ibid.*, p. 268.

7. It will become more evident later how theories of instruction enable the researcher to yield fruitful results from his observations.

8. Thomas F. Green, "A Topology of the Teaching Concept," *Studies in Philosophy and Education* (Winter 1964): 284-319.

9. *Ibid.*, pp. 291-293.

10. John Wilson, "Education and Indoctrination," *Aims in Education: The Philosophic Approach*, T. H. B. Collins, ed. (Manchester, England: Manchester University Press, 1964), pp. 24-46.

11. "Phlogiston" was believed to be an active principle or mystic substance in fire which caused a flame to burn and consume fuel. This theory persisted and prevented progress in chemistry until finally overthrown by the research of Joseph Black, Henry Cavendish, Joseph Priestly, and Antoine Lavoisier.

12. In this connection, Ryle speaks of task and achievement verbs. Task verbs are "running," "jumping," "singing," "teaching," etc.; achievement verbs are "spell," "catch," "solve," "find," "taught," "learned," etc. See Gilbert Ryle, *The Concept of Mind* (New York: Barnes & Noble, Inc., 1949).

13. Antony Flew, "What is Indoctrination?" *Studies in Philosophy and Education* 4 (Spring 1966): 285.

14. *Ibid.*, p. 284.

15. John Wilson, "Education and Indoctrination," *Aims in Education: The Philosophic Approach*, pp. 24-46.

16. Israel Scheffler, ed., "Philosophical Models of Teaching," *Philosophy and Education* (Boston: Allyn and Bacon, 1966), p. 99.

17. See D. B. Gowin, "Teaching, Learning and Thirdness," *Studies in Philosophy and Education* 1 (August 1961): 87-113.

18. Jerome Bruner, *Toward A Theory of Instruction* (Cambridge, Mass.: Harvard University Press, 1967), chapter 3.

19. Jerome Bruner, *The Process of Education* (Cambridge, Mass.: Harvard University Press, 1960), p. 33.

20. Bruner, *Toward A Theory of Instruction*, p. 44.

21. *Ibid.*, pp. 44-45.

22. B. Othanel Smith and Milton Meux, *A Study of the Logic of Teaching*. U. S. Department of Health, Education, and Welfare, Office of Education, Cooperative Research Project No. 258 (7257). (Urbana, Bureau of Educational Research, College of Education, University of Illinois, 1962).

23. Those interested in greater detail are urged to peruse the studies themselves.

24. B. Othanel Smith, "The Need for Logic in Methods Courses," *Theory into Practice* 3 (February 1964): 5-8.

25. *Ibid.*, p. 6.

26. *Ibid.*, p. 7.

27. Arno A. Bellack, *et al.*, *The Language of the Classroom* (New York: Teachers College Press, 1966).

28. Ludwig Wittgenstein, *Philosophical Investigations* (Oxford: Basil Black-well, 1958).

29. Bellack, *The Language of the Classroom*, chapters 4-7.

30. *Ibid.*, chapter 3.

31. Ned A. Flanders, *Teacher Influence, Pupil Attitudes, and Achievement*, Cooperative Research Monograph No. 12. U.S. Department of Health, Education, and Welfare, Office of Education (Washington, D.C., 1965).

32. *Ibid.*, p. 121.

33. *Ibid.*, p. 19.

34. Edward T. Hall, *The Silent Language* (Greenwich, Conn.: Fawcett Premier Books, 1967), pp. 10-11.

35. Basil Berstein, "Social Structure, Language, and Learning," *Educational Research* 3 (June 1961): 163-176.

36. Charles M. Galloway, "Nonverbal Communication in Teaching," *Educational Leadership* 24 (October 1966): 55-63.

Chapter Four
The Educated Man

Introduction

What is the educated man? Is he little more than an antique notion, an
anachronism in our age of specialization and vocationalism? Is the
concept as extinct as the dodo bird, or at least as obsolete and fallacious
as the formal discipline theory? The concepts behind these questions
warrant consideration, and yet, they carry misconceptions that must be
exposed unless notions of the educated man are to be summarily dismissed. The possibility of developing compelling notions of the educated
man is no more remote for our own time than in earlier eras when the
theories of the day enjoyed wide allegiance and a broad consensus. True,
today's specialization and vocationalism frequently have submerged such
ideals by the press to "get ahead" and to secure gainful employment.
This has tended to divert attention to the needs of business, industry,
and public affairs with their own ideals and requisite competencies and
their ability to appeal to talented youth. Specialization and vocationalism

have clouded the picture; they have transformed the ideal of the educated man, rendered it ambiguous and subject to doubt. Either one can redefine the educated man in terms of these new goals and dismiss the older concepts, or else the notion of the educated man can be dismissed as no longer necessary, useful, and viable in a posttechnological civilization. That is, if success is not dependent upon competencies found in past conceptions of the educated man but is related more directly to specialized skills and/or public-relations abilities, then few students will find the older notions of the educated man worth pursuing, especially if such activities would preclude, or at least delay, their advancement in their chosen field. The usual answer is that to strive to become an educated man may not help one to advance in his chosen field (although it may have some indirect bearing in a number of fields), but it will enable one to enjoy and appreciate the Good Life. The Good Life, of course, has various definitions. Most conceptions have in common the conviction that the Good Life cannot be pursued intelligently or result in maximum satisfaction for the individual unless he is an educated person. Somehow the educated man is supposed to be able to live more fully, to savor life's delights and to rejoice in a variety of delectable and challenging pursuits. Thus, it appears to be a common belief that the justification for the ideal of educated man is that it enables man to live more fully, to utilize more of his inherent capacities, and to gain more from the many activities open to him. The defenders of the ideal argue that a narrow specialty and the possibility of some immediate vocational satisfaction is not all that one should expect to gain from life.

Misconceptions About the Educated Man

In order to develop a conception of the educated man, it is important to point up some popular misconceptions about him and to keep these misconceptions in mind when developing criteria. The misconceptions that follow are not by any means exhaustive, but they do represent some of the popular ones familiar to us today.

1. College Education

The educated man is one who has taken a certain number of courses, a certain curriculum, or has a college degree.

This concept may seem plausible to those who have not attended college, except for those among them who believe that life experiences in the business world and the world of the public are the only experiences that truly educate. Most college graduates recognize that a college degree does not reveal as much as we sometimes claim. Colleges differ in quality; departments and instructors within departments differ as well. Students attending the same college—and even those majoring in the same field—do not receive an identical education, for each person brings his unique past experiences and perceptions to bear on his academic experiences. Furthermore, experiences one gains outside the classroom vary. A college degree only signifies that a student has successfully completed a certain course of study at a particular university. His grades, too, are not very revealing. Whether one is a "C" student or an "A" student may only reveal that the latter is better at outguessing the instructor on the types of tests given or that he has a good memory and is willing to spend long hours memorizing. The emphasis on memory work is an indictment either of the lethargy or lack of imagination of instructors. In any case, a college degree does not signify that one has necessarily become an educated person. Whether he is or is not an educated person would have to be determined by other criteria.

That the educated person is one who has taken a certain number of courses or a certain curriculum is difficult to dispute. It has such a long and hallowed ancestry that to question it seriously may appear to some heretical. Its proponents, although differing as to what should constitute such a curriculum, have usually concurred that it would be known as "liberal education." In the course of educational history a liberal education was generally ordained for an elite. In more recent times, it has been marked by a search for common learnings for all those who could profit from them(1).

Obviously, for one to pursue such a curriculum reveals very little about the quality of instruction and student gain from the program. There are no automatic benefits that accrue from exposing oneself to a particular curriculum. A more serious contention is that some programs are more liberal in nature and are more likely to develop educated persons. Certain subjects are believed to engender such results, although there is widespread disagreement. Such disagreements are due in part to the nature of the educated person and what subjects are more likely to affect the desired characteristics. In our own age, the curriculum has generally been divided into the liberal and vocational elements or into general education and specialized studies. The liberal and general education studies were thought to contribute more directly to the making of an educated person. The vocational and specialized studies were designed for career preparation and job skills. Unfortunately, some of the liberal arts courses have been increasingly taught as though every student enrolled planned to major in the field. This has tended to blur the former distinction between the liberal and the vocational education. Furthermore, the interrelationships of the courses and their respective problems and concepts to one another have seldom been made with the necessary intellectual power and clarity needed to enable students to bring subject matter to bear on the problems of life with which they are faced. Because many teachers have an inadequate understanding and ability to bring about transfer of training, a cul-de-sac has resulted. Even if we could designate a certain body of subject matter as contributing directly to the development of the educated person (and no such far-reaching agreement has yet been reached), certain intractable problems persist which must be ameliorated before claims presently being made can be considered defensible(2). This does not mean, however, that all subjects are of equal worth in producing the educated man. Rather, it suggests that significant variables exist that frequently have not been accorded due consideration by those who propound an ideal curriculum. But even if this shortcoming were rectified, it could reasonably be argued that an approach through a set curriculum is the wrong approach with which to begin. It may very well prove more fruitful to look first at the characteristics and competencies of the educated man, and then explore the types of experiences likely to effect such results. It should be noted that the formal curriculum constitutes only one possible set of experiences.

2. Encyclopedic Memory

A popular conception about the educated man is that he has an encyclopedic memory. This conception also appears to be held by those teachers whose evaluations of learning outcomes seem based almost exclusively on items that demand memory ability.

The public is easily swayed by one who can recite a wide array of recondite facts. Widespread public attention was directed to this phenomenon with the advent of the radio and the early T.V. quiz programs. The heyday was reached during the 1950's when millions of people watched as astronomical sums were given away to those who could accurately recite the appropriate facts in response to a particular question. The public was enamored with this phenomenon and approvingly supported the fame and fortune attendant to the success of the memorizers and regurgitators until a shocking exposé revealed that some of their new heros had been prompted by the sponsor with the answers prior to the program.

Surely in the mastery of any subject certain facts must be at one's command. But knowledge of bare facts alone does not constitute mastery. Actually, a fact is not just a miscellaneous datum related in some way to a particular body of knowledge; it is, rather, "a particular ordering of reality in terms of a theoretical interest."(3) For example, one could never say *all* there is to say about a particular student demonstration (or any other event) because he would have to recount in infinite detail all actions of every participant by elaborating each movement and by recording all remarks, expressions, and descriptions of the persons involved. Even a novelist who fills his works with descriptive material must be selective about what material to use. Accounts are selective because of the particular perceptions of the observer, his ideological framework, and his purpose in recording and relating the account. A reporter from a local city newspaper at the scene of the demonstration may perceive the "facts" differently than a reporter from a campus newspaper. More obviously, a journalist representing a periodical on the right would likely recount the events differently than a journalist representing a periodical on the left. This is not to imply that all facts are subjective—they are not. The point is that facts do not stand alone or even make sense apart from some frame of reference by which they can be interpreted. A frame of reference takes the form of a theory (whether well-developed or not) through which the facts are selected as being important and by means of which their significance and possible implications are assessed. Facts do not stand in isolation but are related to other facts or data within a theoretical system through which they gain significance and are employed in the furtherance of new knowledge.

How do these considerations relate to the educated man? A person holding a random collection of miscellaneous facts is not in a position to function intellectually until the collection is organized into a theoretical framework and conjoined with related data that may enter into the process of formulating and testing hypotheses. Thus pertinent facts are merely the starting point in the development of the educated man. The facts that are "pertinent" depend a great deal upon the types of theoretical systems with which a person will need to work and the forms of the experiences necessary to bring about the desired outcomes.

3. Success and Fame

There is a fundamental ambiguity surrounding the twin idols of success and fame. Some believe that one can not realize them except if one is an educated person. However, others contend that education, success, and fame have little in common. The latter belief is deeply rooted in the past of American culture. "Book learning," as it was called, was believed to be remote from the everyday tasks faced by men of action who struggled to grow crops in formerly uncultivated soil, attempted to lay a railroad across the continent, learned to rope steer and herd cattle to market. What did books have to do with getting along in the world? Schooling, particularly secondary and university, throughout most of American history was considered the preserve of an elite group based more on wealth. It was a place to study the classics, to learn the appropriate manners and engage in the proper associations befitting one's station in life. But education beyond the rudiments was not deemed necessary for most people. As late as 1874 in the Kalamazoo Case, an irate taxpayer brought suit against the City of Kalamazoo challenging their right to assess him to support public high schools, which he considered an unneeded luxury for the populace. Although the final decision by the Michigan Supreme Court went against him and was later heralded by historians as a victory for free public education, it did exemplify the common sentiment of the time, and was representative of an overwhelming majority of the populace in many areas of the country. To credit education as the chief avenue to success or fame is a more recent attitude.

Today many persons now believe it necessary to pursue a program of higher education in order to gain fame or success. Entering as we have into a highly complex, postindustrial society where specialized talent is kingpin (in spite of ritualistic lip-service to liberal education), one is encouraged to remain in school in order to develop skills demanded by business, industry, and government. If the key to advancement in today's society is via the route of higher education, there must be some connection between the educated man and success and fame in the larger society. Since the economy demands more and more highly trained specialists, the people—at least in terms of numbers—who get ahead, make a success in terms of pulling down a sizable income, are the specialists. Naturally, there are exceptions. Fame is more difficult to plumb: it fluctuates widely with the vagaries of public opinion and such variables as the talents of one's agent.

Without making the allegation that the specialist is only trained rather than educated, we could first try to take the original argument, as it stands today, to see whether it is credible. Most would admit that one could be an educated person and not achieve success or fame if one's aspirations did not lie in those directions. And it also may be admitted that occasionally we still find high school dropouts who eventually reach great heights in their chosen field, and succeed in doing so by talent, perseverance, connections, cleverness, chicanery, or dishonesty. (Of course many college educated people achieve success through the same means.) Admittedly then, to become an educated person is not a sufficient condition to achieve success or fame. Whether it is a necessary condition would depend on the specialty, but in most cases it does not seem to be a necessary condition unless one considers the specialist the educated man. Whether the specialist and the educated man are incompatible should not be prejudged at this point; however, most leading educators of the past have not defined the specialist as the educated man, although in more recent times specialization has not been considered antithetical so long as the individual possessed other attributes.

4. The Dilettante and the Connoisseur

The dilettante is an admirer or lover of the arts, an amateur who cultivates an art as a pastime or only superficially. He concerns himself with the enjoyment, rather than with mastery of the arts. He may be a dabber and desultory in his approach; his interest is to study the arts for the personal delight they bring. In contrast, the connoisseur is one who understands the principles and techniques of an art and is sufficiently competent to be considered a capable judge; he has scholarly knowledge and developed tastes. His trained tastes enable him to recognize good food and wine or assay the worth of precious jewels. The connoisseur's developed tastes and critical evaluative skills, presumably, lead him to the Good Life at a "higher" level, or at least in a more systematic fashion, then the dilettante.

What is the connection between the dilettante and the educated man? It can best be seen by examining the problems attendant upon certain historical changes that render older conceptions of the educated man no longer viable. The universal man ideal during the Renaissance, as represented in such books as the *Courtier* by Castiglione and exemplified by the life and accomplishments of Leonardo da Vinci, is generally no longer thought to be a reasonable ideal in today's society. Castiglione described the courtly gentlemen who could love, fight, paint, compose poetry, and discuss affairs of state, all with a polished style, ease, and effectiveness. Leonardo brought within his purview the entire range of human experiences and displayed his amazing creativity and originality in most all of the principal areas of human knowledge of his day. However, in the contemporary world with the explosion of knowledge, the far greater complexity of society, and the development and proliferation of innumerable specialties, the Renaissance ideal is no longer feasible. Some believe that their closest approximation to the ideal is to avoid self-encapsulization in their specialty by using leisure time to develop their tastes and appreciations of the arts. They also seek to cultivate versatile abilities by trying their hand at a variety of activities. Those who scoff at the dilettante assert that the helter-skelter pace of activities and diverse pursuits has little connection with the educated man ideal. Nonetheless, unable to realize the Renaissance ideal and lacking the time, ability, or desire to become connoisseurs, they may display a welter of activities and the enjoyment attained as a sign or token, if not the substance, of the educated man.

The connoisseur offers a model for greater understanding and appreciation of the arts for others to emulate. To do so holds out the promise of deepening one's sense of satisfaction and rendering one's perceptions more acute and sensitive than those of the dilettante. The connoisseur sets standards for the more enduring works and activities of society; whereas mass tastes are seduced by Madison Avenue. A rift sometimes develops in cultures where literacy is widespread between mass tastes and "highbrow" with a market appeal to the far more lucrative low and middle range of tastes.

To be a connoisseur sets one apart from the untutored and untrained minds and demarcates one's opinions and evaluations from others as being authoritative. At the same time, to become a connoisseur in an area requires considerable time, effort, and study on a continuing basis that not only automatically limits the number in any given field who would strive and succeed in such an undertaking, but by the very demanding nature of the task would drastically limit the number of areas in which one could become a connoisseur (in spite of the greater amount of leisure time today). Thus one may become a connoisseur in one area—or a few at most—and consider himself an amateur, or perhaps a dilettante, in many of the complex fields and activities of contemporary life; therefore, even the connoisseur is a consumer of the expert opinions of other connoisseurs in most areas of life(4). Where does this leave the Renaissance ideal of the educated man? Probably still back in the Renaissance. It leaves us with a recognition that older ideals can at times prove to be illuminating and capable of generating thought, but they not only need to be interpreted in light of present goals and conditions, they also remind us that the educated man ideal is historically and culturally bound.

5. Wide Reading and/or Broad Experience

Proponents of various educated man ideals may line up on one side or the other as to the chief contributory factor in shaping and assuring the development of an educated person. Some hold that through selective but omnivorous reading of great works the individual will develop his thinking and act with intelligence and foresight. Others are inclined to view a life of varied and significant experiences that influence the individual's self-concept and the way he relates to others and to the world as contributing directly to the making of an educated person.

Advocates of significant reading may be divided over whether such reading can best be done in a formal school system, by means of tutoring, or merely on one's own. Their essential point of agreement is that such readings brings one into contact with great minds and thoughts of the past, the best that has been thought and said. It enables the individual to transcend limited perspectives of his community and of the age in which he lives. It provides a perspective on the problems of the time by offering for consideration the multiple ways men have attacked and dealt with similar problems, and thereby provides a vast experimental laboratory where hypotheses are proposed and plans of action are tested in light of marshalled resources and human ingenuity. Not only are those unfamiliar with the past likely to repeat its mistakes, proponents of reading tell us, but they also tend to lose the strand of continuity from one age to another so that a cult of the modish and fadish gains ascendancy and opts as the chief director in decision-making. Significant reading is vital for the insight to be gained and because it is one of the principal ways by which one becomes a thinking, perceptive person. Since results of this type cannot be obtained by any other means,

significant reading programs are indispensable in developing the educated man.

People who support broad life experiences as the primary educative
influence are not entirely at odds with those who advocate a significant
reading program, but they do point out that there have been innumerable tendencies throughout the history of formal schooling to stultify
rather than liberate the student's development. Often those who conduct
our schools may not be truly educated themselves, and through their
coercive and manipulative practices, bent more on securing order and
exacting obedience, any love for good books and the imaginative play
of ideals are soon extinguished. The student remains on the treadmill
of courses, requirements, tests, and grades with only the diploma to
beckon him on.

Some of the authors of some of these allegedly significant books
have not truly lived life on a broad scale, drunk deeply of its fruits and
sorrows, and savored its splendid delights. Most of us, whatever our
station in life, have scarcely brought within the range of human consciousness a breadth of significant human experience. Too often we
have settled early on the security of a career in a stable firm, leaped
into an early marriage and having a family, and often have been dis-
inclined to stray far from familiar landmarks and places. A price has
been paid for seeking the predictable and the secure in a world where
they are becoming increasingly illusory.

But what sort of experiences, one may ask, will contribute directly
to the development of the educated person? Probably the most important experiences are those that eventually enable the individual to break
away from provincialism, ethnocentrism, dogmatism, and stereotyped
thinking, experiences that enable the individual to be at home in any
company among the diverse cultural patterns of the world's peoples. Out
of this, rich perspectives and flexible and imaginative styles of living are
forged. It takes courage, a sense of adventure, and fortitude and determination to arrive at such sophistication, but it can be reached through
imagination and willingness to repudiate the prosaic styles of life.

Why not, as Malraux suggests, bring within consciousness the widest
range of experience; and if his life serves as an example, both significant
reading and broad experience are needed. Albert Schweitzer is another
example of a contemporary who, with Malraux, approached universal
man stature. And those of the past—such as Leonardo, Leibniz, and
Goethe—were men of thought and action, providing continuity between
past and present and forging a creative link to the future. Wide and

significant reading affords rich theoretical perspectives and the cumulative wisdom of the race as a guide to life, while broad life experiences
become the testing ground for these ideas and offer a sensible contrast
between the actual and the possible, the real and the ideal.

Criteria for Assessing the Educated Man

Several conclusions can be drawn about the nature of the educated man.
First, the obtaining of a college degree or the studying of a certain curriculum will not necessarily lead to the development of an educated
person. Second, encyclopedic memory is a misleading attribute with
reference to the educated man. A good memory is only the starting
point. Third, changes in the notions of what constitutes success and fame
in business and public affairs are related to the needs for specialized
talent. Most of the major conceptions of the educated man hold that
the specialist, especially one who is only a specialist without more
broadly gauged abilities and interests, would not be considered an educated person in the ideal sense. Fourth, although the connoisseur was
found to be more in keeping with ideals of the educated man than the
dilettante, the stringent limitations of becoming a connoisseur in a number of important activities in today's world, render the connoisseur
somewhat equivocal with reference to past ideals. Finally, the values
of wide and significant reading as well as a life of broad experiences
that dispel parochialisms and enable one to be a citizen of the world are
starting points in their contribution to the educated man ideal. A fruitful
combination of both approaches would be best.

The Ideal: Historically and Culturally Relative

Conceptions of the educated man are historically and culturally relative.
Earlier ideals were culturally and historically bound; the best of them
transcended culture and a particular period by proving, at least in part,
to be of worth to later peoples in other nations. However, with the
rapidity of cultural change and the adoption of new goals, earlier ideals
appear less and less appropriate.

Some ideals captured the minds and imaginations of the culture's
leaders because they embodied the very notions that were most prized

at the time. Such an ideal may be seen in Quintilian's writings about the Roman ideal of the orator, a man with a liberal education in the humanities, a practical man who could influence and lead the people and minister to the needs of government through great and elevated oratorical abilities. Cicero embodied this ideal in his activities. Others exemplified, through writing or activity, the ideals of their own age. The northern Renaissance evoked in Erasmus the highest educational ideals of the time. His research and editing of religious and classical manuscripts commanded the respect of the scholarly world; he helped revive a broad study of the classics and represented in thought and action the virtues of reasonableness, tolerance, and moderation in an age that all too often lacked these virtues. Montaigne was another exemplar. He embodied many of the ideals spoken of by Castiglione and Elyot: the courtly graces, a gentleman and a scholar, humanism and naturalism as an outlook on life. Certain individuals represented or propounded ideals of the educated man, and these very ideals are historically and culturally bound. They gain their greatest significance among a particular people during a certain historical period and never seem to have as much import for later cultures.

There were also those who were so far ahead of their time that many of their proposals were ignored, only centuries later to be picked up in various ways. Comenius, who proposed a system of universal education from kindergarten through the graduate school, is such a person. His plan of *Pansophia* or "Universal Wisdom" included the publishing of an encyclopedia of universal learning with leading scholars throughout Europe as contributors. He advocated promoting scientific research by establishing a college in which all the needed research resources would be available; and finally, he sought a method by which all people, to the limits of their ability, might profit from the knowledge in all fields of learning.

These illustrations show that universal and eternal ideals of the educated man have not been constructed—and are not likely to be in the future, unless cultural differences are forcibly dissolved through some unforseen events and conformity is coercively maintained by some tyrannical world governing body. Assuming this state of affairs will not come to pass, it is important that ideals be recognized in terms of their limitations: they are not universal and eternal, but are historically and culturally bound. Therefore, ideals appropriate and compelling for one cultural group during an historical period will not necessarily be so for another. Although the ideals of the United States today are mixed and ambiguous, it is evident that they differ markedly from those of Russia, China, or India. That one country's ideals differ from those of another should not be a cause for censure or a *prima facie* mark of inferiority. Instead, the task for analysis is to see how the ideals function within the culture, whether they are consistent with other basic societal and educational goals, and the social consequences that accrue for the society in pursuing the ideals. This type of analysis is functional-dysfunctional. The objective is to understand the particular culture sufficiently that one can envision the interrelationships between ideals and other cultural values, and explore how the pursuit of a set of ideals influences people and helps in the realization of cultural goals. Some ideals may prove dysfunctional. If, for example, American education upheld the universal man ideal while other institutions ignored or repudiated it, graduates would find the clash of values and life styles even greater than they already do. However, the functional-dysfunctional model is useful for determining whether a culture is able to attain its goals in terms of the resources and human potentials available with the least amount of waste, needless duplication and conflict, but the model is unable to tell us whether the goals themselves are good—and many times this is the most controversial factor and the one open to the greatest disagreements and doubts. How can this problem be settled? Are we to be left with the conviction that each culture is a law within itself, that it can only be evaluated with reference to its ability to attain its own ideals, that ideals themselves cannot be seriously questioned except for their functionality in the attainment of societal goals?

Some have found the latter to be a persuasive argument, for they recollect all too well the dangers of ethnocentrism and chauvinism, the attempt to impose an alien way of life upon another culture, whether in the name of a super race or in the name of democracy. What education has attempted to do—at least in principle—is to foster greater cross-cultural understanding, to dispel parochialism, and to promote a cosmopolitan outlook. To impose universal ideals would be presumptuous; it would indicate that one cultural pattern is superior to another, and missionary zeal or armed might would be necessary to assure its universal ascendancy.

On the other hand, by following this approach would preclude the censure of such heinous cultural practices as found in Nazi Germany. Certainly there must be some transcultural standards or ideals that can be invoked. The Nuremberg trial provided international legal standards, and the United Nations Declaration of Human Rights provides certain

moral standards. These could well be the bridge needed to reduce international anarchy and build a viable means of international law to sustain
world peace, in spite of the fact that heretofore nations only recognize
these and other documents when they perceive them to be consonant
with their own nationalistic ambitions and objectives.

Elitist and Equalitarian Ideals

In many cases in the history of education the ideal of the educated man
was stated in such lofty terms that only a few within a culture could
realistically hope to aspire to it. Furthermore, the means and resources
necessary for the realization of the ideal were available only to a few:
that is, universal education is a relatively recent policy, and throughout
the history of education to this recent point the means to educational
and public advancement has been open only to an elite group. This elite
one founded upon social, economic, political, and hereditary distinctions.

In nondemocratic societies, to restrict the ideal to a select group
would be consistent with their goals and practices. The problem is more
difficult for those societies that consider themselves to be democratic.
Governments in democracies are representative: they are operated by a
select group. Decisions made in the corporate structure are arrived at by
a highly select group. The basic directions that democratic societies take
are determined by an elite. Whether this is an elite of ability is another
question. The fundamental point is that decisions that greatly influence
the life of the masses is made by a select few, and today we see that
some people believe that they lack a sufficient voice in the decisions
that affect them. The call for participatory democracy is a case in point.
Therefore, in formulating the educated man ideal for a democratic
society, should it be formulated in terms of an elite who will assume
positions of influence and power, or should it be stated in terms of conditions that all persons could aspire to?

It is recognized today that many retarded children can be "trained"
to a life of useful service, but they probably cannot be "educated" in
the usual sense that we mean by the term. Thus is it reasonable to state
that the retarded should not aspire to the educated man ideal, for to
focus it at that level would be to vitiate the ideal and make it possible
for average and above-average students to realize the ideal with little or
no effort. Such an ideal should be worthy of the best human efforts and
should somehow demarcate the achievement and abilities of those who

have attained the ideal from others whose aspirations, efforts, or abilities do not carry them as far. It would signify a distinction and a compelling objective worthy of one's best efforts.

There remains the majority of a population. Can this majority, in a democratic society, attain the ideal? Obviously if the ideal is highly stringent and demanding, only a minority could realize it. Assuming that a society wanted to keep the ideal open and accessible to the majority, one necessary condition for doing so would be to actually provide equality of educational opportunity, which all too often is idealized in principle but denied in actual practice. This is the case in the United States today, even though progress has been made toward these ends since the Supreme Court desegregation decision (*Brown v. Board of Education*) in 1954. As long as equality of educational opportunity is not a living reality, millions of minority group members will find that striving for the ideal to be a frustrating and defeating experience, and that the ideal is tacitly open only to a segment of the white majority (the poor would be excluded). To correct this state of affairs would demand widespread and massive social changes that as yet have not been undertaken.

Assuming that the ideal should appeal to and be within the range of the largest possible number of people in a democratic society (excluding only those with severe organic retardation), it is obvious that the ideal would need to be free of various social class biases and artificial and unnecessary distinctions. The ideal should have sufficient breadth to make demands upon and utilize the abilities of many different peoples. It should be sufficiently compelling to sustain the interest and energies of a large number of diverse groups. Due to the complexities of society and the difficulties facing man in the latter half of the twentieth century, multiple ideals may have to be articulated. These ideals will need to have some organic interconnection but would each in turn relate to a particular broad range of behaviors. We are familiar with concepts that focus on certain dominant abilities, such as the contemplative man, social man, political man, and the practical man. Each ideal would need to cut across some of the categories, for surely an educated man is one of both thought and action. But it may make the ideal too broad, demanding, and perhaps inconsistent, to attempt to embrace the multiplicity of traits, characteristics, and behaviors embodied in all of these different types of men. Thus it is likely that multiple ideals are needed. But it will be especially important in a democratic society that invidious distinctions not be applied to an individual who chooses one ideal rather than another. For example, more prestige automatically is attached at the secondary level to those who complete the college preparatory program as opposed to graduates of the vocational or commercial program. In order to avoid such distinction, it will be necessary for persons to develop greater tolerance and acceptance of ways of life which differ from their own. In a highly complex, posttechnological society, many different abilities and styles of life are needed, and one way that our educational systems can deal with this factor is to establish multiple ideals of the educated man.

Thus democratic societies would take a different approach to the problem than nondemocratic societies. One criterion for evaluating an ideal would be to determine the nature of the society and then assess whether single or multiple ideals are used. In the case of democratic societies, one would need to know whether the multiple ideals, taken together, would sufficiently embrace the desired behaviors needed in the society and whether the ideals were sufficiently inclusive and compelling to involve the widest range of participation.

The Viableness of Certain Competencies

In spite of the fact that we have been reluctant to establish a single trait or a cluster of related traits as necessary to the educated man ideal apart from a consideration of the multiple variables involved, there has been some agreement among educators that certain competencies and abilities would be particularly desirable for effective living in the latter half of the twentieth century.

One type of competency or behavioral pattern is dialectical in nature: participation and detachment. The educated man is one who is *in* the culture but not entirely one who is *of* the culture. That is, he lives in the culture, it is his home even though he may at times be alienated from certain tendencies it exhibits, but he is not entirely caught up in and shaped by its activities. In order to remain in touch with the actual affairs of society, he must in some way be a participant—and in many cases a leader. Yet, he cannot become overly immersed in the day-by-day activities of society without being in danger of bewitchment by its hypnotic monotony and paltry goals. He must also find the detachment to serve as a principal critic and evaluator of its basic tendencies and directions, offering through his criticism a clearer vision and a more workable plan and direction for its projects and undertakings. Yet, if he

All instruction should aim at the development of a bold and creative independence in learning.

lacks participation, his criticisms will likely prove unrealistic to present societal affairs and its future promises. This is why an uneasy and dynamic tension must be a working reality. Some fruitful and workable means must be found for living within the tensions (rather than attempting to tranquillize or escape them) and using the tension itself as a controlled and constructive source of power to improve individual and social life.

There are a number of other characteristics or competencies that are considered useful to the educated man living in our complex age. Without a doubt, one scarcely could be spoken of as educated without some of these traits, even though no single trait alone would represent the educated man ideal. One characteristic of great importance is the ability to learn for oneself. A principal objective of all education is to develop on the part of students the requisite abilities and intellectual independence to learn for oneself. Unfortunately, some courses are taught in such a way that the student becomes dependent upon either the instructor or the text, rather than becoming liberated. All instruction should aim at the development of a bold and creative independence in learning. Generally this develops after the student acquires a sound working knowledge of the fundamental concepts and research methodologies of a discipline. There also are personal factors involved, such as a greater need for dependency and following the lead of another. By altering the nature of instruction that fosters needless dependency, it will be possible for more persons to exhibit independent learning abilities.

Another competency that frequently is alluded to as being an objective for any person who considers himself educated is the ability to critically examine beliefs and devise defensible ways of testing their warrantability. This is a competency that is sadly lacking among a large segment of the population. Yet it is essential for one who wishes to live life more intelligently, for life continually confronts one with obdurate problems and difficulties, with conflicting beliefs and ideologies that demand adjudication and intelligent decisions. One arrives at decisions and makes choices by developing the ability to test beliefs for their warrantability in order to know which beliefs to accept and which to reject and to devise intelligent courses of action in light of these outcomes.

A final general competency needed is the ability to construct open, flexible and creative approaches to problems in order to live successfully in today's world. In light of the vast technological changes and the inception of amazing new—and at times unforseen—developments in social, economic, and political life, one needs more than ever not so much the acquisition of a certain body of knowledge and the mastery of a certain curriculum but the cultivation of flexible and creative approaches to problems which will enable the individual to make the needed innovations or reconstructions necessary in individual and social life. Unfortunately, schooling has not been widely recognized for its ability to produce these traits. Therefore, if we hope to effect them on a more widespread scale, profound changes in the formal school system will be needed, for one is unlikely to be able to face radical future developments without flexible and creative approaches to the problems of living in a new world.

The Educated Man: A Reassessment

The significance of the educated man ideal must be predicated on, "What does it mean to be fully human?" Upon closer examination an educated person may appear, at least in part, to be more fully human. This would not bias the issue in favor of those who have completed the most years of formal schooling, for the educated man cannot be neatly equated with the completion of a certain curriculum or the graduation from college or, for that matter, any number of years of schooling. It would still be necessary to know what the competencies of the person are and to what degree the competencies exhibited fulfill the criteria established for assessing the educated person.

To become an educated person, as the term has been defined, is to become in certain important respects more fully human in the sense that the process of becoming an educated person is a movement from underdeveloped to more fully developed competencies, from the undisciplined and uncontrolled human tendencies to the cultivation of more controlled and disciplined tendencies that contribute to growth of the individual's power. Without prejudging what these competencies will be, the very process itself of becoming educated is the fuller development of one's capabilities. Of course there is the question of whether such development is salutary or pernicious. It is well known that development may take many directions: some develop into more highly proficient killers and others may develop traits of greater humaneness and benevolence for one's fellows. Since the possibility that the competencies developed could possible be employed in personally and socially damaging forms as well as for human betterment has just been opened up, it will be wise to connect the idea of the educated man to certain characteristics. This recalls Kant's imperative to treat humanity in every

case as an end and never merely as a means. It also recalls Buber's
"I-Thou" relationship. The arresting problem of our age is that some who
have been highly trained, who possess specialized skills have used these
skills to destroy man. Can any conception of the educated man be eliminated so that before a person could be considered truly educated his
interpersonal relations would have to be shown to follow the dictates propounded by Kant and Buber? If not, persons could use their carefully
honed abilities and highly developed powers in the service of totalitarian
pursuits leading to the enslavement, if not the destruction, of others.
Thus the ideal cannot be neutral. One is not an educated person until
he consistently and characteristically exhibits moral approaches to life
and fellow man. Just as the other competencies of the educated man are
learned, these moral competencies are learned as well. But they may
prove to be the most difficult to acquire in a world which pays them
much lip-service but seldom lives by them. These moral competencies
cannot be argued for on the grounds that it will help one to "get ahead"
or that one will be recognized, praised, and rewarded for living by
them. Either they are morally compelling because they are believed to
be right and because the social good that may possibly accrue is
desirable, or else they are not.

It seems that to be an educated person is to advance far along the
road to becoming more fully human. Yet the two types are not synonymous, for there are many dimensions of being more fully human that
cannot be translated into educational tasks to be mastered. Nor can they
be established as part of a curriculum or as a set of educative experiences to be undergone. To be more fully human would involve many
attributes. Certain ones are illustrative. One must recognize what some
existentialists speak of as the absurd. Its recognition must be appro-
priated in a way that leads to a sensitive awareness of the grounds of
one's tenuous and ambiguous existence. In spite of his ambiguous
existence, one must have, as Tillich has said, the courage to be.

Cross-Cultural Values Reconsidered

The educated man ideal needs to be historically and culturally relative.
However, this raises a fundamental problem as to how ideals are to be
evaluated. A function-dysfunctional model was proposed earlier. The
test was to undertake an internal examination of the culture in order to
ascertain whether various activities, practices, and instrumentalities lead

to realization of cultural goals and thereby serve a functional role. We did not conclude that activities, merely because they existed and endured, were functional. Some activities may prove dysfunctional insofar as they deflect and thwart goal attainment. The function-dysfunctional model, however, cannot be used to evaluate the worth of the cultural goals themselves, because it is the goals which are accepted as given or axiomatic in the system. The problem arises whether each culture is a law unto itself; it raises the spectre of Nazi Germany. Certain transcultural standards were proposed: the Nuremberg trials, the Treaty of London, and the United Nations Declaration of Human Rights. Other standards which we believe to be applicable can be added. The moral standards needed which would cut cross-culturally are Kant's categorical imperative and Buber's "I-Thou" relation. By utilizing these as standards in human relations, would there be danger of ignoring or glossing over cultural differences? Would they in any way foster a Western parochialism as a guise to gain hegemony over the underdeveloped nations of the world? This use is doubtful because it appears that these moral standards do not infringe, abridge, or interfere with distinctive cultural patterns. There is one problem, however. Since these are Westernized standards, it may be necessary that they be reinterpreted in light of meanings found within each distinctive cultural framework. Practices that preclude the realization of these standards would have to be eliminated or substantially modified. In this way, cross-cultural moral standards, as well as international standards of law, can be promulgated and, above all, enforced. They can be enforced when the nations of the world are prepared to invest an international authority with the power to adjudicate disputes, regulate the affairs among nations, and honor the pleas of oppressed people within nations for a tribunal to hear their claims and, when the claims warrant it, to take action to end injustices. Our failures to bring this about are sobering and shocking to the humane spirit. But to preserve mankind under an equitable and just system, we have no other options—for time is running out.

Questions for Discussion

1. Examine several books in the history of educational thought. Assess the educated man ideal within two or more historical periods by determining the ability of the educational system and the culture to realize the ideal.

2. Investigate some of the current popular conceptions of the educated man.
   What criteria would you use to evaluate them? How could they be reformulated in order that they may prove more defensible?

3. What is the conception of your own college or university or the department
   in which you are majoring with regard to their views of the educated man?
   Do you accept, reject, or wish to modify these views? Why?

4. At this moment you have had some opportunity to think seriously about
   the educated man. In what ways do your own conceptions shape your educational plans and life objectives? Are your conceptions realistic and
   adequate for your purposes?

5. Obviously there will need to be new and imaginative formulations of the
   educated man ideal for the future. What types of cultural changes need to
   be taken into consideration before undertaking new formulations?

For Further Reading

One approach to an understanding of the educated man ideal is to gain an
historical perspective. For a collection of selections from the writings of leading educators of the past, see Robert Ulich, ed., *Three Thousand Years of
Educational Wisdom*, 2nd ed., Cambridge, Mass.: Harvard University Press,
1963. Enlightening essays on great educators may be found in Paul Nash,
et al., *The Educated Man*, New York: John Wiley and Sons, 1965. An interesting account of religions and moral ideals in education from the rise of
Christianity to the present day is E. B. Castle's *Educating the Good Man*, New
York: Collier Books, 1962. John S. Brubacher has approached past theories,
ideals, and practices in terms of a problem or topic approach in his *A History
of the Problems of Education*, New York: McGraw-Hill, 1947. And for the
development of different ideals and ideologies of human nature and society
as they affected American education, see Clarence J. Karier, *Man, Society,
and Education*, Chicago: Scott, Foresman, 1967.

Will and Ariel Durant have provided rich and colorful accounts of Enlightenment men in their book *Rousseau and Revolution*, New York: Simon
and Schuster, 1967; and Stefan Zweig has offered some masterful biographies
of writers and poetic men in his *Master Builders,* New York: Viking Press,
1939. For images of what man is and what he can become, Maurice Fried-
man's account through the eyes of some contemporary writers is worth reading, *To Deny Our Nothingness*, New York: Dell Publishing Co., Delta Book,
1967. Finally, for approaches to the problems of knowledge and the curriculum as they bear upon the educated man, see Wayne C. Booth, ed., *The
Knowledge Most Worth Having*, Chicago: University of Chicago Press, 1967.

Notes

1. See, for example, John S. Brubacher, *A History of the Problems of Education* (New York: McGraw-Hill, 1947), chapters 9, 10; Russell Thomas, *The Search for a Common Learning: General Education, 1800-1960* (New York: McGraw-Hill, 1962); and Merle L. Borrowman, *The Liberal and Technical in Teacher Education* (New York: Teachers College Press, 1956).

2. John Dewey called into question some distinctions and artificial separations commonly found in the curriculum in his *Democracy and Education* (New York: Macmillan, 1916), chapters 14, 20, and 23.

3. David Easton, *The Political System* (New York: Alfred A. Knopf, 1965), p. 53.

4. For further discussions of connoisseurship, see Harry S. Broudy, *et al. Democracy and Excellence in American Secondary Education* (Chicago: Rand McNally, 1964), chapter 13; and Broudy, *Building A Philosophy of Education* (Englewood Cliffs, N. J.: Prentice-Hall, 1954), pp. 370-72.

Part Two
The Content of Instruction

Chapter Five
Knowledge and Education

Students' Questions About Knowledge

Students raise many questions, some of which relate directly or indirectly to the concerns that educators and philosophers express about knowledge. However, questions from both groups often do not seem to ask about the same topic because the latter groups express their concerns in technical language that frequently relates to theoretical issues, while students often use a common sense language to raise questions about practical, everyday concerns surrounding their studies. Representative samples of students' questions reveal the types of questions they are and how they relate to the controversies over knowledge.

A frequently heard question is, "Are you sure that you know the answer?" The response requires that one student inform the other student of the degree of certainty by which he asserts the answer is correct. Reliability is an important aspect of the problem of knowledge, for since most of us would like to have reliable knowledge upon which to base decisions, an understanding is needed as to what claims we can make about certainty and how such claims will hold up under scrutiny.

Another type of student question is, "How do you know that X is true?" This is an evaluative question in that it asks the person making the claim to explain the method of evaluation used to arrive at the conclusion. Many times students raise methodological questions: "How would you find the answer (conduct the experiment, research the paper)?" "How will we be evaluated in the course?" "How should I study for the test?" The first question asks for appropriate methods for finding the answer, conducting an experiment, or researching a paper. The second question asks for the methods or evaluative techniques and procedures and how they would be used or applied in arriving at grades. The third question asks for the best method(s) to use in studying for the test, presumably in order to do as well on the test as possible.

Other kinds of questions are instrumental: "What is the best program to take if I want to be a lawyer or teacher or social worker?" "How will this course help me in the future?" The first question focuses attention on the student's career plans; it asks what program will be best as a means to an end (the chosen career). In this sense it is instrumental: the means (program) is desired for the end it will bring about. The second question is also instrumental because it asks about the relation of a course to some future desired state, even though the nature of this future state is not made clear. It is still an instrumental question because the course is looked upon or valued more highly if it helps one to get along more effectively with his future plans.

Three types of questions then that relate to problems of knowledge are: evaluative, methodological, and instrumental.

More and more frequently students are raising such questions as, "Is that course relevant?" In fact, this is becoming the dominant question in the minds of students. It is a complex question because students do not always make clear what criteria they have in mind. One must decide on what criteria are applicable to uncover the significance of the question. Students raise questions about the substantive content of courses: "What is this course about?" They also question the way courses are organized in the curriculum and related to one another. "What is the relation of this course (for example, political theory) to that one (sociological theory)?" These are important questions pertaining to the organization and structuring of human knowledge.

Students always ask questions about sequence or standards: "What courses do I need in order to get a degree?" "What are the requirements of the course?" "What are the prerequisites?" The first question is concerned about requirements, sequence (because the courses cannot be taken randomly), and standards (requirements of any particular program represent standards to be fulfilled). In order to answer the second question, one would need to know the standards of the course since the requirements represent certain standards. The third question pertains to curriculum sequence. Since one sequence is chosen over another because it is thought to be more desirable in developing certain competencies, the sequence represents an order designed to fulfill certain standards.

Students actually raise more questions relating to problems of knowledge than can be dealt with here. There also are some questions which would be more appropriate for others to consider. For example: "Is the course (or teacher) interesting?" is primarily a psychological question that can best be considered in educational psychology courses.

The study of knowledge and education is important not only because students raise questions about knowledge and because educators view problems of knowledge as being of considerable importance, but also because it is worth considering in terms of inquiry into the nature of educated man. The educated man, according to a number of educators past and present, is able to learn for himself. Such study contributes to this end by treating the types of issues that are more likely to promote the abilities needed to gain reliable knowledge through the process of evaluating competing knowledge claims, testing knowledge, and using it intelligently.

The Search for Certitude

Should the school curriculum consist solely of those findings about which we are certain? That is, is it not a purpose of schools to provide students with certain, rather than less reliable, knowledge? At first glance it seems plausible that we need certain or indubitable findings on the basis of which sound judgments may be formed and intelligent decisions may be made. Yet there are genuine difficulties in fulfilling such demands. These problems can be readily seen by examining more closely some of the problems of certitude.

In the process of gaining knowledge of something people commonly make mistakes. These mistakes include fallacious reasoning, misleading and inaccurate perceptions, false inferences, mistakes in the testing and application of ideas. But one may still wonder whether it is possible to gain certainty once these mistakes are eliminated. If this question can be answered in the affirmative, is it not the business of the school to teach only such certainties?

We often contrast illusory perceptions with those which are veridical. That is, in order to know that a perception is illusory we contrast it with one that is not; if we did not have veridical perceptions the word "illusory" would lose its meaning. Standards are derived from trustworthy perceptions by which we may judge new perceptions. Of course we may be mistaken in trusting those perceptions claimed to be veridical merely because we have derived standards from them for rejecting others as illusory. It does not follow that our ability to reject some perceptions render those we accept as true(1). The meaning of certainty must be clearly defined.

Some philosophers have divided statements into *analytic* and *synthetic*. The importance of this distinction is that *analytic* statements were thought to be certain while *synthetic* statements were not. Both types of statements take the subject-predicate form. Analytic statements take the form of $A=A$; $A>B$; $B>C$; then $A>C$. Other examples are: "All bachelors are men." "All brothers are male." To deny an analytic statement would be to contradict oneself.

With synthetic statements, however, there is something in the predicate not contained in the subject. Some examples will illustrate this: "This box is heavy." "All men are selfish." "Boston is nearer to New York than Chicago." In each of these illustrations mere understanding the meaning of the subject does not render the predicate self-evident. Synthetic statements are not known to be true by knowing the meaning of the subject but by some empirical procedures such as observing, testing, or measuring. These statements are contingent upon what the world happens to be like; whereas analytic statements are true by their meaning and are said to be necessary. The statements of arithmetic, such as $2+2=4$, are necessary, while those of science are contingent.

The issue is whether the only statements which we can hold to be certain are those that are necessary. The problem can be rendered more intelligible and amenable to discussion by defining what we mean whenever we say that a statement is certain. There are some factors which sometimes are confused with certainty. Certainty, for instance, is not the same as clarity. Our ability to grasp an idea clearly may cause us to think it is certain. But on the basis of evidence, very clear statements may be open to doubt. Some, on the other hand, may consider as certain those statements which are self-evident. However, it is possible for a statement to *become* certain even though it is not self-evident. Contingent statements, according to Hans Reichenbach, are predictive without limit and future developments may overturn them (2). Technically speaking, even though we may be certain of a contingent statement under some conditions at the present time, future observations may dissolve this certainty. Or, on the other hand, we could withhold certainty so long as any evidence which is revelant to a statement remains unexamined. However, this move is likely to lead to an inability to find certainty at all because, due to the logical connections among facts, the truth-value of a statement may affect an unlimited number of other statements. In order to avoid this problem, it is necessary, in some measure, to determine in advance the relevance and significance of unexamined possible statements to the statement so that inquiry at some point can cease without a loss of confidence that further needed examination remains undone.

At times we are too stringent in our demands for certainty. It really will not do to ask "Is there any knowledge in the world which is so certain that no reasonable, reflective person could doubt it?" What bits of knowledge we would come up with are probably open to question, but it is evident that if universal assent is required without entertaining the least doubt, there would be little indeed that we could call certain. It may be best then to formulate a notion of certainty which, although not requiring universal assent, would ask two or more observers who could maintain a reasonable modicum of objectivity and impartiality to judge whether a statement is certain. Such certainty would not be expected to hold for all time but only within a particular context under conditions which could be specified. Thus we can say that a statement is "certain" when two or more reasonably objective and impartial observers agree after an examination of the evidence in a particular context that a statement is warranted under specified conditions. Two or more persons are involved in order that claims will be open to public verification, and all that is asked is for the persons to be "reasonably" objective and impartial(3). There is no such thing as complete or absolute impartiality and objectivity, and earlier beliefs that scientists could operate in this manner led only to misconceptions about scientific inquiry and ignored the values and the time-place-condition limitations of the person conducting the investigation. We commonly make claims about certainty within a specifiable teaching or counseling situation, but we are, or should be, careful not to generalize the claim to include all teaching and counseling situations irrespective of the differing variables involved.

So far our only candidate for certainty are necessary statements, while contingent statements usually are considered open to fallibility. This duality of statements, however, has been questioned by some philosophers(4). Furthermore, even if we accept this classification, it scarcely represents the many types of statements made in ordinary language. We are familiar with such exclamations as "Watch out!" "Hurry!" and others. These exclamations are in the imperative, rather than the indicative, mood. There also is the subjunctive mood: "It is necessary that he be certified to teach." There also are statements which primarily express emotion: "I love Bach!" Besides these, there are certain types of statements that philosophers and educators are concerned with but which do not fit into the analytic-synthetic distinction. "That is a beautiful vase." "He was wrong to break his promise." The first of these statements pertains to aesthetics, and the second one is a moral statement. Neither statement fits the definitions of analytic and synthetic statements. Yet we still do not wish to reduce all aesthetic and moral statements to either emotive (those expressing emotion) or imperative statements. For if we do, there would be no grounds for making claims, defending claims, developing defensible positions, and adjudicating disputes, which is what we wish to do when we make aesthetic and moral assertions(5). Neither do we wish to say that aesthetic and moral assertions are entirely subjective, entitling each person to his own opinion with each opinion as good as the next. We really do need more substantial grounds for making claims. Undoubtedly, a stringent interpretation of certainty could not be reasonably applied to such claims, but the interpretation stipulated above could be applied — with possible surprising results. For if extravagant aesthetic and moral claims are eschewed, some modicum of certainty may result between disputing parties.

Still, our best candidate for certainty would be necessary statements. However, philsophers have, from time to time, introduced another candidate: sense statements. Such statements are statements derived from the individual's consciousness that constitute psychological certainty. "I have a pain" or "I feel dizzy" are sense statements. Such statements are considered indubitable, not because the individual has assessed all evidence bearing upon the statement, but because there is no evidence that could supersede it. Of course it is not uncommon for one to claim that one has pains which he really does not have or to exaggerate the severity of the pain. This is a common ploy with a spouse who feels neglected. But who knows better than the person who claims to have the pain whether he really does have one or not? If another party doubts the veracity of the statement he can look to outward dispositions: Does the person squirm and moan and complain and show signs of suffering? Does he exhibit by his movements and behavior certain lowered capacity or inefficiency due to his alleged ailment? Only a good actor could fabricate these signs, but some of us are good actors when we want to be. Suppose a student told his teacher that his bladder is distended and asks to leave the room. It would be odd if the teacher asked him how does he know his bladder is distended. However, if the student after returning to class asked five minutes later for permission to leave the class again, the teacher would either ask whether anything is wrong, or question the student as to whether he was telling the truth. But it would be unlikely that the teacher would examine the student's bladder to determine whether he was lying. A more likely method of certification would be the teacher's recollecting past instances which would indicate the student's propensity to lie in order to escape the confines of the classroom.

But the possibility of error holds for sense statements just as it does for other types. Someone may state, "I have a headache," only to notice that the hat he is wearing is too tight, and once it is removed, the original pressure vanishes. In other words, his initial report was predicated on the conviction that he had a genuine headache, but both the pain and his convictions were dispelled upon removing his hat.

Yet if each individual has exclusive access to his own sense experience, how does he get to know what others experience and whether their statements about these experiences actually are true? Obviously he cannot know another's sense experiences directly, but only indirectly. This means that the outside observer must use a different method of verification than the individual undergoing the experience. The outside observer seeks overt behavioral manifestations as signs that can be used for purposes of verification. One sign is a verbal report. The individual who has the pain reports it to the observer. Other signs are found in such overt behavior as writhing, contorting, moaning, tossing, grimacing, and others. When we see these signs we associate them with sensations of pain. They constitute further corroboration of the original verbal report. These signs are usually considered sufficient evidence that the person is experiencing pain. However, the possibility always exists that he really is not experiencing pain, particularly if the individual has a motive for feigning and is adept at doing so. One needs to know something about the individual's past behavior — whether he has a tendency to simulate being in pain — and whether he has a motive in the present situation to feign sense experience. One must also know whether the individual's acting is sufficiently convincing to deceive others. If these conditions do not hold, it is automatically assumed that the individual's reports are true and reliable.

How does the discussion of certainty relate to the school curriculum? Those who believe that schools should only teach what is certain would find (assuming the above analysis is correct) a very limited and circumscribed curriculum, for the analysis has concluded that there are few worthy candidates for certainty. If rigorously applied, such a case would eliminate a large portion of the curriculum at any level of education. But this dismaying conclusion can be avoided if the seekers of certainty who would apply their guillotine to the curriculum could be shown as misguided. It is true that these seekers may wish to eliminate art, music, the humanities, and perhaps even science if they carry their ideas to the logical extreme; or at least the present range of requirements would be circumscribed and considerably curtailed and the remainder of the program would play a secondary role in the educational process. There is a more justifiable approach to the problems of certainty and to the uses of knowledge.

Knowledge, as we presently understand it, cannot take the form of certainty which can be relied upon once and for all time. Analytic statements and sensory reports do afford some forms of certainty; yet the former statements are true but uninformative, while the latter's truth content holds only for a particular moment in time and does not necessarily signify a trend or offer a basis for reliable predictions. More information is needed before trends can be projected and predictions made, and some of this information may be less certain, in the above sense, than the original sensory report. Empirically speaking, the quest for certainty has not yielded the promises that its proponents have hoped. It seems clear that on the basis of our present understanding of the nature of knowledge the quest is a misguided one, even though future advances in knowledge and inquiry may provide greater certainty. However, the direction of future developments remains in the area of speculation. In terms of our understanding of the past and the present status of human knowledge, it would be futile to seek knowledge that will hold true once and for all time. It is true that there are strong psychological reasons for doing so. The quest for certainty throughout history has deep psychological roots. Living today in a highly complex world that moves closer each day toward its own annihilation, man yearns for a certainty that will bolster his sanity. But such a quest is marred by illusions, and man, in order to be more fully human, must learn to live in the world and make his life productive without the certainty that he vainly strives to achieve.

Certainty for the curriculum content can be seen to be a misleading ideal, once we examine the uses of knowledge more closely. The knowledge most important — that which will help us to become more fully human — does not require eternal certainty to be of value. Schools not only presently teach many things that lack certainty (in the sense previously discussed), but it would be a futile and misleading move to limit the curriculum in such a manner. Futile because it cannot be secured, misleading because it would lead in the wrong direction, a direction away from that which is more important and significant for educational institutions to follow.

Schools commonly teach for understanding and appreciation; they also seek to develop skills and inculcate sound habits. Certainty does not apply to learning of this sort. In what sense, we may ask, does certainty apply to the humanities and the fine arts, the sciences and the social sciences? Indeed, an ideal of the sciences, the continual improvement of knowledge, presupposes relative uncertainty of the knowledge on hand. Surely we want knowledge that has some degree of reliability and warrant for its claims, and such knowledge is to be preferred to that which is less reliable and warranted. Part of the educative task in helping individuals to become more fully human is that of developing a greater sensitive awareness of themselves, others, and the significance of existence. This sensitivity can be effectively developed through the cultivation of appreciation and participation in the arts and activities of human culture. As greater sensitivity grows, the old dogmatisms and encrusted prejudices begin to slip away and the spurious certainties that they afford are dispelled with them. At this point, one is face-to face with the greater complexity and forms of human existence and is immersed in a multitude of fruitful uncertainties that generate further growth. In light of these realities, one must learn to live with a minimum of fixed beliefs in order to avoid a premature arrest of one's development, for large clusters of fixed beliefs limit one's choices by prejudging alternatives and different life styles. Large clusters of fixed beliefs lead to a premature closure in exploring the varieties of existence and the multiple possibilities for growth. As Nietzsche asserted: one must learn to hang by slender threads.

An attitude toward knowledge is important. Rather than a quest for certainty, the preeminent task of the educative process is to cultivate openness and wonder in confronting new experience, to develop capacities to think, feel, appreciate, to grow, and, above all, to affirm life in the face of uncertainty and death.

Knowledge and Belief

Children enter school with many beliefs which they have already acquired from the home and their peer group. They also bring with them many different claims to knowledge. As the child matures, the number of beliefs and knowledge claims grows and diversifies. The school experience is where new beliefs are formed and some older ones discarded, where the grounds for knowledge claims can be examined and the ability to gain new knowledge improved. From an educational point of view, statements about belief and knowledge must be defined because they are central in the educational process.

It is generally conceded that to say that someone has a belief is not to imply that the belief is true or could be verified, for there are many beliefs that are false and cannot be verified unless the meaning of truth is grossly distorted. To distort the criteria for truth statements would not serve our purposes because it would no longer be possible to make sharp distinctions between true and false claims. Whenever a belief is proven to be true, one usually says that it is knowledge. To say that we know something to be the case implies that the statement is true and that its truth value could be demonstrated for anyone who is skeptical, which is the basic difference between knowledge and belief.

Much more could be said by way of clarification and elucidation. Whenever a person has a belief, we expect him to affirm his agreement with the belief. Woozley suggests that whenever one has a belief one may have some evidence to support it (although the evidence may be insufficient to establish the belief as true)(6). We would say in such a case that the belief is a rational one because there is some evidence that can be used in its support. The individual recognizes the evidence and is prepared to marshal it whenever the belief is called into question. However, people hold many beliefs which have little or no evidence for their support. We would say in such cases that the belief is nonrational or irrational. Could there be beliefs which have no evidence to support them? People are willing to believe almost anything (as advertising executives have found) so long as the material is presented in a sufficiently persuasive and compelling fashion or fulfills some psychological need. A number of beliefs are not warranted on logical or empirical grounds but are tenaciously maintained, in spite of falsifying evidence, due to a psychological need to hold the particular beliefs. Beliefs which could be characterized as highly irrational, that is, having no grounds for support, are generally maintained in certain personal aspects of an individual's life. These beliefs are acquired usually through custom, family backgrounds, cliques, and other sources, and particularly relate to loved ones, politics, religion, sex, etiquette, customs, and social class expectations. In such cases we may wonder whether any evidence can be offered in their support. Unless the individual becomes emotional over the issue and refuses to talk about it or abruptly terminates discussion, he will offer what he believes to be evidence that supports the belief. In fact, he may say that he knows it to be true, implying that it is more than a belief. When the issue is emotional, the individual will not usually admit any evidence adduced to falsify the belief either by refusing to engage in further discussion once the falsifying evidence is presented or by lapsing into emotional responses or digressive maneuvers. Most people, no matter how false the beliefs they entertain, believe they have evidence for them. But if the alleged evidence is false to fact or irrelevant to the issue at hand, it is technically not evidence. Therefore, it would be misleading to say, as Woozley does, that in order to have a belief one must not only be willing to affirm it but have some evidence to support it. Doubtlessly one may adduce what he believes to be evidence in defense of his beliefs, but the claims put forward as evidence may be false or unrelated to the issue. Thus it is not evidence, and one can readily have beliefs lacking any genuine evidence for their support.

According to Woozley, when one claims that he knows something to be the case rather than merely believes it to be so, he can produce evidence, show that it is sound evidence, and the evidence relates to the conclusion(7). Woozley gives two illustrations of drawing conclusions from the evidence(8). One could accuse a person of forgery by comparing two signatures only to find that the charge was false because the comparisons were not made carefully enough, or one could charge another with murder on the basis of finding his fingerprints in the room where the body was discovered. The person's fingerprints alone would not constitute sufficient evidence to convict him of murder. In other words, an erroneous conclusion has been drawn. One must not only have evidence and be correct that it bears on the matter at hand, but it is necessary to arrive at the right conclusions whenever application is made of the evidence.

Scheffler, on the other hand, outlines the conditions that he believes necessary and sufficient for saying that one knows that something is the case(9). The conditions are that one must believe something to be the case; that the person have adequate evidence to support his belief, and that the knowledge claim itself is true. This, he says, is the strong sense of "knowing that." A weaker sense of "knowing that" may be produced by simply eliminating the second condition. In the weak sense, one needs only to have true belief; it is not necessary for the individual to be able to marshal evidence in support of the belief. The very fact that he believes something to be the case and his belief is a true one, entitles him, at least in the weak sense, to say that he knows it to be the case.

Several further points need to be made about the process of knowing. Knowledge is gained from different sources or through a variety of procedures. People have claimed to gain knowledge through reason, sensory experience and observation, intuition, revelation, and other sources. Some may claim that one of these sources is superior, either because it yields more reliable knowledge or a higher form of knowledge. It is true that historical trends point away from claims of revelation and speculation on the basis of reasoning to the greater use of observation and the scientific method of gaining knowledge. It is also true that some of the developments in science are impressive and the control exercised over nature exceeds the anticipations of previous generations. But still it would be idle to speculate which method was best apart from the uses made of it and the type of knowledge desired. Surely the mathematician needs to utilize observations only minimally whenever he constructs a new axiomatic system. He relies instead on certain rationalistic operations in devising his system. Intuition, too, is still of use in interpersonal relations and is used even by the scientist in uncovering new ideas. The important point is not so much the source of knowledge but the evidence which can be used to support a knowledge claim. Irrespective of how some finding was gained, it still is necessary to subject it to some sort of test or verification procedure to determine whether the claims adduced in its behalf are warranted. Therefore, it would be foolish to limit ourselves to one particular source of knowledge, closing out considerations of other sources, without first considering the type of knowledge desired. Whether a source will yield knowledge for a certain purpose cannot be known prior to the process of gaining new findings and testing them to determine whether sufficient grounds exist for their support.

It should also be noted that the process of knowing is not related to a particular mental state or psychological activity. For example, we cannot be assured that someone knows something because some specific type of mental activity — such as recalling, remembering, imagining, abstracting — is going on in his mind. Knowing is not related to any particular state because there is no logical connection between a mental state and the fact that something is true. One may be undertaking very rigorous and sustained thinking, but that does not assure that the claims he makes resulting from the particular thinking episode are true. The same would hold in the matter of convictions. Merely because someone has a strong conviction that something is the case does not provide the necessary connection that it actually is the case. In fact, strong convictions have been entertained about many ideas, e.g., the earth is flat, bloodletting will cure diseases, etc., that later have been shown to be false.

Another misleading notion about the knowledge process is that when one says "I know" he is in the process of making a report about what it is he knows. It is true that when one makes statements of this sort and someone subjects the statement to question, the individual can report what he knows and then offer evidence to support his knowledge claim. But it may very well be, as J. L. Austin has suggested, that whenever one says that he knows he is also doing something more (10). "I know" has a performance usage. One is giving others his word that he knows; he is asserting his authority for making the statement. In other words, one does not say "I know" idly, for he may be challenged to demonstrate that he can honor his claim. To utter "I know" is not merely a report but is a statement of authority by the speaker that he has grounds for making the statement and can perform the necessary operations to demonstrate the knowledge claim whenever questioned about the statement. With this implication in mind, it is evident that the speaker is only called upon to demonstrate his claim in those instances when his authority is not accepted initially but has to be proved(11).

Forms of Knowing. Gilbert Ryle has spoken of two forms of knowing: "knowing how" and "knowing that"(12). Simply stated, one knows that something is the case when he has propositional knowledge. One knows that New York is east of Chicago, heavy objects fall to earth when dropped from the window of a skyscraper, and that the Declaration of Independence was written in 1776. We know how to do something whenever we can perform certain acts successfully. Ryle, first of all, tries to show why it would be misleading to reduce cases of knowing how to knowing that. This fallacy suggests that before we perform an act we first intellectualize the rules or consider certain propositions. The act does not require the double operation of "considering and executing." Instead, there are many activities, according to Ryle, which are performed intelligently, but rules or criteria for performance remain unformulated. One may not be able to explain how he is able to tell clever jokes. Thus, for many activities there are not two processes — theorizing and doing — but one process, doing. One performs acts intelligently, cleverly, or stupidly. In order to act intelligently, one does not first reflect on how to act, and these reflections, in turn, are not determined by a prior theoretical operation about whether such reflections are intelligent, etc.(13). This would involve an impossible infinite regress.

In the process of learning how to do something for the first time, such as learning how to drive an automobile, one may become acutely aware of the rules of driving, when to put on the brake, when to shift gears, what distance to maintain when following another car, etc. However, once one gains a relatively high degree of proficiency in driving a car or performing some other skill, he has acquired intelligent, coordinated habits which enable him to perform the skill without formulating rules or being self-conscious about what he is doing.

Ryle notes another distinction between knowing how and knowing that(14). In terms of knowing that, one either knows or he does not know. It would be odd to say that a person only partially knows that Albany is the capital of New York state: either he knows or he does not know this fact. In knowing how, one can speak of a person having an ability in a limited degree. That is, we can speak of someone as having some, but a limited, ability to ski. Knowing how can be evaluated in terms of different degrees of ability to perform a series of acts. One learns a certain truth at a particular moment, but one learns a skill over a period of time.

Not everyone has accepted Ryle's distinction between knowing how and knowing that. Hartland-Swann argues that knowing that is a sub-species of knowing how(15). Hartland-Swann suggests that this relationship can be seen if knowing that is considered a dispositional term. Dispositional terms, according to Ryle, are used when we describe glass as brittle or sugar as soluble(16). We ascribe these characteristics to glass and sugar because whenever certain acts are performed, glass will break and sugar will dissolve. So, in reference to knowing, to say that someone knows something does not mean that at the present moment he is thinking about it or reciting it. Rather, it is to say that he has the capacity to demonstrate that he knows whenever the occasion calls for it. "Know," in other words, is a capacity verb. For Hartland-Swann, knowing that can be translated into knowing how: for example, when asked, "Do you know the capital of New York state?" it would appear to be a case of knowing that Albany is the capital. One either knows it or he does not. However, one could say that he knows how to give the correct answer when he responds by answering, "Albany." In other words, whenever one gains propositional knowledge, that is, learns that something is the case, he also, if he has learned it correctly, knows how to respond whenever someone asks him the appropriate question. Therefore, whenever one knows that something is the case, he knows how to state the answer correctly or demonstrate that he knows on appropriate occasions; otherwise, one could be said to know something and not be able to answer correctly.

There are a number of possible objections to the above interpretation(17). Even though one may know something, he may have a tendency to avoid responding with the correct answer when given the appropriate question (as in the case of a spy captured by an enemy). There are other less extreme cases where fears or inhibitions may prevent one from responding. However, in such cases, it would be impossible for the questioner to know whether the person actually had the information, so there would be no way of verifying it.

On the other hand, a person may give a response which he really does not accept as true, either because he made a lucky guess or because he wishes to please the questioner by responding in ways designed to evoke approval. A child, too, may know the truth about a situation but refuse to reveal it for fear of provoking censure from an adult. In such cases, however, one is not seeking truth, but only conformity to adult demands. The adult in the illustration is not seeking truth; his interest lies in seeing that the child is sufficiently tractable to comply with commands and, for the time being, eschew truth statements or, in some cases when a certain question is asked, to deliberately offer false or misleading responses. The most obvious case is when the child is told to answer the doorbell, and is told: "If there is a man there who looks as though he is selling things, tell him your mother is not at home." There are many instances when the truth is undesired and illustrations must be chosen in which the objective is that of gaining the truth. The remarks above apply as well to instances of restraint and coercion in totalitarian states where one's personal security and well-being would be jeopardized by publicly stating the truth about the political regime.

Knowing Oneself

Importance of Self-Knowledge

There are those who believe and would argue that a knowledge of oneself or self-understanding is the most vital knowledge of all. It is not that other forms of knowledge — such as knowledge of others, of things, of the organized disciplines — are unimportant or unessential; rather, the case could be made that knowing oneself is primary among all epistemological tasks. Furthermore, all too often the other forms of knowledge have been granted priority over self-knowledge when in actuality, their usefulness and value would be more thoroughly enhanced when added to a foundation of self-knowledge.

There are several questions which need to be raised and explored. More explicitly, why is self-knowledge important? To state the case negatively, one can avoid many mistakes, false moves, and embarrassments by having a sound understanding of oneself. One catches himself, from time to time, saying "I am surprised I did that; I really thought I knew better. I don't know why I did it." There are occasions when we find ourselves surprised at our own behavior and lacking a suitable explanaton for it. This unawareness causes disturbance whenever our acts have untoward results. Whereas when we do something unexpected for which we have difficulty explaining but which leads to desirable

outcomes, our reaction is likely to be one of elation and pleasant surprise that is free from recrimination. It is unlikely that we would examine these desirable outcomes — or, at least, not in as much detail —
because no feelings of guilt, remorse, or self-criticism are involved.
However, perhaps when we had the good fortune to unexpectedly win
money or material goods we may want to examine our acts more closely
in order to discover how to do it again. In any case, we need to understand ourselves to avoid making costly mistakes and to be able to explain why, at times, we have the happy knack of doing the right things
but cannot explain why we do them. Nevertheless, we would like to
formulate them more carefully so that such acts can be repeated in
some predictable form whenever the appropriate occasion arises.

On the more positive side, better understanding of ourselves presumably will enable us to live life more effectively, more fully, and
with greater enjoyment and satisfaction. It will help us to set more
realistic personal goals and attain them more quickly with less expen-
diture of energy. It should also help us to enjoy better interpersonal
relations because a lack of personal understanding may be projected
into our social affairs and cripple our ability to relate effectively to
others.

Do these positive benefits seem plausible? One argument that may
be used against these claims is that some persons seem to get along
in life well but also seem to lack any great or profound understanding
of themselves. In response, it could be said that their actions appear
to exhibit these characteristics. Yet we may immediately need to ask
what it means "to get along well in life." What criteria do we use to
evaluate such claims? However, the same question could be raised
about our own claim that self-understanding will enable us to live more
effectively. It is unlikely that either side could support its case if the
question remained in the general form in which it has been stated.
The usual way of treating it would be to take situations or particular
life functions and raise these questions in each instance, assuming that
some criteria will already be built into the situation and can be used
in making an evaluation. For example, does self-knowledge or understanding help or hinder a person overall in his marital relations? Are
some of the problems of marriage created by one or both partners who
lack a good understanding of themselves? Is this one of the primary
causes of divorces? Another illustration would be to ask to what extent
does an understanding of oneself help one to work effectively, smoothly,
or fruitfully with his associates or superiors in his occupation? Here we

may need to explain self-understanding by offering a tentative definition which later will be amplified further. Self-understanding is the ability to grasp and explain one's major propensities, goals, and desires as expressed in important relationships. What relationships are important depend upon the individual's goals, but they are found in certain fundamental relations between the sexes, in the family, occupational structure, church, civic and political participation, and among one's close friends. With this definition in mind, if we can answer the above questions affirmatively (as well as questions of a similar form applied to other basic relationships), then it can be said that in most cases greater self-understanding is a worthy goal for which to strive.

There is, however, another objection which could be raised, a serious objection which, although not always taken seriously by philosophers and educators, cannot be readily dismissed or glossed over. There is the intellectualist bias that more knowledge and its widespread dissemination will dispel ignorance, superstition, bigotry, and will enable people to live more intelligently. A tacit assumption operates which holds that the more knowledge we can gain the better we can lead our lives. Now the objection to this widely held view is that, at best, it is only partially true. It is obvious that some knowledge, such as knowing how to do something, may be indispensable. To preserve life, it is necessary to know how to avoid being hit by a car, what to do when one accidentally takes poison, how to treat frostbite or sunstroke until the doctor arrives. There are numerous forms of knowledge essential merely for the preservation of life, not to mention those forms which are useful in embellishing and enhancing life. But this does not contradict the argument, which is based upon an objection to the intellectual's categorical belief that more knowledge is good and the school should see that this function is fulfilled.

Under what conditions would more knowledge be undesirable? One usually would claim its undesirability when the knowledge would disclose to the individual certain information that would cause aversion, revulsion, or generate tendencies toward psychological illness or lead to destruction of one's self-concept. More knowledge, in other words, is not invariably good. There are many things one does not wish to know and such revelations may only inhibit one's ability to function fully. Even if true, one does not want to hear that his mother was a prostitute, his father a common criminal, that his spouse committed adultery, or that his country committed unprovoked, brutal and iniquitous acts against a group of people or a nation. Most persons do

We need to develop the ability to assess not only knowledge, but also the illusions that will enable us to become more fully human.

not have a great deal of intellectual curiosity; even among the few who do, their curiosity would be unlikely to extend to subjects enumerated above unless the individuals had pronounced masochistic tendencies. This brings us to the tenuous line between truth and illusion that some contemporary playwrights, such as Albee, Pinter, Williams, and Miller, have exploited so well.   One needs illusions to get on in the world — illusions about oneself, and relations to the larger culture. The trick is to make one's illusions work in one's behalf so that life can be lived more abundantly and enjoyed more fully rather than the converse. Since a great dependency upon multiple illusions may lead to a psychosis, great care must be exercised to avoid that untoward result. However, it is doubtful whether anyone who has been reasonably sane has ever been free of all illusions. As one strips away more illusions than he can psychologically withstand, the tendency, first of all, is to become highly cynical. Later, serious psychological disturbances may ensue unless the process is arrested. Nietzsche vacillates somewhat in taking a strong position on the truth and illusion theme, but he has Zarathustra tell us that man must learn to hang by slender threads. Apparently the fewer the illusions the greater the strength. But Nietzsche does not say that man can have no illusions. In fact, there are some useful fictions. It seems that the problem is not so much to strike a balance between truth and illusion, but rather to strip oneself of all illusions except those that contribute to man's ability to become more fully human. In conclusion, merely more knowledge of ourselves is not all that is needed, for some knowledge may be harmful to ourselves. We need to develop the ability to assess not only the knowledge but also the illusions that will enable us to become more fully human. One problem is that illusions are more fragile than knowledge claims and the more closely and painstakingly we examine and analyze them, the more likely they are to shatter and expose themselves for what they are, making use of them much more difficult, even though we may wish to do so.

Developing Self-Knowledge

Keeping the previous qualifications in mind, there is a certain amount and type of self-knowledge needed by each person in order to live more fully and effectively. The questions we wish to raise are: What forms of self-knowledge are most valuable? and How do we go about acquiring and using this knowledge?

There are many types of self-knowledge, ranging from the basic autobiographical facts of one's existence to more profound understandings of one's inner motivations, desires, and life goals. Obviously one needs to recall some basic autobiographical information merely to maintain a minimum sense of identity, but for the most part this recall is an automatic process that causes no particular problems except for the amnesia victim. There is some autobiographical information that we would like to forget because its recollection elicits feelings of guilt, shame, or remorse. Most psychoanalysts tell us that whenever memories of past events become too painful to bear, they are repressed into the unconscious but still may exert a maladjustive influence over our behavior. A considerable part of the problem is that society labels certain acts as immoral, corrupt, or sinful, and the individual may tend to repress knowledge of his participation in such acts. Therefore, hypothetically speaking, the more repressive a society becomes, and the stronger the individual's conviction that society's mandates are legitimate and should be obeyed, the greater the amount of repression on the part of the individual. On the other hand, a society may be highly repressive, but if the individual does not accept many of its principal mandates as legitimate, there will be far less tendency to repress incidents in one's past life. Although somewhat oversimplified and not sufficiently inclusive as categories, we could think of the white middle class of the middle age and elderly generation as illustrative of the former group, while the students on the left would be more characteristic of the latter group.

There is little or no problem to acquiring autobiographical information. The issue is how it will be used. Two variables operating, according to our analysis, are repression and legitimacy. What will be repressed is culturally determined; the extensiveness of repression depends upon legitimacy. Although this analysis deviates from Freudian orthodoxies, it may prove valuable in promoting an understanding of the uses made of autobiographical information.

In responding to the question, "What forms of self-knowledge are most valuable?" we can say that autobiographical information is essential for maintaining some sense of identity and a modicum of continuity from past to present. Not all autobiographical information, however, is needed to successfully conduct our activities and fulfill our goals. Many events in the life of the individual are trivial and prosaic, and their recollections would have negligible effects upon present plans and future goals. Other events, which were taken by the individual to be significant at the time they occurred, are no longer vested with significance (although it is possible that they may be evaluated differently in the future). Thus what is autobiographically significant in the life of the individual would be those recollections that provide him with a sense of identity and continuity in time, along with other past information which helps the individual to formulate his plans and achieve his goals. What autobiographical material this will be would obviously depend upon the individual, his objectives and aspirations.

Possibly, however, the individual may not interpret this autobiographical material correctly. Questions of interpretation arise when two or more people get together to reminisce about certain past events in which they jointly participated. One person may relate what he did or said in the situation and what occurred as a result of these actions. The other parties may object that his story is inaccurate or grossly distorted, for they may allege that the events were quite different. They may accuse the individual of a lapse in memory or a tendency to exaggerate, deceive, or jest. There is no conscious motive in a lapse of memory, but if any of the other ascriptions are correct, the parties may be accusing the individual of exaggerating, deceiving, or jesting due to some motive. Although one could accidentally exaggerate, or without thinking or consciously formulating what he is doing give an inaccurate story as a basis for humor, we would not usually speak of him as deceiving unconsciously. But we could say he unintentionally mislead us.

This means that our autobiographical information may be faulty and that any inaccuracies or distortions may be brought to attention by other parties who were witnesses or participants in the same events, or inaccuracies may be corrected by ourselves whenever we reassess past events and attempt to recollect them more accurately. But suppose we doubt the accuracy or veracity of the other parties' account and continue to hold tenaciously to our own contentions? What would be needed then would be to determine whether the other parties were in a position to observe as accurately or more accurately than the individual who made the autobiographical claims. Are there any reasons to question the veracity of the parties involved? Are there any records to show that the events occurred? Would any of the claims be inconsistent with other connected events which have already been accepted as reported? Are there any reasons to suspect that the individual could not have done what he said he did because such acts were beyond his ability to perform at the time? There are other questions that may be raised in trying to establish the accuracy of autobiographical information whenever it is challenged. However, the questions enumerated above should be sufficient to convey the idea of how one would proceed to support or refute such claims.

In addition to autobiographical information, we need other forms of knowledge which will provide the basis for developing a sense of identity and a realization of our place in the world. A sense of identity means how the individual conceives of himself as a person in his relation to others and the demands of his culture. In other words, clarifying one's sense of identity enables him to make a connection between this conceptual framework and his idea of his place in the world. We are aware that this sense of identity is shaped largely by the socialization process. A number of observers, such as George H. Mead, have described the initial stages of this process in terms of developing a concept of self. This process begins in early childhood as the child begins to imitate the roles others play. It then develops further as the child begins to see himself as others see him. At this point he begins to grasp the relationship of himself to other members of his family, and learns to play the roles that his parents and other adults expect of him. Whenever he is aware that he misbehaves, the awareness indicates that he has learned to conceptualize a certain limited range of role behavior. One's self-concept is further amplified, embellished, and refined in the socialization process in the school, home, and other institutions.

In light of the great influence exerted by the culture on the development of a self-concept, one may very well wonder whether his "own" identity consists entirely of the cumulated social roles, rules, and prescriptions imposed by the culture. He may ask "Am I nothing more than what the culture has made me?" Could each person be little more than the movie star whose celluloid image is the fabrication of a role and whose public image is whatever the publicity agent wants to make it? Perhaps in a computerized world of artificial needs and simulated goods our anxieties are so great they we are becoming more like robots than distinct and unique human beings. The question of identity is a genuine concern in our time. Our problem is to uncover who we are and to discover whether this person who is "I" has any identity apart from the way the socialization process has shaped him.

This question cannot be answered prior to gaining a sense of self and sorting out the divergent influences that shape one's basic beliefs and prevailing behavior patterns. How does one gain insight into his identity? Does he, first of all, examine the multiple influences on his life as they unfolded within chronological sequence? Or does he begin with his present way of life and draw upon autobiographical material whenever necessary? Let us utilize the latter course and see what progress we make. Although some continuity usually exists, we are assuming that the individual is actually what he has become at the present; he is not just what he was. In a limited sense of the word, he also is what he can become and aspires to become insofar as these ideals enter into and guide his present behavior. Thus, although the individual enjoys a modicum of continuity over time, he is not merely what he was when someone knew him at a previous date; neither is he just a totality of his past experiences, for some experiences can be redirected and transformed by the individual so that they will be more serviceable for present experiences and future aspirations.

The problem of reconciling how one perceives himself and the way others do is a fundamental difficulty. This problem does not arise for those who have slavishly followed the dictates of others; but for those more independent in their thought and actions, some discrepancies may be revealed once the individual has scrutinized the problem carefully. A psychological problem also arises when those who are influential in our lives view us somewhat differently than we do, for, unless we are strong-willed, we have a tendency to make our views conform to theirs. To gain a sense of identity we must examine closely what we claim to believe most deeply, our basic value system and outlook on life. Then we can try to see if we live by these values or only give them lip-service. Of course, one does not always have opportunities to apply all that he believes in practice. But taking this proviso into consideration, and assuming that the lack of opportunity is not of one's making due to lack of diligence or moral courage, an analysis of one's value system, coupled with an examination of one's actions, should help in uncovering his sense of identity. In addition, one should examine his goals and aspirations, along with the activities undertaken to realize them. Understanding and insight into these factors will begin the process of constructing a sense of identity. Autobiographical information will be useful at certain points whenever it appears relevant; so, too, will the conceptions others, whom we have reason to believe know us well, have of us. But the individual's first responsibility is to develop himself and his own sense of identity, so that whenever his self-concept conflicts with that of others, his own sense of identity will not be relinquished unless conclusive evidence shows him to be mistaken.

There are other factors which may contribute to one's self-understanding. A knowledge of the findings and theoretical studies in the social and behavioral sciences contributes to a greater sophistication as a student of human behavior and promotes the development of conceptual systems for the analysis of interpersonal relations. But knowledge of this type alone is not enough, for an individual could score high on a test measuring his knowledge of human behavior and principles of interpersonal relations and still not have a good understanding of himself. The reason for this discrepancy is that knowledge of behavioral science is not personal knowledge. Knowledge of behavioral and social sciences is in the form of empirical findings, generalizations, and theoretical systems which apply to certain groups, classes, and categories of people under certain specified conditions. That one could have a good grasp of such knowledge, use it to make sound analyses of interpersonal relations, yet still be unable to apply it to himself is no mystery. Such knowledge is usually presented in the form of objective, impersonal, meticulous studies that seem to desiccate the personal, human, and idiosyncratic characteristics of the individual. The student is likely to conceptualize this knowledge in terms of the form in which he finds it. It becomes a knowledge to be applied to "the other" — other persons, groups, organizations, and institutions. One may even consider himself something of an "expert" in human behavior, yet exhibit abysmal ignorance of his own inner strivings. These so-called experts are highly painstaking and thorough in their analysis of human behavior, but their powers of understanding dramatically atrophy during those rare moments when they become reflective about themselves. On those occasions it is likely that they never break through their facade, a facade erected not just to protect them from others but primarily to protect them from themselves. Since the process by which the facade is erected is likely to be more unconscious than conscious, elaborate systems of projection and rationalizations are marshalled to buttress it.

Thus, there are difficulties in using findings from the social and behavioral sciences to foster greater personal understanding; however, the barriers are far from insuperable. Even when the barriers can be overcome, the application of this knowledge alone is insufficient to foster the sense of personal identity needed, although it can prove to be of considerable worth.

The problem of gaining personal knowledge was expressed well by Nietzsche in *Thus Spoke Zarathustra:* "For whatever is his own is well concealed from the owner; and of all the treasures, it is our own that we dig up last . . ."(18) But as Nietsche adds: "He, however, has discovered himself who says, 'This is *my* good and evil' "(19), not what is good and evil for all, for the mass, for the majority, but what is good and evil for me. Man must reevaluate all existing values, create his own and live by them courageously. But until he takes the necessary steps to create his own values, his self-understanding will be greatly limited.

There are, in addition, other procedures by means of which greater personal knowledge may be gained. One way to approach these processes is in terms of those instances when one's speech and actions are less guarded. These moments may arise when one is speaking freely and candidly to intimate friends and associates whom he feels have his welfare at heart. Other instances are also found in situations in which one feels free to do what one pleases, be oneself without fear of disapproval, guilt, recriminations, or punishment.

Certain situations of a different type may also prove instructive. During birth, marriage and death, inhibitions are reduced and the facade shown to the world may temporarily vanish. There are also situations in which the individual finds himself under considerable strain or even subject to mild trauma, such as an accident or the duress of war, when a side of oneself is revealed that hitherto remained undisclosed. One may find a shocking side of himself that does not coincide with his self-image. On the other hand, one's behavior in crisis may reveal a positive facet of himself with which he had not credited himself. Situations of these varied types all contribute to our most important knowledge — self-knowledge.

In conclusion, there are several impediments to self-knowledge which can be analyzed to show why it is so difficult to acquire and put into practice. Greater self-knowledge can be gained in a variety of ways: from the social and behavioral sciences (with a number of qualifications); autobiographical information; one's value system and outlook on life and one's actions that issue from these systems; those instances where speech and action are less guarded; observations of one's behavior during rites of passage, and also under stressful and mildly traumatic situations.

Relevant Knowledge

There is much discussion today among some students about making their studies "relevant." However, what they mean by this term is not always clear. One approach by which the term may be clarified is to determine how it is used when applied in a context of opposition to present university curricular and instructional policies. In other words, since students who use the term have not usually developed alternative programs with sufficient clarity and detail, it may be easier to first examine the types of practices to which they apply the term "lack of relevance."

In terms of curricular organization, some students oppose what they consider a rigid, lock-step system of parceling out knowledge in bits and pieces in the form of courses, and the requirement of accumulating these courses as credits toward graduation. Disciplines become highly specialized, subareas are generated, and courses are instituted which deal with "more and more about less and less." Not only is knowledge not integrated, but interrelations among fields and subspecialties which treat overlapping problems in several areas are seldom related to one another. The curriculum has become highly atomized and any attempt at integration must be made by the student or not at all. Furthermore, in our scientific age, everything examined must be "objectified" to the point of desiccation and sterility. Although many students would recognize the need for specialization of knowledge and the development of scholarly pursuits attached to one's discipline, these very tendencies, when carried to the extremity found in some of today's universities, lead to an exaggerated compartmentalization of knowledge and the commitment of the faculty to their discipline rather than a concern for teaching and students. That such highly specialized courses will relate meaningfully to the problems of contemporary society and living in today's world is highly unlikely according to more vocal students. The value of the college experience in contributing to a liberating education and humantistic study has largely been lost.

Some system is needed to break the lock-step of atomized knowledge, the inexorable round of papers to be written and tests to be taken, where no time is left for genuine thought and exploration, where the fear of poor grades and their possible effect on vocational aspirations keep students racing feverishly on the academic treadmill. The "free university," which has sprung up to rectify these shortcomings, was conceived largely by students alienated from the academic "rat-race." Each free university likes to actualize in its own way an informal design which will provide students with a learning environment and types of exploratory educative opportunities which they believe to be sorely absent from the multiversity. Programs in the free universities vary, but many of them feature courses on sex, drugs, Viet Nam, socialism, Marxism, radicalism, the military-industrial complex, Zen, and courses pertaining to various aspects of personal growth. The programs are voluntary, and there are no required courses, no diplomas, no research papers, and no grades. Tuition fees are minimal. Classes and discussions are characteristically much more informal than regular university arrangements, breaking completely from the lecture-assign-recite-read-research-grade pattern.

In light of these developments, what students have in mind when they speak of "relevancy" becomes evident. To this demand for relevancy should be added the demands of blacks for black study programs designed to develop a greater knowledge and appreciation of their history, culture, and accomplishments, as well as pride in their race. From the point of view of some of the protesting students, the university has developed into a colossal knowledge factory for the production of robots while engaging in active support of the militaristic mentality, succoring the military-industrial complex, and, by secret research, promoting the development of bacteriological and chemical warfare. Apart from the massive university reforms needed in its relation to the larger society, curricular reforms, too, would be great and far-reaching. Some of these reforms have already begun at several major universities. Black study programs of various types have been initiated. A pass-fail system in some areas of the curriculum has been instituted for exploratory purposes. Honor program arrangements have been extended to other students on an experimental basis. Requirements in certain programs have been given more flexibility permitting more freedom of choice. There have been rudimentary developments in broad field courses that attempt some degree of integration of knowledge across the boundaries of related disciplines. These developments have arisen primarily in response to the growing wave of dissatisfaction among students. Of course, these developments are still a long way from what some students are demanding, but they do indicate that some universities are willing to change in response to certain types of pressures.

What does the above discussion mean in terms of the idea of "relevant knowledge?" When protesting students speak of the need for "relevant knowledge," they expect the university curriculum to relate more directly and effectively to the need for two types of knowledge: personal knowledge and knowledge about the significant issues of our time, in addition to how these issues relate to the lives of the younger generation, and what youth can do about them. The importance of personal knowledge and the form it is likely to take have previously been indicated. However, its place in the larger university setting must be

Students desire an understanding of the
significant events of our time.

clarified. Presently this knowledge is more likely to be gained in association with one's peers than in the classroom. This is principally due to the reasons previously mentioned: the atomization of knowledge, its objectification, rendering it less amenable for personal use, the commitment of instructors primarily to their discipline rather than to students and teaching, the lock-step procedure of getting a college education, the excessive pressures it imposes upon students, and the consequent preclusion of leisurely process of reflection and indepth appropriation of the material.

Students desire an understanding of the significant issues of our time, how these issues affect them, and what they can do about the problems. The distrust of anyone over thirty stems not just from the fact that society's elders have made a world in which youth are not consulted (a situation faced by every new generation), but also from the fact that many in the older generation, particularly society's leaders and influentials, seem to operate with a different value system and outlook on life than youth. No longer do some youths want the materialistic values and the sacrifices that go with them in order to experience a deceptive sense of security, to be accepted in the "right" circles, to have a home in the suburbs, a fairly secure but uninteresting job with good fringe benefits. Even more seriously, our elders have created a society verging on nuclear annihilation, a society where youths are conscripted for undeclared wars which they oppose and consider unjust.

Part of the problem is that those who disseminate knowledge in our universities, if not exactly the same ilk as the other elders, have, in some cases according to students, sold themselves out to the military-industrial complex. This sell-out means that knowledge is not likely to be organized and presented in such a way that it goes to the roots of today's most significant issues. For those who have a large stake invested in present arrangements, both in the university and the larger society, are not likely to expose the shortcomings of these institutions or present material that could be employed in some way to dramatically change society. For this reason and others cited earlier, students will have difficulty in gaining the forms of knowledge from organized instruction needed to understand and deal effectively with what they believe to be the significant issues of our time. As a result, demonstrations occur over the curriculum and related issues, free universities are established, and other action is taken.

Knowing how to use personal knowledge depends, at least in part, upon an understanding of contemporary society. Living as we do within a social and cultural framework, one's goals and aspirations may continually be thwarted due to an inadequate understanding of the social conditions and forces in one's environment. Thus personal knowledge alone is not enough if one hopes to live meaningfully as some students envision. Personal knowledge must be meshed with an understanding of the significant issues of our time. An adequate conception of relevance should relate not only to vital social issues and personal knowledge, but also to the knowledge that may help us understand and control ourselves and society, as well as to the methods used to improve knowledge and the criteria used to validate knowledge. To understand how this knowledge can best be gained, it is necessary to know something about the organized disciplines and fields of knowledge: their methodologies, objectives, and how they may possibly be reoriented or modified in order to yield more abundantly knowledge of the significant issues which can be used by the individual to live with greater awareness, participation, and meaningfulness.

Questions for Discussion

1. The questions which students raise about knowledge differ, at least outwardly, from those expressed by educators. In what areas do the two groups express similar interests and concerns? Where they differ, should the students' interests be reformulated so they coincide with those of educators, should the converse be pursued, or are there other alternatives?

2. To what extent can we hope to gain certainty? Should certainty be a criterion in selecting curriculum material? If so, should it take precedence over other criteria that you would use in curriculum construction?

3. Should educators aspire to eliminate all false beliefs and illusions? Can one still be considered to be an educated person and hold many illusions? How do we determine whether illusions impede an individual's educational development?

4. Are there any forms of knowing other than "knowing how" and "knowing that?" If so, how are they expressed and employed in education?

5. How does an individual ascertain what is "relevant knowledge" for him? How can he use his findings to determine what type of education is best for him?

For Further Reading

Two lucid introductions to epistemological problems which are accessible to the beginning student are: A. J. Ayer, *The Problem of Knowledge*, Baltimore: Penguin Books, 1961; A. D. Woozley, *Theory of Knowledge*, New York: Barnes & Noble, 1966.

Some of the problems of knowledge and education raised in this chapter are treated from a number of varied perspectives in other works. An analytic treatment is provided in Israel Scheffler's, *Conditions of Knowledge*, Chicago: Scott, Foresman, 1965. An approach through an experimentalist point of view is found in H. Gordon Hullfish and Philip G. Smith, *Reflective Thinking: The Method of Education*, New York: Dodd, Mead, 1961. Alternate approaches to the above positions are available in Harry S. Broudy, *Building A Philosophy of Education*, 2nd ed, Englewood Cliffs, N.J.: Prentice-Hall, 1961, chapters 5-7; and Philip H. Phenix, *Philosophy of Education*, New York: Henry Holt, 1958, chapter 17. Finally, for the original development of "knowing how" and "knowing that," as well as many other significant epistemological issues, the student could profit by studying Gilbert Ryle's *The Concept of Mind*, New York: Barnes & Noble, 1949. Many of the selections listed at the end of Chapter One are directly relevant for the topic "personal knowledge."

Notes

1. A.J. Ayer, *The Problem of Knowledge* (Baltimore: Penguin Books, 1961), pp. 37-38.

2. Hans Reichenbach, *Experience and Prediction* (Chicago: University of Chicago Press, 1938).

3. The public cumulative character of scientific knowledge is obtainable in various ways, sometimes by people observing the same event, or replicating experiments, or by one person checking on the predictions made by another, etc.

4. Philosophers such as Morton White, Nelson Goodman, and Willard Van Orman Quine have seriously questioned the distinction between analytic and synthetic statements. Some philosophers would say, e.g., that the

statement "A cat is an animal " might best be regarded as "analytic" only in some senses or contexts—that to illustrate what is necessarily true *now:* that if anything is to be a cat, it *necessarily* must be an animal. The fact that cats are animals is an historically learned fact, the *meaning* of animal has changed and probably will change as knowledge develops.

5. Most philosophers now agree that logical principles and truth claims can be used in thinking about moral and aesthetic problems at least to some extent.

6. A.D. Woozley, *Theory of Knowledge* (New York: Barnes & Noble, Inc., 1966), p. 191.

7. *Ibid.*

8. *Ibid.*, p. 190.

9. Israel Scheffler, *Conditions of Knowledge* (Chicago: Scott, Foresman, 1965), p. 21.

10. J. L. Austin, "Other Minds," Anthony Flew, ed., *Logic and Language*, 2nd series (Oxford: Basil Blackwell, 1961), pp. 142-147.

11. P.F. Strawson develops the performative theory of truth in his essay "Truth," *Analysis*, vol. 9, no. 6 (1949). Reprinted in M. McDonald, ed. *Philosophy and Analysis* (New York: Oxford University Press, 1955), p. 260. Strawson holds that to say "the statement is true" is to perform an act of endorsing, agreeing with, granting, or confirming the statement.

12. Gilbert Ryle *The Concept of Mind* (New York: Barnes & Noble, Inc., 1949), pp. 25-61.

13. *Ibid.*, pp. 29-32.

14. *Ibid.*, p. 59.

15. John Hartland-Swann, *An Analysis of Knowing* (London: George Allen and Unwin Ltd., 1958), pp. 56-65.

16. Ryle, *The Concept of Mind*, p. 43.

17. See Scheffler, *Conditions of Knowledge*, pp. 76-90. However, Scheffler's arguments pertain to beliefs (even though he examines and uses arguments about forms of knowing) while our analysis is concerned with the reduction of knowing that to knowing how.

18. Walter Kaufmann, ed., *The Portable Nietzsche* (New York: The Viking Press, 1954), p. 305.

19. *Ibid.*, p. 306.

Chapter Six
The Sciences

Scientific Approaches to Knowledge

Aristotle noted that men by nature have a desire to know; they take delight in the use of their senses, not only for purposes of action, but also for the mere use of them. The delight in the use of our senses, he believed, is indicative of this basic desire to gain knowledge.

Man has progressed a long way from the time of Aristotle in the development of sophisticated methodological procedures for gaining knowledge and in the growth of organized bodies of knowledge designed for the understanding, prediction, and control of natural phenomena. These developments are in many ways cumulative insofar as they build upon previous laws and theories of the natural world. It is commonly said that the ordinary schoolboy can see further into the reaches of space and time than Galileo and other early scientists due to their works and the discoveries since that time. It is in this way that science is cumulative, and one's knowledge and ability to explain natural phenomena advances as the work in science progresses in many nations throughout the world. The so-called "scientific community" is an international community of researchers pursuing inquiries by commonly recognized methodological procedures and communicating to others in the language of science, so that a new discovery by scientists in one part of the world constitutes an advance for scientists elsewhere (except in such cases as classified research done under the auspices of various national governments, or officially, culturally prescribed ideologies that distort intrepretations of scientific findings). This cooperative characteristic of scientific inquiry, in spite of an increasing amount of secretive research even within the university, has been one of the chief reasons for the rapid advancements of science.

In contrast to the majority of civilizations from the beginning of recorded human history, we are living in an age of science. It is well known that science and its technological applications dominate our times and permeate our lives. Prior to the rise of modern science men also sought to explain the imponderable events in the world around them. They called upon myth, custom, folklore, religion, and common sense to provide the explanations needed. That these explanations frequently proved unreliable, particularly when dealing with complex events, is too well known to elaborate further. However, during the eighteenth and nineteenth centuries, some men of letters, social philosophers, and an occasional scientist were so highly enamored of the prospects for scientific advancement that they claimed that science, given more time and access to greater resources, would be able to embrace all human knowledge and render all phenomena amenable to scientific investigation. They believed that science would dispel superstition, prejudice, ignorance, and idolatry, overcome poverty and disease, and usher in a virtual utopia on earth. The heavenly sectarian city of theology during the Middle Ages had been transformed into the heavenly secular city of science during the Enlightenment. The *Philosophes* of the eighteenth century and the positivists of the nineteenth century had virtually unlimited faith in the power of science(1). As the social sciences developed in the nineteenth century, there was a tendency for them to fall under the spell of "scientism." Scientism is the proposition that the methods of the natural sciences should be used in all areas of investigation. This has led some of the social sciences to ape the methodology of the physical sciences. Scientism manifested itself early in the present century as a confusion of scientific method with scientific techniques, so that the techniques themselves became the necessary and sufficient conditions for scientific standing. It also had the effect, especially in educational research during the 1920's, of emphasizing the measurement function of science as if it were the sole function of scientific investigation.

Our concern in this chapter is not so much the treatment of sciences from the point of view of the specialist, but, rather, the role of science in the larger society, in the lives of people, and as part of general education. But in order to discuss these relationships intelligently, it is necessary to know what the scientist is about. What are his objectives? How does he know when he has atttained them? Is there a way of answering these questions without an advanced knowledge of one or more of the sciences? The answer is "yes" if we think of ourselves as intelligent nonspecialists who believe we need to deal with some of the rudiments of scientific inquiry in the contemporary world.

Laws, Theory, and Measurement

It would be more accurate to say that the objective of science is to discover the laws of nature rather than to study nature. In order to uncover laws, it is necessary to develop an appropriate system of methodology. Therefore, the first task in gaining an understanding of science is that of examining the characteristics and uses of laws and measurements. Then the role of theory in science must be determined.

Scientists seek to find certain regularities in nature by which natural phenomena and events may be explained. There could be no science if all events in nature were random and occurred by chance, for no patterns and regularities of natural phenomena could be observed, no explanations could be offered for events, and no predictions could be made about future events. Chance does not rule the universe. Rather, the universe is amenable to human understanding by the establishment of natural laws through procedures that provide man with an understanding of the fundamental events and regularities of nature.

A universal law expresses an invariant relationship among properties or events. If an event is explicable in terms of a law, the event is invariably associated with other events and must occur if other events occur. For example, if a book is pushed from a table, it will fall to the floor. If a baseball and a marble are dropped from a window simultaneously, they both will fall to earth at virtually the same rate. This was a phenomenon first observed by Galileo. Occasionally, however, laws may seem to conflict. For example, Galileo's observation may seem to conflict with Newton's Law of Inertia, which states that if matter is at rest it tends to remain at rest, and if matter is in motion it tends to remain in motion unless blocked by some force outside itself. To look at it another way: there is a resistance of a body at rest to being set in motion, and of a body in motion to being retarded, accelerated, or changed in direction. To this Newton added a second law that states that if the same force is applied to two bodies of different masses, it will produce greater acceleration in the smaller than in the larger body. Now the problem arises of how to explain why bodies move horizontally at a velocity determined by their mass but move vertically at the same velocity irrespective of their mass. Newton's solution is found in his Law of Gravitation which states that all bodies have a mutual attraction for one another. If a body is small its inertia is small — but so is the force that gravity exerts upon it. However, if a body is large, inertia is great, but the force that gravity exerts upon it is also great. Therefore, gravity is always exerted in the exact degree necessary to overcome inertia.

As in the above illustration of laws and assuming certain contexts, certain invariant relationships are expressed among events. Laws are not stated in the indicative mood but in the subjunctive conditional. In other words, a law is not stated as follows: "This book falls to the floor when I push it off the table." This statement cannot be universally verified because not everyone can observe the process of someone pushing a particular book at a specific moment off a certain table. But the experiment can be performed by others for purposes of verification when stated in the subjunctive conditional as follows: "If *a* book is pushed off a table it will fall to the floor." Universal agreement can then be obtained. Of course, this is a very simplified illustration, but even though scientific experiments are usually far more complex, the basic method of stating laws enables others to attempt to verify them. Since a problem determines the method appropriate to its resolution, the scientist must devise experimental conditions in light of the problem with which he is working.

Science is able to explain when events are examples of general laws, universal or statistical. One understands why a marble and a baseball, when dropped from the window of a ten-story building, will fall to earth at virtually the same velocity by showing that the event is an example of the Law of Gravitation. The event is also invariant since, under similar conditions, it can be repeated an indefinite number of times with the same results. This invariance is also why science is not only able to explain but also can predict. For one can usually project the same experiment an indefinite number of times in the future and expect the same results. Thus, by understanding the laws of science, one is able to appreciate the regularities of nature and explain and predict certain types of events.

These conclusions can be illustrated by another law. One may assume that by burning or boiling some substance he is destroying matter, and if we project this alleged fact on a world-wide scale, the destruction of matter by people will eventually destroy all matter on earth. However, the Law of Conservation of Matter states that matter can neither be created nor destroyed. By heating a pan until the water boils away completely does not mean that the water was destroyed. It has been converted into vapor and, upon being cooled, the vapor will condense to form the amount of water formerly in the pan. One is able to explain the process by subsuming it under the Law of Conservation of Matter, and one can safely predict that whenever these operations are performed under the same conditions in the future the same results will obtain(2).

It is necessary to be able to measure or distinguish phenomena with a considerable degree of precision before laws can be established. Measurement is the process by which numbers are assigned to represent properties, a process which has been central in distinguishing properties in many sciences; measurement makes relations among variables more precise and hypotheses more testable. However, not all existential states are measurable. One's joys and sorrows, feelings and attitudes, as well as such qualitative distinctions that some thing is more beautiful or desirable than some other thing are not generally thought to be measurable. Also considered immeasurable is attempted measurement in which results are not considered convincing, except for those who are willing to reduce such states to readings recorded on various measuring devices. Many domains may be worthy of investigation — either to satisfy scientific curiosity and promote greater understanding or for the possible utilitarian outcomes and applications of inquiry. But investigation cannot proceed very far until some processes are devised for discriminating or measuring the properties to be investigated and determining the relations of properties under various conditions (in this determination measurement is often central, never sufficient). But that which is measurable will differ from one time period and one generation to another, so that the province of scientific investigation in Galileo's time, for example, was more restricted than today's science due to the state of development of mathematics and measurement through the years.

Physical scientists have found certain limitations insofar as their ability to establish precise and invariant measurement as expressed in natural laws. These limitations, however, were not always recognized. These difficulties go back to early Greek science. Democritus asserted in the fifth century B.C., "Nothing is chance, but everything happens for a reason and of necessity." He also held that the universe consisted of atoms and the void. These beliefs would later lead to a strict deterministic and materialistic world view. In the hands of early modern scientists determinism assumed the form that for every event that occurs in the universe, there is a cause operating. It was characteristically materialistic because all things were conceived as matter. Yet these views did not prevail for many centuries following Democritus' death principally because of the vast influence of Aristotle's thought. Aristotle enunciated a teleological view of nature, a view which ascribes design and purpose to natural events. This perspective, which ostensibly retarded scientific advancement, was not rejected by scientists until the Renaissance. Aristotle had denied the atomism of Democritus and sought purposes rather than causes in nature, leading to an anthropomorphic view. Beginning with the Polish astronomer Copernicus in the early sixteenth century, there was a return to a deterministic, materialistic world view which was supported and reinforced by the work of such later scientists as Galileo, Kepler, and Newton. Newtonian physics held sway throughout the nineteenth century and the task of measurement was conceived as that of precise formulation of invariant laws. Although Newton believed that the laws of the universe held for both the macroscopic and microscopic world, quantum mechanics was later to find that this microscopic world of atomic particles, not accessible to the unaided senses, could not be treated in the same manner as the macroscopic world. Rather, statistical laws, based upon large numbers of experiments with elementary particles, were designed to predict the *probability* of the occurrence of certain events. No longer was the relationship expressed as an invariant one. Relativity theory no longer recognizes a macroscopic world of absolute space and time but a system in which measurements are made relative to observers who could theoretically occupy positions on different heavenly bodies and could communicate signals by sound or light waves, or observers at rest as compared to those in rapid motion.

Now it is true that scientists employ many different measuring procedures. They measure by means of balances, clocks, rulers, and other instruments, and also use various mathematical systems in their work. At times scientists develop their own system of mathematics and, more commonly, they borrow from mathematicians. Newton found it necessary to devise the infinitesimal calculus (along with the philosopher Leibniz, who devised it independently) in order to perform the mathematical calculations needed to establish certain natural laws of the heavenly bodies. On the other hand, Einstein found Euclidian geometry inadequate for his purposes and adopted Riemannian geometry.

Mathematical operations relate directly to the development of laws. This relation is particularly evident in the development of statistical laws, which are needed because older laws based upon a mechanistic view of the universe do not hold for microscopic phenomena. This factor became evident in the development of quantum mechanics by Max Planck and also by Werner Heisenberg's indeterminacy principle. Heisenberg showed that it was basically impossible to measure simultaneously the exact position and velocity of a microparticle. In the very act of observing the position of a particle its velocity is changed; conversely, the more accurately the velocity is measured, the more indeterminate the position becomes—and this element of caprice in subatomic particles is not due to the lack of refinement of scientific instruments. There exists a certain fundamental discontinuity in the types of laws which can be formulated in the microscopic as opposed to the macroscopic world. Whereas in the latter world, laws expressing an invariant relationship can be formulated, statistical laws which are stated in terms of different probability levels are the type appropriate to the microscopic world. On the basis of thousands of experiments the behavior of billions of subatomic particles are stated in a lawlike fashion which would predicate a probability level that certain future behaviors would occur under similar experimental conditions.

Although it may be thought that laws state serial relations where one event precedes another in time and may or may not be a cause or one of a series of causes of the later event's occurrence, numerical laws as well as statistical laws do not state relationships of this type. A numerical law is discovered whenever a relationship is established between two or more numbers which measure different properties and when the established relationship is maintained under further experimental conditions of a similar type. This relationship indicates an interdependence between two or more variables, so that a variation in one is concurrent with variations in the other(s). This interdependence is illustrated by Boyle's law which states that the volume of confined gas at a constant temperature decreases in proportion to increase in pressure. The scientist can observe the interdependence of the two variables by reading the measuring instruments and noting that the relationship holds. Or, as Ohm's law states, an electrical current is proportional to the pressure between its ends. We know that if the pressure is doubled the current is doubled. The events are simultaneous, not serial.

Both statistical and numerical laws differ from those earlier formulated known as causal laws. A causal law states an invariant relationship among a serial or sequential state of affairs so that it could be said that one event occurring earlier in time caused another. Releasing a rock from the window of a building causes it to fall to earth. Of course it would not fall except for the field of gravitational force. Dropping a match in a tank of gasoline results in an explosion because gasoline is a flammable mixture. And leaving certain types of steel exposed to moist air over a period of time will cause them to rust through a process of oxidation(3).

Scientists use different procedures to discover laws; the procedure appropriate depends upon the problem with which they are faced. A scientist generally proceeds by restricting his attention to a limited class of phenomena, raising questions as to why these phenomena behave as they do, entertaining hypotheses, making observations, and seeking connections between certain variables. Once a relationship is mathematically formulated, the scientist states a law governing the selected range of phenomena. This connection may not be discovered upon initial investigation but may entail hundreds of experiments, after which the relationship may still only be a highly plausible hypothesis needing further testing for confirmation. If the hypothesis is refuted, it is replaced by one that fits the measurements better. The process of establishing a natural law is incomplete until there has been confirmation by independent observers.

A word about the relation of laws to theories: the purpose of theories is to provide a system of interconnected general laws stating determinate relations from which other laws can be derived. In a very highly developed science, new laws may be less likely to be derived from making observations and conducting experiments than as a side effect of devising theories to explain older laws. One prominent test of the value of a theory is its ability not only to explain old laws but to generate new ones. However, there are some laws — known as experimental laws — which are formulated more obviously on the basis of experimentation; therefore, they lack a strict or unique theoretical explanation. But in a highly developed science, one has more confidence in laws which are derived from theories. Of course, even then the law still is not firmly established until it is confirmed by rigorous testing.

It would be misleading to say that, in order to be accepted, a theory must be subjected to rigorous experimentation, for there are cases of the acceptance of experimental laws which later are shown to be explained more adequately by a new theory. For example, Boyle's Law and Gay-Lussac's Law were known before the kinetic theory of gasses. The theory provided a pictorial representation of the gas molecules, thereby, afforded additional explanation of the two laws. A single theory may explain certain existing experimental laws and may prove heuristically valuable in suggesting new laws. From Newtonian theory one could derive two of Kepler's laws of planetary motion; it also suggested a wide variety of laws, such as laws of tidal action, freely falling bodies, the thermal property of gasses, and others. Thus, it is a characteristic of general and leading theories in the natural sciences, such as Planck's quantum theory, that many new and unforeseen laws can be derived from them.

Laws are usually formulated in a single statement and express certain uniform relations among phenomena, whereas a theory sets forth ideas not contained in the laws which it explains. There are certain hypothetical ideas or fundamental axioms and postulates in a theory which are not completely determined by experiment. These usually are expressed in terms of mathematical equations. Theories also possess two other characteristics not found in laws: a model (or models) and rules of correspondence. Since the fundamental axioms are mathematical equations not completely determined by experiment, a model or analogy is needed to provide visualizable and more familiar conceptual material. Additionally, correspondence rules are devised to assign some empirical content to the basic postulates so that certain postulates will have a counterpart which can be observed under experimental conditions. For example, in the Bohr theory of the atom, electrons are depicted as moving in elliptical orbits around the center of the atom's nucleus, with occasional jumps of an electron from one orbit to another. These jumps correspond with what can be observed under experimental conditions as a spectral line. These three characteristics, then, indicate some of the features which distinguish theories from laws.

To this point our analysis has been based on activities and operations found in the natural sciences, particularly those which deal with non-living things. Biology is subject to the physio-chemical laws of nature; it also has some unique characteristics not found in the physical sciences. Obviously animals and plants are subject to the law of gravitation, the laws governing heat, electricity, radiation, as well as various chemical processes in the atmosphere, soil, and within the organism. It may seem that the behavior of plants and animals may be reduced to certain physical and chemical laws—except that there are certain unique features of living organisms that may preclude these processes.

One characteristic is that organisms exhibit certain types of behavior directed to the achievement of certain goals. Organisms are able to regulate, maintain, and reproduce themselves; they attempt to avoid deterioration and death by carrying out certain fundamental biological processes. Organisms also have different internal systems which operate conjointly to maintain homeostasis and promote well-being. Among the higher organisms we find circulatory, digestive, respiratory, lymphatic, and reproductive systems, each of which serve certain functions essential to the maintenance of life. Many of these systems function in concert to serve essential life processes. This functional, purposive or teleological nature of living things is not a characteristic found among the nonliving properties and phenomena that physical and earth scientists study.

Another characteristic of organisms which is not found among nonliving phenomena is their organization into a living system. Moreover, this system cannot fully be explained by analyzing the separate parts, their structures and functions. It is necessary for the biologist to study the total organism as well to see how the various functions are orchestrated to maintain, regulate, and reproduce the system. Scientists frequently assert that biological systems are hierarchially organized so that an explanation of the isolated parts at a lower level would not be sufficient as an explanation for the higher levels. Organisms consist (in moving from simple to more complex) of cells, tissue, organs, and systems. This hierarchy shows that to explain the function of certain tissues does not offer an adequate explanation for the function of a biological system.

These two characteristics seem to indicate that the study of living organisms cannot be reduced to physio-chemical laws. But opinion is still divided. The controversy is probably seen most sharply in discussions following the discovery of the DNA molecule. DNA (deoxyribonucleic acid), found in the nucleus of cells, is believed by some scientists to transmit the patterns of heredity from one generation to another. Genes are thought to be composed of DNA molecules. DNA is supposed to send out coded instructions to an intermediary, RNA (ribonucleic acid), which triggers a pattern of protein synthesis.

A major controversy was ignited in biology after the discovery of DNA. The discovery, followed later by the far-reaching claims by some biochemists and other scientists, has divided biological inquiry between two approaches to biological research. The older approach studies the total cell as the basis of life, holding that only by cellular study can scientists hope to gain a full understanding of the life process.

The second and younger approach, which focuses on DNA and other molecules, assumes that the key to life processes can best be revealed by a study of certain chemical constituents that can be separated from the nucleus of the cell. This new molecular approach has shifted a considerable amount of research away from the cellular, more classical, approach and its interest in living organisms to a search for and an attempt to isolate a chemical substance which will unravel the mystery of life processes and the genetic code itself.

This issue illustrates a controversy discussed earlier: can biology and the life processes it studies be reduced to physio-chemical laws? The molecular approach, in searching for a chemical basis for inherited characteristics, is based on the assumption that this reduction, in one form or another, can be made. The cellular approach supports the position that there are certain unique characteristics to be found in those disciplines which study living organisms that render it inherently unamenable to reduction. The cellular biologists, of course, do accept the fact that living organisms obey fundamental physio-chemical laws of the universe that regulate nonliving phenomena; however, they still demur at any attempt to derive complete explanatory systems of living things from the laws of the physical sciences. The controversy remains at this point at the present time and is not likely to advance significantly until more definitive evidence is forthcoming.

Science and Human Affairs

Generally speaking, the quest to promote freedom of inquiry and gain acceptance for scientific knowledge in civilizations of the past appears to have been a long and arduous struggle. Early science encountered resistance whenever its findings, real or imagined, conflicted with established customs, traditions, or religious dogma. The clashes of Copernicus, Galileo, and Bruno with religious authority are examples of this conflict. The Copernican system, on which modern astronomy is based, held that the sun is the center of our solar system, rejecting the medieval Ptolemaic system which proclaimed the earth as the center of the system. In light of its obvious challenge to religious cosmology, Copernicus withheld his manuscript with instructions that it be published upon his death. The experiences of Galileo and Bruno were far more harsh. Galileo published his astronomical investigations, which confirmed the Copernican theory; later, during the Inquisition, he was forced to recant out of fear for his life. But Bruno—who challenged dogmatic authority and absolutism with his own beliefs that the world consists of irreducible elements (monads) governed by pantheistic principles and that knowledge, rather then circumscribed by an absolutistic system, is virtually unlimited—had to be silenced. He was convicted of heresy and burned at the stake(4).

The silencing of these men was not the end of controversy between science and other institutions of society. Explosive debates arose over the theory of evolution or the disputes initially surrounding the propagation of the germ theory of disease or the early shock and outrage with psychoanalysis. However, resistance to new scientific findings no longer was vested primarily in the church but came from various groups and institutions, even though their opposition in many cases was on religious grounds.

The Renaissance witnessed the rise of modern science, the advent of nation-states which clashed with the Church over sovereignty in the affairs of man. And with it came a growing secularism and the emergence of early forms of capitalism. These new forces, more often than not, viewed science as an ally in conquering nature, promoting economic growth, developing new material resources and providing the necessities and the comforts of life.

The intellectuals of the Enlightenment believed that, given time, science would disseminate knowledge and dispel superstition, myth, and prejudice. It would eliminate sickness, suffering, disease, and usher in a virtual utopia on earth. Who would challenge this, other than certain literary figures or theologians, in light of the undreamed of contributions that science, by the eighteenth century, had already made?

But the technological creations of the nineteenth century were even more spectacular as industrialism emerged as the dominant economic force in the West. Positivism became the outlook of a number of scientists, mathematicians, and philosophers. It was a philosophy which used a limited conception of science as a paradigm for all knowledge, and its methodology and verification procedures were proposed for other disciplines. For Auguste Comte, the Frenchman frequently referred to as "the father of sociology," civilization had passed through three stages of development: theological, speculative, and positivistic. The theological was associated more with myth-making and religion, the speculative with metaphysics, and the positivistic with the emergence of modern science and its methods of inquiry. The positivism of the late nineteenth century, which rejected metaphysics and maintained that all knowledge is based on sense experience, culminated with the movement in the 1930's known as logical positivism. A group of scientists, mathematicians, and philosophers met in Vienna to discuss issues of common scientific concern the outcome of which was the development of a joint positivistic statement which became epitomized by the Verification Principle. The Principle initially stated that the meaning of a statement is its method of verification. However, after discussion and debate during subsequent years, the Principle was progressively modified so that it would be less restrictive. Nonetheless, the movement had the effect of relegating all statements and claims which could not be verified by sensory or physical means to the realm of either meaningless or emotive statements. Religion, which had once persecuted scientists for their "heresies," was considered for the most part by the logical positivists as consisting of empty or meaningless statements.

The attitude of the logical positivists toward religion illustrates how the forces and institutions of the modern world have shifted. Organized religion once held uneasy sway over other institutions. Its chief threats came from the emergence of national states, the growth of secularism, and the findings of the early scientists. The scientists were branded as heretics and were persecuted. Today, however, the positivist can relegate religion to a "no-man's land" and espouse the scientific method as the touchstone for all forms of inquiry.

This outlook raises the specter of scientism, a position that becomes idolatrous of science and its achievements. Any discipline which purports to yield knowledge must either do so by means of the scientific method or abandon its claims as empty. Meanings and values, which scientism contends are not amenable to scientific investigation, must be abandoned to the humanities. Quantitative techniques and measurement become the hallmark of academic respectability. Computers and equations, charts and graphs reduce the indeterminate to the determinate, render the imponderable in precise mathematical terms.

The reduction of all life and its varied manifestations to the probings of science and the equating of all verifiable knowledge with scientific, has probably finally been recognized for its excess. In fact, there seems to be a rejection of science and its promise by many of the youth of today. Science, which experienced the wrath of organized religion for uncovering and promulgating heretical findings, gained a position of cultural dominance which was formerly held by religion and promptly found religious knowledge-claims to be empty and meaningless. But even a scientist who practiced some form of religious observance and belief in his private life could not accept the "evidence" that the theologians and their followers advanced if the test was that of scientific verification. Except for the study of psychological and sociological factors of religion as a social institution, it is doubtful that religion's knowledge-claims could be treated scientifically. But since the scientific method is generally accepted today as the most reliable and productive method of gaining knowledge, religious claims are placed in an invidious position. Although a large minority of scientists profess fairly orthodox beliefs, history has come full circle: religious claims are heretical in scientific circles.

The Role of Science

Many persons envision the role of science in contemporary society as strictly utilitarian. Proponents of this view usually are enamored of technological advancements which have dramatically altered their style of living. They extol, among other things, modern medical advances and their conquests of many contagious diseases, creation of rapid transportation and communication, the improvement of creature comforts in homes and offices, and the development of machines to reduce human toil. The welter of inventions and their application have altered the face of industry and of the world. It is with these and many other advancements that the case for science rests. Advocates of the utilitarian view are generally unsympathetic to the needs for basic research and the demands of "pure science," for in their eagerness for tangible results and pecuniary gain, and lacking sufficient knowledge of science, they usually fail to understand the importance of theoretical research.

This same view can be used to support the belief that the scientist and the technician are the servants of society and should create whatever society desires, whether it be new inventions which produce greater creature comforts or more devastating weapons of destruction. Private research laboratories utilize the fruits of scientific research for the advancement of industry; the federal government contracts university scientists to conduct research in both domestic and international affairs. Some of the government research, particularly those projects connected with the Department of Defense, is classified.

There are people, on the other hand, who view the work of the scientist more as a worthy end in itself rather than in utilitarian terms. The scientist, according to this position, should remain unfettered to pursue scientific inquiry wherever it may lead strictly for the sake of the advancement of knowledge. Scientists work best with few external restrictions and pressures; utilitarian concerns and the molding of research activities to fit limited, preconceived notions, whether by government or industry, lead to a truncated view of the role of science in society. Advocates of this position concede that even though utilitarian interests may likely continue, it behooves these interests to recognize that the vitality and growth, developing new material resources and providing the necessities vide substantial support to basic research. Without this support, the well-springs of both science and technology will dry up.

Proponents of this view generally jealously guard freedom of inquiry from all outside encroachments. Many are mixed in their feelings as to the advisability of becoming engaged in classified research, for they recognize that although some of the research contracts of this type may be justified in terms of national interests and defense, the secrecy in which they are veiled precludes application of one of the essential tenets of the scientific community: free and open inquiry and the dissemination of results to the international scientific community. Not only is this one of the canons upon which science was erected, but the quality of research is seriously jeopardized whenever research cannot be subject to examination and testing by a broader scientific community. Indeed, large-scale involvement of scientific research on classified research, in research designed to promote mainly the abilities to kill, sell, and consume, is destructive of science as well as of man.

What responsibility should the scientist and technologist share for the uses made of their discoveries? Should they create whatever the corporate structure and public officials desire, or do they have a wider responsibility for the public's general welfare? Fundamental conflicts have arisen between the demands made upon scientists by elites in industry and government and the broader public interest. If the public interests were more adequately informed about the technical consequences of the uses of sciences, they would probably protest and seek means for the redress of grievances. Today, pollution of the atmosphere, land, and bodies of water is generating serious problems. The former aboveground testing of nuclear weapons presented serious health hazards, and the development of lethal bacteriological and chemical weapons of warfare, their testing, transportation, and storage at various sites constitute matters of considerable gravity. The development of new food products, drugs, detergents, and other commercial products periodically escape rigorous testing needed before their distribution for public consumption. Many mechanical inventions, including the automobile and other modes of transportation, have many unsafe features which may result in serious injury or death. These and other applications of science have engendered a growing distrust of science in our time.

It is difficult to state precisely when public interest finally elevated science to a supreme place in American culture, and one is also hard-pressed to specify with exactness when this interest began to sour. There are some who have never accorded this accolade to science, even though their lives have been dramatically altered by scientific and technological developments. Some refused to accept the Industrial Revolution as an unmixed blessing. This attitude was found particularly among literary figures of the nineteenth century who railed against the wretched working and living conditions resulting from rapid industrialism. Their rancor was directed not merely at the industrial tycoons who shaped the early designs of an industrial economy, but also against certain gross insensitivities by scientists toward the public welfare. The scientist, on the other hand, could well point to the many advantages afforded to the public by the shift of the economy from an agrarian to an industrial society.

The most serious questions for the general public arose with the development and testing of nuclear weapons. For some time the extensiveness of radiation hazards was obscurely divined or underestimated, and the secrecy surrounding government research in this area prevented the full scientific community from subjecting to careful examination any of the classified knowledge of the small coterie of scientists involved in this secret research(5). Yet many of the grave dangers of radioactive fallout and accurate assessments of the extent of these dangers could not be determined until the veil of secrecy was partially lifted to permit the scientific community to examine the evidence. The secrecy has been so great in the case of the Atomic Energy Commission that a survey article on uranium fission published in a scientific journal in 1940 and available to the scientific community at large, along with the 133 studies it reports, has been declared classified material and will remain so until the Commission decides to declassify it. As Gerald Piel asserts: "This is not secrecy; it is statutory taboo."(6) These and similar decisions are indicative of the general atmosphere that surrounds these projects. It tends to keep the public sealed off from essential information on which to make intelligent decisions and offer proposals for suitable policies.

In light of the unnecessary secrecy which serves neither the public interest or the defense posture of the nation, the scientific community has been unduly hampered in assessing the effects of radioactivity and other hazards, and the public has been unable to base its thinking on a realistic appraisal of the scientific evidence. However, this difficulty is not the only one in shaping intelligent public policy. In spite of increased years of formal schooling, opinion polls indicate that the American public is generally not well informed on social and political issues and that most Americans do not usually read widely(7). Thus, the public's general lack of intelligent choice in political affairs and the absence of widespread awareness of the issues of moment cannot be borne entirely by the secrecy of government.

Still, a growing disenchantment with science, which at an earlier period would have been considered heretical in some quarters, has begun to spread across the land. A suspicion has grown that science is not the social benefactor that formerly it was reputed to be; rather, the horror movies and the science fiction stories are becoming a reality. Science has unleashed a Frankenstein monster, which, ostensibly beyond human control, will ultimately destroy its maker. This time he will take himself and all civilization with him. The unending spiral of the nuclear arms race and its spread to other countries, if not brought under rigorous control, inspection, and eventual disarmament through an international body under law, will lead to a world holocaust. Scientists have served the munition makers; they have also been, as some suggest, a willing tool of the industrial magnates who seek greater profits irrespective of the social consequences(8). This willingness in turn has led to the widespread exploitation of nature culminating in a situation where the delicate balance of the biosphere is disturbed as a result of indiscriminate use of insecticides, detergents, and chemical pollutants.

In some cases with every gain there is a correlated loss. The introduction of pesticides into farming controlled insects and various scavengers for the first time. But it also poisoned other species of life and disrupted the balance of nature. The use of detergents proved to be of considerable advantage for washing in hard water; at the same time, the manufacturers did not sufficiently test them to discover that they would not dissolve by the usual chemical processes, and hence, would pollute our rivers and streams.

Because of his specialized knowledge, the scientist is in a position to appraise not only leaders in government and industry but also the public as to the likely benefits and disadvantages in the use of new scientific inventions and processes. As a scientist he cannot set the goals for society to follow. But he can make available in the language of the nonspecialist the needed scientific information, without which intelligent decisions cannot be made, and he can act as a private citizen in participating in the debate over the proper goals for society. Since scientists are highly specialized and have no special monopoly on wisdom in social and political affairs, it would be unreasonable to expect them to lead the way in formulating priorities and goals. They would participate just as other intelligent citizens would be expected to participate. Hopefully more scientists will join their more vocal (and some would say the "more sensitive") colleagues in providing the needed knowledge on the possible effects of the application of their specialty to human welfare. Only when this knowledge dissemination comes about will the growing suspicion and distrust of science and its role in contemporary affairs begin to abate. A more balanced and realistic perspective of the uses of scientific knowledge for human betterment will likely be clearly conceived and applied to the affairs of nations at that time.

Science and the Curriculum

There has been a movement in the past decade to upgrade and restructure the teaching of science in the public schools. Leadership in this movement has come from many well-recognized university and research scientists who have been bent upon effecting an assessment, reappraisal, and revision of the content of science courses. In making these revisions there has been an attempt to deemphasize former descriptive treatment of physical phenomena and their technological applications. Importance has been given to key conceptual ideas which constitute the basic structure of the disciplines, to the ability to grasp these ideas in terms of their interrelationships with other ideas and explanatory principles, and to practice in using the basic modes of inquiry by means of which fundamental laws and theories are discovered. Rather than emphasize laboratory manipulative skills, stress is placed upon acquiring an understanding of the interrelations in the various sciences and their connection with technology. At the secondary level, a characteristic feature is the relegation of scientific information to a position of lesser importance to that of acquiring an understanding of scientific inquiry.

That less emphasis is placed on information and manipulative skills seems less significant than the assumption that it is possible to teach youth to think and investigate (although obviously on far less complex scale) as a professional scientist. The percentage of secondary school students who are capable of mastering the key concepts is questionable, especially as they are to be discovered in terms of utilizing the scientific method in classroom and laboratory investigations. Furthermore, the lower 50 percent of the high school population is likely to experience considerable difficulty in adapting their thought to and learning the modes of inquiry used by the scientist himself. Abilities, as we are well aware,

are exceedingly diverse and varied. A secondary program that hopes to retain all youth of high school age may well frustrate and eventually drive out youth who have limited scientific aptitudes, especially those programs that fail to differentiate the range of abilities and to formulate curricular policies in light of such factors. This is not to imply that the new programs in science which have by now replaced the older programs do not mark an advance over the older programs in the areas indicated above (even though some of the outcomes in the older programs have been deemphasized). What is suspect, however, is the ability of a considerable precentage of the high school population to profit significantly from the new programs.

Alternate objectives for science education have been proffered. Some students have thought that their science courses could prove more profitable if they offered more practical and utilitarian outcomes. Among these outcomes are the abilities to perform minor repairs on one's automobile, radio, television set, and on various mechanical devices in the home. Those who espouse this objective are not usually aware that cultivation of skills is generally not thought to be the purpose of science education. But some may wish to argue that such skills should be substituted for certain segments of the high school population in lieu of the regular science program. Once again we are faced with the problem that only a certain number of students have the manipulative aptitudes to profit by a program of this type. Among those who have the ability to profit from a study of either program, it could be argued, especially for those who plan to attend college, that the regular scientific program would be of greater value—in fact, they would be seriously handicapped without it and may be denied admission at some colleges. There are also those who cannot profit from either program and who may be better served by pursuing a two-semester course in general science. The remaining group who could profit most by a more utilitarian program may wish first to enroll in the general science course in order to acquire a background of understanding of the rudiments of science, to be followed, in turn, by shop and vocational courses leading to a career as a technician in the servicing of machines and various types of industrial equipment. They will also need to pursue a postsecondary school program in order to develop the specialized abilities. Those students who lack ability or interest in careers of this type but who still wish to pursue a science program which will enable them to be a general repairmen should probably be discouraged from such aspirations on several grounds. First of all, they are better served by entering the regular science program, if they have the required ability, for they can very well use the understanding and the scientific thinking to which they will be exposed to live more meaningfully in our complex scientific age. If they lack the ability to profit from the regular science program, it is highly doubtful that they would be more suited to the role of general repairman, because our age precludes the successful development of such skills by the vast majority of students. This development of skills is due to the fact that machines and mechanical devices are becoming increasingly complex and in most cases, require the services of a specialized technician whenever repairs are needed. Thus, many people become slaves to machines, for once they depend regularly on the performance of mechanical devices to fulfill the onerous tasks humans formerly discharged, they perforce must bear the costs for their maintenance and repair.

Living as we do in an age in which scientific discoveries and develop-ments exert vast influences over our lives, it behooves every citizen to acquire a minimum level of scientific understanding and ability to inter-pret the literature. The scientific journals are intended for scientific spe-cialists: the average citizen should not expect to peruse them with any degree of comprehension. How, then, is the layman to grasp the essential scientific developments on which his very life may depend? Since many students will not attend college and will have little more than a general science course at the secondary level, it is exceedingly important that a strong interest be aroused in the role of science in the contemporary world in this course and in previous work of a more elementary nature. It is important, too, that rudimentary understanding of the progress of scientific discovery and the application of its findings be provided. Devel-opment of interest and understanding is much to ask of these limited curricular experiences; however, once interest is piqued and understand-ing is broadened, the range and variety of scientific developments re-ported in the mass media and in books and articles which treat these developments for the intelligent laymen should be sufficient to keep the initial interest alive. There is no shortage of good scientific books for the layman, but the mass media, with some notable exceptions, have scarcely performed the educative function of which they are capable. This failure is critical in light of the fact that many people do not like to read and read very little (either in spite of or because of their school experiences). It is likely that in our electronic age people will read less in the future (even though there will still be a market for printed mate-rial due to the growth of population and the large number of youth in school). Unless the mass media upgrade the quality of programming considerably, we are likely to find ourselves with a population abysmally ignorant of some of the critical developments on which the very future of civilization rests.

Those who attend college can be divided into three categories on the basis of career plans: scientific, technical, nonscientific. The program suitable to those who will become scientists and technicians is best left to the judgement of specialists in their respective fields. Those who plan to become technicians will begin their studies in high school and follow up with more specialized training at a technical institute, a community college, or in some cases in a four-year college. The length of their training will increase as skills demanded in their prospective careers become more complex. Those aspiring to become scientists, on the other hand, will need a lengthy period of advanced study leading to a doctorate in their specialty, plus various forms of postdoctoral study to maintain, upgrade, and improve competencies throughout their careers.

Our concern here is for the majority of college students who do not choose to become scientists or technicians. These persons constitute a reservoir of talent for government, industry, business, and the professions. Some of them will be called upon to formulate policies some of which will require a broad, general understanding of the world of science. Their college experience should provide a basic background on which they can continue to build.

A minimum of one year of study in science would be needed for these students. Obviously, if one has the time and inclination, he could acquire more (but not more of the obsolete courses or poor teaching already available). How this year will be organized is open to debate. Other than various honor programs, the two principal proposals are a strict discipline-centered program or a broad-fields program.

The proponents of the discipline-centered program argue that one needs to focus his attention for an entire year within the structure and methodology of a discipline (such as biology, chemistry, physics, geology, or astronomy) to grasp some of the basic laws and concepts and to learn to think and operate with the scientific methodology peculiar to the field as the scientist himself does.

The other proposal is to offer broad field courses which cut across departmental and disciplinary lines in order to faithfully pursue integrative concepts and common problems. These courses could be structured around the concepts and problems or they may be found under the rubrics of "life science," "earth science," and "physical science." The life sciences would relate material from botany, zoology, kinesiology, biochemistry, physiology, health, and other fields. The earth sciences would be devoted to geology, mineralology, and physical geography. Finally, the physical sciences would be concerned with at least physics, chemistry, and astronomy.

The strengths and limitations of the two approaches may already be apparent. The discipline-centered approach enables the student to concentrate for one year on a single discipline rather than spread himself thin over several. It also enables him to acquire an understanding of and a rudimentary working ability with the scientific methodology of the discipline. Of course the question as to which science should be required arises. Some have argued that physics is the most advanced of the sciences, and its study would enable the student to begin to appreciate how complex theoretical systems can be used to explain a multitude of phenomena. Others have contended that biology should be required because it is closer to daily human problems and health concerns. Differences of this type are not easily settled, and so a common compromise is to require one year of science and permit the student to elect the discipline or to divide the required work between a physical and biological course. This approach may not be the most satisfactory one, but with competition between departments as is presently found, it may be the best approach until something better can be agreed upon.

The broad-fields approach offers the nonspecialist a wide survey of certain fundamental problems and concepts that relate to several disciplines. It avoids the problem students frequently experience in the discipline-centered approach in which the instructor teaches the course as if each student is planning to become a specialist in the field. Since time in one's college program is limited, the broad-fields approach enables the student to grasp the interrelationship of concepts; and since in his own life he will likely need far-ranging concepts and information on which to base decisions, the likelihood of a broad-fields approach being useful is ostensibly great.

On the other hand, it may also prove to be superficial and culminate more in a smorgasbord sampling rather than something substantial. It does not permit the deeper grounding in a single discipline and its methodology as is characteristic of the discipline-centered approach. Since scientists are trained as specialists, it also becomes more difficult to find scientists with the background and inclination to teach such courses. The inclination is lacking because status comes from one's identification with his discipline. There is more status in graduate than undergraduate teaching, and in terms of the latter, the least status would likely be accorded to broad-field courses and other course structures which do not draw more or less exclusively upon one's specialized knowledge. However, there is nothing inevitable about this state of affairs so that academicians may decide, due to future needs for integrative courses, to award greater value to the broad-fields approach.

One promising development is the emergence of the history and philosophy of science as fields of study. Majors are offered in these areas at several universities. Courses in these areas at the advanced undergraduate and graduate levels have provided breadth of understanding of the sciences within the larger cultural and historical framework, both for prospective scientists and nonscientists alike. Although these fields usually presuppose basic knowledge in one or more of the sciences and, hence, are inappropriate for freshman and sophomores, their value can be especially great for those with the requisite background.

In conclusion, a thorough reappraisal of the undergraduate science requirements for nonscience majors is in order. This reappraisal may well lead to more integrative experiences during the early college years, while those with a stronger science preparation may secure the integration through the history and philosophy of science as they relate to cultural and cross-cultural studies of other social institutions and their roles within a broad humanistic orientation to life.

Questions for Discussion

1. Although it may be misleading to speak of the scientific method, there seems to be some overlapping of methodology and general objectives by practitioners of the various scientific disciplines. What is it that they would have in common?

2. Is the methodological approach to the discovery of knowledge as used by science one that can be utilized in all areas of inquiry and human concern, or is it limited strictly to empirical phenomena which can be observed or measured? What significance attaches it to the general fad that different studies have been considered empirical or scientific in different cultures and periods of history?

3. What are the scientist's responsibilities for his discoveries and their application? Does the scientist have a special role to play in public affairs, or should he restrict himself to his work and let others determine how and for what ends his findings will be employed?

4. To what extent and in what manner can the problems which face education be treated scientifically? Do we have many educational problems today principally because scientific research has not advanced far or has not been utilized well, or are the problems obdurate and persistent due to other factors?

5. Taking into consideration the wide range of individual and cultural differences in the population while at the same time recognizing the importance of science in this age, what type of scientific program of studies would you recommend in the public schools and in higher education? How would you justify your decision?

For Further Reading

There are a number of useful introductory books on the nature and function of science written with the intelligent nonscientist in mind. Among them are Jacob Bronowski, *The Common Sense of Science,* Cambridge, Mass.: Harvard University Press, 1953; James B. Conant, *On Understanding Science,* New Haven, Conn.: Yale University Press, 1947; A. N. Whitehead, *Science and the Modern World,* New York: Macmillan, 1927.

F. S. C. Northrop's essays are valuable in formulating more precisely the methodology of science and its relation to other areas of inquiry. His book is titled *The Logic of the Sciences and Humanities,* New York: Macmillan, 1947. The more advanced reader will find a comprehensive treatment of the philosophy of science in Ernest Nagel's *The Structure of Science,* New York: Harcourt, Brace and World, 1961. For an application of the principles of scientific method to the social sciences, one can profit from Abraham Kaplan's *The Conduct of Inquiry,* San Francisco: Chandler Publishing Co., 1964.

As for science and public affairs, Barry Commoner has discussed many critical issues perceptively and uttered a stern warning to scientists and public officials in his *Science and Survival,* New York: Viking Press, 1967. Gerald Piel's essays are particularly valuable for highlighting problems of censorship and restrictions on inquiry. Piel's essays are titled *Science and the Cause of Man,* 2nd ed., New York: Vintage Books, 1961. Among other books in this area the reader could profitably consult: Eugene Rabinowitch, *The Dawn of a New Age,* Chicago: University of Chicago Press, 1963; J. A. V. Butler, *Science and Human Life,* New York: Basic Books, 1957; A. Cornelius Benjamin, *Science, Technology and Human Values,* Columbia, Mo.: University of Missouri Press, 1965.

Apart from the specialized studies of the science curriculum, three books particularly provide a broad perspective of the issues discussed in this chapter. Science in the secondary curriculum is evaluated in terms of different uses of knowledge in Harry S. Broudy, B. Othanel Smith, and Joe R. Burnett, *Democracy and Excellence in American Secondary Education,* Chicago: Rand McNally, 1964. Daniel Bell in his *The Reforming of General Education,* Garden City, N.Y.; Doubleday Anchor Books, 1968, discusses perceptively the role of science in general education in our colleges and universities. An attempt to depict science in its relationships with other domains of human knowledge in the curriculum is found in Philip Phenix's *Realms of Meaning,* New York: McGraw-Hill, 1964. Those interested in the teaching of science should not overlook Joseph J. Schwab and Paul F. Brandwein's *The Teaching of Science as Inquiry,* Cambridge, Mass.: Harvard University Press, 1962.

Notes

1. Carl L. Becker, *The Heavenly City of the Eighteenth Century Philosophers* (New Haven, Conn.: Yale University Press, 1932).

2. The process is actually more involved than this and is developed at length in Ernest Nagel's, *The Structure of Science* (New York: Harcourt, Brace and World, Inc., 1961), chap. 3.

3. For a further discussion of other types of laws, see Nagel, *The Structure of Science,* pp. 75-78.

4. Some of today's heresies are the discussion of scientific theories which run counter to the official scientific theories of the state (Soviet Union), and the unwillingness to disseminate classified scientific information, such as surrounds nuclear testing, which bears on the virtual life and death of the population (United States).

5. See Barry Commoner, *Science and Survival* (New York: The Viking Press, 1967), pp. 16-19, 52-54.

6. Gerald Piel, *Science and the Cause of Man,* 2nd ed (New York: Vintage Books, 1961), p. 138.

7. See Burton R. Clark, *Educating the Expert Society* (San Francisco: Chandler Publishing Co., 1962), pp. 36-37.

8. Industrial magnates and militarists, along with considerable public apathy, also stand indicted.

Chapter Seven
The Humanities

The Meaning of the Humanities

The humanities have a significant role to play in contemporary society. However, disagreement exists as to what that role should be, just as differences arise over interpretations of the substantive content. These differences are not surprising in light of the fact that conceptions of the humanities reflect the concerns of historical periods. Examples of this reflection can be found in a more restricted centering of the humanities around theology during the Middle Ages. Many of these restrictions were removed and others imposed as the secular vitality found in Greek and Roman classics was eventually recaptured during the Renaissance. New interpretations of the humanities arose in more recent times as a revolt occurred against an exclusive classical curriculum. Each period chooses various elements of human life as most significant and to emphasize for study. No age is entirely oblivious to the past, although past contributions are always used with a high degree of selectivity. The Renaissance man, for instance, repudiated what he considered the superstitions, barbarisms, and unenlightened ways of the medieval mind and devoted his attention to revivifying the Greek and Roman masters. On the other hand, contemporary man generally finds himself in an ambiguous position. Should he preserve certain humanistic concerns of earlier periods, or, in light of unprecedented social, political, and technological developments of this century, seek to create new modes of humanistic disciplines designed expressly for his own times? Competing voices clamor to be heard and disorder emerges out of this cacophony, in spite of which, uneasy islands of agreement exist within the center of the conflict.

Part of the problem is to be found in our mixed views about man himself. As heirs to Greek, Roman, Hebraic-Christian, and Enlightenment outlooks, our own culture cannot accurately speak of itself as holding to one in preference to the others. Rather, through the process of selectivity we have built conglomerate perspectives that not infrequently are internally inconsistent. The bold, unqualified optimism of the Enlightenment has been undermined by the chaos and violence of our time, while secular technology and vast changes in the economic system have vitiated organized religion as a significant and central force in cultural life and the affairs of nations. We are confronted by a palpable baseness in complex social relations while at the same time, recollect former beliefs in the inherent dignity and goodness of man. As a result of these cleavages in our cultural outlook, some seek new directions for the humanities in hopes that they can usher in a more unified and compelling perspective on which to base human affairs.

The humanities as organized fields of study are presently identified with certain disciplines: literature, music, painting, sculpture, architecture, languages, philosophy, and history (although the latter discipline is sometimes placed among the social sciences). By singling out certain disciplines and dividing organized bodies of knowledge generally into four major areas—the humanities, natural sciences, social sciences, and professional studies — the impression is left that the concerns of the humanities are to be found only in those disciplines so designated. This impression is misleading.

Since the humanities concern themselves with the full range of thought, action, and the creations of man, humanistic investigations should not be limited to certain disciplines, even though this traditionally has been thought to be the case. All areas of study have some potential to reveal important findings about man. The physical sciences focus on nonliving phenomena in an attempt to discover laws and develop explanatory theories. Various professional studies, due to their highly specialized nature, are also limited in their applicablity to broader humanistic concerns. The social sciences, on the other hand, patently appear to be of direct humanistic concern since their focus is upon man and his institutional behavior; yet their objectives and methodology diverge from those disciplines previously delineated as the humanities.

This divergence raises a critical question: Are there distinctive objectives and methodologies of the humanities? The social and behavioral sciences aspire, above all, to be as scientific as possible. Most practitioners in the respective social sciences are devoted to making their discipline a science. Putting aside the question whether these disciplines can ever attain the scientific status of the natural sciences, it can be noted that this overriding objective is not shared by persons in the humanities. In order for the social scientist to make his discipline a science, he must seek to uncover laws or law-like statements to explain the empirical data which has been gathered. As these disciplines become more highly developed, theories are devised to explain a multiplicity of laws. The social sciences, in contrast to the physical sciences, have had to rely upon the statistical quantification and interpretation of data rather than the precise uses of measurement.

The objectives and methodologies of the social and behavioral sciences as adumbrated above are not shared with the disciplines commonly referred to as the humanities. True, both areas concern themselves in certain ways with man, but the centrality of focus differs. The scientific thrust and the quantification of data have led some humanistic scholars to question the value of some of the studies in the social sciences. And at times these scholars think of themselves as the last protective outpost of man, holding the fort, so to speak, against the onslaught of mechanization, bureaucracy, and totalitarian thought-control.

The Origin of the Humanities

Although certain emphases on the study of man and his works can be found in both ancient Greece and Rome, the humanities emerged as a distinctive aspect of the curriculum during the Renaissance. The curriculum advocated during that period was known collectively as the *studia humanitatis,* the humanities—consisting of grammar, rhetoric, history, poetry, and ethics, all of which was studied in the classical Greek and Roman manuscripts. This program was in conflict with the Scholastic curriculum of the Middle Ages, which stressed natural philosophy, metaphysics, and logic. Whereas the medieval curriculum was designed to prepare men for the professions of law, medicine, and theology in particular, Renaissance humanists conceived a broader education which emphasized the full development of the individual—mind, body, and character—for social responsibilities and civic participation.

At its best, this new humanism was highly creative and imaginative. But there were also those scholars, out of their reverence for the classical texts and their glorification of the classical tongues, who developed a narrow formalized literary humanism. Cicero became the epitome of style. "Ciceronianism," as this movement came to be called, emphasized the style and sentence structure of classical writers—primarily Cicero—without evidencing an integral concern for the thought and concepts found in the works. The idea behind the movement was that in order to be creative, one must first imitate models of the best style. Unfortunately, most students never advanced beyond the stage of imitation. Pedantic, slavish imitation of the old master was one of the factors that precipitated the demise of Latin as touchstone for all school learning once reaction finally set in.

There are several examples of Renaissance ideals. Petrach (1313-1375) is generally conceded to be the first major figure of the Italian Renaissance. The date of his birth has been a convenient point to mark the advent of this period, although historians today are more likely to view some of the developments of the twelfth century as more or less continuous with the Renaissance. Petrach was a critic of scholastic education and repudiated the other-worldliness of the monasteries for a love of the ancient manuscripts. He collected and copied many of the Latin works, but never mastered Greek. He helped revive an interest in the classics while, at the same time, elevated eloquence and style to a higher position in the educational firmament than it deserved.

The northern response to the Italian Renaissance took the form of religious revolt and a mystical, rather than a secular-naturalistic, approach to life. In Erasmus (1469?-1536) we find developed the highest ideals of humanistic culture combined with a great understanding of the religious ideals of the time. He edited Greek and Latin masters, including the Church Fathers, and was the leading figure in northern Europe in restoring the ancient tongues. His thorough research and scholarship commanded the respect of the scholarly world, and his Latin schoolbooks were used as texts by numerous students. Erasmus sought to refine taste, elevate moral standards, and promote the peace and unity of Europe. The aim of education, he believed, was a moral one, to develop the "good man" who would be informed and refined by a study of classical literature. But Latin was not an end in itself, and he was sharply critical of the Ciceronians. He gave great impetus to an education that would restore individuality to a central place in the educative process as did Montaigne and Rabelais later in the sixteenth century.

There were a number of books in the fifteenth century of the prince and the courtier. Of all of these, Castiglione's *Courtier* was the most popular and widely read in southern Europe. In England, Thomas Elyot was the first to use his native language in all his writings, and his work, *The Governor,* became the first work on education in English. Just as Quintilian had employed the ideal of the orator for ancient Rome, Elyot elevated the governor as an exemplar for the Renaissance. Governors consisted of a number of public officials—judges, ambassadors, royal secretaries, and others. Political power rested in the hands of these men; therefore, it was thought that their education was of considerable moment.

Quintilian's educational thought was widely admired and applied in Renaissance education; it is not surprising to find many of Elyot's proposals for the education of governors in essential agreement with Quintilian's position. Both the orator and the governor were men of public affairs who exercised power over their subjects in the affairs of the state. The future governors were drawn from boys of the nobility; their education contained the diversity needed to provide the requisite skills and talents for their calling. Following Quintilian's advice, early childhood was safe-guarded by selecting a nurse who would prevent the child from assimilating evil influences. At the age of seven the conduct of his education was assumed by a male tutor who would see that the boy learned to speak Latin as preparation for writing Latin when he became older. Among the Greek and Latin authors studied were Homer and Virgil, as well as Aesop's *Fables.* The tutor's responsibility was to see that the program was balanced and diversified by teaching the youth to play a musical instrument and to engage in physical exercises and sports befitting a gentleman. These activities not only helped prepare him for his future role, but they were also conducive to the needed balance which would avoid intellectual fatigue and overwork with books. From the ages of fourteen to seventeen the youth studied logic, rhetoric, and geography, and at the latter age he began his work in philosophy, which included some biblical and theological writings. In Elyot's plan, education was designed to develop the whole man by an emphasis on intellectual, moral, aesthetic, and physical dimensions. In addition, the necessary social graces and demeanor befitting the youth's future role were inculcated.

The ideals of Renaissance humanism and many of the educational programs which stemmed from them not only permeated many parts of Europe but also found a place in early American education. That some American educators adopted some of the more rigid and pedantic practices bespeaks more of their lack of imagination and the weight of unexamined tradition, for some of the original European programs had considerable balance and emphasized the complete development of the individual. In spite of the strengths of Renaissance education and its nurture of individualism, there are several reasons why it cannot serve as an exclusive guide for education today in the humanities.

Ralph Barton Perry indicates that Renaissance humanism opposed itself to science, humanitarianism, democracy, romanticism, and modernism(1). Actually, the Renaissance attitude toward science was a mixed one and not a clear-cut case of opposition (even though Perry does not indicate this). On the one hand, the humanists contributed to the development of science by translating many scientific writings of antiquity, by introducing the study of Plato and his mathematical conceptions of the universe, and especially by emphasis upon concrete experience in art. However, some aversions to abstract thought can also be found. The cultivation of a polished style of writing and the elevation of selected classics to a supreme place in the curriculum led to conflicts with emerging developments in science. The classics dominated secondary and college programs in America through the eighteenth century. The Academy, another type of secondary school which was made famous by Benjamin Franklin, partially broke with the Latin grammar school, which had dominated secondary education throughout the colonial period, by offering practical and commercial courses along with a study of English, while simultaneously providing some work in the classics. The Boston English High School in 1821 was a further departure from the classical pattern, even though the classical approach was still used in the program and the enrollment was still drawn from an elite segment of the population.

There were many conflicts during the nineteenth century between the new sciences and the classics as to which should enjoy the dominant role in American higher education. The classicists had aligned themselves with an aristocratic tradition and sought to bar the gates to any encroachments upon their required classical curriculum. Sporadic breaks in the strict classical pattern could be found in various parts of the country during the early nineteenth century, but the real break came during the 1850's when the scientific school became popular. Between 1860 and 1870, twenty-five institutions opened scientific departments(2).

During this time the classicists not only resisted the enlarged curriculum that the sciences were forging, but they also opposed the introduction of romance languages and other new disciplines in the humanities. The older classical notions began losing their hold against these new developments. Latin slipped further when the decision was made to model graduate education in America after the German universities. Later studies, such as those by William James and Edward Lee Thorndike, exploded the formal discipline theory that conceived the mind as similar to the muscular system, hence, could be improved and strengthened by certain difficult subjects such as Latin and mathematics.

The humanities at times have enjoyed an uneasy truce with the sciences. On other occasions open hostilities have erupted with no sensible resolution of the conflict, or even clearer understanding resulting. Since both the sciences and humanities are vital to man, a detailed examination of the nature of this dispute can uncover fresh possibilities for more cooperative and fruitful relations.

At this point, however, Renaissance humanism must be noted to have not only found itself in conflict at times with the new sciences but also to have demonstrated an opposition to humanitarianism. Humanistic education was devoted to cultivating man's abilities and striving for perfection of human potentialities. Failures in the past to accomplish this usually were blamed upon the Church and its preoccuption with preparation for an after-life. The superstition and barbarism which some humanists ascribed to the Middle Ages led them also to associate many of the acts of Christian piety and brotherhood to the same context. Of course, this opposition need no longer be the case today if humanistic ideals are to be extended to all mankind. But this inherent shortcoming of Renaissance humanism was due to its aversion to the Middle Ages and the fact that its program was elitist in character.

The education of the courtier and the governor was designed to prepare young boys from noble backgrounds for the responsibilities demanded in their role as a public official. Universal education was unknown at the time, although Luther later advocated certain rudiments of elementary studies for German youth, and Comenius devised a more comprehensive plan of education from kindergarten through the graduate school. Renaissance ideals excluded not only those from less elite backgrounds—that is, the vast majority—but it also neglected the education of women. Today, however, our problem is to construct meaningful approaches to education of all youth through a judicious balance between the humanistic and scientific.

The classical humanist, according to Perry, has also opposed romanticism and modernism. Romanticism was a movement which advocated a return to nature and a more natural life. It exalted the emotions and the senses over reason and proposed that human feelings and emotions were essential areas for study. The classicists conflicted with the romantics because the former identified with the ancient Greek works which were generally based upon a rationalistic approach to life. The classical humanists would be mistaken if they identified romanticism with a sickly sentimentalism, just as the romanticists would be if they attached the label of "Ciceronianist" to humanism. Yet misunderstandings and conflicts have arisen for these very mistakes. Each is more of a caricature than an accurate representation of a total movement. Each group can learn from the other by serving as a corrective for excessive emphasis on certain aspects of man and human experience. Surely man's reason, his feelings, and inner strivings should serve as material for constructing a more complete perspective of the individual; therefore, although it may prove difficult to integrate the two movements into a single, unified perspective—perhaps in terms of an organism of forms developed by Alfred North Whitehead or Lewis Mumford, the two movements should strive for greater cross-fertilization.

Classical humanism has also found itself in opposition to modernism as a result of the fact that the core of its program is devoted to classical studies. It can rightfully object to a cult of contemporaneity whereby all that is past is denigrated by a quest for the fads and fashions of the moment. The classical humanist is quick to point out the shallowness of such pursuits and to stress that the value or worth of a particular literary or artistic work must stand the test of time. Man loses a sense of continuity and perspective, the humanist would assert, when he fails to comprehend the relation of the present to historical forces and the ideas that have shaped the course of nations.

At the same time, however, it could justifiably be argued that an preoccupation with classical studies will not properly equip youth for our postindustrial age. In light of the fact that vast social, economic, and technological changes have occurred in the past fifty years, and that the rate of change is accelerating precipitously, educators would be negligent if they did not plan programs which would help students deal meaningfully with present critical problems. In actuality, there is no reason why the humanities should be, in some circles, notorious for their neglect of the contemporary world and its pressing problems. But often these problems are excluded from examination and discussion. The humanities, however, if they aspire to serve men of today, must relinquish these preoccupations and become a vigorous force for a more relevant education.

Reinterpreting the Humanities

We may not necessarily agree fully with Gilbert Chinard that "humanism is not a subject which can be taught, but a state of mind and a discipline which permeates all human activities."(3) Unless one formulates a constricted definition of teaching and subject matter, there is no reason to believe that certain types of well-conceived courses cannot contribute to humanism and a humanistic education. Humanism becomes an approach to the world, an outlook and demeanor that guides and influences one's actions. It is also possible to find a type of spirit in a multitude of diverse activities, even though, more often than not, such a spirit is sadly lacking. Most importantly, the humanities are not *merely* a set of activities to be found in certain types of classes or a form of knowledge or insight transmitted by certain types of instructors. Humanism can not only be found in all areas of life, but the acquisition of a humanistic perspective can result from a wide variety of social relationships, both in and out of the formal educational system.

Perhaps Ralph Barton Perry expresses it most precisely. "Any agency or relationship or situation or activity which has a humanizing, that is, liberalizing effect, which broadens learning, stimulates imagination, kindles sympathy, inspires a sense of human dignity, and imprints that bearing and form of intercourse proper to a man, may be termed 'a humanity'."(4)

It has been thought that only the study of the Greek and Roman classics would bring about such outcomes, but this kind of thinking is far too constricted and limiting. Many experiences of life may contribute significantly to a broadened outlook, although obviously not the daily commonplace events in which the individual can rely primarily upon habit and routine, for these relations are mechanical and lacking in reflection. Those experiences in which one meets persons who hold value systems differing from one's own, or whose cultural background is sig-

nificantly divergent are the ones that contribute most. Even in such experiences, however, outcomes are not automatic, especially when one does
not enter into a meaningful relationship with such persons by attempting
to comprehend the diversity and to see why these individuals live, act, and
think the way they do. Because of the divergence of value systems, it
may be natural at first for the untutored and unsympathetic to consider
the ways of others as strange, odd, or bizarre. One task for a humanistic
education, both in its formal and informal aspects, is to provide the
reflective abilities which enable one to secure the necessary background
material for an initial understanding, while also cultivating an openness
of mind to be receptive to human differences without prejudging and
stereotyping.

These are large demands that can only be met when one's schooling
and informal educational opportunity cross-fertilize and supplement one
another in contributing to such ends. To achieve these ends youth need
to be provided many educative relationships that a large number
today are not receiving. The unhealthy, prejudicial, conventional, and
narrow-minded environment in which some youth are raised largely precludes the humanistic development needed. For such development we
will need teachers who possess these humanistic characteristics. We will
need a reorganization of educational systems so that they may more
effectively provide an atmosphere which contributes to the cultivation
of such characteristics. We will need more informed, less parochial and
demeaning child-rearing practices. Finally, we will need communities in
which a humanistic way of life is nurtured and rewarded. There are many
disadvantaged youth—not just those from the ghetto. Many white middle-
class youth are disadvantaged because their environment, both in school
and out, impairs the development of a humanistic way of life.

Although the humanities traditionally have been considered as that
part of the curriculum expressly designed to have this humanizing or
liberalizing effect that Perry speaks of, there is no reason why the natural
and social sciences cannot also contribute to such ends. Many of the
interdisciplinary courses, as well as work in the history and philosophy
of science, could have strong humanizing effects. While it is recognized
that courses designed to prepare specialists, scholars, and persons for
the professions are essential for the type of world in which we live, there
is a low probability that these courses will have the desired humanistic
outcomes. Yet in any discipline, in addition to courses which interrelate
concepts across traditional subject-matter lines, offerings are springing
up which attempt to delineate the relationship of the discipline to the

. . . we will need teachers who possess these humanistic characteristics.

concerns of the larger society. Studies of art and literature within a larger historical and cultural perspective are cases in point. Other examples are courses in professional schools, such as medicine or law, which seek to show the relationship between the profession and the larger society. In this regard we find not only courses in professional ethics, but also instruction, sometimes provided by social scientists, in the role and responsibilities of the profession in the broader concept of a changing culture.

The dimensions of the humanities and their respective functions must be shown more precisely. This not only will enable us to distinguish the humanities more sharply from the natural and social sciences, but it will also demonstrate whatever power the humanities have for producing humanistic outcomes.

Dimensions of the Humanities

The following four dimensions can be ascribed to the humanities whenever they are found to be organized within a conceptual or disciplinary framework: the creative, appreciative, normative, and synthetic. These are not necessarily mutually exclusive dimensions for there are times when they overlap and interpenetrate one another.

The Creative Dimension

There is no single definition and interpretation of creativity that is universally agreed upon. Rather, there are several major approaches to creativity each of which enjoys its own band of followers(5). Creativity may be considered an infrequent idea which is adaptive and carried to fruition. Some investigators approach it through the psychic life of the individual in terms of various types of inventive responses. Abraham Maslow has emphasized the flash of insight as the significant aspect of the problem(6). Getzels, instead, emphasizes the envisionment of problems(7). However, it should be pointed out that in the problem-solving approach, there is more genuine creativity when the subject discovers the problem than when he finds it already at hand. The task of unconventional thinking, then, is not only to solve problems but also to demonstrate the ability to formulate the problem itself. Creativity is also thought to involve divergent rather than convergent thinking(8). The latter process refers to new information maximally determined by existing information, while divergent thinking is new information minimally determined by existing information.

Creativity in the humanities can be approached from the point of view of the artist or the observer of the work. Looking first at the artist (and we are using artist in the broad sense to include all forms of creative achievements in the humanities), the creative process may be studied in terms of the early formulations, conceptualizations, imagery, flashes of insight which ignite the creative process. Quite often, prior to the inception of a new creation, the artist may undergo a period of incubation where his thoughts and imagery fail to distinguish a clearly-defined direction. This may be a period of listlessness, aimlessness, or frustration, during which time, however, ideas may be germinating imperceptibly. There may be periods of false starts and unproductive attempts to bring ideas to fruition. Whatever the hidden stimulus may be (if there is one), the artist suddenly, and sometimes feverishly, divines his project and leaps forward to forge its proportions, to shape and direct it, and bring it to fruition(9).

Besides the initial stages of the creative act and the explorations and shapings of ideas or materials in the process, the final product is appraised as a work of art, a work with varying degrees of excellence and certain shortcomings. Whether or not a work is adjudged of high artistic merit is determined by its ability to fulfill certain standards deemed appropriate for the genre or movement. The standards themselves are developed and applied by those knowledgeable in the field. Of course, the "experts" themselves may disagree on occasion, leaving the untutored observer with a sense of bewilderment. However, the disagreements of authorities may well prove to be instructive, and it is out of such disagreements that new standards are developed and new approaches explored.

Whenever a product is evaluated as a work of art, it is implied, assuming the evaluation is correct, that the artist performed a creative act. Such an act is the converse of the commonplace, banal, and imitative that proliferate profusely in any society. Although creativity, if interpreted broadly, is not rare, the creation of a work of art, whatever the medium, is an infrequent event. Obviously creativity is not by any means limited to the humanities but is found in various forms in all organized disciplines as well as within the framework of occupations. There is little point in making much ado over creativity in the humanities, then, unless it exhibits certain distinctive characteristics.

There is, however, a certain creative focus in the humanities that can be delineated. This focus may be found in the attempt to penetrate and explore the inner-life of man: his hopes, joys, sufferings, aspirations, and failures. The social and behavioral sciences, on the other hand, direct their inquiries toward the development of a science of man and society by uncovering law-like statements which govern social behavior. This procedure is carried out by the application of a variety of empirical methodologies which lead to the quantification of findings. The pursuit of humanistic inquiries is generally eschewed by the social sciences because it does not fit into any existing scientific framework. But since there are diverse and fundamental inner-expressions of man, some of which have universal dimensions, it is left to the humanities to capture and record them in some inimitable form. These forms or media are aural, visual, and linguistic. The aural is found in music; the visual in painting, sculpture, ceramics and architecture; and the linguistic in literature, poetry, languages, and philosophy. Some creative expressions are found in all three: dance, cinema, theater, etc. By use of the appropriate media as its chief mode of expression, the respective disciplines are able to creatively convey their own interpretations of the inner-life of man.

But it should be noted that the creative process is not limited solely to the artist: his work challenges the sensitive observer to think or to perceive creatively in order to grasp the full significance of the work. Since all great works make such demands, many persons avoid them either because they are unwilling or unable to marshal the necessary qualities of mind to interpret or preceive them sympathetically, or because they believe that they lack requisite background which would make such efforts worth the exertion.

The creative response is elicited from the observer due to his inability to use habitual, stereotyped, or conventional approaches in the act of interpretation or perception. An essay or philosophical work will require sustained thought in order to follow the principal arguments and trace their ramifications and implications. It may be necessary for the reader to hold in abeyance certain personal preconceptions that may cloud his thinking or bias him prematurely in order that the work will be given a fair hearing. So, too, with a painting or a musical composition. Too often we apply our tastes, which for many of us are more limited than we imagine them to be, and reject a work out of hand because of its incongruence with these tastes. But the humanities also teach us that man is not a completed being, that he is in a state of becoming. In

... man is not a completed being, he is in
a state of becoming.

order to appreciatively to grasp new and diverse modes of expression which strive to capture multiple manifestations of man as he makes himself and his future, it is necessary to maintain openness, receptivity, and flexibility. Fixed attitudes, cocksure solutions, imitative behavior, and respectable role-playing we have in abundance. It is the quintessence of the humanities to evoke creative attitudes and modes of behavior in the service of a more profound appreciation of the inner-life of man and the extensiveness of human possibilities.

The Appreciative Dimension

Art also has the power to evoke an appreciative awareness on the part of the beholder. The humanities provide works which are not merely descriptive and critical, but highly expressive as well. This expressive feature has the power to elicit appreciative feelings whenever there is some synchronization or complementariness between the work itself and the observer's past experiences, his mind-set, and his aesthetic sensitivity.

Thus there are multiple factors which enter into and contribute to the process of creative awareness. The background needed by any individual to appreciate a humanistic work would tend to vary with the type of work itself. One may very well gain an appreciation of certain paintings or sculpture without a knowledge of art history, even though some argue that it is impossible to gain a "full" appreciation without such knowledge. The first part of the argument is sufficiently clear that it can be affirmed without equivocation, for there are cases every day of persons who lack a working knowledge of the technicalities and finer points of the fine arts but who demonstrate appreciative capacity. The second part of the argument is more difficult to support until standards are produced by which the level, extensiveness, depth, and intensity of appreciation can be evaluated. It is true, of course, that the expert has a working knowledge of the standards applicable to a particular humanistic work in his speciality, but the ability to use standards intelligently is not synonymous with the quality of appreciation. Difficulties, however, are far greater for the untrained observer when he confronts poetry and philosophy. Too often with these disciplines he is closed off from an appreciative awareness by his lack of the requisite background and competencies needed to perceptively enter into these regions of the mind.

The appreciative dimension of the humanities cannot be stated in quantifiable terms and, at times, not even in terms which could be communicated accurately to others. This lack of communication is due to the large element of subjectivity present, which becomes apparent whenever the personal background, tastes and interests of the individual are considered. Each individual brings with him to a humanistic work certain attitudes and values that he has acquired from his culture and also from his social class and various affiliations within society. These influences contribute to a common outlook with others of a similar social and cultural background. Yet individuals bring certain unique capacities to a humanistic work; otherwise, it would be a contradiction in terms to speak of them as individuals rather than automatons (unless, of course, they could compensate by exhibiting unique approaches in some other aspect of life). Appreciations emerge from a subjective personal awareness of the qualities that a work elicits within the individual. The experience remains subjective until one attempts to communicate his feelings to others. Success in doing so is a factor of the ability to symbolize vividly and precisely so as to evoke a sympathetic sharing of the original feelings on the part of others. But since a large number of people lack such facility, their appreciations remain subjective. Another limiting factor is the background of the hearer. He may be lacking experiences sufficiently similar in quality or kind to relate to the feelings communicated. Without the convergence of these experiences in the background of all parties, concerned sharing of feelings is likely to be precluded.

Another facet of appreciation is that the process is generally accorded intrinsic value. Other than those occasions in which the purpose of appreciating a work is principally to be *au courant* in order to impress someone or to be accepted into certain social circles, the act of appreciation is thought to need no external justification and is worthwhile for its own sake. A scientist may also look upon his investigations as of intrinsic worth, but it is more likely that he undertakes the research to achieve certain external ends. Science is more concerned with bringing a wide range of phenomena under experimental or theoretical laws in order that they may be explained more adequately; whereas, the humanities focus their attentions more closely upon the types of human values, interests, and appreciations which are not readily amenable to measurement and quantification.

Those humanistic works which are designed to effect certain explicit external ends may be appraised, if of a sufficiently high quality, as of great cultural worth during a particular historical period within a particular culture. These works may aim to promote piety, foster patriotic sentiments, or expose the weakness or corruptness of some aspect of the social system. But it is most likely that these works will not prove as significant to later generations (although notable exceptions may be found) as those artistic creations which have no external aim in mind. They are of value and can be enjoyed for their own sake.

Enjoyment is a subjective affair and difficulties arise in conveying one's feelings to others. The power of a great humanistic work lies not only in its ability to promote understanding and alter perspectives, but also in its capacity to bring about an aesthetic experience. It is true that an individual may enjoy a work without undergoing an aesthetic experience in the process—and such experiences defy prediction. However, part of the basic attraction of humanistic works lies in their ability to generate such experiences. These experiences, although differing in quality and intensity with different individuals as well as within the same individual at different times, can be characterized as a heightened sense of perception, an elevation of feeling, a purification of emotions, and a sense of exhiliration and release from mundane cares and problems. However, it would be fallacious to conclude that whenever an aesthetic experience occurs, the individual has been immersed in a great humanistic work. The beauties of nature, the aesthetic by-product that sometimes accompanies or follows the creative process (in any field of endeavor), and those rare, but simple and poignant acts in which one learns to relate to others in new and more fruitful ways, all carry strong aesthetic overtones. There also are some who, on occasion, enjoy an aesthetic experience with works of questionable quality. The humanist, then, could not argue the uniqueness of such experiences for his field. Rather, he could more defensibly point to the possible profundity of these experiences and the high potentiality of humanistic works to evoke these experiences frequently in persons of varying backgrounds. There are virtually unlimited possibilities in humanistic works to evoke profound aesthetic experiences, while works of highly questionable quality have far fewer possibilities in this regard, and the experience is likely to be more superficial and evanescent.

So far we have discussed the expressive, subjective, intrinsic, and aesthetic aspects of the appreciative dimension. There are times, however, when the act of appreciation is not only one of finding and prizing a work to be desirable from a personal standpoint, but also one may engage in appraising and evaluating the work. One may evaluate a work and find it desirable and enjoyable as a result. On the other hand, one may find upon completing the evaluative process that even though he does not personally enjoy the work, he can now understand why the work is considered to be outstanding. The observer has not rejected the work out of hand due to a lack of enjoyment, but has learned to "appreciate" or at least to understand the significance of the work and its relationship to other works of its type, even though studying or contemplating the work does not engender an aesthetic experience. In this case one appreciates only in an external sense by applying standards and determining whether the work fulfills the standards. Thus, the evaluative process may be strictly external, or one may also enhance his enjoyment and generate an aesthetic experience which depends upon the individual, the work, and the circumstances surrounding it.

The evaluative process, referred to as the normative dimension of the humanities, must be examined more closely.

The Normative Dimension

A humanistic work is evaluated in terms of its ability to fulfill certain standards. The set of standards appropriate to the process of evaluation varies not only among the respective disciplines but also within a discipline itself. For example, the standards employed in evaluating Romanesque architecture would not be exactly the same as those used in assessing Baroque creations. By the same token, different sets of standards may be appropriate in evaluating novels of social realism as opposed to those used in evaluating the romantic novel.

The term 'standard,' according to *Webster's Third New International Dictionary,* applies to "any authoritative rule, principle, or measure used to determine the quantity, weight, or extent, or especially the value, quality, level, or degree of a thing." Although both quantitative and qualitative evaluations are made of humanistic works, the latter are usually of principal concern to the humanistic scholar.

Standards may be employed in terms of different points of view: economic, political, historical, and aesthetic are the most common points of view among humanistic works. There are those works which are developed to serve certain political ends, or are inadvertently used for a political function, such as to promote patriotism, bravery, or loyalty to the state. The work is then evaluated for its ability to fulfill these functions. Works of this type may be short-lived when the political movement which gave rise to it is eclipsed.

One can also appraise a work from an economic point of view. The appraiser thinks not so much of its aesthetic worth but the economic value of the work in a given market. Many works which today are considered of unusually high quality were economic failures at the time of their creation. One may recall the difficulties Van Gogh had in selling his paintings, or the fact that forty copies of Nietzsche's *Thus Spake Zarathustra* were sold and seven were given away. The list could be multiplied many times. On the other hand, due to varied and diverse reasons relating to each case, some artists achieved renown and economic success during their own lifetime. There is a bias among the literary intelligensia that any book or novel that becomes a bestseller, or at least enjoys large sales, cannot prove to be of any lasting value. This distinction is a rather dubious one, especially when used to prejudge a work. In any case, although appraisals from an economic point of view have their own importance, our concern is with the aesthetic point of view.

One may also approach a humanistic work from an historical point of view. This point of view frequently uses a particular cultural theory and various historical concepts in the act of interpreting and evaluating a work within a certain period or movement in addition to historical movements and the study of biographical information about various artists. One usually begins by locating and observing a set of records, determining how they should be dated, and then ascertaining how they should be organized. Discerning whether a work is an original or a forgery is also a problem when dealing with records.

Finally, the aesthetic point of view looks at a work in terms of its artistic worth and value. One aspect of this point of view is whether the work promotes enjoyment and is conducive to an aesthetic experience. Another aspect is to determine, by applying appropriate standards, the quality of the work. Standards are selected in terms of appropriateness to a particular movement or genre. Multiple standards are applied and the evaluator assays the ability of the work to fulfill the standards. Since a standard is not likely to be satisfied completely, it is necessary to grade the work. This may be expressed in such terms as 'excellent,' 'very good,' 'below average,' or in other terms such as 'highly original,' 'lacking originality,' etc. However, in making evaluations, a humanistic work is usually compared to other works of a similar type. In so doing one is thereby ranking the work by making a comparison with another work whose quality is already known. It may then be evaluated with respect to particular standards as 'better than' or 'inferior to' another work. Thus, it is possible for a work to rank high on some standards and low on others, whereas, some works may actually rank consistently low or consistently high. To make an overall appraisal of a work once the work has been evaluated with respect to the separate standards, it is necessary to determine the weight to be given each standard. Of course, if the standards carry equal weight, it is a simple task to arrive at an overall evaluation. Yet the standards will more than likely not be weighed equally; therefore, it is necessary to see how the work was ranked on each standard, assign the weight, and arrive at an overall grade or evaluation of the work.

Obviously the standards selected for evaluation must be carefully chosen so that they are appropriate to the work under examination. Usually several qualified persons will evaluate a work in order to cross-check multiple evaluations, offer criticisms, and reappraise the work whenever needed. Thus, when appropriate standards are chosen, when the work is compared with others of the same type in which the same standards are relevant, and when qualified persons who attempt to be fair and impartial appraise the work, an overall worth and quality of a work may be determined with a reasonable degree of accuracy. The overall evaluation itself is never final. It is not uncommon for works to be reappraised at a later date, particularly when new evidence is brought to light that may have originally been neglected. There are occasions when a work is reevaluated from a different ideological position, such as Marxism, Freudianism, or existentialism, and this new evaluation usually leads to a new interpretation and appraisal of a work because standards differ according to the ideological or philosophical framework employed. Finally, a work may be evaluated differently in a later generation due to widespread social and cultural change and the overall tenor of the times. This type of reevaluation has resulted in a number of writers such as Nitzsche, Melville, and Poe being evaluated more highly in a subsequent generation, and others, such as Scott Fitzgerald, to drop in esteem.

The Humanities and the Sciences

For many years now the sciences and humanities have alternated between outright hostilities to an uneasy and unstable truce. What seemed to some to be a new conflagration resulting from C. P. Snow's Rede Lecture(10) was actually only a revival of older mistrusts, concerns, and suspicions. What Sir Charles' lecture did was to bring into the open the doubts and questions that many scientists and humanists had secretly harbored for some time. Snow's own explanation for this phenomenon appears to be essentially correct. His explanation is to be found in his "second look" essay, which was prepared as a comment on the world-wide response to his lecture. In the essay he stated— modestly, but no doubt correctly—that original ideas do not carry so fast, and evidently many people must have been giving this issue thought for some time; otherwise, it is unlikely the response would have been instantaneous and widespread(11).

In his lecture Sir Charles noted that for many years in his careers as both scientist and novelist he had had abundant opportunities to circulate in the circles of both groups. In spite of the facts that both groups were similar in intelligence, social origins, race, and income, they seemed to be very far apart in their intellectual interests and attitudes toward life. He dubbed this phenomenon "the two cultures," consisting of the literary and scientific culture. A "gulf of mutual incomprehension" had developed between the two, and sometimes open hostility among the younger members. This was not merely unfortunate, but a critical matter in light of the problems with which societies presently are faced.

Although Snow did not find one of the two groups exclusively responsible for this condition, he did attribute more of the blame to the literary culture. Neither group was conversant with developments in the other's culture. Perhaps some of the scientists had read a little Dickens or occasionally listened to classical music. But this taste was the extent of their delving into the humanities. The literary culture, on the other hand, was even more ignorant of the scientific world. When Snow asked his friends in the literary culture to describe the Second Law of Thermodynamics, their response was "cold" and "negative." Yet, according to Snow, this was like asking the scientific equivalent of: "Have you read a work of Shakespeare's?"(12) Evidently there is no point at which the two cultures join forces or share common concerns.

Yet, in spite of the wrongheadedness of some scientists, the principal culprit is—at least for Snow—the literary culture. What are the charges against this culture? Literature is slower to change than science and does not have built-in corrective mechanisms. More specifically, there are some forms of early twentieth-century art which evince expressions of antisocial feeling. Whereas the scientific culture is future-oriented, the literary culture "responds by wishing the future did not exist."(13) The scientific culture is more rigorous than the literary and is conducted at a higher conceptual level. The social charges that Snow amasses against the traditionalist or literary culture are also serious. He tells us that the traditionalists were never able to understand or accept the industrial revolution, that their programs in English education helped solidify rigid social class distinctions, and finally, that science rather than literature is the only real hope of dealing with the great social problems of our time: nuclear warfare, the gap between the rich and poor nations, and overpopulation.

In reassessing the charges, it appears that Snow has overlooked some of the shortcomings of science while somewhat magnifying those of the literary culture, although it should be kept in mind that Snow was speaking primarily of England; hence, the gap between the two cultures may not be as wide or as unbridgeable in the United States. The charges against the literary culture are best sustained when this culture becomes classical and Ciceronian. Its worship of past masters accompanied by its neglect of the present and the future, its elitism and antidemocratic tendencies, and its tendency to lapse into a sterile pedantry are warranted charges against classical, Ciceronian forms. On the other hand, we have already discussed some of the best features of the humanities, and Snow's critics were also quick to bring to the fore these features. The shortcoming of the sciences and technology have been expressed amply in the preceding chapter; therefore, there is no need to reiterate them.

The debate took an unexpected turn when F. R. Leavis, the renowned British literary critic, in a closed session at Cambridge, attacked Sir Charles with uncontrolled vituperative fury. The story leaked to the press and soon created something of a temporary sensation resulting initially in an outpouring of letters to the papers sympathetic to the Snow position. Leavis' lack of emotional control apparently inhibited his ability to respond to the issues as effectively as we would be led to expect by his previous literary criticisms, although he was able to show that Ruskin and other figures had clearly recognized in their distinction between wealth and well-being that the industrial revolution was not an unmixed blessing. Other writers were able to respond more fully and objectively to the issues and come to the defense of the literary culture by a presentation of the activities and achievements of the humanistic scholars(14).

Actually the present debate has deep historical roots. There were many persons during the nineteenth century who spoke or wrote about the sciences and humanities, their effect on the curriculum, and the benefits and dangers of the industrial revolution. Among the most notable figures were the luminaries Matthew Arnold and T. H. Huxley. In contrast to the more recent debate, both men addressed one another in temperate and respectful tones and endeavored to interpret the other's position fairly and judiciously. Huxley, who had been one of the foremost and effective champions of Darwinism and an opponent of supernaturalism, delivered an address in 1880 titled "Science and Culture." He argued that classical education is not of sufficiently great value for the student of physical science to justify his pursuing such a curriculum and that a scientific education is just as effective as a literary one in its contribution to real culture.

He noted that in the English tradition it is commonly believed that not just a study of literature but principally an education in the works of Greek and Latin antiquity that would provide the student with culture. One versed in other disciplines, no matter how deeply, is still considered a specialist, a person without the stamp of culture, hence, not an educated man.

At this point, Huxley quotes the famous expression of Arnold that the meaning of culture is "to know the best that has been thought and said in the world." Arnold approached literature as a criticism of life, (as Leavis, following in this tradition, was to do later). Huxley interprets Arnold as holding that the essence of culture is a criticism of life, and that literature alone is sufficient for such a criticism. Huxley assents to the former statement, but demurs from the latter. He contends that nations are not likely to advance without utilizing scientific knowledge. In spite of this fact, nineteenth century humanists rest their case upon classical education as the sole approach to culture just as though they were still living in the Renaissance. Yet the modern world is more sharply separated from the Renaissance than the Renaissance was separated from the Middle Ages. This separation is due to the rise of modern science. Huxley observes that science, in contrast to classical studies, appeals not to authority but to nature; it focuses inquiry upon things rather than words, and it is always open to new evidence. Yet the classicist worships ancient Greek culture but ignores their use of reason and scientific method.

Huxley states that in light of human diversity and opportunity, there will be educational paths appropriate for some which will not be so for others. This diversity means that it is equally acceptable, depending upon the individual and his aspirations, for some to pursue a literary and others, a scientific education. Those planning to become scientists or physicians, as well as those "who have to enter early upon the business of life" would be mistaken to pursue a classical education. Yet he warns his listeners that he does not "question the importance of a genuine literary education" (and from his remarks it is evident that in such an education contemporary literature and modern languages of English, French, and German should be offered). In conclusion, a man with an exclusive scientific training will have a "mental twist" as surely as one with an exclusive literary training.

Matthew Arnold delivered an address in 1882 titled "Literature and Science" in response to Huxley's lecture. Arnold's reply is predicated upon his statement that in our culture "the aim being to know ourselves and the world, we have, as the means to this end, to know the best which has been thought and said in the world." He proceeds by first indicating what he means by the process of knowing Greek and Latin antiquity. It should not be a superficial and decorative humanism; neither should it be merely a knowledge of vocabulary, grammar, and so many portions of authors in these languages. Rather, one should know their lives, activities, their genius, and what of value we can learn from them. When one studies the Roman Empire he should focus on more than *belles-lettres;* he should come to understand the political, legal, administrative, and military aspects of the lives of the people. The same type of learning holds with ancient Greece. One should understand their art, mathematics, science, and their use of reason and the scientific method — not merely their literature and histories. Arnold adds that he is also in favor of studying modern works. He then observes that he and Professor Huxley have no real disagreement because both hold that the scientific study of nature should be an integral part of one's education just as literature and art should be.

But there is one area of disagreement remaining. Arnold objects to the proposal by some reformers to make natural science the main part of education. Humane letters enjoys the distinctive functions of engaging the emotions, and provide us with a sense of conduct and of beauty. As men's minds are cleared by scientific thinking and its results, humane letters come to be studied for what they truly are — "the criticism of life by gifted men." Thus, there need be no invidious comparison between humane letters and the natural sciences. However, those who have no great talent for the study of nature will be better served by a study of letters, for it will "call out their being at more points, will make them live more."

Some advocate the removal of Latin and Greek from education. However if the instincts for beauty and conduct are served by these literatures, society, in fulfilling its own self-preservation instincts, will strive to preserve them. It may be that humane letters will temporarily lose their preeminence, but they will in time reestablish their leading place in the curriculum. Human nature being what it is, man will always find them irresistibly attractive. In fact, the need to study them is even greater today, according to Arnold, "as they have the more and the greater results of science to relate to the need in man for conduct, and to the need in him for beauty."

Doubtlessly, we would not have the present gulf between the cultures if more of the contingents were as sane, sensible, and humane as Arnold and Huxley. The issues that they raise are still the same today, even though the details and the protagonists differ. If more humanists conceived their undertakings with the liberality of vision shown by Arnold, then such criticisms that more commonly are directed against them would not apply. And if more scientists could see the worth of humanistic studies when placed in a more balanced arrangement with the sciences, then it is likely that mutual suspicions would be considerably mitigated.

The difficulty of the humanists, particularly the literary humanists, is that they wish to sanction practices which were elitist, undemocratic, and slavishly imitative of past masters. Not realizing that the past only comes alive and takes on significance in its continuity with present concerns and problems, the humanists too often lapses into a sterile classicism. Since the idea of "classics" did not emerge until the Renaissance and since ancient Greeks had no "classic," and did not pursue such a course of study, it is highly questionable that they would have ever developed to the heights that they did.

In light of Arnold's thesis that the distinctive role of the humanities should be that of providing us with a sense of conduct and of beauty, it is sometimes difficult today to see exactly how some humanists are serving such ends. The knowledge explosion, although greatest in the physical sciences, has also had profound effects upon the humanities. This explosion has led to highly specialized studies in the humanities whose audience is a small body of fellow specialists. Although the studies may be meticulous and may result in uncovering certain minor facets of a former great writer's life or work, they scarcely contribute to the ideals Arnold so eloquently espoused.

At the same time the problems of specialization in the sciences are even more acute, the point has been reached in which scientists in the same discipline may experience difficulties in communicating their research to one another. The few humanists who wish to acquire a better knowledge of modern science often find themselves bewildered by the esoteric terminology and statements of experimental design. This barrier exists because they lack a strong foundation in the particular science with which to interpret scientific research, and this problem is rendered more acute by their deficiencies in advanced mathematics.

During the period in which Huxley was writing, one of the principal problems was the relation of science and industrial development. Today we can see that starting first with the work of a few inventors, and then later with a systematic application of scientific findings to industrial processes, the industrial age was ushered in. It brought both great economic and material advances as well as much grief and suffering. Scientists such as Snow have emphasized the advances that the application of science made possible, while such humanists as Charles Dickens sought to arouse people to ameliorate the wretched urban conditions resulting from rapid industrialization in England. Although Snow can rightfully speak about the great medical advances in the Western nations which have virtually eliminated epidemics, decreased human suffering, and prolonged life, he is amazingly silent over the barbarities inflicted upon mankind as a result of the mushrooming of scientific inventions of destruction.

Some scientists do claim that their task is to pursue truth and to uncover new knowledge. The use of this knowledge, especially for purposes which they had not conceived or intended, is not their responsibility. But this evasion of responsibility is the very point at issue today. Science has placed no real check, except for several exceptional cases, upon their researches; they have embraced the questionable conviction that everything that can be known ought to be known. The problem today is for scientists to decide among all the things which can be done the ones which rightfully should be done. This statement is not a plea to curtail theoretical research; rather, it points to the need of scientists to be more selective in determining their projects and to refuse to work on those projects results of which can be employed for wholesale human destruction. As Price has said, "it cannot be worth while sacrificing all else that humanity holds dear in order to allow science to grow unchecked for only one or two more doubling periods."(15) What is needed is an international body under law with sufficient power to bring the nuclear arsenals and other weapons of scientific destruction under rigorous inspection and control, and to destroy those weapons less amenable to control. But so long as science is in the throes of a spiraling arms race with opposing sides presently capable of unleashing and delivering enough megatons to destroy their opponents 100 times or more, science is fueling the fires of a nuclear holocaust. There have been notable scientists who have spoken out against this suicidal race, but other than an agreement on the banning of above-ground testing, little progress has been made. This advocation of arms control is not to minimize or detract from the work of some scientists in helping to bring about an international test-ban treaty. The important point is that the scientific community, in general, aided and abetted by the military-industrial complex, will try to discover anything that can be known and will permit these discoveries to be used for political purposes.

The scientific community needs to undertake new projects with far greater care in order that their discoveries will benefit mankind rather than lead to its eventual destruction. Whenever new discoveries may be put to practical uses, scientists should be concerned that these uses contribute to the type of cultural environment in which men can grow, be productive, and relate themselves to one another in a spirit of trust and cooperation. A vision of what a truly creative culture may be is needed. This need is where humanists and scientist can join forces.

Of course, it is commonly said that science itself is neutral, that it is concerned with means not ends. Science does not tell us how to act or how to live; it deals not with values but only tries to uncover the laws of the universe. For Arnold as well as others, the humanities purportedly serve the functions of providing an appreciation of beauty and direction in moral affairs. Science makes no commitment to a form of government, according to Snow, because the scientific enterprise can prosper in the Soviet Union as well as in more democratic countries. What Snow overlooks, however, is the amount of control that officials exercise over science, so that research in many areas of the social sciences and psychology, unless arriving at conclusions which support the official party line, are strongly inhibited.

It would be a mistake, however, to consider values to be the exclusive preserve of the humanities. First of all, values may be found in terms of the ethics of the scientific community. Values also frequently occur as subject matter for scientific inquiry. And finally, values enter science in terms of the selection of problems, the order with which they are dealt, and the resources expended on their solutions. Although some scientists, particularly some in the social sciences, ignored or denied these facts due to the sway of scientism, they need not have adopted this posture because it is only when values prejudge solutions, not when they dictate problems, that they make for bias.

Scientists also share certain beliefs which have value overtones. They believe, if only pragmatically, that nature is characterized by certain regularities (although they may only be of a statistical character in the microscopic world). They value certain types of proof, the elimination of error, and the observance of parsimony.

Since scientists deal with values in a manner appropriate to their own inquiries, the question presents itself as to the respective roles that the sciences and the humanities play in this matter. Since the fruits of science have been used not only to destroy human life but also to improve it, we need to determine how to bring about the latter conditions. Science in its broadest sense is probably best able to inform us how to reach the goals we seek, although the insights of the humanities should not be minimized in such a capacity. With our goals in mind, science can show us how to make our cities habitable, how to provide better health care, how to raise the standard of living of underdeveloped nations, and how to provide needed material comforts. Applied science is not error free, but with a willingness to take some risk and to contribute the necessary resources to achieve success, science today is in a position to dramatically alter human cultures. Some have suggested that science may be capable of resolving the basic value problems that divide men and need not defer the issue to the humanities. This position has been supported by John Dewey, Erich Fromm, and others. It has been strongly opposed, for different reasons, by most humanists, the positivists, and by a large majority of scientists and social scientists.

One approach to such an undertaking is to employ the values already given in human experience and test them through the use of the scientific method by observing what possible social consequences result when they are put into practice. The test of any set of values is their effect upon the lives of people and the social conditions which they bring about. Every culture has its own value systems which, heretofore, have been sanctioned by folklore, tradition, and institutional interests. What is needed is to subject these systems to scientific testing to determine whether the claims made in their behalf can actually be supported. By this means, modes of inquiry which have transformed other aspects of human culture can be brought to bear upon men's most vital concerns.

This position holds that ethical premises are to be found operating within the context of experience, and since there are many different types of experiences undergone by each individual, the ethical premises utilized will be chosen for their appropriateness to the particular context. Once the disputants agree on general ethical premises applicable to the situation, the scientific method enables them to choose the means which offer the greatest possibility of bringing about the desired social outcomes. But it should be noted that ethical principles which are accepted in one situation may be questioned in another context. "Honesty" may be an ethical principle in one context, but it may be inappropriate in another. For instance, if Mrs. Vanderbilt asks you while attending her party whether you like her new hat, you are averse to tell her that it is rather ludicrous, even though it looks that way to you. On a more serious note, you have just been told by your friend's physician that your friend has terminal cancer and that any shock will likely cause sudden death due to a weak heart. Your friend asks you to reveal to him the physician's diagnosis of his case. In this context would honesty apply? Thus, we can see that no ethical principle is infallible; all are open to question, but some may never be discarded, even temporarily.

The difficulty with the contextualist position is that it does not explain why we should regard known ethical beliefs as justified. In other words, the contextualist position takes certain ethical principles as unquestioned within a particular situation, observes the possible consequences of various courses of action, and, after assessing them, chooses the one that will realize the ethical principle to the highest degree. But it does not follow that starting with given principles which may entail certain types of consequences when acted upon, the consequences are justified. At best, they may prove to be consistent.

This survey attempts to show that values need not be considered the exclusive domain of the humanities, that the sciences, once they have cast off positivism and scientism, are capable of making important contributions in this area. At the same time, the limitations of science have been briefly analyzed; the justification of ethical principles, as matters presently stand, seems to be beyond their ability to perform, at least in terms of their methodologies and working assumptions. It falls to the humanities to develop justification for ethical principles. The most direct approach to this task is found in philosophy where an analysis is made of major ethical systems and the grounds for their support. It is also true that entire ethical systems are called into question in plays and novels. Here a wide range of styles, forms, techniques and dramatic devices can be employed that frequently reach audiences averse to a study of philosophical treatises.

Arnold also cites the humanities not only for providing direction to moral conduct but also for cultivating a sense of beauty. Although the humanities are preeminent in aesthetic matters, it would be mistaken to consider the sciences oblivious to these. The sciences, even though they do not usually undertake systematic studies in aesthetics, have their own aesthetic canons. An hypothesis may have great heuristic value. A mathematical proof or scientific theory may be spoken of as "elegant." A creative act in which a breakthrough on an obdurate and inveterate scientific problem is achieved is also spoken of in aesthetic terms. Scientists. and especially engineers, create technological structures some of which manifest considerable aesthetic worth. They also create mathematical and theoretical systems which, although less tangible then technological achievements, possess their own aesthetic components and overtones that may be observed and enjoyed by those sufficiently knowledgeable in the field.

There are other similarities between humanists and scientists. Both attempt to find, as Bronowski claims, a sense of unity within disorder. Beauty, Coleridge says, is "unity in variety," and for Bronowski science itself is the quest "to discover unity in the wild variety of nature—or more exactly, in the variety of our experience."(16)

Susan Sontag argues persuasively the growing similarities between the arts and the sciences(17). The arts, she says, are increasingly becoming an area for specialists; hence, the creations of artists demand a specialized language in order that they may be grasped. Music, dance, philosophy, and other fields are cases in point; only the novel is an exception. Specialization and abstruseness, then, are characteristics today of both the sciences and the arts. Art also parallels the sciences in its historical-mindedness, for contemporary art is replete with references to its history, while science, too, displays an historical interest in terms of tracing cumulative discoveries and in new explorations in the history of science.

According to Sontag, the arts—dance, architecture, painting, sculpture, and music — draw widely upon science. Only when literature is employed as a model for the arts do we fall into a discussion of two cultures and speak of a gulf between them. With emphasis in the arts on coolness, exactness, and its sense of "problems," they are closer to science than ever before. The notion that the function of a work of art is to convey moral sentiments and ideas is misleading, especially for today's art. The new art, for Sontag, is not just a criticism of life, but an extension of life—it represents "(new) modes of vivacity" and the "analysis and extension of sensations."

Developing the thesis that each culture places a premium on some senses and permits or encourages others to atrophy, Sontag notes that the new art makes serious demands upon these unused senses, therefore, may prove at times to generate painful rather than the pleasurable experiences that we usually associate with art. There still is, of course, the element of play in the arts, but the present seriousness of the arts precludes some of the familiar pleasures, as is the case with the sciences.

Whether the present developments represent more than a transient transformation is difficult to say; but it is increasingly evident that Matthew Arnold's conception of the humanities, with its formulation upon a literary model, is not fully adequate to capture the full range of artistic and humanistic works found today. There is also considerable overlapping in functions once believed to be exclusively the domain of science, and science can make some contribution to the fulfillment of these functions. Science and the humanities are, in some ways, moving closer together. Finally, what may be emerging is a new unitary sensibility in the humanities and the sciences.

Questions for Discussion

1. In what way and to what extent can the humanities in their present form contribute to the students' demands for "relevant knowledge" (as this term is used in Chapter 5)?

2. What present characteristics of the humanities need to be changed in order that they may more fully contribute to this ideal?

3. Are there certain experiences, knowledges, skills, and insights that all persons, irrespective of their future careers, need to acquire before they could be considered an educated person (as developed in Chapter 4)? How would these experiences differ, other than that of greater complexity, as a student moves through the public schools and into his college work?

4. To what extent are Snow's critcisms of the humanists justified? Are the charges leveled against the scientists supportable (such as those presented in Chapter 6)? How can the existing suspicions and disputes between the two groups be alleviated?

5. There are great and even unprecedented changes occurring in the larger culture. What responsibilities do the humanities have for helping the individual to interpret, understand, and modify these changes?

For Further Reading

Some works especially valuable for interpreting the meaning and significance of the humanities in today's world are: Theodore Meyer Green, ed., *The Meaning of the Humanities,* Princeton, N.J.: Princeton University Press, 1938; David H. Stevens, *The Changing Humanities,* New York: Harper

& Bros., 1953; Howard Mumford Jones, *One Great Society*, New York: Harcourt, Brace and World, 1959.

Standards of criticism and studies in aesthetic values are treated in the following works: Herbert Read, *The Nature of Literature*, New York: Grove Press, 1958; I. A. Richards, *Practical Criticism*, New York: Harcourt, 1929; Vernon Hall, Jr., *A Short History of Literary Criticism*, New York: New York University Press, 1963; Melvin Rader, ed., *A Modern Book of Esthetics*, 3rd ed., New York: Holt, Rinehart, and Winston, 1960; Monroe C. Beardsley, *Aesthetics*, New York: Harcourt, Brace and World, 1958; Curt John Ducasse, *The Philosophy of Art*, New York: Dover Publications, 1966; John Dewey, *Art as Experience*. New York: Minton, Balch, 1935.

Art and aesthetics in education are discussed in: *Art Education*, National Society for the Study of Education, 64th Yearbook, Part II, Chicago: University of Chicago Press, 1965; Elliott W. Eisner and David W. Ecker, *Readings in Art Education*, Waltham, Mass.: Blaisdell, 1967; Herbert Read, *Education Through Art*, London: Faber and Faber, 1943; Ralph A. Smith, ed., *Aesthetics and Criticism in Art Education*, Chicago: Rand McNally, 1966.

The classical essays by Huxley and Arnold on the conflict between the sciences and the humanities can be found in most textbooks on British prose and poetry. Snow's controversial ideas on this topic are in *The Two Cultures: And A Second Look*, New York: The New American Library, 1963. Among the other works of especial interest are: Martin Green, *Science and the Shabby Curate of Poetry*, London: Longmens Green, 1964; M. E. Prior, *Science and the Humanities*. Evanston, Ill.: Northwestern University Press, 1962; David K. Cornelius and Edwin St. Vincent, eds., *Cultures in Conflict: Perspectives on the Snow-Leavis Controversy*, Chicago, Scott, Foresman, 1964.

Notes

1. Ralph Barton Perry, "A Definition of the Humanities," Theodore Meyer Green, ed., *The Meaning of the Humanities* (Princeton, N.J.: Princeton University Press, 1938), p. 26.

2. Frederick Rudolph, *The American College and University* (New York: Random House, 1965), p. 233.

3. Gilbert Chinard, "Literature and the Humanities," Greene, ed., *The Meaning of the Humanities*, p. 153.

4. Perry, "A Definition of the Humanities," p. 30.

5. Among the different interpretations, see the following: Jacob W. Getzels, "Creative Thinking, Problem-solving, and Instruction," E. R. Hilgard, ed., *Theories of Learning and Instruction,* 63rd Yearbook, NSSE (Chicago: University of Chicago Press, 1964), pp. 240-67; Brewster Ghiselin, ed., *The Creative Process* (New York: New American Library, 1952); D. W. MacKinnon, "The Nature and Nurture of Creative Talent," *American Psychologist* 17 (1962): 484-95; A. H. Maslow, "The Creative Attitude," *The Structurist* 3 (1963): 4-10; A. Newell, et al., "The Process of Creative Thinking," H. E. Gruber, et al. eds., *Contemporary Approaches to Creative Thinking* (New York: Atherton Press, 1962), pp. 63-119.

6. Maslow, "The Creative Attitude."

7. Getzels, "Creative Thinking, Problem-solving and Instruction."

8. J. P. Guilford, "Traits of Creativity," H. H. Anderson, ed., *Creativity and Its Cultivation* (New York: Harper and Row, 1959), pp. 142-61.

9. At least this exposition is similar to the creative process gathered from certain autobiographical material of leading figures in sciences as well as humanities. See Brewster Ghiselin, ed., *The Creative Process.*

10. See C. P. Snow, *The Two Cultures: And A Second Look* (New York: The New York American Library, 1963).

11. *Ibid.,* p. 54

12. *Ibid.,* p. 20.

13. *Ibid.,* p. 17. If true, this presumably is due to the classicism and its worship of historical exemplars that we spoke of earlier.

14. See, for instance, Lionel Trilling, "Science, Literature & Culture: A Comment on the Leavis-Snow Controversy," *Commentary* (June 1962), pp. 461-77.

15. Derek Price, *Science since Babylon* (New Haven, Conn.: Yale University Press, 1961), p. 117.

16. J. Bronowski, *Science and Human Values* (New York: Harper, Torchbooks, 1959), p. 27.

17. Susan Sontag, *Against Interpretation* (New York: Dell Publishing Co., 1966), pp. 293-304.

Part Three
The Role of Education in Society

Chapter Eight
The New Left and Conflicting Roles of Higher Education

Since the issues concerning the role of education in society are large and complex, it will be necessary to examine them here only at certain crucial points which are likely to indicate significant changes and new directions for the future of education. Chapter Eight will investigate the New Left and its influence on the role of higher education in the larger society. Chapter Nine will view the fashioning of new roles and responsibilities in terms of the struggle for equal educational opportunities as it affects policy decisions on the control of education. Finally, Chapter Ten will assess projected trends and developments in terms of their likelihood of influencing and changing future roles of education.

The issues surrounding the New Left and its influence upon the roles of higher education in the United States can best be viewed by laying a background for an understanding of present roles and by examining how the present roles became accepted. Through such an examination, it is possible to see the many conflicts that arose and the reasons these conflicts and disagreements still exist today.

241

Role Conflict in the Development
of the American University

American higher education exerts considerable influence on the larger society. The magnitude of influence has probably never been greater than it is today. The nature and direction of this influence, along with the many interconnecting links and alliances with other institutions, are presently being challenged. The outcome of this challenge is likely to result in various redefinitions of the role of higher education. In order to see what possible new roles may develop, what the existing roles are and how they are being challenged must be clearly defined. To understand these roles, it is important to comprehend how they have come to take their current form.

Three dominant conceptions of higher education were found during the late nineteenth century; a fourth conception—that of mental discipline—had by that time declined from its erstwhile position of ascendancy. The three dominant conceptions at that time were liberal culture, utility, and research(1). Certain unique features in the liberal culture ideal at the turn of the century which do not coincide with the discussion in the preceding chapter make it necessary to explore the conception momentarily.

The Liberal Culture Ideal

Some ideals in American higher education, such as the utility ideal, were more or less indigenous to the culture. Others, such as the research and liberal culture ideals, drew heavily from western Europe. The scientific research ideal was brought back to this country principally by American scholars who visited or studied in Germany; the liberal culture ideal, on the other hand, was modeled more after the British system. But each of these ideals was to be reinterpreted in light of the American experience.

Actually, the proponents of liberal culture were in a minority in the late nineteenth century, but they compensated for lack of number by being more vocal and active in academic affairs than some of their colleagues in scientific research. They tended to exert more influence in the small liberal arts colleges than in the multipurpose universities. Some of the older classicists including religious educators who dominated the church-related colleges who conceived of their task as building moral character and mental discipline were eschewed, while other classicists, recognizing the errors of their ways, began to adopt the liberal culture ideals. Too often religious educators and classicists supported the formal discipline theory (which was coming under severe attack); therefore, they were accused of a narrow interpretation of the curriculum and an obsolete theory of learning.

The liberal culture proponents were advocates of studying modern languages from a literary standpoint. Many classicists were not prepared to accept this innovation. Other opponents were the philologists, who sought to convert the study of languages into a science. The fine arts had not as yet assumed a sufficiently large place in the liberal arts curriculum to be of any great help to the literary men, but philosophers of the idealist persuasion could be counted on for sympathetic support. However, idealism was to decline in philosophy departments during the early part of this century as positivistic and pragmatic tendencies expanded.

The outcomes of liberal culture were extolled in such phrases as "breadth of learning and understanding," "sensibility and artistic feeling," and "serenity and solidity of mind."(2) The student would combine broad learning with aesthetic tastes and moral development. A study of literary models and philosophical works was used to contribute to character development rather than reliance upon religion. Ethics rather than religion became the basis for the formation of character.

In seeking breadth of learning, it was important that the breadth not degenerate into a mere dilettanteism. The breadth that was sought could be attained, advocates thought, by a study of the standards of past civilizations. In this quest they opposed the narrow religious fervor of the fundamentalists, the emphasis upon a utilitarian accommodation to the demands of a bourgeoning industrial economy, and the highly specialized scientific studies found in the graduate schools. Both science and the "lower" vocational and utilitarian demands represented to them an impoverishment of the human spirit. The vocationalism and practicality of higher education was looked upon as pandering to crass materialistic interests. Scientific studies were viewed as pedantic and making little or no contribution to the development of the whole man, while the fear and suspicion of the scientist's claim to account for the whole of reality led literary men to attack this presumption. They were aware that science and utilitarian concerns were beginning to dominate the university, but scarcely did they divine the vast influence that science and technology would exert over American life and education during the next fifty years.

At the center of the literary men's ideals was a fundamental uneasiness and unrest with certain democratic notions. The cultivated man, they believed, was a gentleman, a man of polish and style. They recognized that it was easier to develop a gentleman if the young man was well-bred and came from the proper background. This belief led them to identify with certain aristocratic strains of thought and created aversions toward attempting to reshape middle class youth. This belief also carried over to the hiring practices of some departments, so that the prospective candidate's manners and style took on more importance in some instances than his academic qualifications. The clash of the gentleman ideal with the concept of the dignity and worth of the common man was never really reconciled.

Literary men of the period were usually receptive to and prided themselves on an understanding and appreciation of current developments in European thought. Uppermost was English letters, but they also knew of the work taking place in France and among German idealists and romantics. The classical tongues were still to be taught but more as a means to know what civilized man had thought and said rather than as little more than grammatical exercises, as was the wont of the classicists. Through studies of civilization, of modern languages, letters, and philosophy not only could the gentleman be created, but it was earnestly hoped that this broad culture would somehow trickle down to the masses, and society would eventually be uplifted. This approach rather than direct political action was the literary men's plan for elevating the national character and the boorishness of political life. But since some recognized the great magnitude of such a task, they frequently turned away from the sordid affairs of everyday life and sought repose and renewed strength in their university sanctuary.

This movement, both at the turn of the century and today, has never been a genuine force for social reform. It also found itself more sympathetic and at home with Plato's, rather than Locke's or Paine's, political ideas. Its position has been eroded through many social and technological changes and by the greater need today for specialized talent. It is customary to find a university administrator invoking the liberal culture ideals while simultaneously channeling funds into the sciences. There is no question that the literary man is on the defensive today as he sees his former influence vitiated, and the centers of power either opposing or ignoring his demands. The explosion of knowledge and the need for specialized manpower have wreaked havoc to the cultural ideal, but just as damaging in another way is the literary man's own failure to exemplify the ideals of broad learning that he espouses (as was noted in the previous chapter). One sign in his favor is that as the work-week is progressively shortened, a larger segment of the population will turn to reading as a form of liberal learning. However, there is little reason to believe that people will turn to such pursuits merely because they have more free time; in fact, a concerted campaign aimed at reeducation will be needed—and the mass media do not seem to be cooperating. Not only is the magnitude of the task likely to be discouraging but also the time it would take away from specialized scholarly pursuits would be large. But more important, the belief in "high-brow," "middle-brow," and "low-brow" culture is not expected to enamor the literary man with the masses.

That the liberal culture ideal is not actually defunct in certain liberal arts colleges is not to be denied. However, such programs have little appeal to the majority of college students, and it is unlikely that enough of the "higher" culture will seep down to the masses to bring about a transformation in character. Although the concept of broad learning and liberal culture is still considered by a small minority as the most vital role for higher education to pursue, today it has given way to the greater influence of other roles.

The Research Role

The research function is such an integral and significant dimension of higher education today that it is difficult to imagine a time when this role was practically nonexistent. Yet early programs of higher education, more limited and restricted in their functions, scarcely envisioned a place for basic research. American higher education from its earliest days offered a classical education for the development of the gentleman and for the shaping of character. Vocational preparation was largely the task of apprenticeship programs outside the formal educational system. Only the professions of law, medicine, and theology, it was believed, merited preparation in higher education. As many new church-related institutions were founded in the nineteenth century, character training became associated in these institutions with formal religious training as an integral part of college life, while the formal discipline theory, more often than not, was used as the psychological guide for organizing and directing learning activities.

But during the latter-half of the nineteenth century this pattern was strongly challenged: first, by the development of land-grant colleges and, second, by the introduction of the research function. Germany had made considerable progress in developing graduate education and promoting scientific research, and as word of its accomplishments spread, a number of American students and scholars traveled abroad to study for their Ph. D. degrees. Apparently there were other attractive features. At the time one could live in Germany for a year of study at approximately one-third the cost of a year at Cornell, Harvard, or Johns Hopkins(3), and some of the provincial German universities were, relatively speaking, diploma mills(4). As young American scientists gained inspiration from German universities, they interpreted the German ideals in a rather unique fashion, since there were distinct departures from the ideals as they were transplanted to American soil. Investigation and writing as opposed to teaching could just as well include studies of Hegelian idealism for German scholars, and statements by scientists of their aims usually paid homage to those ideals. Not so in American universities, where more positivistic, painstaking, and highly specialized scientific investigations became common. True, this trend could also be found in some German universities, but it actually constituted only one aspect of German graduate education. German methods became wedded to British empiricism in the research activities of American scientists(5).

The single event during the 1870's which symbolized the German ideal of research was the founding of Johns Hopkins University in Baltimore. Through the leadership of its president, Daniel Coit Gilman, doctoral programs were established based upon the research ideal, and the belief in pure scientific research was espoused as a worthy role for the university. In fact, Gilman was prepared to argue in the face of a skeptical audience the utility of pure research, citing many of the new technological inventions that were transforming industry and everyday life as a result of basic research and applied mathematics(6). The Hopkins experiment encouraged many scholars to visit or study in Germany; it also proved to be an influence on the developing state universities as they modified the ideal to suit their own needs and objectives.

In light of these developments the conception of science began to change. Earlier science had been considered any well organized body of principles within an area of knowledge. Thus, philosophers and classicists could speak of the scientific organization of subject matter in their disciplines. But science now became associated with the search for evidence of nature's workings and the uncovering of basic laws which would explain the data of scientific investigation. Such popular designations as "natural history" and "natural philosophy" were replaced by a conception of science which specifically denoted the uncovering of laws governing the material universe.

In a Darwinian age in which organized religion considered itself threatened by heretical interpretations of creation, the new scientific spirit which swept through the graduate schools afforded little comfort to fundamentalists and more orthodox educators. The scientific spirit of inquiry was conceived of as a skeptical, questioning attitude toward accepted beliefs. Many long held preconceptions, whether originating from deductive systems, religion, or custom, would fall before scientific discoveries. These views, in any case, were held by many of the young scientists, and such ideas served as an iconoclastic force in higher education. Yet most scientists did not enter into an uninhibited battle against the established values of society, and though they were less religiously orthodox than the majority of their fellow citizens, they usually attempted to retain those religious beliefs which were reasonably compatible with their scientific outlook(7). Scientific research led to greater specialization in the university and encouraged scholars to consider it academically respectable to investigate minute topics exhaustively. The new graduate programs also led to striking differences in the way students were treated.

At Johns Hopkins, President Gilman urged that only students sufficiently prepared to provide the faculty with challenging stimulation be admitted to the program(8). This shifted the burden found in the older colleges where the faculty was expected to take students, some of whom were of unexceptional talents, and stimulate their intellectual and moral development. The ideal that scientific investigation was the chief aim of the university spread in a somewhat diluted form to other universities, hence, faculties should no longer be burdened with untalented and immature students. In time this emphasis led to researchers placing a low value on their role as teachers. By the turn of the century the Ph. D. degree was mandatory for employment at the leading institutions. The next step was to insist upon scholarly publication as a requirement for advancement. Thus, the "publish or perish" doctrine was installed, and the research emphasis of the university had gained a position of dominance by 1910(9). This emphasis was reinforced by the formation in 1900 of the Association of American Universities, an elite organization established by university presidents and deans who wished to discuss policy-making in matters of higher degree programs. Only a dozen of the top institutions were originally admitted to membership, leading other excluded universities to covet membership, which they could only gain by emulating certain standards. The AAU agreed that vocational training and research are two worthy functions for institutions to fulfill, while the latter function was thought to merit special attention and promotion. Thus, those institutions seeking membership in the AAU would perforce have to strengthen their graduate and research programs.

The research role has continued to grow within the past fifty years in our leading state universities, land-grant institutions, and prominent private universities, and the expansion of this role has involved the university more intimately and directly in the affairs of the larger society, particularly in the corporate structure and in the military-industrial complex. These new alliances began to be seriously questioned on a widespread scale during the 1960's, and the challenges posed by the New Left to the hegemony exerted by the military-industrial complex, including its involvement and influence over some of the scientific research conducted in universities, has led to open clashes on several campuses. Out of these confrontations may come a reinterpretation and reappraisal of university policies governing their research functions.

The Utility Role

What seemed to be a sense of unity, whether real or imagined, appeared to vanish as colleges in the late nineteenth century became universities and assumed new and contrasting—if not conflicting—functions. The belief that some subjects and programs had inherent value and were essential to the molding of an educated man became increasingly questioned until some claimed that each subject is of as much worth as any other. As universities assumed new roles while at the same time attempting to maintain older functions which occasionally were modified in various ways, diversity of faculty outlooks widened and an uneasy truce among the different groups was sometimes secured by discussing only "safe" issues. In other cases, however, underlying suspicions ignited clashes between different factions. The older harmony of outlook that found only occasional dissenters became an historical relic. Research, liberal culture, and vocational service were the multiple ideals that divided faculty loyalties and commitments.

The utility ideal, although present to a minor degree before the Civil War, emerged during the land-grant movement in the 1860's as an ideal sufficiently strong to challenge any competing ideal which vied for administration and faculty loyalty. Utility-minded educators became ensconced within the system rather than, as formerly the case, having it make their views heard from their stations outside of the ivied walls. Utility educators began to be found in large numbers in the applied sciences and the social sciences. They also were able to substantially strengthen their position by placing men of their persuasion within the administrative hierarchy.

The spirit of vocationalism coupled with the incorporation of new professional programs within the university structure assured the ideal of utility a secure and significant place in higher education. Besides the land-grant movement, a great deal of technical knowledge was needed to fulfill the needs of a rapidly developing industrial economy. Industrialism also meant a greater division of labor and a need for specialized abilities. Vocational preparation, which was once handled largely through apprenticeship programs and had no connection with university responsibilities, became incorporated within higher education. The older colleges had prepared men for the professions of law, medicine, and theology; teacher preparation was relegated to the normal schools and teacher institutes. But with the installation of many new vocational programs, a blurring of the former sharp distinctions between vocations and professions occurred. The label "profession" had formerly been reserved for those occupations requiring preparation within higher education(10). The apprenticeship route was being supplanted for a number of careers, and the scope and responsibility of the university was greatly widened. By the admission of many new vocations, a leveling tendency occurred among occupations so that those considered superior in their social prestige due to the requirement of advanced study were leveled to a position of greater parity while the new vocations continued to rise in status. Still, all careers were equal in principle, as democratic or Jacksonian rhetoric would have it, but in actuality the older professions still retained some of their distinctive status.

Besides the need to develop technical knowledge for industry and to prepare specialists, the utility ideal expressed itself in divergent ways. Some educators attacked the monkishness of scholars and the artificial and pedantic problems with which they dealt. The educator, they argued, should maintain close contact with the life of the larger society, which was more "real" than the life of the university. They called for practical men, not pedants, men who could grapple with the problems of life. The university would serve society by preparing practical men with the needed technical competence, and the university itself would disseminate technical knowledge to the home, farm, and factory. Some advocated that the university assume whatever functions requested by the citizenry. Pressures were often brought to bear on educators by politicians and vested-interest groups to lower their notion of "practicality" so that preparation for a motley array of new trades would become part of the university curriculum.

The problem with the ideals of utility and practicality, just as today, was that educators, administrators and the public usually failed to agree upon the meaning of these ideals in terms of actual policies and practices. Some wanted the universities to instill various civic virtues or develop leaders who would clean up politics. Other scholars concentrated on applying knowledge which held promise for social reform. Several administrators interpreted utility in terms of the crassest materialistic desires, and some conceived utility in ethical terms as a crusade for public service. Rather than turning to the new American philosophy of pragmatism, educators usually thought in terms of "social efficiency." This notion was able to mesh the scientific with the practical for purposes of organizing the university for community service(11). Yet the ideal functioned in the hands of administrators more as a slogan and rallying cry for instituting new programs and adopting new policies rather than as an explanatory theory with the power to order a whole range of phenomena.

Many of the same ideals can be found today in higher education, even though the former ideals of utility, practicality, and social efficiency may no longer be invoked. What can be observed is that a wide array of vocational programs are now securely a part of higher education, that programs preparing students for technical specialties compete with the pure research ideal and the liberal culture ideal. That the vocational ideal is dominant in higher education is shown by a study of the objectives of students on eleven campuses. The study revealed "that 68 per cent of the working class students" considered preparation for a vocation to be their primary goal in college(12). The need for specialized, highly-trained manpower has grown as technology has become more complex while at the same time, labor leaders have desired to keep youth from flooding the job markets. Thus, youth have been delayed in securing full-time employment, embarking on careers, and becoming economically independent. A period of time is now set aside for career preparation for the young adult who, a generation earlier, would be on the labor market.

Manpower is considered today more in light of national goals. During the late 1950's when fears abounded that the United States had fallen behind the Soviet Union in the space race, cries went up that our educational institutions, rather than the priorities established by the federal government during the early 1950's, were the cause of the debacle. The charge was that an insufficient number of scientists, mathematicians, and engineers had been prepared. This fear lead to the passage of the National Defense Education Act, which was designed to correct these deficiencies.

Besides the turn toward national manpower needs, there also is the widespread conviction today that one must go to college if he wishes to secure a good job. The information is usually cited in a cause-effect relationship that the college graduate earns so many hundreds of thousands more in a lifetime than the high-school graduate. This sounds strange to many older citizens who remember their program of apprenticeship, rather than college, training and the small number of youth in their generation who completed high school. Naturally the composition of the student body in higher education was vastly different than it is today.

Other University Roles

Of the three basic functions of higher education and three ways that education serves and influences the larger society—liberal, culture, research—the latter two roles have expanded while the former has diminished.

Universities serve the function of preserving knowledge, not only by the maintenance of records, archives, and libraries, but also by the transmission of knowledge to students. Emphasis is greater today on extending knowledge through organized research, which is in sharp contrast to the purposes of American colleges up to the late nineteenth century when the transmission and preservation of knowledge was a dominant function. This latter function has been maintained today, but with the expansion of research facilities and the greater magnitude of the university's research enterprises, the teaching function has declined in prestige.

Higher education has also fulfilled a socialization function. Earlier colleges were not only expected to transform callow youth into responsible adults, but they also were given a character education function to perform. In other words, college masters were expected to supervise the conduct of youth outside the classroom as well as in, from formal curricular programs to extracurricular activities. This supervision took a strong religious bent at church-related colleges, consisting of various sermons, chapel services, and the infusion of religion into the curriculum. At the secular institutions, while religion was appealed to from time to time, various character molding devices were used. Mental discipline was called upon. Abstention from vice was implored. Exemplars were studied in history and literature so as to inspire the young to more upright behavior. The faculty was expected to maintain surveillance over the morals of youth and keep them from temptation and unsavory worldly influences, particularly those found in rapidly growing cities. Proponents of urban values argued at length with the upholders of the virtues of rural life. Urban educators could accuse their rural counterparts of parochialism and impeding progress while, in turn, the city was stigmatized for its vices and corruptions.

The larger socialization function of shaping the morals and character of students, although still conceived by some liberal culture proponents as essential in aiding students in acquiring a certain life-style, has largely been tossed by the faculty to the administration(13). The faculty no longer wishes to assume this function and many have expressed doubts that it actually is a proper function for universities to be involved in in the first place. Research oriented professors conceive socialization as strictly an intellectual one: the development of high level research abilities in their graduate students. The personal lives of students are their own business unless activities in this sphere interfere with their opportunities and progress toward becoming an able researcher. American higher education is unusually diverse and the above-mentioned emphasis does not apply to church-related colleges, junior colleges, and some private colleges. Regional differences also exist, and the socialization function traditionally has been more broadly conceived of in the deep South and historically in New England as regulation over the complete conduct of students than it has in other regions. But even in these cases the former range of faculty and administrative authority has been, in more recent years, relaxing its scope. The concern here, however, is with the major universities which not only reflect some of the values of the larger society but also are agents for bringing about new values.

Universities also influence the larger society in several other important ways. As universities have expanded the scope of their activities and the range of their interests, they have been in a better position to offer a multitude of services. Universities maintain museums, offer concerts, art exhibits, entertainment, sports events, and provide extension and adult education classes. In most all of the smaller college towns, the state university is the center of cultural activity for the community and provides cultural activities and entertainment for faculty, students, and local citizens which would otherwise be unavailable. This influence opens the possibility of raising the cultural level and refashioning the outlook of the people.

Universities have also exerted considerable influence on the larger society by providing various consulting services to people in local communities. Some of these services first became prominent with the establishment of the land-grant institutions; most notably, agricultural and home demonstration agents have exerted great influence in rural areas of the nation. The growth of American agriculture to its present place of preeminence is due to a considerable extent to agricultural research and the ability of the university to get farmers to adopt new and improved farming techniques. As schools of business administration grew, new approaches to management, advertising, investments, sales, and distribution of goods were devised. Specialists in business administration and in economics have consulted with business leaders and helped to promote new business operations and new modes of thinking about the economy. A notable example of university influence in this area was President Franklin Roosevelt's "brain-trust" which brought in many of the newer economic ideas, particularly those of Keynes. Since that time the advisory role of university economists and other specialists to government has continued to grow. The use of university specialists was particularly prominent in the Kennedy and Johnson administrations.

In addition to the above services, universities provide hospitals and medical centers for the advancement of medical practice and for the improvement of community health. They also provide legal and social welfare services through their schools of law and social work. Many new engineering and technological projects in industry and government are planned by university specialists in science and engineering.

Finally, the university has exerted vast influence over the larger society by new discoveries and technological inventions which have changed

living conditions for all citizens. Basic inventions in the areas of transportation, communication, industrial production and automated factories,
building materials, and weapons of warfare have brought America into
a postindustrial age.

The university has been said to consist of a community of scholars in
search of truth. Perhaps, too, it is a bevy of administrators searching for
funds. In any case, whether the scholarly search is entirely dispassionate
and motivated by no ulterior desires is beside the point in terms of the
atmosphere of the university as compared to that of the larger society.
In spite of the obvious imperfections, shortcomings, and violations of
this atmosphere, it still is basically a place where ideas—many of them
controversial—can be explored without recriminations and censorship.
There have been numerous breaches of academic freedom and, more
particularly, the freedom for students to learn. Nonetheless, the university stands in stark contrast to the larger community as a whole where
the spirit of open inquiry is sharply limited whenever controversial material is presented which would call into question some of the basic value
assumptions by which certain groups in the community live.

The university is also supposed to represent the endorsement and
application of democratic principles in practice, and it is generally alleged
that it is less open to the charge of discriminatory treatment than is the
case of other community institutions. The observance of democratic
principles has certainly been true in some cases, and whenever it is,
the university can serve as a model for the local community. However,
the university's record on this score and in providing needed freedoms
for students can still be improved. It is evident, in any case, that without
strong support for academic freedom the remarkable advancements in
human knowledge observed in many disciplines during the past several
decades could never have been accomplished.

It is clear that universities fulfill not one but many functions. These
multiple functions are not necessarily complementary and mutually supporting, generating conflicts and open competition for funds among the
various contingents. "One way to determine the central purposes of an
institution," according to Jencks and Riesman, "is to ask whether a given
function could be eliminated without changing its name." This definition
of purpose, however, may be difficult to ascertain when we recall that an
increasingly large number of institutions in recent years have attached
the label "university" to their name and eliminated their former designa-
tion as "college," "teachers college," or "A & M." Many of these are
universities in name only and scarcely resemble those institutions which

for many years have been considered universities. But if we take these latter institutions as illustrative of the Jencks and Riesman formula, it is doubtful whether one could eliminate the research institutes, the graduate schools, and various professional programs and still rightfully consider them universities. Of course, there is nothing to prevent the growth of new institutions serving rather different functions from calling themselves universities; there is no monopoly on the term. However, as universities have been conceived since the late nineteenth century, we would have to say that the functions and roles enumerated above are basic, central, and distinguishing features.

The Impact of Student Movements

Not only has the university exerted great influence in recent years on the larger society, but developments in other institutions have also served to shape the pattern of some university programs and activities. With a rapidly changing economy, its need for highly skilled manpower, and the desire of labor to keep the job market from being flooded with youthful candidates, higher education is now considered a necessity for all who wish to secure a good position. At the same time the competitiveness for places in the better institutions has sharply increased along with the intellectual tensions that accompany the struggle to remain in the program by securing the needed grade point average and courses required for graduation. With the rapid growth of enrollment in higher education, universities have become bureaucratic systems. Some students see the university as a factory with assembly-line techniques of turning out a product—the graduate. It is, according to some students, a knowledge factory which uses mechanical and dehumanized means of production. For Mario Savio, a leader in the Berkeley revolt, the university "is a factory that turns out a certain product needed by industry or government."(14) This view is reinforced by the former president of Berkeley, Clark Kerr, in his discussion of the "knowledge industry." Using the terminology of industrial processes to refer to education, Kerr relates that 29 per cent of the gross national product is involved in the "production, distribution, and consumption of knowledge," and the growth rate for this industry is nearly twice that of the other parts of the economy(15). With discussion such as Kerr's, a growing bureaucratization of higher education, and administrative officials and faculty who appear increasingly inaccessible to some students, that the university seems to resemble a factory should not be surprising.

It is also a well known fact that a significant amount of funded research by leading universities is under contract with the Department of Defense. By its considerable involvement in the invention and construction of weaponry, the university has supported the military-industrial complex. Youth is always the most directly involved in warfare, so it is not surprising that students have demonstrated and brought to the attention of elders possibly still enamored with the patriotism and heroism of the second world war the hypocrisies of military adventures.

The course of student movements in the United States is generally well known due to widespread publicity, even though there still are widespread misconceptions. The public usually overestimates the number of active militants; they generally fail to recognize that the students involved are representatives in most cases of the upper-middle class and most of the participants are academically more able students. The white middle class has frequently looked at symptoms rather than causes and has been quick to support administrators and politicians who take a strong "law and order" stand. Public interests have not always been served well by the mass media which, more often than not, have emphasized the more sensational elements and failed to treat underlying problems in depth.

Emergence of the Student Movement

Student movements are not unique in the United States, but have been characteristic of universities on many continents since the rise of universities in the late middle ages. In our time student movements have succeeded in overthrowing governments in South Korea, South Vietnam, and Turkey. They have played a key role in independence movements in Vietnam, Algeria, Burma, and India, and they have been active in Latin America, Portugal, Spain, Italy, and West Germany(16). In 1968 they helped precipitate the demise of the de Gaulle regime in France. The issues and conditions which generate these movements naturally differ from one country to another, but in the underdeveloped nations students frequently have organized to support movements toward independence. In the developed Western nations, some of the generic economic, political, and social conditions that afflict the United States are causes for agitation in these other nations as well. The vast changes attendant upon the emergence of postindustrial societies, the instabilities of economic systems, and the threat of nuclear warfare are conditions which all of these nations share. Since youth has inherited the vast problems of our age and will have to find some way of dealing with these problems more effectively than today's leaders, it is only natural that more perceptive students would manifest great concern. The attempt to envision these problems differently is due in part to the testing of new life styles which differ sharply from the model of the "organization man."

Doubtlessly the two most significant factors in the rise of the New Left in this country have been the civil rights movement and the Vietnam war. The activities of the late Martin Luther King, Jr. and his nonviolent protest, the work of CORE and SNCC, all showed the discrepancies between professed ideals and actual practices. From the initial bus boycott in Montgomery, Alabama, which energized King's movement, to the sit-ins, freedom rides, episodes in Little Rock, Oxford, and Selma, to the period when the movement was carried into the North, an indelible impression was left in the minds of many youth. Some students spent their summer in the deep South working on voter registration and other projects, and they learned through harsh experiences that deep-seated bigotry and intolerable discriminatory practices had long been a way of life in some parts of the United States. But the civil rights movement was also to find racism prevalent in all sections of the country. The riots during the summer of 1967 were investigated and published in the U. S. Riot Commission report. These riots occurred in Tampa, Cincinnati, Atlanta, Newark, Detroit, and other American cities. The Report concluded that, "White racism is essentially responsible for the explosive mixture which has been accumulating in our cities since the end of World War II."(17) It warned that, "The nation is rapidly moving toward two increasingly separate Americas. Within two decades, this division could be so deep that it would be almost impossible to unite."(18) This division would take the form of white society located in the suburbs while blacks occupied the central cities.

In addition to the acute problems of civil rights and the denial of equal opportunities, the conscription of youth to serve in undeclared wars which they consider unjust has been the second major factor which has increased militancy on the campus. Venerable patriotic sentiments are despoiled within a context of mass killing and destruction for purposes which are, according to some students, unjust and insupportable. Protests have taken many forms: destroying draft cards, organized draft evasion, moratorium marches, teach-ins, stopping the movement of troop trains, distributing anti-war leaflets at military bases, and other activities. Former Selective Service director, Lewis B. Hershey, has taken punitive action by reclassifying some of the protestors to 1-A status and rendering them immediately subject to induction. This action along with other factors, such as the belief of many white middle class people that protest demonstrations are treasonable acts because they play into the hands of the enemy by giving the illusion that we no longer have the will to "win," have served to exacerbate the conflict over the course and disposition of the war.

There have been several new developments in the university in response to the civil rights movement and the Vietnam war. In terms of the former, blacks have attempted to get black studies programs introduced into the curriculum, have sometimes sought separate living quarters, and have attempted to modify admission policies in order that potentially able but disadvantaged minority groups can enter the university. They also have sought to increase the number of black professors on the faculty, to increase the size and budget of the black studies program, and to give students an opportunity to concentrate in black studies for full credit.

The policy of more open admissions poses some intractable problems because it involves a clash between proponents of different theoretical outlooks: egalitarianism vs. meritocracy. The meritocracy approach has viewed schooling as a selective system by means of which the less academically able are weeded out and only those demonstrating certain desired academic traits are permitted to remain. Those who graduate, by implication, have met minimum standards and are thereby prepared to offer certain specialized skills to the manpower market. Ideally, factors such as race, religion, nationality, family background and other extraneous factors should not enter the admissions and selection process; only sheer academic ability and motivation to do college work should count (although the latter factor is not measured by college admission tests). If this ideal was a working reality, it also would mean that labor, industry, business, and government would only promote on the basis of demonstrated ability rather than seniority, race, religion, politics and other factors. Obviously a meritocratic system is far from operative today, even though it has been attempted in the academic world(19).

The egalitarian approach takes various strategies. In some cases it supports open admissions for disadvantaged minority groups in which these groups would not be required to take admission tests and would not be judged by their rank in their high school graduating class. Anyone who desires a college education should be given an opportunity.

Egalitarians usually oppose admission tests on the grounds that certain cultural biases are built-in, particularly against those who come from bilingual homes. They also are in favor of assigning students to programs on the basis of their own preference. The egalitarian vs. meritocratic views have been debated at the City University of New York system and other institutions(20).

So far internal changes in higher education brought about by the civil rights movement and black militancy have been discussed. It should also be noted, however, that the university has influenced other institutions in the larger society by the activities of students in behalf of civil rights, by the work of scholars on civil rights studies, and by the advisory services by the academic community to the different branches of federal and state government.

In terms of the Vietnam war, the university's influence in the larger society has been sharply challenged by the New Left students. Leading universities have become increasingly involved in various types of research for the Department of Defense. M.I.T.'s laboratories alone had $120 million in military research contracts in 1969. University social scientists have undertaken studies of counter-insurgency strategies for the CIA. A large pool of CIA funded research was uncovered at Michigan State University by *Ramparts* magazine. Another dramatic example came to light in February 1967 when the press revealed that the executive director and the treasurer of the American Political Science Association were officers in a CIA-funded research organization known as Operative and Policy Research, Inc(21). Thus, the universities "at the time that they should have been creative centers for the development of strategies for peace, disarmament, and world unity, they were busy with defense departments contracts."(22)

Student protest against such activities is predicated on the belief that secretive research runs counter to the ideals of the university, which is based on the free pursuit of ideas and the dissemination of findings to all interested parties. Furthermore, the university's participation in military research places the university, whether intentionally or not, behind the war machine and the use of new and more ominous weapons. The secrecy surrounding contracts and missions for intelligence agencies, as well as the refusal by researchers to discuss the purposes of the research, is a mockery of the professed ideals of organized inquiry in the university.

Students have also protested against ROTC and other military programs on campus. Some have urged that these programs no longer be offered for academic credit which can be applied toward graduation; others have demonstrated to remove all such programs from campus.

Chemical companies, which manufacture napalm, have also been the object of the students' ire when recruiters have visited campuses. Recruiters for the army, navy, and air force officers training programs, too, have been the target of demonstrations and sit-ins.

What do these developments mean? They point to the great involvement of our leading universities in the military-industrial complex, an involvement that has grown rapidly since the second world war. Since students no longer blindly accept this country's military adventures and the expansion of its hegemony in Latin America and Asia, war research and military activities are vigorously opposed on a number of campuses. But researchers and administrators are loathe to relinquish their lucrative contracts, for it brings massive outside funds and offers the researcher the prestige of directing or participating in large-scale projects. The research director, should he be lured away by the greater advantages offered by another institution, takes his grant with him. He becomes an attractive prize to aggressive administrators.

But student protestors, such as those at M.I.T., are getting the authorities to reappraise their massive involvement in war-related research, so that plans may be developed as to how the research may be phased out and be replaced by projects designed to make a contribution to the solution of our vast domestic problems. These protests are likely to intensify at leading universities until the university's role in this area is so thoroughly and mercilessly exposed that this form of research will be abandoned for a return to more humanistic inquiries. Students, then, will have precipitated a major change in policies and role relations the university assumes with the larger society. If nothing else is accomplished by student militance, this change in itself will be a significant achievement. But it should also be noted that widespread protest may effect a reappraisal of foreign policy. This reappraisal, too, would be an important development because U.S. foreign policy during the past twenty years has been accused of having no long-term planning or direction, other than being "dedicated to delaying or preventing social change throughout two thirds of the world. . ."(23)

The Intellectual Basis of Student Militance

In addition to the two major events having a radicalizing effect on students—the civil rights movement and the Vietnam war—there have been local issues such as those which erupted at Berkeley and San

Francisco State College. However, the ability to interpret events in political terms and the willingness of certain students to commit themselves to political action designed to challenge existing roles, are due in large measure to the dramatic and transforming effects of civil rights and Vietnam on students' values. As egregious shortcomings and the hypocrisies of American domestic and international policies have been exposed, a growing sense of alienation has spread. Ways of life accepted as natural, right, or inevitable by the white middle class have come to be repudiated as a sellout to materialistic ambitions and the maintenance and extension of existing injustices. Students have turned to a diversity of ideological positions as possible sources for developing a counter position and new ways of life.

"The New Radicalism," according to Jack Newfield, "is authentically new in its vague weaving together of anarchistic, existential, transcendental, populist, socialists, and bohemian strands of thought."(24) Assuming that Newfield's interpretation is essentially correct, the ideological picture we get of the young militants is that they are not united behind one ideological position, and any attempt to label their thinking as a total group would be, at best, simplistic and misleading. This spread of ideologies does not mean, however, that no substantive observations can be advanced as to students' ideological roots. A caveat that should be observed is the students' rejection of many older ideologies, particularly those of the 1930's when some American intellectuals flirted with Marxism or became Marxists. Although some students do read Marx and Lenin, they seemed to be more impressed with some of the recent leaders, such as Mao Tse-tung, Guevera, Debray, and Fanon. In this spirit, Herbert Marcuse has reinterpreted the older ideologies in light of contemporary social and political developments, and has become probably the leading intellectual spokesman, both in western Europe and the United States, for students on the Left. Marcuse attempts to demonstrate that, since American democracy is built upon a theoretical cultural foundation that supports one dimensional thinking by repudiating the Hegelian dialectical process, the U.S. government through mass media imposes coercive and restrictive totalitarian practices on its citizens(25).

The beat and bohemian elements of the student culture in the 1950's were those who withdrew from the sordidness that they found in the world to repair to coffeehouses to read poetry and the ways of Zen. Their counterparts living in the 1960's were the hippies and flower children who sought to live naturally and practice a code of love and mutual aid. They were not and are not part of the militant student groups, but their ideas are important for the New Left because their way of life exemplifies a distinct alternative to the dominant ethos of the larger culture. Thus, if we view militant student movements as designed not only to restructure existing social institutions but also to develop a counter culture which offers more meaningful and less hypocritical ways of living, then the hippies and flower people are exemplifying counter styles of life. They do not have more among their numbers as yet because the values of the larger culture are still dominant and a part of the life style of most college students. However, since the early 1960's we have witnessed an increasing number of students become politically radical. Some observers contend that once America's involvement in Vietnam is ended, the radicalization of the student culture will sharply decline, presumably degenerating to the level of apathy found on college campuses during the 1950's. This apathy, however, is unlikely in light of the fact that the movement has gone too far and deeply affected too many students to retrench other than momentarily. Furthermore, after the United States' engagement in Vietnam is ended, the need for massive action on the domestic front will be greater than ever.

Probably the most influential militant group on American campuses is the Students for a Democratic Society (SDS). Distrusting the bureaucratic organizational forms found in the university and the larger society, they have been since their founding a loosely-organized, nearly leaderless group based upon the notion of participatory democracy. This concept is not only the one man-one vote idea, but it reduces leadership and office-holding to a bare minimum while generating the basic programmatic decisions from the membership. The SDS was founded in 1960 at a New York convention sponsored by the League for Industrial Democracy, and in 1962 they issued their now famous Port Huron Statement(26).

The Port Huron Statement repudiates both communism and the paranoid anti-communism found in America during the early 1950's and at other times. It is a broad critique of the bureaucratic capitalism system, the shallow materialism of the general culture, and the lack of thoughtful, amelioristic planning by government. It is also an indictment of apathetic students and their willingness to settle for security and "low success" rather than a willingness to set goals and take risks in order to reshape the conditions under which they live and study. It is a call for "participatory democracy" by rectifying the conditions which have separated the people from power and from a base for decision-making(27).

While it is difficult to assess the exact influence of the SDS in terms of its ability to effect changes in the university's role, it is well known that its local chapters have instigated militant action at Columbia and other universities. Some of these activities have resulted in changes in the administrative hierarchy and in university policy itself (at Columbia, for instance), while on other campuses the protests have been less successful due to their generating a strong "back-lash" from the administration, faculty, or students. In any case, besides assessing the specific episodes in which the SDS has been involved, the organization has sought—and with some success—to radicalize the student population. And although the majority of students are more conservative and some are still enamored with the middle class values of their society, the overall influence of the SDS has been that of bringing to the fore issues which hitherto have been dormant and also of moving a considerable portion of the student body further toward the Left.

As a viable organization, however, the SDS has been in serious trouble and its future is presently in question. The June 1969 convention of SDS in Chicago became a shambles as a result of an attempted putsch by the Progressive Labor Party, which served to split the organization into clashing factions. Its future was further clouded later in the year when different factions took up violent and ostensibly aimless protest in the streets of Chicago. Presumably their marauding was aimed at the trial in Chicago of the protest leaders who were indicted following the 1968 Democratic Convention in that city. Although the SDS has instigated campus confrontations which have eventuated in various reforms and has served to move many students further toward the Left, its future effectiveness on college campuses is clearly in doubt. Probably some of the activities will be taken over by other organizations.

Among the other organizations is the Progressive Labor Party (PLP), which adheres to Marxist-Leninist principles. The PLP membership is small and its ideology focuses on the old Marxist theme of capitalist exploitation. It differs from the SDS in ideology by the fact that the SDS has been more diverse and amorphous and less committed to one position. Many in the SDS were suspicious of the old hard-liners, whether Marxists or capitalists. PLP is also more puritanical in its life style than SDS and campus students in general. Because of its hard-line Maxism and its puritanism, it is not likely to become a significant force on college campuses.

Another organization, the DuBois Clubs, founded in San Francisco in 1964, has little more than 2,000 members concentrated in New York and San Francisco areas. The members think of themselves as Marxists and, in contrast to the Progressive Labor Party, are more like Soviet, than Chinese, Marxists. They identify more with reform rather than revolutionary movements. They still identify with the liberal wing of the Democratic Party and organized labor in particular, at a time when the SDS has clearly recognized that these two are no longer forces supporting great changes. Probably the two largest politically active groups on campus are the Young Democrats and the Young Republicans. As their names suggest, they are the youthful representatives of the Democratic and Republican parties and, thereby, seek to effect or inhibit change through the traditional party apparatus. The SDS, on the other hand, does not believe that existing political parties are capable of leading the nation in such a way that the reorganization and restructuring of its society will become a reality. The SDS sees the two parties as heavily bureaucratized, rigid, and unresponsive to the demands of the people. Various observers on the Left have debated whether the present parties, even with considerable reform, could ever become a force to address themselves to the great domestic and international problems in such a way that a new sense of priorities and commitment to new goals could be achieved(28). The Young Democrats and Young Republicans, on the other hand, serve to bring about greater political awareness among students while focusing their political concerns within the framework of the existing major parties. The two organizations serve as a moderating influence on campus political dialogue and act as a brake against attacks challenging university policies which may call into question the university's external roles in the larger society.

An organization of more recent vintage is the Young Americans for Freedom (YAF) group composed of a variety of conservative and reactionary students who seek to counter the militancy of the SDS and other groups. They have attempted to do this by mounting their own publicity campaign through the use of public meetings and the mass media. One of their tactics is to threaten to initiate suits against militant students who block egress to classrooms and offices, as well as any other activities which threaten to slow down or bring about a temporary cessation of any university activities. To date, the YAF has been only a minor force as far as its effectiveness on campuses; however, if student militants increasingly threaten or antagonize the larger body of politically inactive students, there may be a "back-lash" which would incline some of the moderates and inactives toward the YAF position. On the other hand, administrators and faculty who treat students' demands in an authoritarian and insensitive manner are likely to precipitate the radicalization of some of the more moderate students.

It should be noted that the mobilization committees that organized the peace marches as protests of the United States' policies in Vietnam were able to successfully bring together persons of diverse backgrounds, young and old, committed to the rapid withdrawal of U.S. forces and a cessation of fighting. Since these marches, first the one on October 15, 1969, and later the march on Washington, and San Francisco November 15, 1969, involved the largest simultaneous demonstrations in American history, and since these marches were amazingly nonviolent (except for sporadic outbreaks by some militant groups in Washington), it seems that they have demonstrated the ability of student groups to organize large masses of people successfully for peaceful protests. Demonstrations of this type, undoubtedly, will continue to prove effective in awakening the consciences of people and stimulating the government to defend and, perhaps, reappraise its policies. However, such demonstrations are no substitute for a viable organization on the Left—perhaps even a new political party—which will organize the diverse and splinter elements into a coherent whole for the purpose of setting and carrying through new domestic and international priorities and helping to make the watchwords of justice and equality a reality.

Humanistic Roles for Higher Education

The establishment of colleges and universities symbolizes the institutionalization of rationality. However, "institutionalization," says Alasdair MacIntyre, "can be used to try to isolate the practice of rational criticism and to prevent it being exercised upon the social order, and there is a continuous pressure upon universities and other institutions to make the practice of rational enquiry merely instrumental to the purposes of government."(29)

Whatever the historical merits of MacIntyre's proposition, if rational criticism can be isolated within the universities and this criticism, in turn, can be directed primarily to specialized studies within the scholar's discipline, then governments are free, for the most part, from searching criticism. This tendency, of course, assumes that the press, organized labor, special interest groups, and Congress can not be counted on to perform this critical function in a consistent and thorough manner— and this claim is at least partially true today. Due to the scholar's preoccupation with his specialty, he fails to make a contribution to the analysis and clarification of broad social and political issues. This criticism is not to demean specialized inquiries for select audiences; it only points to the fact that both types of studies could be successfully conducted, even though scholars may need to be rewarded for addressing themselves to broader social and political issues.

The practice of rational inquiry, as MacIntyre indicates, has also been made instrumental to purposes of government. Social scientists especially have fallen into this trap by conceiving their work as neutral with respect to values. They have striven to make their studies objective and dispassionate in order to be scientific. They have aped the methodologies of the physical sciences whenever possible. They have eschewed values because they thought involvement with them would be unscientific and would bias their investigations. What most social scientists have failed to understand is that values frequently occur as subject matter for scientific inquiry which, since their existence and not their validity is the concern of inquiry, do not make for bias. Also, values which occur in terms of the ethics of the scientific community do not make for bias. Values enter science in terms of the selection of problems, the order in which they are dealt with, and the resources expended on their solution. It is only when values prejudge solutions, not when they dictate problems, that they make for bias.

Government officials have given social scientists the goals to be achieved and have asked them to conduct studies designed to implement the goals most expeditiously. Social scientists have been averse to criticize the goals they are asked to implement because they have misconstrued their own responsibilities and relationships with value concerns.

There are other reasons as well. Equilibrium models are commonly employed in the social sciences. These models are developed to show how social systems can be optimally organized. From these models, social disorganization can be predicated when a sufficient number of key people fail to perform prescribed roles adequately, resulting in the inability of the system to fulfill its functions. This outlook takes the social systems in society as given so that disorganization and deviance can be ascribed irrespective of how corrupt and unjust the system may be.

Universities cannot perform their role of social criticism adequately when such models are employed, when value concerns are misconceived, and when scholars believe that they should avoid undertaking inquiries into the basic social and political issues of our time. A reassessment by social scientists of their role in government is needed, as well as a reappraisal of the functions of the academic community. The more militant students are pushing academicians to reexamine their roles. These same students have also brought about greater student participation in policy decisions in a number of universities which affect their lives by showing administrators that their oligarchial tendencies are not always in the best interests of the university community.

Predictions of future developments are at best a combination of imagination and the projection of present tendencies; however, it could well be predicted that the university's involvement in defense and classified research projects will appreciably decline in the near future, and, in lieu of such involvement, research contracts with the federal government will focus principally upon pressing domestic problems. The research function of the universities will continue to grow, but it will move away from classified contracts. Without the pressures applied by student militants, it is doubtful that these changes would have come about nearly so soon, if at all.

Only in recent years have the occasional criticisms that scholars directed to institutions in the larger society been turned toward the university itself. Even scholars who have been perceptive analysts of other social systems were scarcely aware of the involvement of their own institution in the military-industrial complex as was shown during the demonstrations at Columbia. During the 1960's more scholars have become interested in the field of higher education as a legitimate and worthy area of study. Much more is known about other institutions than is known about higher education. This neglect should soon be rectified. Before the rectification can be successfully accomplished, however, professors will need to recognize not only a commitment to their discipline but also to that of bringing rational inquiry to bear upon the activities, operations, and policies of the university.

Higher education will need to define more precisely its utility function. State universities frequently have been willing to assume any new function and institute any new program that at the moment is in demand rather than developing clear-cut objectives and long-range planning undergirded by a defensible sense of direction. It is true that the state institutions have found themselves under pressures from the legislatures and the public, and they have at times had to assume new functions which they could only embrace less than enthusiastically. Each state, however, needs a master plan by which institutions of various types—from the junior college to the land-grant institution—have distinctive and clearly specified roles to play, and that these roles, in turn, are organized so that they coordinate well with one another and avoid unnecessary duplication. Alternative vocational training programs are needed in business, industry, and organized labor to provide skills which need not be gained in college, for a college degree should not be the objective of every youth in order to secure gainful employment. Proper steps must be taken to plan vocational programs more intelligently than has been the case in the past.

In conclusion, because of the shortage of funds coupled with enrollment bulges, colleges will have to develop clear-cut objectives, and long-range planning guided by a clearly conceived rationale. It is idle to ask whether students will affect the external roles of the university, for they have already done so. On some campuses student protest has wrought significant changes in the university's internal operations as well, such as curriculum, grading, student representation on various administrative bodies which determine the students' future, etc. Administrators may cavil that the university must stay out of politics, which is another ploy to be used to discourage dissent. But the university is already and has always been involved in politics: with state legislatures and politicians, in government research contracts, through the use of loyalty oaths, in consulting work with business, industry, and agriculture, in town-gown relations, in the quest for grants and subsidies from foundations, special interest groups, and private individuals, and in decisions as to whether or not controversial political figures will speak on campus. This list is representative and by no means an exhaustive one. That higher education is involved in politics is obvious, and it is essential that our institutions of higher learning avoid degenerating into mirror-images of some of the worst practices found in the larger society. If this mirroring is to be avoided, it is necessary for faculties to recognize that values determine the questions asked rather than outcomes and solutions; therefore, it is vital to the future of society and the university that scholars be genuinely committed to humanistic values, both in thought and action. Only when this commitment is made will the university become a significant force for social amelioration and regeneration.

Questions for Discussion

1. What are the chief external roles of the university today in its relations with other social institutions? Why are they significant?

. . . it is vital to the future of society and
the university that scholars be genuinely
committed to humanistic values. . . .

2. In what way do you believe that these roles are changing, and for what
   reasons? What effect will these changes have on the future direction of
   the university and its role in society?

3. Contrast college students of the 1950's with those of the 1960's in terms
   of their awareness and sensitivity to political events and social issues.

4. What are the principal causes of student militance, and what are the
   goals and purposes of student protestors?

5. We have heard of the importance of academic freedom for the faculty.
   What rights do students have in the classroom, on campus, and in the
   community? Are there certain prominent areas in which student rights
   have been abrogated?

6. What rights do students have to demonstrate and protest, whether on or
   off campus, against policies and practices with which they disagree? What
   are the legitimate limits of student protest?

7. Some have suggested that the activities of militant students are the most
   significant force for bringing about more humanistic values in higher
   education. Others, however, disagree. What are your beliefs on this issue?
   Explain and support them.

For Further Reading

Among the studies of higher education, there are those which deal with
its history, others which deal with present institutional characteristics and
trends, and some which pertain to the nature of the student population. For
a history, see Frederick Rudolph's *The American College and University,*
New York: Vintage Books, 1965. For further historical studies see his bibliography.

As for the present characteristics of higher education in the United States,
Paul Woodring's *The Higher Learning in America: A Reassessment,* New
York: McGraw-Hill, 1968 highlights its diversity and uniqueness while, at
the same time, displays a lack of sympathy for student militance. Christopher
Jencks and David Riesman's *The Academic Revolution,* Garden City, N.Y.:
Doubleday, 1968 is a much more comprehensive account written from the
viewpoint of sociology of education. Those interested in the different philoso-
phies of higher education could well consult John S. Brubacher, *Bases for
Policy in Higher Education,* New York: McGraw-Hill, 1965. For an essay
on the multiversity and a book which has aroused the ire of militant students,

see Clark Kerr, *The Uses of the University,* New York: Harper, Torchbooks, 1966.

There have been a number of important studies in recent years of students, their characteristics, and the influence of their college experiences upon their lives. A number of these studies are contained in Nevitt Sanford, ed., *The American College,* New York: John Wiley and Sons, 1962. Among the other studies are Kenneth Kenniston, *The Uncommitted: Alienated Youth in American Society,* New York: Harcourt, Brace and World, 1965; Joseph Katz, *et al., No Time For Youth,* San Francisco: Jossey-Bass, 1968; and Arthur W. Chickering, *Education and Identity,* San Francisco: Jossey-Bass, 1969, a book which uses Erik H. Erikson's personality theory to build a set of developmental tasks for colleges.

A book which challenges the faculty and their disciplines to become more relevant to the lives of students and the great issues of our time is *The Dissenting Academy,* Theodore Roszak, ed., New York: Vintage Books, 1968. Among the numerous writings dealing with student politics and protest, the following are especially recommended: Seymour Martin Lipset, ed., *Student Politics,* New York: Basic Books, 1967; "Students and Politics," *Daedalus* 97 (Winter 1968). These publications analyze student movements in countries throughout the world. Other books which focus more exclusively on aspects of student protest in the United States are Seymour Martin Lipset and Sheldon S. Wolin, eds., *The Berkeley Student Revolt,* Garden City, N.Y.: Doubleday, 1965; Christopher G. Katope and Paul G. Zolbrod, eds., *Beyond Berkeley,* Cleveland: World Publishing Co., 1966; Michael V. Miller and Susan Gilmore, eds., *Revolution at Berkeley,* New York: Dell Publishing Co., 1965; Jack Newfield, *A Prophetic Minority,* New York: The New American Library, 1967; Paul Jacobs and Saul Landan, eds., *The New Radicals,* New York: Vintage Books, 1966; Michael Cohen and Dennis Hale, eds., *The New Student Left,* Boston: Beacon Press, 1966; and Theodore Roszak, *The Making of a Counter Culture*, Garden City, N.Y.: Doubleday, Anchor Books, 1969.

Notes

1. Laurence R. Veysey, *The Emergence of the American University* (Chicago: University of Chicago Press, 1965).

2. *Ibid.,* p. 186.

3. *Ibid.,* p. 130.

4. *Ibid.*, p. 131.

5. *Ibid.*, pp. 126-27.

6. Frederick Rudolph, *The American College and University: A History* (New York: Vintage Books, 1965), p. 273.

7. Veysey, *The Emergence of the American University,* pp. 137-38.

8. Rudolph, *The American College and University,* p. 271.

9. Veysey, *The Emergence of the American University,* p. 177.

10. Rudolph, *The American College and University,* pp. 338-39.

11. *Ibid.*, pp. 116-17.

12. Quoted in Burton R. Clark, *Educating the Expert Society* (San Francisco: Chandler Publishing Co., 1962), p. 206.

13. Christopher Jencks and David Riesman, *The Academic Revolution* (New York: Doubleday, 1968), p. 28.

14. Mario Savio, "An End to History," *Revolution at Berkeley,* Michael V. Miller and Susan Gilmore, eds., (New York: Dell Publishing Co., 1965).

15. Clark Kerr, *The Uses of the University* (New York: Harper Torchbooks, 1963), pp. 87-88.

16. Seymour Martin Lipset and Philip G. Altbach, "Student Politics and Higher Education in the United States," *Comparative Education Review,* 10 (June 1966): 320.

17. *Report of the National Advisory Commission on Civil Disorders.* (New York: Bantam Books, 1968), p. 203.

18. *Ibid.*, p. 407.

19. For a vision of what such a system may look like and the problems which may be generated, see Michael Young, *The Rise of the Meritocracy, 1870-2033* (Baltimore, Md.: Penguin Books, 1961).

20. See "Plan to Admit All High School Graduates Stirs N.Y. Storm," *The Chronicle of Higher Education,* 4 (November 10, 1969): 3.

21. Marshall Windmiller, "The New American Mandarins," *The Dissenting Academy.* Theodore Roszak, ed. (New York: Vintage Books, 1968), p. 122.

22. Harold Taylor, "The Academic Industry," Seymour Martin Lipset and Sheldon S. Wolin, eds., *The Berkeley Student Revolt,* (Garden City, N.Y.: Doubleday, 1965), p. 62.

23. Kathleen Gough, "World of Revolution and the Science of Man," *The Dissenting Academy,* p. 150.

24. Jack Newfield, *A Prophetic Minority* (New York: Signet Books, 1967), p. 132.

25. See the following for an amplification of this and other points: Herbert Marcuse, *One Dimensional Man,* Boston: Beacon Press, 1964; Robert Paul Wolff, *et al.,* eds., "Repressive Tolerance", *Critique of Pure Tolerance,* Boston: Beacon Press, 1965; Herbert Marcuse *An Essay on Liberation,* Boston: Beacon Press, 1968.

26. The Port Huron Statement can be found in Mitchell Cohen and Dennis Hale, eds., *The New Student Left* (Boston: Beacon Press, 1967), pp. 9-16; and also in Paul Jacobs and Saul Landau, eds., *The New Radicals* (New York: Vintage Books, 1966), pp. 150-162. (The latter has fewer deletions from the original document).

27. The Port Huron Statement bears the impress of Thomas Hayden, former President of the SDS. His views can be found in "A Letter to the New (Young) Left," Cohen and Hale, eds., *The New Student Left,* pp. 2-9; and "The Politics of 'The Movement,'" Irving Howe, ed., *The Radical Papers* (Garden City, N.Y.: Doubleday, 1966), pp. 362-377.

28. For divergent views see: Christopher Lasch, *The Agony of the American Left* (New York: Vintage Books, 1968) and Michael Harrington, *Toward a Democratic Left* (New York: Macmillan, 1968).

29. Alasdair MacIntyre, "On Marcuse," *New York Review of Books,* 13 (October 23, 1969): 38. Reprinted with permission from *The New York Review of Books.* Copyright © 1969 The New York Review.

Chapter Nine
Equal Opportunities and the Control of Education

One of the most volatile and controversial issues surrounding the public schools is the question "Who shall control public education?" Many interest groups correctly recognize that the answer to this question will determine the character and direction of public education and its promise for the future. Much of the controversy has resulted from the rapid changes that have taken place both in schools and in other social institutions during the past decade, leaving many persons bewildered in the face of unprecedented turns of events.

Citizens have debated with school board members in recent years over their rights to approve or reject certain curricular innovations, such as the new science and mathematics programs, sex education and controversial material in the social studies. In metropolitan areas there have been notable cases, such as in New York City, in which citizens have attempted to wrest some of the control of local schools from what they believe to be an entrenched and unresponsive bureaucracy. Many arguments have also arisen over the role of the federal government in education. Some have feared that various forms of federal aid will lead to federal control as to how local school districts should be operated. Others have attempted to counter arguments of this type by indicating that without federal aid there would be no way to equalize educational opportunities between states. Local citizens also have been disturbed by the powers of state departments of education to organize and abolish school districts and set accreditation standards. These citizens would like to have the determination of such matters back in their own hands, or at least conducted by their elected representatives in the local community.

Misconceptions Over the Control of Education

There are a number of misconceptions that should be examined. Early forms of educational organization in the United States were based on a district system in which local communities controlled school affairs. This control stemmed from the fact that education was not mentioned in the Constitution and according to the Tenth Amendment "the powers not delegated to the United States by the Constitution nor prohibited by it to the States, are reserved to the States respectively, or to the people." This system differs from the more centralized pattern of some European nations. Its basis was partly due to a fear of a strongly centralized government and partly an historical accident. Although many Americans extol local control and decentralization as distinctive features of American education, it should be noted that education was most likely not mentioned in the Constitution because the signers did not have a concept of universal education. Other than among a few radical thinkers, one could not find the idea of universal education being entertained. A different treatment may have been accorded education if such a convention had met during the late nineteenth century after the concept of universal education was rather widely accepted.

There has also been a tendency in this country to associate decentralized control with democracy and to associate centralized patterns with autocratic and undemocratic designs. But this concept is far too simple. One has only to look at western Europe to observe more centralized patterns within governments which are basically democratic. Perhaps the problem lies in conceptualizing democracy in limited and stereotyped terms and also in associating it more or less exclusively with a form of capitalism. But, as is well known, democratic arrangements cannot be exclusively associated with a particular type of economy.

Some citizens, although they feel the federal government has made inroads in gaining control of education, still believe that public education is principally under the control of the local community. They fail to realize that due to dereliction by local boards, as well as other reasons, control of education is now vested primarily in the state government. The derelictions were many. It was not uncommon to find a number of the wealthier local districts refusing to tax adequately to provide sufficient revenue to support the schools. There were gross irregularities in the length of school term. Some schools were in session for nine months each year, others for seven, some for five. Districts in rural areas usually closed schools during harvesting season to enlist students as field hands, and would reopen after the crops were gathered and on their way to market. Great disparities existed among the qualifications of teachers in various districts within a state, and there was little agreement on the standards of selection and retention. Uniform curricular patterns and standards for graduation were rarely found. Due to these and other reasons, the state government began to assume far greater responsibility in public education, and had made large inroads by the early part of this century in wresting the control of public education from local school districts. Today education is a state function and is principally under the control of state government. The states have assumed the most important functions of education and, as a result, greater uniformity of standards and curricular offerings have become a reality. State departments of education are now in charge of the certification of teachers, accreditation of schools, have established compulsory school attendance laws, minimum length of school term, have provided financial subsidies to local school districts to help equalize pupil expenditures within the state, and have the power to establish, reorganize, or abolish school districts.

The Basis of Social Control

Every society must exercise sufficient control over its institutions in order to maintain stability and avoid the threat of chaotic breakdowns in its various social systems. Social controls are instituted to facilitate the realization of institutional goals, and are designed to maintain the optimum order within a social system which will permit it to attain its goal in the quickest and most economical way.

Two generic forms of social control are the formal and the informal arrangements found in all but the preliterate cultures. Formal controls are associated with laws, the legal system, and the legislative process; the informal pertains to the mores and folkways of a society. Through these two types of controls together with appropriate sanctions (rewards and punishments) different groups in society restrain and discipline their members and shape their behavior. For Emile Durkheim the essence of group life is that it exercises constraint or coercive power upon the individual(1). The group acts as a conservative agent, limiting individual variations and deviations from the norm. There is of course a certain amount of deviation from the norms in every group. Groups generally permit slight deviation so long as it does not threaten group solidarity. For a group to attempt to regulate all forms of deviance would overly tax the resources of the group, prove too time consuming and costly. Therefore group leaders attempt to gain compliance with the norms by providing appropriate rewards (such as recognition, promotion, etc.) and punishing only those individuals whose acts pose a serious threat to group stability. There are, however, considerable differences in the amount and kind of deviance permitted. The more secure and stable the group and its leaders are, the less they will be intimidated by minor deviancies. There are also other factors involved. Much depends upon the ability of the individual to produce exonerating circumstances in the situation. If, for instance, an administrator is charged with carrying out a particular school board policy but does not do so because of great likelihood of failure due to insufficient resources, he is likely to be excused if he can convincingly demonstrate that the particular policy would fail and should be replaced with an alternate policy which is more likely to succeed. It should also be noted that the prestige of the individual and his power in the system are also factors in determining the amount of deviation in the group. Those people with more power and prestige are more likely to be able to deviate without punishment; conversely, those lower in the hierarchy are more stringently regulated and their deviancies are less likely to be tolerated.

Another variable is the freedom from threat to the group's stability. During times of crisis the individual's freedom is more limited. If a group is under attack from some other group and the attack is perceived as threatening by the group's leaders, it is likely that new restrictions will be placed on its members and less tolerance will be exhibited even for minor deviancies. This tightening of control can be seen more clearly at the national level when a country goes to war. In such cases some of the former freedoms of speech and action granted to citizens during peacetime are withdrawn whenever it is feared that their exercise might undermine the war effort. The same control is true in group life. Members are instructed by their leaders to present a solid front to the opposing forces and to comply without exception to emergency policies. It could be added that whether threatened or not, whenever there is an urgent issue before the group there is less tolerance of nonconformity.

The principal means by which control is gained is through the socialization process whereby the individual learns and adopts the expected ways of behaving. The object of socialization is to get the individual to internalize the norms so that the need for policing members and applying sanctions will be reduced to a minimum. We usually think of socialization occurring, first of all, in the home with the young child as he learns the role behavior prescribed by his parents. Later, as the child moves out of the home into the larger community, the socialization process continues in the school, church, and among peer groups. Parents hope that other groups and institutions will complement and reinforce the basic value system acquired in the family. Conflicts arise between the generations when this complementation does not occur (as in the case of some university students). It is more likely that the value systems will be complementary in small, relatively homogeneous communities than in large metropolitan areas.

Socialization also takes place in college, on the job, in the military, and in a host of other social systems. Whether going to college for the first time or taking a new job, one has to learn the rules and social expectations of the system(2). Those desiring to advance in a particular system do so by internalizing the norms and adopting the expected role behavior. However, since some systems are more innovative than others and deliberately seek new ideas, they are more prone to accept deviant thought and action whenever it results in innovations which help the system achieve its goals more expeditiously.

Since many individuals belong to several groups, the individual will experience divided loyalties whenever the norms of the different groups conflict. Although there is a tendency to choose one's group membership in terms of congruence between group norms and one's own value system, such selection is not always possible to accomplish because of the demands of earning a living, joining a union or professional organization, and the necessity to associate with certain organizations which may be deemed desirable by one's employer. The most acute conflict usually arises, however, when one begins to question the basic values which he has been taught and, as a result, explores new groups which identify with different, and often conflicting, values. This exploration is the problem of some university students today.

Types of Controls

There are different types of controls or different forms that controls may take. Controls may operate either directly or indirectly. In the former case, the subject is informed of a law, rule, or directive and urged to comply. Such controls as the laws surrounding the payment of income taxes, traffic laws, posted rules as to the prescribed uses of school property would be illustrations of direct controls. Indirect controls, on the other hand, are often unseen or undetected. Usually the individual is placed in a social situation in which the possible alternatives are limited to those which are consonant with the types of behavior desired. In the economy, there are a large number of fiscal and market regulations about which the average citizen is not fully aware; but by the very fact that he is a consumer or home owner, he comes under the influence of these regulations. There are also teachers who, overly concerned with the maintenance of a certain type of order and stability in the classroom, prearrange the classroom environment so that there will be a greater likelihood that only certain desired student responses will occur. Obviously indirect controls are more insidious because the individual is usually unaware that he is being controlled — or at least unaware of how he is being controlled and to what ends.

The limitations of controls are often seen in such complex social systems as state and federal government, organized labor, and metropolitan school systems. Since there are multiple subsystems and an intricate chain of command, there may be mutually contradictory orders or policies issued to subordinates due to the breakdown of communication in the hierarchy(3). This situation engenders frustration and decreased respect for administrators. It will also lead to contradictory outcomes when the conflicting policies are implemented; hence, it becomes self-defeating and impedes the system in attaining its goals. Of course, there is a possibility of serendipitous results. However, the unpredictability and erratic nature of these events offers little comfort in the long run to the managers of a system whose controls are operating inadequately.

Controls are generally applied not so much to specific persons but to categories of relationship. In other words, one comes under certain controls whenever he enters into new relationships. If a person becomes a homeowner for the first time he comes under a set of government regulations that he has not previously experienced. If he takes a job with the federal government, he comes under civil service regulations. If he decides to become a teacher, he must adjust his preparation for the job to accord with state certification requirements.

Pervasiveness of Controls

Some tend to attribute to the regulations they abhor the objective of instituting thought control. Actually, thought control is not usually the case, because it has been attempted in only a few societies and these societies have experienced limited success. The most notorious case in recent years was by Chinese during the Korean War(4). However, not only would thought control be inconsistent with expressed democratic sentiments of some Western societies, but democracies have found, according to some observers, more subtle and indirect ways to bring people around to the thinking of their leaders(5). One way is to get people to feel that their well-being — in fact, their very life — is tied up with their newly won affluence, gadgets, and the style of life that such gadgets offer. One can come to identify unquestioningly with an inequitable system so long as it continues to offer a high standard of living and all the positive benefits that such a standard entails. One's sense of identity becomes attached to the things and gadgets which the society makes possible by rewarding those who help keep the system operating and expanding so that it can provide a larger quantity of goods with more profits for the investors. Those who grow comfortable and complacent from such largesse become the unwitting prey of the manipulative aspects of the culture. Regulation is thereby greatly simplified by leaders having at their command an army of acquiescent role players who consider dissent against the system to be heretical or an act of tyranny.

Yet, as far as direct controls go, they are not as pervasive as some people think. There is a diffusive but restive fear in the land that government — particularly the federal government — has spread its tentacles into every nook and cranny of the individual's life, that "government is best which governs least." People sometimes recall a time when control was not so pervasive, when government was smaller and less centralized and the number of regulations was geometrically smaller. But they often fail to consider that as a society becomes larger and increasingly complex, the number of regulations must grow. The real question is whether existing regulations help to promote democratic ideals, basic rights, and human welfare more effectively than an alternate set of regulations, since there is no way to have a society without regulations and controls.

As for direct controls, government and other institutions do not regulate all aspects of a person's life, notwithstanding opinions to the contrary. Decision-makers must choose among alternate goals and a number of possible means. In a complex, decentralized society it is often difficult to implement policies successfully. Whenever there are multiple goals to attain, it is necessary to establish priorities among them because time and resources are always limited. The human imagination always outstrips the resources at one's command, even for those who allocate the resources within the system. There is also the possibility that when striving for multiple goals simultaneously, there will be conflicts among the goals which may prove self-defeating for all but the most astute planners. Even dictators cannot exercise complete control over their subjects. Information about a problem may be faulty or misleading. The design of a program sometimes breaks down. Regulations may be implemented poorly or ineffectively. Goals may conflict or may fail to receive proper priority. There is a limit to the ability of social systems to enforce regulations, which is evident in the failures of enforcement by principals over teachers, university administrators over faculty, and certainly, teachers over students. The government, too, has its enforcement problems. The U.S. government has difficulties in prosecuting draft evasion and tax delinquencies. The government has also had limited success in regulating monopolies and prosecuting corporations for illegal practices. Thus, there may be a lack of incentive or sufficient reward to abide by regulations on the part of citizens, or the regulations may be viewed as conflicting with more desirable personal goals. Whenever these conditions prevail, they may lead to sabotaging the attempts to enforce the regulations, or they may take the form of evasive action which could remain undetected. Thus, it is evident that there are numerous limitations to which decision-makers may fall prey in attempting to enforce regulations and execute policies.

Bureaucratic Educational Systems

It is a common assumption that bureaucracies are autocratic, cluttered with "red tape," self-serving, inefficient, and run by curt time-servers. Actually, the term "bureaucracy," as used by the social scientists, is not employed in this pejorative sense. Rather, for them, bureaucracies refer to the social structure of large scale organizations. Bureaucracies are designed to carry out complex tasks more efficiently than nonbureaucratic organizations by means of their specialization of roles and functions, division of labor, and the employment of modern management techniques. According to Max Weber, bureaucracies are designed to eliminate irrationality and emotional elements, facilitate speed, precision, and continuity, and subordinate personnel to the administrative hierarchy in order to reduce costs and personal friction(6). Bureaucracies are organized in a hierarchy with each office under the supervision of a higher office (which can be viewed on an organizational chart as a chain of command). Bureaucracies employ specialists to fulfill tasks, which creates a complex division of labor and an intricate communication network.

Another characteristic of bureaucracies is their attempt to eliminate partiality, prejudice, and favoritism in employment. This nonpartisanship is accomplished by specifying in writing the standards of competence required for each position, and to base advancement upon achievement, seniority, or both. Employment in the organization constitutes a career, and the employee is protected by a pension plan and through safeguards against arbitrary dismissal.

The characteristics enumerated above hold for large school systems and universities just as they do for industry and government. There are, of course, obvious differences in these social systems, but the similarities of organization are sufficiently clear to refer to each of them as bureaucracies. The question to be raised for public education is: "Do bureaucratic systems perform their tasks efficiently and economically as they are designed to do, or have they generally failed to fulfill their goals?" It is not possible to review their success in attaining all of their diverse goals. However, one of the most critical and complex goals is promoting equality of educational opportunity. An educational system, no matter what other goals it achieved, would not be successful unless it demonstrated substantial success in bringing about equality of educational opportunity. Equal opportunity is undoubtedly our most critical domestic issue today, and the continued inability to make concerted and sustained progress in this area leads not merely to a worsening of the problem itself but to the prospect that American society will be torn asunder by the various contingents. Immediate massive action is needed not only because of these dire forebodings, but also and more importantly, because the provision of equal opportunity is just and right. A society cannot continue to espouse democratic ideals and deny equal opportunities if it hopes to survive in any form other than a police state.

To what extent, then, do the bureaucratic controls in our large educational systems promote equality of educational opportunity? Since "one-fourth of the nation's school systems educate nearly 80 per cent of the U.S. population,"(7) a focus should be on these metropolitan schools.

In any large school system it is necessary to standardize a number of operations in order to have common procedures which are acceptable and to have a common basis for evaluating the different units within the system. This need has meant that curricular offerings, testing, promotion policies, age grading, and numerous other aspects of the system have been standardized, which has led, on the one hand, to the application of uniform criteria whenever the relevant policies have been properly executed. On the other hand, it has led to a neglect of human diversity and individuality that has particularly proved harmful with minority groups.

Theoretically speaking, bureaucratic organizations can accomplish large scale tasks better than any other form of organization. Yet there are numerous complaints today that many of our metropolitan school systems have become inflexible and ossified, no longer able to attain their stated objectives and make flexible adaptations to new demands. Some of the reasons for the failures to regulate social systems successfully can be applied. New York City's school system has been accused of being a "sick" bureaucracy(8). Among the charges are its overcentralization, fragmentation of units, protectionist and expansionist policies of administrative subsystem irrespective of the system's overall welfare, compulsiveness in observing and enforcing rules, rebellion of lower level supervisors against office directives, insulation of administrative personnel from the public in order to pursue their career interests, and the inability to hold any person responsible for policies due to the fact that nearly all decisions are made in committees. These conditions, however, are not unique to the New York City system; they can be found in various forms in other metropolitan systems(9).

The Concept of Equal Educational Opportunity

Equality and the Political System

In democracies, educational policies are usually established to insure that all young people will have an opportunity to pursue an education. This policy is thought to be necessary, politically speaking, because the welfare of democracy is best served when citizens are informed of the issues which affect their lives and learn to participate intelligently in the essential tasks of citizenship. As the argument goes, if educational opportunities are not widely and impartially distributed, there is a strong likelihood that a segment of the population will be unable to perform their citizenship tasks; it will, in other words, prove to be a handicap to the adequate workings of the democratic process.

There are some who would suggest, however, that studies of democracy, particularly American democracy, fail to show that widespread political activity is essential to the success of democratic governments; rather, the elite or policy makers and shapers are the main bulwark against the breakdown of the system(10). The policy makers are the chief apologists for democracy because the system itself has enabled them to gain power. They, in turn, secretly fear widespread participation in the political process because it may upset the stability of the system. The system works best when the political entrepreneurs can compete openly in the struggle for power to see who runs the system, while the citizenry remains basically passive and apolitical. The elites utilize the machinery of the system to elevate themselves into power by learning how best to appeal to the masses at election time. Democracy, then, becomes a method of decision making by means of which the system is administered, power is allocated, and favorable public opinion is elicited prior to election day.

The elitist theory also views the notion of consensus, which is commonly appealed to in democratic thought as essentially misleading. The consensus notion states that democracy can operate effectively only when leaders are able to unify the people by gaining their assent on issues that are critical to the successful operation of society. In order to gain widespread support, elites are aware that political parties which appeal to a narrow spectrum of interests are not viable. It is essential that their platforms cut a broad swath across the center of the population, appealing to the largest possible number of people. If possible, the party should frame its platform so that it appeals to labor, management, civil service employees, small and large businessmen, farmers, homemakers, the elderly, and young adults. Obviously an appeal this broad is generally not possible, even though political parties would like to elicit such widespread support. By attempting to engineer consent by offering something to each of these diverse groups, the party gains public support and its candidates are successful in being elected.

The elitist theory presents evidence against the consensus notion by pointing to the fact that most citizens are apolitical: their prime interests are their job, family, and recreational pursuits; few actively participate in precinct politics, contribute to political campaigns, are active as lobbyists. To argue that citizens are watchdogs over the political process, seeing to it that democratic values are realized is implausible. Rather than consensus as the aim, the continuation of general apathy is needed in order to insure that disagreements will not involve large numbers of people or get out of hand; otherwise, the stability of democracy is threatened. The elitist theory can point to the tendency of the masses to be easily swayed by demogogues whenever inflammatory issues arise, posing the threat of overthrowing the system and replacing it with a totalitarian one. The political elites are the best protectors of democracy because the system has brought them power and all the possibilities that power carries with it.

That the system operates this way today is true; but it does not follow that this is the only way it can operate to insure democratic values. We would also need evidence from democratic societies where citizens were more politically active to see whether this activity tended to subvert the democratic process. More widespread participation may actually promote a greater realization of democratic ideals and result in an amelioration of some of the inequities presently found in American society.

Thus, universal education may be said to have some bearing on the successful operation of democratic forms of government. But suppose the elitist theory is correct. Certainly it does not follow that public education is no longer needed, for it would still be necessary to train potential leaders. Since the elitist theory is not based on invidious distinctions of wealth, birth, race or religion but, rather, on a meritocracy, it would be logical to use the public schools as a screening device for the discovery of talents (in fact, this is exactly what has been done —

although quite imperfectly — for many years). One could not leave
the education of the younger generation in a meritocracy up to parents
— not only because some parents are not wise about such matters, but
also due to the fact that if public schools were not provided, only those
who could afford to do so could send their children to private schools.
Such a process is too haphazard to be useful in selecting a elite; therefore, a system of education must be provided at public expense that
utilizes an equitable form of taxation. American society is, in many
ways, far less than a meritocratic system because the ability to advance
is not determined solely through merit but on the basis of seniority,
influence, family background, political bargaining, and other factors.
There already exist many meritocratic factors in some bureaucratic systems, although many of these systems have frequently failed to live up
to professed meritocratic standards. Yet the trend is toward instituting
and enforcing more systematic and comprehensive meritocratic standards in our social system.

Thus, whether we accept elitist theory or a more classical conception
of democracy which insists on a widespread public participation as
essential to the health of democracy, public schooling is necessary. The
content of the program may differ in certain ways depending upon which
theory one adopts. The importance of public schooling need not rest
upon civic participation; it is frequently argued for on other grounds
as well. Some find a connection between public education and the Good
Life (however it may be defined). Others are more specific about the
ingredients that compose the Good Life. They may cite the importance
of vocational skills, preparation for family life, appreciation of the arts
and sciences, and ability to use leisure time wisely. There are proponents for each of these educational outcomes, and some proponents further argue that such abilities are needed by all persons if democratic
societies are to prosper. They hold this position for a number of reasons: humanitarian grounds, the consistency of these ideals with the
needs of democracy, or the fact that their denial is a restriction of basic
human rights.

Arguments Against Equality

It is well known that equal educational opportunities are related to
democratic values, but considerable confusion still surrounds the notion
of equality. There have been various fears expressed about equality.

If instituted, equality will lead to mass conformity. Equality constitutes a leveling process by which the wealth may be redistributed and incentive destroyed. By its very nature equality is impossible to attain due to the obvious differences among men. Finally, equality restricts human liberty.

The mass conformity argument rests on the belief that a thoroughgoing egalitarian system tends to erase social, political, and economic differences among men that in other types of societies bring out distinctive human features. These features are often based upon the social and economic differences among men associated with existing social classes where social mobility is far more difficult. One is born into a certain station in life and the sphere of one's activities and his group membership are determined by his birth. It was only under exceptional circumstances that a person, during his lifetime, can elevate himself into a class higher than that of his parents in such a system.

Although Western democracies today manifest different degrees of social mobility, all of them are characterized by systems offering greater mobility than that described above. In fact, this greater measure of mobility is usually thought to be one of the favorable features of democracies. Yet it is true that in any system where a greater degree of equality becomes an actuality, there may very well be a tendency to minimize the differences, such as economic inequalities. This minimizing may lead, for instance, to a large middle class which enjoys similar products, tract houses, and tastes in entertainment and recreation. This situation is becoming increasingly true today of the American middle class, but it has been abetted by the mass media and the advertising industry.

On the other hand, it could be argued that if we are speaking of equality of opportunity, a greater diversity will utimately prevail in society because it permits each individual (within certain limits) to develop his abilities. Apart from great social pressure to force human development into predetermined channels, there are considerable possibilities that diversity and human differences will be accentuated if, of course, sufficient liberty is present to permit individuals to choose the paths they wish to pursue. Thus, it is evident that liberty must supplement equality, unless equality is defined in such a fashion that it permits freedom of choice in certain areas of life.

Some observers, such as de Tocqueville, do not see that equality will bring about a mass uniformity(11). There are, according to de Tocqueville, various factors — education, fortune, tastes — which will maintain the differences among men. Through private societies or voluntary associations that men establish they will avoid a mass uniformity. In contrast to aristocratic nations which confine citizens to associate almost exclusively with members of the class of their birth, democratic societies offer men the opportunity of wider and less restricted associations, hence, promote diversity. Rather than supposing that in democracies all men will live in common, de Tocqueville was afraid that "they will end by forming only small coteries."(12)

But, undoubtedly, the forces that issue in mass conformity are greater than in the 1840's when de Tocqueville visited America. Regional differences today are no longer as great, thanks to television and other media, rapid transportation, and communication. Voluntary associations are more numerous than ever, and while some groups promote healthy differences, many more reinforce norms which transcend the particular group and assimilate broader social class interests.

There is a danger in equality, however, that de Tocqueville correctly divined. He saw that in a state of equality no men are required to come to the aid of another or expect much support from another. There is no *noblesse oblige*. Each is independent but lacking in power. The citizen looks to a strong central government to correct this disability. Whereas in a democracy citizens are wont to be suspect of those who proclaim some form of superiority, their state of power allows them to submit to a master in the form of the state(13). It was de Tocqueville's belief that "equality singularly facilitates, extends, and secures the influence of a central power . . . Democratic nations often hate those in whose hands the central power is vested; but they always love that power itself."(14) The history of the United States, we could add, seems to support this idea, although it would be folly to attribute it as the sole cause—or perhaps not even the primary cause—of the growth of a strong centralized government. Many people, particularly during the depression of the 1930's, came to believe that there were many tasks that the government could best perform for them. The immense power today in the federal government, most notably in the military, was unanticipated by most people during the 1930's. But to say that equality was a principal cause of these developments would not only prove exceedingly difficult to demonstrate, but would also overlook the great inequalities in American society. These inequalities were more pronounced when de Tocqueville visited America, but probably due to the marked contrast he found with European society, he tended to overlook their pervasive and intractable nature.

A second argument against equality is that it results in a leveling process by which wealth may be redistributed and incentive destroyed. This argument, of course, is one used against the personal income tax: that the wealthy are taxed to support the poor, and that those who have worked hard (or who are gifted at financial chicanery) have their assets redistributed. However, this argument means very little so long as large loopholes remain in the income tax system. The middle income groups are the ones who actually take a beating.

This debate presupposes some form of economic equality, and we find very few reformers, other than those who advocate a pure form of communism, espousing this position. However, some view such activities of government as progressive taxation, Social Security, Medicare, welfare, and other programs as a move to bring about economic equality. Actually, these programs are consistent with one of the long-held beliefs of liberalism that a duty of government is to minimize and prevent needless suffering. By instituting programs of this type, it can be claimed that, in spite of whatever abuses and inefficiencies presently exist in these programs, suffering is decreased and human well-being is promoted. In other words, differential treatment is granted persons with the appropriate disabilities for relevant reason of suffering. If one should ask why this reason is appropriate, he would be referred to the basic tenets of democracy. The argument may not stop at this point, but it could be claimed that, although democracy is accepted as the best form of government, the notion of preventing suffering is not one of its tenets. If the prevention of suffering is admitted as a tenet, it could still be argued that the programs themselves are not the most appropriate or desirable ones to fulfill the tenet because of existing resources. There may be people who do not accept democracy as the best form of government and reject the tenet out of hand. All that can be done at this point is to debate the merits of different systems of government.

Presumably if more equality exists today than ever before, there should be, as the argument goes, a greater redistribution of wealth. The middle class is larger percentagewise. Still, the very situation that is feared — redistribution of great wealth to the masses eliminating the wealthy class — has not occurred(15). In fact, there are more people in America with great wealth than ever before.

That equality will destroy economic incentive has not discouraged the many who have made their fortunes since World War II. But the concept is a seemingly plausible rationalization for the failures among the materialistically ambitious. Without a modicum of equal opportunity, incentive is decisively destroyed whenever those who attempt to rise out of poverty confront continual failure. Yet many people still believe that those on welfare lack ambition and a willingness to work hard, that as long as people are given hand-outs they will never have any incentive to become successful. In spite of the shortcomings of the welfare system, a study of those on welfare indicate otherwise. Analysis discloses that "out of the 7.3 million Americans on welfare, only 50,000 males may be capable of getting off — even if every program, public and private, were adequately staffed and efficiently run."(16) The reason is that of the people on welfare a large number are over 65 (2.1 million); 700,000 are blind or severely handicapped; 3.15 million are children bereft of parental support; 1 million are the children's parents, and only 50,000 of these are capable of acquiring vocational skills(17).

A third argument is that equality, by its very nature, is impossible to attain due to the obvious differences among men. Men are not equal, there are great physical, intellectual, moral, and social differences among them. To consider men equal is to falsify empirical evidence open to everyone. But when Jefferson wrote in the Declaration of Independence that all men are equal, he did not mean that there exists a literal equality of attributes among men. Some infer that Jefferson was referring to the Christian doctrine because he made reference to the Creator, and with Christianity being the dominant religion of the colonies, he could be establishing equality on sectarian grounds. However, even though there are certain egalitarian tendencies in Christianity, there also is the problem of some being saved and some being damned. In addition, it is doubtful that this connection could be made because Jefferson and other Founding Fathers were deists.

By the very fact that men are human, they ought to be treated equally. Here we note that it is not because of any alleged similarity of attributes among men that warrants equal treatment, but the fact that they are human beings possessed of many differences but sharing the characteristics of rationality, aesthetic sensitivity, ability to assume responsibility for actions, self-consciousness, and the ability to plan and create a culture. Thus, unless there are exceptional circumstances in which there are relevant and justifiable reasons for not doing so, men should always be treated equally. There are, however, possible arguments against this justification of equality. For the moment, though, to point out this one possible response to the argument against equality based on the obvious differences among men is enough.

Another response to the argument is to acknowledge the differences among men but support equality on the pragmatic grounds that it is essential to a democratic system, for without it democracy would fail.

Therefore, those who accept democracy as the best way of life will accept the concept of equality in order to be consistent. For it could be shown that one could have the various freedoms associated with democracies, but without equality great limitations would be placed on one's ability to enjoy them. Liberty without equality would degenerate into privilege; equality without liberty would lead to mediocrity.

A fourth and final argument against equality is that to institute it would lead to a curtailment of liberty. To establish and enforce policies of equal opportunity may result in restrictions upon the liberties of those more fortunate who are in a position to enjoy more of the privileges and the goods and services of life than their fellows. Introducing equal opportunities in industry has forced management to change its personnel policies in this area; in education, it has restricted school boards from enforcing segregated schooling. It would be mistaken, however, to label these two instances as a denial of liberty, for one has no "right"—legal, natural, or otherwise—to discriminate(18). What would constitute discrimination, moreover, is determined by an evaluation of basic rights, particularly the right of equality.

There are possible social arrangements that offer equality at the price of freedom, however. We could imagine a ruler who would arrogate all power to himself and organize society into two groups: himself and the masses. The people would be given equality but denied liberty. All would have equal, but limited, opportunities within a circumscribed range of activities that in no way conflicted with or impeded the ruler's privileges and his ability to exercise power. In such a society, equality would be vitiated by the lack of other essential rights which would strengthen it and give it substance. In other words, equality becomes meaningful in a society by the mutual support it enjoys with other rights.

The illustration used here could be characterized in another way. The social system employs a form of "exclusive equality" in the sense of a group, class, or caste sharing equality but not necessarily sharing it with others. The type of equality which is more desirable is an "inclusive equality" which is extended to all members of a society rather than limiting it to certain groups(19).

Equality Reassessed

Equality is actually more of a prescriptive than a descriptive concept. To talk about equality does not imply that two or more persons have

identical or the same weight, height, speed, strength, intelligence, creativity, or any other characteristic. What is generally meant by the concept is that one *ought* to accord equal treatment to all persons unless
there are relevant and sufficient reasons for not doing so. By treating
people differently rather than similarly in certain situations, one is not
denying equality so long as differential treatment under the given circumstances is justifiable. To determine whether distinctions should be
made in the treatment of individuals, one must examine the situation
or context, the individuals involved, and the circumstances surrounding
the situation. Whether we are evaluating the treatment to be accorded
to juvenile delinquents, job applicants, or candidates for graduate school,
it is necessary to observe the rules relevant to the situation to see how
they apply to the persons under consideration. For example, suppose
that a college requires two semesters of physical education of all incoming freshmen. What do those in charge of the program do if a
student is physically handicapped and would experience considerable
difficulty in completing the courses? If the rule requires all students
irrespective of their physical condition to complete the course, such a
rule would be discriminatory to those who were physically handicapped.
Equal treatment would mean that the rules should be formulated in a
manner in which special provisions would be made for the handicapped.

For admission to graduate school in many universities, an acceptable
score on certain standardized tests are required. These tests usually are
weighed along with other factors, such as grade point average. What
policy should be followed on these admissions tests with respect to those
students whose native tongue was a language other than English?
Since graduate schools in the major universities receive applications
from many students for whom English is a second language, should these
students be required to meet the minimum score on these test for admission which are used with English-speaking students? The tests, as we are
aware, presume considerable facility with English, and they also are
usually speed tests. Are there sufficient and justifiable reasons for differential treatment in such cases?

Although the concept of equality is essentially prescriptive, there may
be some descriptive aspects. These descriptive aspects do not occur
with the initial interpretation of equality which concerns equal treatment
for all persons, because this part of the interpretation does not depend
upon the individual having a particular characteristic (such as, strength,
quickness, musical ability, etc.). Rather, equal treatment is accorded
for the very reason that the individual is a human being. In order to

know whether differential treatment should be accorded, one must look at the characteristics of the individuals involved (descriptive) with reference to the situation and the rules governing it.

The question has been debated whether equality of opportunity should be based on need or merit. Equal opportunity initially is not on the basis of merit but on need. Everyone "needs" equal opportunity in order to become more fully human. Merit does not relate so much to one's humanness as it does to one's special talents and capacities which give the individual his uniqueness. Humanness does not refer to uniqueness and idiosyncratic features; it pertains to what all men have in common, that one is a human being. Because one is a human being, he should not be deprived arbitrarily or capriciously of opportunities available to others.

As for merit, some individuals are given opportunities to pursue certain lines of endeavor because they meet the standards governing the activity (e.g., higher education). However, the standards should not be arbitrary or capricious; they should be derived in such a way that they apply strictly to competencies governing the activities and not to irrelevant factors such as race, religion, sex, etc. Irrelevant factors should not be used because they limit opportunities on grounds that have no connection with merit.

In a system that utilizes a considerable number of meritocratic criteria, the application of these criteria should *not* be construed as indicating those whose achievement is highest in certain valued fields of endeavor as being "higher" as human beings. Rather, their status is high only in the field in which they excel. The only hierarchy pertaining to persons is a moral one. If this hierarchy is the case, some members of a number of minority groups are more fully human because they have been the only persons who have consistently fought for equal opportunity *for all*.

Equal opportunity based on need is applicable at the beginning of our principle of equality. Each individual should have opportunity to further develop himself as a person, that is, his humanness. Based on need, then, there is a minimum income, varying from one society to another, below which no individual should fall; otherwise, the individual cannot become more fully human. Government, therefore, has a moral obligation to see to it that no individual falls below this level (this obligation is usually construed as providing sufficient income to keep families above the poverty line). In order to provide the opportunity to move away from this minimum level so that the individual's total energies and talents are not absorbed in securing the bare necessities of life, hence, leaving no

**Educational programs should be broadly conceived
so that the multiplicity of talents among students can be
brought to fruition.**

time to develop oneself, it is necessary for society to provide opportunities for each person to learn and pursue a vocation(20). The range of vocations should not be limited. Otherwise, the retarded and handicapped will never have a genuine opportunity to move sharply away from the poverty level. Society must provide vocational opportunities for the full range of human abilities: the average normal, talented or gifted, retarded, and the handicapped. These proposals are based on the *need* of each person to become fully human. We should also include equal access to education. However, once a person takes a job or enters the educational system, considerations of equality are governed by *merit*. Educational programs should be broadly conceived so that the multiplicity of talents among students can be brought to fruition, and also to insure that merit is not interpreted in an overly restrictive fashion by limiting it to a narrow range of programs which only call forth the talents of a limited few. To take an historical example, when secondary schooling was based on a classical curriculum, it severely constricted the range of merit that could be recognized. Those who lacked the talent or motivation for classical studies could not benefit by the programs, hence, their abilities could not be developed through organized schooling. The same could be said today about programs which place too great an emphasis on the college preparatory program, leading to limited opportunities in vocational and commercial areas.

The concept of equality is based on both need and merit, but merit considerations refer to one's level of achievement rather than one's merit as a person. Initially merit is not a criterion in personhood since each person has a right to certain equal provisions and opportunities as a human being. Later, after these provisions and opportunities are distributed equally, we can evaluate one's personhood on the basis of merit by his acts which have moral significance. The minimum criteria on which this moral evaluation could be made is to see whether the individual grants to all other persons, by recognizing their essential humanness, equality of treatment and the basic freedoms which complement and insure that equality with liberty will become a living reality.

Problems of Desegregation

An enormous amount of progress must still be made in the area of desegregation (or, preferably, integration) of the educational systems of the nation if society is not to be torn asunder by internal strife. Furthermore, we scarcely measure up to our professed ideals of equality of educational opportunity. Part of the problem lies in matters of social control and bureaucracy. First of all, the controls exercised, in many cases, are designed to maintain existing arrangements, even though inadequate, and to take punitive measures against reformers who prove overly threatening to those in positions of power. Although controls are exercised imperfectly in maintaining existing power arrangements, they usually result in further disorder, frustration, and confusion between the administrative hierarchy and personnel in the field, when they go awry.

The growth of bureaucracy, rather than bringing about greater efficiency of operation and impartiality in employment and retention as its proponents claim, has, more often than not, degenerated into an obstacle course of poor communication, "red-tape," slavish following of rules, and even an inability to implement desirable desegregation plans developed by the administration and board. There have been numerous proposals as to how the cumbersome machinery of metropolitan school systems can be rejuvenated—from new alliances of power blocs and personnel to far-reaching desegregation of the entire administrative system. There is no surefire solution to the problems that afflict our cities, educational, political, economic, or other types of problems. A known fact is that our educational systems are in trouble, and those measures which have been tried and found wanting in the past must be discarded and replaced with more rewarding ones rather than penalizing those with original and promising ideas which tend to threaten existing power structures. Some have suggested that before metropolitan school systems can be successfully rebuilt so that they can secure the objectives for which they were designed to serve, restructuring many of the institutions in the larger society will be necessary. If these observers are correct (and considerable disagreement still exists on this point), educators cannot afford the luxury of waiting, something must be done immediately to marshal great resources and to solicit vigorous public support. What major changes should be effected are conditioned by a number of factors. Obviously we need to survey and assess the particular school system, its objectives, most pressing problems, the resources at its disposal, and the political and community support that it can command. However, to know something about the empirical studies of desegregation and their bearing on policy formation is necessary.

Undoubtedly the most important study of desegregation problems in recent years has been the Coleman Report(21). The Report has been widely discussed by educators and other interested persons, and as is usually the case of a major study dealing with a critical issue, it has elicited strong support from some quarters and drawn pointed criticism from others(22). The Report, which included data on 600,000 children and 60,000 teachers in 4,000 schools, also formed the basis for a U.S. Civil Rights Commission Report(23). Rather than corroborating the belief that school facilities for minority group children are unequal and that these inequalities are related to student achievement, differences were found to have little discernable relationship to student achievement. The Report did reach two conclusions which differed from what many educators expected: 1) As measured by standardized tests of mathematical and verbal skills, the most significant determinant of educational success is the social and economic background of the student; 2) Irrespective of the races involved, those children from disadvantaged backgrounds learn more when they are integrated with children of advantaged backgrounds. The learning performance of the latter group, contrary to popular belief, does not drop when placed in an integrated learning situation.

The Report diverges from other studies by emphasizing "outputs" rather than educational "inputs." Inputs are those factors which are placed in the system to improve quality and include such things as better facilities, smaller classes, higher-paid teachers. The Report interprets equality of educational opportunity in terms of outputs or the effects of schooling. It was found that considerable differences in achievement exist between Negro and white students. To bring out equal opportunity, one would not aim to make the achievement levels of the two groups identical but only the averages for the two population groups would come to be identical.

Two economists, however, claim that if the methodology of the study had been reversed, so would the conclusions(24). In other words, if such inputs as teacher training had been controlled, the social background of students would make little difference. Others have suggested that rather than concentrate exclusively on equalization, it is also important to emphasize and develop the diversity of strengths of each ethnic group(25). For example, Jews score higher, relative to the general population, on verbal skills but do not do as well on space conceptualization. For Chinese students, on the other hand, the strengths and weaknesses are reversed. Information is also available on other ethnic groups. Perhaps an important goal of schooling should be that of maximizing these strengths.

It could be argued that the Coleman Report presents some of the most cogent data for integrated education ever assembled. A prima facie case could then be made that an inherent conflict exists between the Coleman Report and the Bundy Plan(26). The Bundy Plan calls for city-wide decentralization and community control. However, Coleman, in an essay, rejects the view that only through integration will Negro academic achievement be brought up to the level of whites(27). He also recognizes that integration is not likely to be achieved soon. There is also evidence in the Coleman Report that would support efforts to instill black pride. It was found that one's self-concept, his attitudes of interest in school, and a sense of environmental control show the strongest relation to school achievement. "Environmental control" refers to the extent that students feel they have control over their own destiny(28). Thus, metropolitan public schools, as well as those in smaller cities, seem to have failed to provide an educational context in which blacks can develop favorable attitudes toward schooling, a favorable self-concept, and a sense of environmental control. These facts would indicate the desirability of black studies and other promising attempts to instill black pride. The sense of powerlessness of the disadvantaged in highly centralized school systems may also be ameliorated through decentralization and greater community control. Although decentralization would lead to a form of separatism in with each ethnic group dominating a geographical area of the city would run its own schools, many of the existing centralized systems are racially imbalanced, and in spite of promising desegregation plans (which usually fail at the implementation stage), many of our schools are essentially separate and unequal as they stand. Due to the intransigence of many whites, resulting from what the Kerner Report calls "white racism," it is unlikely that significant steps will be taken in our cities in the very near future to bring about widespread integration. Since community control has promise, but has never been tried on a large scale, it deserves to be given a chance. This need is further buttressed by the failures of existing arrangements and the unlikelihood of widespread integration in the near future.

Proposals for Desegregation

Although there have been continuous and concerted efforts to prevent the desegregation of schools in the deep South since the Brown vs.

Board of Education decision in 1954 and the U. S. Supreme Court statement in 1955 that school systems are to desegregate "with all deliberate speed," the lack of progress in this region led the court in 1969 to urge "immediate" desegregation. Previously there had been threats to cut off federal aid if U. S. Office of Education guidelines for desegregation were not complied with. However, with a relaxation of pressure on the South during the early years of the Nixon administration, what former progress had been made had slowed to a trickle until the Supreme Court mandate.

The prospect that it will take many decades to correct the racial imbalance in the public schools of the South and an unknown period of time to rectify the damages of *de facto* segregation in other parts of the country remains. That a number of metropolitan school districts have instituted compensatory education programs, while others have tried and dropped them after finding they failed to measure up to their early promise should be noted. Many educators had bright hopes that compensatory education would help to provide some of the needed experience lacking in the background of disadvantaged youth; however, a number of observers believe that these programs have failed and that it will be necessary to try other proposals for equalizing educational opportunities(29).

There are a number of other proposals which have been made to correct racial imbalance, some of which have been tried with varying degrees of success. One policy employed is that of "pairing," which would involve merging the attendance areas of two or more schools in order to achieve better racial balance. Two elementary schools whose attendance areas are drawn in such a way that one is predominantly Negro in enrollment and the other white are paired so that children of both attendance areas enroll in each school by grade. Thus, where each school was K-6, one school is now K-3 and the other 4-6. By pairing, one school building may become a central facility for a small community. A similar arrangement can be effected in larger communities by making the entire district a single attendance zone for every student in one or two grades. This arrangement tends to preclude the reoccurence of segregation whenever there are shifts in residential patterns of housing.

Another plan—that of open enrollment—permits parents to send their children to underused schools outside their attendance district. Open enrollment has not been successful in some cities either because of the difficulties and "red-tape" involved in making transportation arrangements, or else because those least able to pay are expected to shoulder the costs of paying a private transportation system for services. That many white parents have openly resisted plans of this type and have precipitated their collapse is well known.

Another plan to alter racial imbalance is to select building sites for new schools which are strategically located between neighborhoods whose racial composition is predominantly of one race. Since this plan is characteristic of housing patterns in many of our cities, it tends to break up the concentration of a single race in a neighborhood school. There also have been efforts to place Negroes in some underused suburban schools. It has also been proposed that educational parks be created which would link the inner-city and suburban school systems. If federal funds were allocated for new housing throughout metropolitan areas rather than exclusively in the ghetto, a major step would be taken in overcoming the segregated housing patterns which now exist and which contribute to racial imbalance. Financial incentives from federal and state aid could be tied to the proportion of children from low income groups enrolled in suburban schools.

In addition to proposals for community control (which would temporarily maintain segregated patterns while offering citizens a greater voice in school affairs), alternate and competing school systems provide another approach to the problem. However, the full plan would be to give redeemable tuition grants to each child, which could be used at any approved school. As envisioned, some of the programs may be operated on an experimental basis, and some of the acceptable schools may be under private auspices.

Paying private learning industries a specified amount for each child, who within a year comes up to a certain achievement level, and reimbursing the school whenever the child fails to advance to this level is also practiced. This proposal is not one to desegregate schools, but it may be one approach to overcoming the high rate of failures in racially imbalanced schools. It could be used until the transition is finally made to more integrated schools.

The public schools will be faced with acute problems for some time, and great improvements are unlikely as long as, according to the Kerner Report, "white racism" infects American society. Progress has been made in the past decade in providing more equal educational opportunities, but sustained and concerted effort is essential—along with a shifting of national priorities to the urban domestic scene—by all levels of government, business and industry, the mass media, and the attitudes of white America before the democratic ideals, which are so fervently espoused, will become a living actuality.

Questions for Discussion

1. What are the predominant forms of social controls utilized in your community? In the school system?

2. Are there certain forms of social control presently used in education which are inherently undesirable or harmful, or can any type of control be used by a skillful person with desirable results (with "desirable" meaning, in this context, that which best promotes learning)?

3. Since power is unequally distributed in society, in what way should the social and political elites change their policies in order to bring about greater equality of educational opportunity?

4. Can bureaucratic educational systems regain their efficiency and impartiality or will it be necessary to decentralize school systems into small units in order to promote equality and to improve learning opportunities for all students?

5. Explain how you would set up a school system whose policies are based on both equality of need and merit.

6. Do you agree with the findings of the Coleman Report? Compare it to other studies which are addressed to the same issue.

7. During the interim period before integration is achieved, what policies do you believe will best alleviate the racial imbalance in the schools?

8. What major changes will be needed in our social institutions and in our way of life before full-scale integration of education becomes a reality?

For Further Reading

Treatments of politics which stress control are George E. G. Catlin, *A Study of the Principles of Politics,* London: George Allen and Unwin, Ltd., 1930; Charles E. Merriam, *Political Power,* New York: McGraw-Hill, 1934; Harold D. Lasswell, *Politics: Who Gets What, When, How,* New York:

McGraw-Hill, 1936. For sociological approaches to control, see: George C. Homans, *The Human Group,* New York: Harcourt, Brace, and World, 1950; and Richard T. LaPiere, *A Theory of Social Control,* New York: McGraw-Hill, 1954.

Among the many effective studies of bureaucracy are Chris Argyris, *Personality and Organization,* New York: Harper and Bros. 1957; Peter M. Blau and W. Richard Scott, *Formal Organizations,* San Francisco: Chandler Publishing Co., 1962; Ronald G. Corwin, *A Sociology of Education,* New York: Appleton-Century-Crofts, 1965; Amitai Etzioni, ed., *Complex Organizations: A Sociological Reader,* New York: Holt, Rinehart, and Winston, 1961; James G. March and Herbert A. Simon, *Organizations,* New York: John Wiley and Sons, 1958; James G. March, ed., *Handbook of Organizations,* Chicago: Rand McNally, 1966; Robert Presthus, *The Organizational Society,* New York: Alfred A. Knopf, 1962.

In order to effect many of the changes mentioned in the chapter, one needs to understand the workings of politics in education. There are a number of studies that treat politics at different levels: Roald F. Campbell, *et al., The Organization and Control of American Schools,* Columbus, Ohio: Charles E. Merrill Publishing Co., 1965; Richard F. Carter, *Voters and their Schools,* Stanford, Calif.: Institute for Communication Research, Stanford University, 1960; Richard F. Carter and John Sutthoff, *Communities and Their Schools,* Stanford, Calif.: School of Education, Stanford University, 1960; James S. Coleman, *Community Conflict,* New York: The Free Press, 1957; James B. Conant, *Shaping Educational Policy,* New York: McGraw-Hill, 1964; Robert A. Dahl, *Who Governs?* New Haven, Conn.: Yale University Press, 1961; Neal Gross, *Who Runs Our Schools?* New York: John Wiley and Sons, 1958; Floyd Hunter, *Community Power Structure,* Chapel Hill, N.C.: University of North Carolina Press, 1953; Ralph B. Kimbrough, *Political Power and Educational Decision-Making,* Chicago: Rand McNally, 1964; Robert S. Cahill and Stephen P. Heneley, eds., *The Politics of Education,* Panville, Ill.: Interstate, 1964.

The concept of equality has been treated from a number of perspectives by several writers. Among them are "Justice and Equality," chapter 5, S. I. Benn and R. S. Peters, *The Principles of Political Thought,* New York: The Free Press, 1965; R. S. Peters, "Equality," chapter 3, *Ethics and Education,* Chicago: Scott, Foresman, 1967; John Martin Rich, *Education and Human Values,* Reading, Mass.: Addison-Wesley, 1968, pp. 50-51; Bernard Williams, "The Idea of Equality," chapter 5, Peter Laslett and W. G. Runciman, eds., *Philosophy, Politics, and Society,* Oxford, Eng.: Basil Blackwell, 1962; B. Paul Komisar and Jerrold R. Coombs, "The Concept of Equality in Education," John Martin Rich, ed., *Readings in the Philosophy of Education,* Belmont, Calif.: Wadsworth, 1966, pp. 312-330; Gregory Vlastos, "Justice and Equality," Richard B. Brandt, ed., *Social Justice,* Englewood Cliffs, N. J.: Prentice-Hall, 1962, pp. 31-72; I. Berlin and R. Wollheim, "Equality," *Pro-*

ceedings of the Aristotelian Society, supplementary volume (1955); William T. Blackstone, "The Principle of Equality and Educational Opportunity," *Proceedings of The Philosophy of Education Society,* Lawrence, Kan.: 1965, pp. 69-74; John Martin Rich, "Rights and Education," *Journal of Educational Thought* 2 (December 1968): 167-174.

Finally, some of the problems, policies and politics of desegregation can be studied in the following works: James S. Coleman, *et al., Equality of Educational Opportunity,* Washington: U.S. Government Printing Office, 1966; U.S. Commission on Civil Rights, *Racial Isolation in the Public Schools,* Washington: U.S. Government Printing Office, 1967; "Equal Educational Opportunity," *Harvard Educational Review,* Special Issue 38 (Winter 1968); David Rogers, *110 Livingston Street,* New York: Vintage Books, 1968; Marilyn Gittell and Alan G. Hevesi, *The Politics of Urban Education,* New York: Frederick A. Praeger, 1969; Robert L. Crain, *et al., School Desegregation in the North,* Chicago: National Opinion Research Center, University of Chicago, 1966; Marilyn Gittell and T. Edward Hollander, *Six Urban School Districts,* New York: Frederick A. Praeger, 1968; Peter Schrag, *Village School Downtown,* Boston: Beacon Press, 1967; Robert L. Crain, *The Politics of School Desegregation,* Chicago: Aldine, 1968; and two studies by Mario Fantini and Gerald Weinstein: *The Disadvantaged,* New York: Harper and Row, 1968; and *Making Urban Schools Work,* New York: Holt, Rinehart, and Winston, 1968. For a comprehensive review of research findings see "Education for Socially Disadvantaged Children," *Review of Educational Research* vol. 40, no. 1 (February, 1970).

Notes

1. Emile Durkheim, *The Rules of Sociological Method* (Chicago: University of Chicago Press, 1938).

2. This does not necessarily mean that the rules are good, right or just, or that they are applied impartially, but is merely to report how the system functions.

3. This has frequently occurred in the New York City school system (although it obviously is not unique to that system). See: David Rogers, *110 Livingston Street* (New York: Random House, 1968).

4. For a discussion of thought control, see Robert Jay Lifton, *Thought Reform and the Psychology of Totalism* (New York: W. W. Norton, 1961).

5. See Herbert Marcuse, *One Dimensional Man* (Boston: Beacon Press, 1964).

6. *From Max Weber: Essays in Sociology,* trans. and ed. by H. Gerth and C. Wright Mills (New York: Oxford University Press, 1958); *The Theory of Social and Economic Organization,* trans. by A. M. Henderson and Talcott Parsons (New York: Free Press, 1957).

7. Quoted in Ronald G. Corwin, *A Sociology of Education* (New York: Appleton-Century-Crofts, 1965), p. 41.

8. David Rogers, *110 Livingston Street,* p. 267.

9. Robert J. Havighurst, "Chicago's Educational Needs," *Educating an Urban Population* (Beverly Hills, Calif.: Sage Publications, 1967), pp. 37-59; Marilyn Gittell and T. Edward Hollander, *Six Urban School Districts* (New York: Frederick A. Praeger, 1968); Peter Schrag, "Boston: Education's Last Hurrah," *Saturday Review* (May 21, 1966): 56-58ff.

10. See David Truman, "The American in Crisis," *Political Science Quarterly* (December 1959): 481-97; V. O. Key, Jr., *Public Opinion and American Democracy, Part IV* (New York: Alfred A. Knopf, 1961); Robert A. Dahl, *Who Governs?* (New Haven, Conn.: Yale University Press, 1961).

11. Alexis de Tocqueville, *Democracy in America,* Richard D. Heffner, ed. (New York: New American Library, 1964), pp. 247-48.

12. *Ibid.,* p. 248.

13. *Ibid.,* pp. 293-94.

14. *Ibid.,* p. 295.

15. See Ferdinand Lundberg, *The Rich and the Super Rich* (New York: Bantam Books, 1969).

16. Joseph A. Califano, Jr., address before Washington Chapter, Sigma Delta Chi, Washington, D.C., April 19, 1967.

17. *Ibid.*

18. There are, however, legal systems which do not prohibit unequal treatment which is discriminatory and a denial of equality. In this case, one can legally refuse to observe equal treatment; equality would need to be argued for on moral grounds and, as a result, some may choose to attempt to change the laws which bear on equality.

19. See Clinton Collins, "Equality, Justice, and Desegregation" (Lawrence, Kan.: *Proceedings of Twenty-First Annual Meeting of the Philosophy of Education Society,* 1965), pp. 103-4.

20. Whether this is done through formal schooling, industry, or both is not of concern at this point.

21. James S. Coleman, *et al., Equality of Educational Opportunity* (Washington: U.S. Government Printing Office, 1966).

22. See "Equal Education Opportunity," Special Issue, *Harvard Educational Review* 38 (Winter 1968).

23. U.S. Civil Rights Commission Report, *Racial Isolation in the Public Schools* (Washington: U.S. Government Printing Office, 1967).

24. Samuel Bowles and Henry M. Levin, "The Determinants of Scholastic Achievement — An Appraisal of Some Recent Evidence," *Journal of Human Resources* (Winter 1968).

25. Susan S. Stodolsky and Gerald Lesser, "Learning Patterns in the Disadvantaged," *Harvard Educational Review* (Fall 1967).

26. Mayor's Advisory Panel on Decentralization in New York City Schools, *Reconnection for Learning: A Community School System for New York City* (November 1967).

27. James S. Coleman, "Toward Open Schools," *The Public Interest* (Fall 1967).

28. Coleman, *Equality of Educational Opportunity,* pp. 23, 319.

29. Coleman, *Equality of Educational Opportunity;* David Rogers, *110 Livingston Street;* Mario Fantani and Gerald Weinstein, *The Disadvantaged* (New York: Harper and Row, 1968).

Chapter Ten
Future Prospects for
Education and
Human Development

The future will not wait. Time moves onward in an inexorable cycle of birth, growth, decay, and death. It causes some people to hold more tightly to infrequent present moments of bliss. Others look back nostalgically to a real or imagined idyllic, former age. A few attempt to anticipate future developments and devise ways to cope with them intelligently. A frequently heard saying is that the only thing we can be certain of is change itself. From this perspective, change is the one factor we know will characterize the period in which we will live out our lives. But this bit of information does not reveal much, for it is only natural that man would like to know what principal changes are likely to occur during his lifetime so that he may plan more intelligently and make the most of whatever opportunities accost him. The ability to foretell the future has been desired by men of all ages, and they have recruited shamans, fortunetellers, soothsayers, and others who purported to possess hidden powers to divine the future. Obviously, knowledge of the future would be an invaluable gift, not only to assure a fortune on Wall Street, but to assure a high probability of success in all

. . . yet the scientist, too, is limited in his predictive powers.

one's undertakings. Today the sorcerers are not the religious and mystical men of the past—at least not in the West—but the scientist himself. Since science has transformed the culture during our very life-time, it seems only logical to turn for direction to those who have such seemingly magical gifts. Yet the scientist, too, is limited in his predictive powers. He can forecast what is likely to occur if present experiments prove successful with the necessary breakthroughs being achieved. On the other hand, many of the most significant inventions, such as elec-tricity, telephone, laser, etc., were not anticipated by the scientific com-munity. We have found, however, that they have exerted an inestimable influence on human life. What new and unforeseen inventions are likely to occur before the turn of the century which will transform the way men relate to their environment and their fellows? These are the question marks with which science leaves us.

The prospects for human development—for becoming more fully human—between now and the year 2000 through formal education and other social institutions is of great concern(1). In order to evaluate these prospects, the preeminent dangers which threaten man and which may precipitate the demise of civilization as we know it must be ana-lyzed and steps taken immediately to reduce their ominous portent and bring them under the widest range of social control.

Imminent Perils to Man's Future

1. Lack of International World Government. In spite of efforts by states-men and political leaders to develop an international governing body that can deal effectively with the world's problems, such an international organization has yet to come into being. The League of Nations col-lapsed for various reasons. One reason for its failure was the lack of support by the United States. The United Nations was formed after the second world war, and though UNESCO and some of its subdivi-sions have had important influences on the nations of the world, the United Nations has had little notable success in its peace-keeping func-tions. These functions have not been fully supported by the two super-powers—the United States and the Soviet Union—and the policies propounded by the international body have been supported only when they were conceived to be in their self-interest.

An international body with sufficient strength to enforce its mandates is important because the world's nations could better regulate economic

policies, control pollution, effect population controls, distribute resources more equitably to the underdeveloped nations, eliminate epidemics, contagious diseases, offer medical services, and, finally, provide
agricultural aid which would elevate the nutritional level of the world's
peoples.

An international body is needed to regulate small wars by providing
troops drawn representatively from the countries of the world in order
to bring about a cessation of hostilities and prevent a small war from
becoming a major one. It should also provide a just and equitable forum
for negotiation and the airing of grievances.

The most perilous issue is the spread of nuclear, bacteriological, and
chemical weapons of warfare, and the present incapacity of the major
powers to bring them under international control. As more nations
secure these weapons and effect the means of delivering them, the probability of a world holocaust becomes greater. There will be no future for
man and all other living things on this planet if such weapons were to
be unleashed. At present the nuclear arsenals of overkill contain the
destructive equivalent of a number of tons of T.N.T. for every man,
woman, and child on earth — and the arms race continues. Thus, other
issues are meaningless unless a rigorous system of international control
and inspection is developed. Petty nationalistic interests, hopefully, may
be put aside for the sake of survival.

2. Pollution.   In addition to the grave threat of nuclear, chemical, and
biological warfare, the spread of pollution has developed so rapidly
that it now constitutes one of the gravest problems faced by industrially
developed nations. A long-term study by the Atmospheric Sciences
Research Center in Scotia, New York, indicates that the last vestige
of clean air in the United States, which was found near Flagstaff,
Arizona, disappeared in 1963(2). In other words, all air in the United
States is polluted in varying degrees. Polluted air is that which has 2,000
particles in a section half the size of a sugar cube. Metropolitan areas
today average about 15,000 particles. This number is growing at the
steady rate of 1,500 particles a year. The lethal level for humans is
35,000 particles. Scientists at the Center predict that in 1980, 10,000
people will die in one metropolitan area due to inundation by a cloud
of pollution. In ten to fifteen years, every person will have to wear a
breathing helmet in order to survive outdoors. Most of the animal life
and much of the plant life will be dead. By 1990 in the Northern Hemi-

sphere man will live in domed cities if the present pollution rate continues; he will need to wear a semi-space suit to roam around over a dead and deserted countryside.

What can be done to avert this catastrophe? We must begin immediately to effect legislation which will control pollution. Legislation should be passed to do away with the internal combustion engine by the mid 1970's. This legislation will give Detroit a little—but not much —time to come up with an alternative engine for transportation which does not pollute the atmosphere. The costly process of converting factories and industries to pollution free processes must begin immediately. Prohibitive fines for those who fail to convert their operations within the alloted time will be needed. New techniques for the disposal of garbage—some of which are presently known—will have to be employed as substitutes for existing processes which pollute the atmosphere. All of these measures, and others, will have to be taken by the mid 1970's to avert these perils to civilization.

3. Overpopulation.   Population trends are projected by making certain assumptions about birth and death rates. If the birth rate does not decline during the 1970's and then remain at a lower level, the U. S. population may be over 250 million by 1980 and close to 350 million by the end of the century(3). The world population could range from a low of 6.4 billion to as much as 7.2 billion by the year 2,000(4). These figures mean that the population of the world will more than double in the next thirty years, and although substantial growth will be registered in both the developed and underdeveloped nations, far larger increases will occur in the latter countries. This growth means that the critical problems faced by these nations will seriously worsen in the decades ahead unless long-term measures are taken now. Their progress in agriculture, industry, education, and other areas is likely to retrograde in the years ahead without effective population control. At first, the concern of population experts was that birth control practices were too difficult to administer properly and were overly complex for the native population to understand and put into practice. But in cases in which some measure of success has been achieved, another problem presents itself. Although it is possible to teach different peoples how to use birth control devices correctly, the custom in many countries is that of large families. Thus, once the family consists of the number of children desired, birth control is practiced successfully. The problem today for both the developed and underdeveloped countries lies in the customs and traditions surrounding family size. Even though family size has dropped appreciably in the developed nations since the turn of the century, most families still desire three or four children. In the underdeveloped nations, the desired family size is larger. To curb the dangers of the population explosion, one must attack the root of the problem — traditions surrounding family size. How to accomplish such ends is still an open question, but since overpopulation has widespread political repercussions, it becomes a matter of considerable import for national governments. It could be invested with patriotism for people to have small families or, for some, no children at all. National campaigns could be mounted to inform families that it is in the welfare of the country to have small families, that to do so is a responsibility of citizenship, and that those who refuse to regulate family size will be stigmatized by their fellows as shirking citizenship responsibilities. Whether more formal punishments by the state can be exacted which do not hurt the children is open to question. But people must be convinced that they no longer have a "right" to have large families.

Since the growing emancipation of women in the developed nations, it is possible to view other means by which this goal could be realized. As women are granted equal status with men and no longer are dependent upon men for support and protection, and as men are no longer dependent upon women to perform the household chores (since these increasingly will be taken over by machines), new relations between the sexes will be formed. Since the state has no genuine interest in marriage other than the protection of children, new types of relationships will likely be formed among the sexes for companionship and sexual enjoyment without the objective of parenthood. Only when a couple wish to unite for the purposes of procreation should the state regulate the relationship. Since it will be some time before enough is known about genetics to determine those who would transmit the most desirable genetic endowments, it is unlikely that the state will exercise much greater control (other than propagandize in favor of small family size) until more definitive knowledge is available.

Besides the usual couple arrangement, group marriages may be sanctioned in many of the developed nations as they are in Denmark. Less stigma will be attached to those who remain single. It should only be a short time before these nations also begin to eliminate laws prohibiting two consenting adults from practicing homosexuality in private. The last vestiges of Puritanism should fall in the decades ahead. One possible reversal of these trends would be that the political authorities believe, as in the case of a number of Communist nations, that such practices divert the citizen from his primary duties and allegiances to the state. However, with the reduction of the work week and the consequent growth of leisure time, it is unlikely that governments will press for Spartan regimes due to fear of possible dissatisfaction, discord, and strife.

4. Overurbanization. With the growth of urban areas, the rise of the megalopolis has occurred. These are urban areas of great population adjacent to or joined to one another; eventually the open space between these areas diminishes until it appears to be one metropolitan conglomerate. Three such areas are likely to be found in the United States. The first will be an area which extends from Washington to Boston and will contain almost one-fourth of the population. A second will be found in the Great Lakes area, stretching from Chicago to Pittsburgh and north to Canada. It will include Detroit, Cleveland, Toledo, Akron, Buffalo, and Rochester, and will probably contain one-eighth of the population. The third megalopolis will extend from Santa Barbara (or even San Francisco) to San Diego and will likely contain one-sixteenth of the population.

Even if pollution is somehow brought under control before it becomes lethal, there are grave problems facing these and other over-urbanized areas. Scientists know that animal life deteriorates under conditions of overcrowding that does not recognize territoriality(6). Territoriality refers to the way animals lay claim to a geographical area and defend it against others of their species. There are numerous functions served by territoriality in the animal kingdom, the most important of which is to regulate density which prevents the overexploitation of the environmental resources needed by an animal to survive. Overcrowding among animals has resulted in aggression, abnormal behavior, and premature death.

Although knowledge is incomplete, there are considerable dangers which may accompany human overurbanization. Scientists know that when people are exposed to noise of high decibels over periods of time, that they become less efficient in their activities, more tense and irritable, and develop various psychosomatic symptoms, including a proneness to ulcers. Even though man is communal, he also needs a measure of privacy, not only freedom from arbitrary search and seizure, but the privacy to think and conduct himself as he chooses. Whenever these conditions are largely absent, psychological health is impaired. The inability for man to achieve a healthy balance between his communal and private existence poses grave dangers for the future well-being of society.

Proposals to ameliorate these conditions have generally taken two forms. One proposal is that of improving the existing environment without disrupting present living patterns. Such a proposal would mean that noise and atmospheric pollution would be stringently regulated. Zoning would be used to prohibit certain types of vehicles in population centers. Parks, playgrounds, and recreation areas would be built in the center of the city. Public services and educational facilities would be improved and expanded. These proposed changes still await a system of adequate financing for urban areas.

The other proposal seeks to utilize existing space in the country more adequately by designing new cities in less populated or unused areas of the country, particularly the Midwest and the West. New cities can be created which offer adequate provisions for human needs, encouraging rather than coercing people to settle there. With present technological know-how, there is little reason to believe that needed development of industry, transportation, communication, and other public services cannot be created within a relatively short period of time.

What must be guarded against is the spiraling random growth which afflicts today's urban areas. Human welfare must be placed ahead of the pell-mell race for profits and the accumulation of material goods at all costs. The priorities of the federal government must be reassessed so that the urgent domestic problems of the nation will no longer go unattended. Long-range planning and a massive reallocation of resources will be needed at the earliest moment to stave off the deterioration of our cities and the despoiling of human life.

5. Neglect of Domestic Problems for Foreign Wars.   The 1960's were divisive years in American life. Besides the quest for social justice by minority groups, American military might sought to police the world and extend its hegemony on other continents. To do so it often supported dictatorships out of fear of a Communist menace. It committed itself in a highly costly undeclared war in Vietnam. During the early years of the war, most Americans thought it unpatriotic not to support its country's military adventures, especially since it supposedly was done to assure self-determination for a people by helping them turn back the Communist threat. But many American youth who were not nurtured on World War II heroics and a belief in "My Country, right or wrong" dissented from the growing involvement in Vietnam by countless marches, demonstrations, and protests, culminating in the nationwide moratorium in the fall of 1969.

The Johnson administration's "Great Society" program for the domestic scene was rapidly undermined and submerged by the administration's growing commitment of men, material, and resources in an Asiatic war. Defense took more than half the total budget, and never before in peacetime had so much of the nation's resources been committed to the military. The dangers of "the military-industrial complex," which Eisenhower fleetingly warned about when leaving the presidency, were not heeded. The vast resources needed to deal with our massive domestic problems have not been unleashed because our priorities are still fixed on war, defense, and the Cold War nemesis. Without agreement on nuclear disarmament and inspection, those who goad the fears of the Communist menace can continue many costly programs (such as the ABM) after the Vietnam war ends, and with the disparity between defense and domestic appropriations, the conditions in the latter sector may worsen to a point of no return. Thus, unless there is a serious and thoughtful reappraisal of priorities leading to a total national commitment dealing with human problems first — before profits and material accumulation — it is unlikely that the future of this country will be very bright.

6. Domestic Strife. The generation of the sixties awakened and perceived the enormous discrepancies in society between word and deed, between professed democratic ideals and actual practices. Some youths joined with minority groups in an attempt to secure greater social justice. The civil rights movement and the Vietnam war were two of the principal forces which girded youth for action. But as protest demonstrations on campuses and in the streets gained nationwide attention through the mass media, reaction set in among a large member of the older generation who felt that youth and civil rights groups were trampling upon the ideals they felt sacred. The older Puritanism, with its emphasis on cleanliness, Godliness, hard work, association of sex and sin clashed with the new styles that youth so ostentatiously displayed. There was also the "white backlash" against the civil rights movement, due to what the Kerner Report referred to as "white racism."

Many of the things that need to be done on the domestic scene do not cost anything: the granting of equal opportunity, respect for individual differences and the honoring of democratic ideals and the Bill of Rights. But since these things are not being done and minority groups are no longer as intimidated as formerly by the majority's threats against "getting out of line," the divisive tendencies in society are likely to continue until human rights are fully honored. Whether society should expect today's youth to gain positions of power in which they can correct some of these wrongs is open to question on two grounds: Can we afford to wait that long? Will youth become disenchanted with their present ideals and become corrupted by the power of the system itself? One factor is certain: When a large number of people no longer voluntarily abide by the laws and mores of a society but increasingly must be coerced to comply, the society already manifests the seeds of its own dissolution.

7. Inability to Develop a New Political Philosophy for Our Age. Some writers have suggested that in light of new knowledge and theoretical advances a new political philosphy is needed for our age(7). The original political thought on which this nation was founded was based to a considerable extent on Locke's conception of representative government, which was consistent with the Newtonian world view dominant at the time. But now we have moved in the physical sciences from the Newtonian absolute space machinery to relativity and field theories which finds an integral place for the observer within the system. However, our thought about government, man, and society is still too often entrapped in obsolescent nineteenth century notions. A need exists to bring these areas up-to-date by developing a political philosophy more appropriate to the theoretical knowledge presently available.

A strong current of liberalism runs through American political and social life. Liberalism itself has been modified, both in theory and policy, since the beginning of the republic. Starting with Locke and the ideals of the Enlightenment, reconstructions of liberal thought have been made by Mill, Bentham, and T. H. Green, among others. These reconstructions have served to move liberalism away from a laissez-faire conception to one based more upon the interdependence of persons in society. Changes have also been made in terms of policy beginning with New Deal legislation, which conceived a large interventionist role for government to play in the economy and in the broad area of welfare. Classical liberalism, with its hostility to governmental regulation, has declined since the time of John Stuart Mill(8).

One of the important political highlights of the 1960's was what some youth believed to be the exposure of the bankruptcy of liberalism. It was liberalistic policies that enjoined us to engage in a calamitous war in Vietnam and to seek to police the world while gaining greater hegemony over the underdeveloped nations to exploit them economically. Liberalism, too, became a fervent "cold warrior," leading to the adoption of intransigent positions internationally and fueling the fires of a spiraling arms race. Liberalism was also the voice of what students referred to as "the Establishment," which claimed that grievances could be aired and considered through the process of rational discussion and debate, leading to corrective action after all sides had been given a fair hearing. However, New Left students claimed that such proposals were only guises, that many times in the past they had presented grievances to the administration; the grievances were perfunctorily heard and nothing further was done about them. Only after months, and in some cases even years, of futile attempts to effect what students believed to be sensible and needed changes did they begin to resort to more dramatic means of bringing their grievances to public attention. True, as the 1960's wore on, some student groups did not attempt to placate authorities by pursuing the procedures that the latter preferred. Rather, they began immediately with various types of demonstrations, which they felt would bring substantive results. Without sanctioning all of the diverse and sundry tactics employed, many of the most significant changes in higher education during the past decade can be attributed to the reaction to student protest(9). Students claimed that there was something wrong with the liberalism that undergirded university policies if the only way substantive changes could be made which challenged existing policies was to bring pressure on the authorities via various types of demonstrations.

Could it be that liberalism was not actually operative but only some subverted form of liberalism? Could liberalism stand condemned for its susceptibility to being perverted? If true, this perverted form constitutes that which liberalism has been forced to take by the political and social elites, a form that it may likely sustain until the latest thinking becomes more closely attuned to the needs of society. Frequently youth is criticized for exposing the weaknesses of social institutions without offering suitable alternatives. Although they are exploring new styles of life, they have not as yet provided a new political philosophy even though they have generally espoused various forms of socialism and anarchism(10). But it would really be asking too much to expect them to develop such a philosophy when we recall the fact that liberalism was developed and refined over several centuries. However, the great problems of our time are pressing, and we can no longer afford the luxury of waiting for generations for such a philosophy to come to fruition. It would be misleading for society to expect youth alone to perform this vital task, for it surely is a responsibility of other minds in society to address themselves to this project, and it is in the interest of all citizens to see that the task is promptly undertaken.

8. Inadequate Planning.   One of the salient shortcomings of both education and government is the lack of adequate long-range planning. More often than not, planning has been on an *ad hoc* basis designed to deal with problems which have been permitted to grow disproportionately and become aggravated. In many instances, little is done to anticipate problems and possible exigencies, much less to engage sustained thought directed to future goals and alternative models for the types of educational systems and social institutions most desirable. Many of our greatest problems today were either dimly comprehended a generation ago, or on those few occasions when they were foreseen, little long-range planning was undertaken to see that the necessary resources were allocated toward their resolution. All levels of government must assume systematic and coordinated planning functions on more than merely a year-by-year basis. Education, also, needs long-range studies. One proposal that could be implemented now calls for leading universities to develop centers for studying and planning for the future. This arrangement would offer the needed detachment from the press of immediate crises, as well as the resources for conducting systematic research and the freedom to make policy recommendations apart from the pressures of political considerations.

Planning consists of several dimensions. Agreement is needed on the objectives to be attained, and since there are multiple objectives envisioned by complex social systems, priorities must be established among objectives in order to avoid conflicts and to allocate resources effectively.

Research must be undertaken to determine the significance of the operative social variables and the possible effects of the alternative plans on the population involved. Research brings into focus the emerging problems and needs of a system and how these can best be met. However, one's objectives often determine what problems will be apprehended. For example, if educators do not articulate the desegregation of the educational system as an objective, then segregated schooling is not viewed as a problem, even though outside observers may say that it *ought* to be.

The factor of time is one of the great problems with which we are faced today. Many social and educational problems have mushroomed out of proportion because of lack of adequate planning and priority given to other concerns. Time is now running short to bring these problems under control before permanent scars are left in institutional life. We need knowledge to deal with these problems effectively, and we need the skilled personnel who can conduct these planning functions effectively. At the present we are short on both personnel and adequate knowledge. Besides these factors, there has been resistance to planning among those who still hold a laissez-faire outlook and who tend to associate planning with a planned society characteristic of totalitarian regimes.

Today's planning will have to become more systematic and continuous than in the past. It should be based on a clearly conceived and agreed upon set of objectives with each objective being appraised in terms of its relative priority. Centers for planning need to be established and coordinated for all levels of government and education, and adequate financial resources need to be allocated to these centers in order that they may have the resources and personnel needed. Radical and courageous thinking is needed if we hope to cope with the vast social and technological changes.

Education, Productivity, and the Meritocracy

One of the problems of our posttechnological age is the change in the meaning and nature of work and productivity. With the advent of many of many technological and social changes, the needs in employment will differ markedly from those of the recent past.

In the past private industry and the manufacture of goods and products for personal consumption have been associated. Today the economy is shifting toward service industries. Cybernated systems are also being introduced and in the near future may be applied to a larger number of service industries, such as banks and supermarkets. While these developments have been taking place, the unions have not sufficiently readapted their policies and administrative structure to the changes in the economy. As a result, they have lost membership in recent years, in spite of their efforts to attract white collar workers.

The key economic values of the past were derived from industrial institutions and the entrepreneurs, and they were centered on the production of goods. But as production becomes routine, according to Daniel Bell, the major new institutions of society will be intellectual ones(11). These institutions could take the form of scientific laboratories, nonprofit corporations, and universities with scientific centers. As defense needs continued to mount after the second world war, scientific laboratories — Argonne, Brookhaven, and others — grew rapidly. If greater priority is given to domestic problems, new types of research and intellectual institutions are likely to spring up to meet the demands. Research scientists, computer technologists, mathematicians, and economists will guide these new institutions.

These developments tend to presage the numerous expected changes in the world of work. The impact of cybernation will be felt more acutely during the next ten to fifteen years, resulting in the usurpation of jobs not only of the unskilled and blue collar workers but engineers and managers as well. Youth will find that career decisions will have to be made on the basis of societal need and demand rather than subjective preference. Since highly qualified professionals and well trained technicians will likely be in short supply, they may be called upon to work 60 or more hours per week while other workers will enjoy a short work week, more extended and frequent vacations, and earlier retirement. There will still be a need for some relatively unskilled workers whose jobs are not eliminated by cybernation, but since the supply will undoubtedly exceed the demand, many will have to acquire marketable skills.

The demands on professionals will be severe, not only for their services but because they will spend a lifetime acquiring new knowledge and skills. This task will indeed be a great and demanding one in view of the knowledge explosion, and it will sorely stretch the capacities of professionals, making life more competitive, hectic, and a vital challenge. The problem will be further accentuated by the fact that those who will have more leisure time to develop skills will not be the ones whose jobs are highly demanding. The professional and the highly skilled technician will need to find some way during a lengthy work week to meet the pressing responsibility of acquiring new skills and abilities. But some will need the free time to learn a new career since the average worker may have to retrain for as many as three different careers during a lifetime.

Another revolution in work is taking place: the rise of the meritoc-racy(12). The rewards in a meritocratic system go to those who achieve, on demonstrated performance, rather than on the basis of race, religion, nationality, seniority, family background, politics, and other artificial distinctions that are still commonly used in a number of areas. The artificial and arbitrary system of perquisites and rewards found in cap-italistic and other economic systems would be prohibited in a meritoc-racy. Instead, the abilities, skills, and types of performance to be rewarded would be evaluated on the basis of merit. The abilities and skills deemed most desirable and worthy of reward would be determined by the priorities and highest values of the society. Hence, not all abilities are worthy — either in a meritocracy or in our present system. Among the wide range of human abilities, certain abilities are honored and others are disregarded or, in some cases, people are punished for exer-cising them. If art is thought to be of little worth in a particular society, then even the most talented artist will find his works disregarded and his efforts unrewarded. In our own society scientific, rather than artistic, achievement is more highly rewarded. Some abilities are also strongly discouraged: Plato, in his *Republic,* wished to prohibit children from reading such poets as Homer and Hesiod. In the Soviet Union today, the practice of psychoanalysis is prohibited, most likely because it poses certain theoretical conflicts with Marxism.

But assuming many developed nations move more toward a merito-cratic system, one may wonder what exactly would be wrong with doing so? Is not a meritocratic system more just, fair, and impartial than present modes of operation? There is usually resistance in any social system whenever new changes threaten the members' security, estab-lished ways of doing things, and opportunities for advancement. Those who have profited from established arrangements are naturally loathe to accept changes which would disrupt the pattern. Those secure in their jobs may soon be very insecure and unhappy; they may even find themselves without a job until newly demanded skills are acquired.

On the other hand, there are those people who claim that they would accept a meritocratic system on principle but object to its implementation because it will prove to be a failure when put into practice. There are too many vagaries and personal biases, they say, for such a system to work successfully. Evaluators and supervisors may use inappropriate standards or apply them incorrectly; favoritism and politics are prone to enter any evaluation. Many teachers take this tack whenever discussing merit raises.

Another approach taken in discussing a meritocratic system is to argue that it is essentially unfair until equal opportunities become fully implemented; otherwise those who have not been denied opportunities will have a decisive advantage over others who were not so fortunate. Other than a small number of exceptional cases, those who rise to the top, are those whose opportunities were not denied. Since it may be a generation or more before equal opportunities are fully provided, to institute a meritocratic system prior to that time will, in principle, be ineffectual and a denial of the basic concept of merit. We need not reiterate the importance of equal opportunity; however, while many wait for such practices to become widespread, evaluation of performance will continue, either on the basis of artificial distinctions or in terms of a quasi-meritocratic approach. Some would prefer to take their chances with the latter, believing that at least it is more just and equitable, in spite of its ostensible shortcomings.

A meritocracy values competitiveness, willingness to learn and adapt quickly to new situations and tasks. It would tend to devalue gregariousness and advancement through political manipulation, even though it may not be able to entirely eliminate these factors. Education is of vital importance because one will no longer be able to depend upon artificial distinctions for advancement.

A meritocracy feeds on specialized talent. The need for specialists to communicate with one another and with the policy makers will grow more acute as specialization and competition are accentuated. A need will exist for broadly educated generalists who can fill the communications barrier caused by these trends. Unfortunately, our universities are preparing few persons who can capably assume this important role. But since policy decisions often demand an ability to deal with findings from several disciplines, policy decisions are unlikely to be handled as intelligently as desired until this deficiency is overcome.

A meritocracy would appear to prolong dependency due to the lengthy period of specialized education required and the inability of students during this period to hold a full-time job. This problem may give rise to ambivalent tendencies in youth: on one hand, they wish to live their own lives and think of themselves as adults while, on the other, their financial dependency and obligations to their parents may mean that their parents still consider them in need of their counsel as to how life should be lived. For some students this tends to breed a sense of distrust and alienation. It is likely that a meritocracy will subsidize youth while they attend school. A meritocratic society will invest in ability and intelligence rather than property, commodities, and weaponry. Since shortages of these skills exist in any population, it will be essential that talented youth are recognized early and provided the best education possible. But in order to make this possible, teachers themselves will have to represent some of the most outstanding talent in society. If we are to attract such talent to the teaching profession, it will be necessary to pay them as well as scientists in industry. Furthermore, schools will need to be reorganized so that the administrative machinery facilitates and promotes, rather than impedes, learning.

Artificial distinctions in industry, including seniority, will gradually have to yield to merit for the system to be complete. A meritocracy, more than any other type of system, will find the young occupying the important positions of power. This shift is due to the fact that a rapidly changing society quickly renders the skills of the older generation obsolete, and since it is easier to learn skills for the first time than to unlearn obsolete skills, the young have a decisive advantage. The young, however, are faced with the same problems as they grow older, and those who are highly flexible, who have continued to learn through the years, may be in the best position to avoid having their positions unsurped by a younger generation. Furthermore, the educational system will be expected to prepare the young with flexible talents, as well as the interest, intellectual curiosity, and the requisite abilities for successful lifetime learning. But since talents of this type, too, are limited in any population, many persons will find themselves displaced by more youthful talent as they approach middle age.

As the barriers to equality of educational opportunity progressively fall, people who fail to measure up to meritocratic criteria will be left without the psychological props which formerly sustained them in their failure — discrimination on the basis of race, religion, nationality, or family background. Society will need to protect these persons by resocializing them and offering them a role to play which will provide a modicum of self-respect. It may be that those who fail at the intellectual tasks may succeed at the physical tasks (even though here some will lack the intelligence or the requisite abilities). These people may become sports heroes or offer entertainment. Others, with different skills, will likely be employed in service industries: as caretakers, domestics, in restaurants, transportation, entertainment, and other areas.

It could be urged that the schools should cultivate all human talents whether or not they are needed at the particular time in society. But this task would be unrealistic, for societies have always selected certain abilities to reward, others to ignore or discourage. It is unlikely that a meritocracy will be any different, except its talent demands are more severe than traditional systems of vocational advancement; therefore, a large segment of the population will have to be resocialized to accept merit and reconcile itself to positions of lower status. Since it will be several decades before many of these changes come about, it will provide educators and policy-makers time to reorient and resocialize the population (assuming, of course, that adequate planning is quickly undertaken).

Autonomy and Full Humanness

In collectivized, postindustrial societies, there are many threats to personal autonomy. Not only is life more urbanized and other-directed, but privacy is threatened by such developments as electronic eavesdropping and proposals for a national data bank which could provide detailed information, from birth to death, on every citizen — and citizens may not be permitted to examine and correct false and damaging information. Computers have made possible for the first time the storage and transmission of vast amounts of data. Such data are valuable to demographers, employers, credit unions, and many other groups. That the data will be used wisely with due respect for the individual's right to privacy is a question that remains unanswered at present. However, unless policies are quickly established to strictly regulate the use of data, abuses will doubtlessly occur.

Personal autonomy, however, is far more than respect for the individual's right to privacy, even though this is a necessary ingredient. The basis for autonomy lies in the ability of the individual to choose intelligently for himself the essential direction for his life. Such a choice means that he has to make independent value judgments and assume

The basis for autonomy lies in the ability
of the individual to choose intelligently for
himself the essential direction of his life.

responsibility for them rather than shift the blame to others or to the group whenever the judgment and the course of action which follows prove to be faulty. The individual comes to feel that the center of evaluation lies within himself. This feeling does not mean that he ignores others or shuns the findings of authorities in various fields. Rather, it is the individual's task to assess the validity of the various sources of information and the different findings and value systems available to him and decide — after all the information is gathered and evaluated — the best course of action for himself. To do so necessitates resisting social pressures to go along with the group and engage in respectable role-playing in order to avoid the loss of personal autonomy.

It has been said that "man's reach exceeds his grasp." This saying applies not only to his material desires and his quest for happiness, but equally as well to his ability to use his intelligence. In spite of the many social and technological advances made possible through the wise use of human intelligence, the philosophical systems and religious perspectives which have been constructed to explain the world have failed to demonstrate that any of these taken by themselves have the explanatory power to answer all of the perennial questions that man puts to himself. The problems of human existence transcend the logical categories that man has constructed. But it does not follow that reflective thinking is of little avail. Actually, it will carry him as far as the conceptual and theoretical schemes will permit, and as extant systems prove inadequate, more adequate ones will need to be devised.

Man also recognizes another facet of his existence that is not always encompassed by his rationalistic systems: that the world is essentially indifferent to human aspiration, that the world is inhospitable to the person. Existentialists inject the further point that there is no sufficient reason for things being what they are rather than something else. Man lives, as they would say, in a senseless or absurd world. Turning from an ontological to a social and political level, this feeling is exacerbated by the forces of cultural life which engender alienation, a sense of dehumanization, and a lack of genuine community. Some of this alienation can be ameliorated; but man's state in the universe remains unaltered as one of the obdurate facts of his existence unless, of course, we adopt an ontological perspective more hospitable to man. Assuming that man's ontological predicament is as suggested, one need not resign himself to his fate; rather, he can rebel against the forces that would render existence senseless. It is through the comic spirit that man can laugh at himself. It enables him to accept without defeat, without fear

Man must be a creator as well as a receiver of values.

or illusion the facets of his existence which cannot be changed. At the same time, his growing sense of personal autonomy will enable him to guide his life in terms of his own choices; it will provide a sense of controlling rather than being controlled. As much as his power and judgment permit, the individual will be in charge of his own life and what he can become.

The tragic vision of one's ontological position in the universe is tempered by the fact one is not fully alive, not fully human unless he is fully conscious of the great joys and sorrows. Rather than living as some do in a gray world of depression in which the full range of human feeling has been closed off, man needs to be open to the full range of human feelings. He must taste tragedy before he can fully appreciate joy.

Man must be a creator as well as a receiver of values. Therefore, he needs a productive orientation to life in order to create, whether it be in the home, school, or community. This orientation is maintained by the full use of one's abilities, as well as by overcoming the natural and cultural forces which serve to vitiate productivity and despoil human creations. By cultivating a sense of identity, along with a productive orientation, one avoids the stifling of human ability by the alienative forces in the larger society. But there are limitations: "Time is a wrecker, Death a murderer," but within them much is still possible(13).

For man to have dignity, the constitutional rights of all must be protected and guaranteed. Too often the protagonists in this struggle have been few in number. Those who struggle for their own freedom by seeing that others can enjoy their rights are still all too rare. It is true that a few who have dedicated their lives to these ends, as well as their own full development, have become more fully human than their fellows: among them are Bertrand Russell, Martin Luther King, Jr., Albert Schweitzer, and Gandhi. It is through the actions of men united by the common goal of guaranteeing basic human rights for all persons that human dignity survives the forces of enslavement. Only in this way can fraternity acquire its true significance. We should strive, as Franz Fanon suggests, to provide the conditions where each of the oppressed can "be a man among men . . . to come lithe and young into a world that [is] ours and to help build it together."(14)

Questions for Discussion

1. Of the many critical problems facing society in the immediate future, which ones concern you the most at the present time? Why?

2. In what way do you believe that you can contribute to the solution of these problems? To what extent has your formal education prepared you to deal with these problems?

3. What are the most significant changes that need to be made in our educational systems if they are to meet the challenges in the decades ahead?

4. How will the growth of meritocratic systems affect you, especially in terms of developing a productive orientation to your work and your career?

5. Do you believe it will still be possible in the immediate future to maintain a sense of personal autonomy in spite of the many alienative and dehumanizing forces in the culture? If affirmative, how can it best be accomplished?

For Further Reading

An assessment of problems and possibilities for this decade is made by Robert L. Heilbroner, "Priorities for the Seventies," *Saturday Review* (January 3, 1970): 17. Some believe that there is still much to be learned from history which can be applied to the present. Others, such as Margaret Mead, believe that in many respects our age is discontinuous with the past and, perhaps, youth is the only age group capable of successful adaptation. She argues these and other points in her "Youth Revolt: The Future is Now," *Saturday Review* (January 10, 1970): 23. The immense changes which have occurred in our generation are dramatically presented and analyzed in Alvin Roffler's "Future Shock" *Playboy* 17 (February 1970): 94.

An important study that developed out of the deliberations of the American Academy of Arts and Sciences is found in the special issue "Toward the Year 2000: Work in Progress," *Daedalus* 96 (Summer 1967). A projection and assessment of various trends in the future may be found in Donald N. Michael's study, *The Next Generation,* New York: Vintage Books, 1965. For a discussion of some of the problems ahead for the university see "The Embattled University," *Daedalus* 99 (Winter 1970).

Planning for change is a vital task in preparing ourselves for the future. Of help here is Donald Michael's *The Unprepared Society*, New York: Basic Books, 1968. A series, which was conducted in the Rocky Mountain region, is titled *Designing Education for the Future*, Edgar Morphet and Charles D. Ryan, eds. Those which bear upon the concerns of this chapter are *Prospective Changes in Society*, no. 1; *Implications of Education for Prospective Changes in Society*, no. 2; *Planning and Effecting Needed Changes in Education*, no. 3. Each book was published by Citation Press in New York in 1967.

In the same genre as such anti-utopian novels as Orwell's *1984* and Huxley's *Brave New World*, is Michael Young's imaginative and witty book, *The Rise of the Meritocracy, 1870-2033*, Baltimore: Penguin Books, 1961. Among other comments on the meritocracy are David Riesman's "Notes on Meritocracy," *Daedalus* 96 (Summer 1967): 897-908; and John Martin Rich, "Mass Man, Popular Education, and the Meritocracy," *The Educational Forum* 32 (May 1968), 495-99.

Notes

1. Technological developments will not be of immediate concern unless they bear directly on the social and educational issues discussed. For a list of one hundred technical innovations likely by the year 2000, see: Herman Kahn and Anthony J. Wiener, "The Next Thirty-three Years: A Framework for Speculation," *Daedalus* 96 (Summer, 1967): 711-716.

2. Associated Press release (December 21, 1969).

3. Philip M. Hauser and Martin Taitel, "Population Trends — Prologue to Educational Programs," Edgar L. Morphet and Charles D. Ryan, eds., *Designing Education for the Future No. 1* (New York: Citation Press, 1967), p. 54.

4. Kahn and Wiener, "The Next Thirty-three Years," p. 727.

5. *Ibid.*, pp. 718-19.

6. Edward T. Hall, *The Hidden Dimension* (Garden City, N.Y.: Doubleday, Anchor Books, 1969).

7. Lawrence K. Frank, "The Need for a New Political Theory," *Daedalus* 96 (Summer 1967): 809-816.

8. For an analysis of the strengths and weaknesses of liberalism, see: Kenneth R. Minogue, *The Liberal Mind* (New York: Vintage Books, 1968).

9. For some of the changes in higher education purported to be brought about by student protest, see "The Fruits of Protest," *Change in Higher Education,* vol. 1, no. 6 (November-December 1969): 9-10.

10. See Theodore Roszak, *The Making of a Counter Culture* (New York: Random House, 1969).

11. Daniel Bell, "Alternate Futures," *Daedalus,* 96 (Summer 1967): 667.

12. Michael Young was probably the first to coin this term in his imaginative and witty work, *The Rise of the Meritocracy, 1870-2033* (Baltimore: Penguin Books, 1961).

13. This is an expression used by Bernard Shaw in his *Man and Superman* (Baltimore: Penguin Books, 1952).

14. Franz Fanon, *Black Skins, White Masks* (New York: Grove Press, 1967), pp. 112-113. Copyright © 1967 by Grove Press, Inc. Published by Grove Press, Inc.

Index

ABM, 315
Absurd, the, 50
Academy, 210
Acculturation, 9
Admissions tests, 259
Adjustment as goal, 21
Adler, Alfred, 14
Aeschylus, 52
Aesop, *Fables*, 209
Aesthetic overtones, 222
Aesthetic point, 224
Africa, 23
Albee, Edward, 54
Alger, Horatio, 70
Algeria, 256
Alienation: diminish, 86;
    function of expectation, 66, 68, 73,
    76; Marx, 28-30; production, 24
Altizer, Thomas J. J., 36
Ambiguity, 49
America, nineteenth century, 70
American Indian, 29
American scientists, 246

American university, role conflict in
    development, 242-255
Analytic statements, 148
Anglo-American theologians, 43
Animal behavior, 10
Anomie, 73
Anxiety, 44-45
Appreciation, 153, 220, 221
Appreciative dimension, 222
Apprenticeship, 245, 249, 251
Argonne, 320
Aristocratic thought, 244
Aristocratic tradition, 210
Aristotle, 9-10, 53, 178, 184
Arnold, Matthew, 228, 229, 230, 234, 235
Art, 125, 126, 127, 235
Artistic feeling, 243
Asceticism, 33
Asia, 23
Assignments, 64
Association of American Universities
    (AAU), 248
Atheists, existentialist, 47

Athens, Periclean, 53
Atlanta, 257
Atmospheric Sciences Research
    Center, 310
Atomic Energy Commission, 194
Attitudes, 72
Augustine, Saint, 43
Authentic person, 49
Awareness: appreciative, 220;
    existence, 48; sensitive, 153

Back-lash, 264
Back to Methuselah, 42
Bacon, Francis, 18
Bacteriological warfare, 172
Basic drives, 7
Beckett, Samuel, 55
Behavior: learned, 9; nonverbal, 111-114
Behavioral sciences, 6, 207
Behaviorism, 16-20, 21
Behaviorist, 71
Being, existentialist term, 50
Being-itself, Tillich, 46
Belief, 136, 154-160
Bellack, Arno A., 108-109, 117, 118
Bentham, Jeremey, 316
Bergson, Henri, 43
Berkeley, 260
Berlin University, 26
Biogenesis, 38-40
Biological factors, 8
Biosphere, 40
Black militancy, 259
Black study programs, 172
Bonhoeffer, Dietrich, 35
Boston English High School, 210
Boston public schools, 78
Bo tree, 33
Bourgeoisie, 26, 54
Boyle's Law, 186
Brahmanism, 33
Brecht, Bertolt, 54
British empiricism, 246
Broad field courses, 172, 199
Bronowski, J., 235, 238
Brookhaven, 320
Brown vs. Board of Education, 299-300
Bruner, Jerome S., 94, 102-105
Bruno, Giordano, 189
Brunstein, Robert, 54
Brutalization, 74
Buber, Martin, 84, 138, 139
Buddha, 32, 33
Buddhism, 32-35, 57
Bultmann, Rudolf, 35

Bureaucracy, 283, 297
Burma, 33, 256

Cambodia, 86
Camus, Albert, 47, 50, 54
Capitalism, 26
Capitalist, 27
Career plans, 199
Careers, embarking on, 251
Castiglione, Baldassare, Conte, 126,
    130, 209
Categorical imperatives, 82
Causal determinism, 15, 51
Causal law, 185
Certainty, 150, 152, 153, 154
Certitude, 147-154
Ceylon, 33
Chance, 181
Character: shaping, 252; training, 245
Chauvinism, 131
Chekhov, Anton, 54
Chemical warfare, 172
Chicago, 263
China, 33, 86
Chinard, Gilbert, 213
Christ, 32, 44
Christian piety, 211
Christian revelation, 44
Christian theological perspective, 43
Christianity, 32
Christology, 36
Church-related colleges, 243
CIA, 259
Cicero, 130
Ciceronian, 227
Ciceronianism, 208
Ciceronianist, 212
Cincinnati, 257
Civil Rights Commission Report, 298
Civil rights movement, 259, 260, 315
Class conflict, 26
Classical humanist, 212
Classicists, 210, 211, 243
Classics, 210
Classroom, dehumanization in, 74-80
Classroom climate, 109-111
Classroom discourse, 106
Class system, 28
Class war, 26
Coleman, James S., 297, 299
College education, 120-122
Colleges, liberal arts, 242
Colonial period, 210
Comenius, 130, 211
Comic spirit, 55

Communication, 72, 108, 111
Communism, 28
Communist nations, 315
Communist Party, 29
Community control, 301
Competencies, 134-137
Comte, Auguste, 18, 190
Concepts, use of, 96
Conditioning, 17
Conditioning skills, 100
Conduct code, 57
Conformity, mass, 288, 289
Confucianism, 32
Connoisseur, 125-127
Consciousness, 39, 80
Consensus, 286
Conservation of matter, 183
Constitution, 276
Consulting services, 253
Contemporary society, 174, 192, 204
Contextualist position, 234
Contingent statements, 149
Controls, 280-282
Copernicus, 189
CORE, 257
Cornell, 246
Cosmic self, 33
Courses, broad field, 199
Courtier, 126, 209
Creative dimension, 216-220
Creative focus, 218
Creative intelligence, 79
Creativity, 22, 216, 217
Criticism, 134, 136
Cultural differences, 112
Culture, defined, 8
Culture, liberal, 242, 249
Curiosity: intellectual, 164; retreats
    from self, 49
Curriculum: classical, 210; misleading
    ideal, 153; reorganized, 66; school,
    152; science, 196-201; students'
    concerns, 66
Czechoslovakia, 29

Dakota Indians, 79
Darwinian age, 247
Darwinism, 228
Das Kapital, 26
Da Vinci, Leonardo, 126, 128
Death, 86
Death at an Early Age, 78
Death of God Movement, 35-38, 54
Debray, 261
De facto segregation, 300

De Gaulle, Charles, 86, 256
Dehumanization, 26, 65, 74-80, 86
Dehumanizing force, 24
Dehumanizing situations, 76
Democracies, Western, 288
Democratic Party, 264
Democratic principles, 254
Democratic societies, 134
Democritus, 183, 184
Denmark, 312
Department of Defense, 192, 256, 259
Depersonalization, 68
Deprivation, 19
Descartes, 47
Desires, 165
Detachment, 134
Detergents, 195
Determinism, causal, 51
Detroit, 257
Dewey, John, 141, 233
Dialectical materialism, 26
Dictatorship of the proletariat, 27-28
Dignity, 87, 328
Dilettante, 125, 127
Dimension, appreciative, 220-223
Diploma mills, 246
Discipline: mental, 242; teachers, 78;
    theory, 243, 246
Discipline-centered program, 199
Disciplines, 206
Discontinuity, 40
Discoveries, university, 253
Divine Incarnations, 32
Dogmatism, 128
DNA molecule, 188
Domestic problems, 314-315
Domestic strife, 315-316
Drive, 19
DuBois Clubs, 263
Dukkha, 33
Durkheim, Emile, 73, 278

Earth science, 199
Economic equality, 290
Economic point of view, 224
Economic values, 320
Educated man: assessing the, 129-139;
    misconceptions, 120-129;
    reassessment, 137-138
Education: college, 120-122; conditioning,
    17; principal objective, 136
Educational factors, 7
Edwards, Paul, 46
Egalitarian approach, 258
Egalitarians, 259

Ego, 12, 14
Eightfold Path, 34
Eisenhower administration, 29
Elitist: ideals, 132-134; theory, 286, 287
Elizabethan England, 53
Ellison, Ralph, 77
Elyot, Thomas, 130, 209
Emerson, Ralph Waldo, 112
Empiricism, 19, 246
Employment, full-time, 251
Encyclopedic memory, 122-124
Ends, 232
Engels, Frederick, 24
England, Elizabethan, 53
English tradition, 228
Enjoyment, 222
Enlightenment, 30, 47-48, 70, 180,
   190, 206, 316
Entropy, 42
Episode: classroom discourse, 106;
   coordinate, 107
Equalitarian ideals, 132-134
Equality: arguments against, 287-292;
   political system, 285-287; reassessed,
   292-296; term, 29
Equilibrium models, 266
Erasmus, 130, 208
Eros, 11
Erotic individuals, 14
Error, elimination of, 233
Esslin, Martin, 56
Estes, William K., 92
Eternal soul, 33
Ethical premises, 233
Ethnocentrism, 128, 131
Europe, 23
Existentialism: drama, 55; perspective,
   47-52; Tillich's, 43-47
Existentialists, 326
Existential revolt, 54
Experience: broad, 127-129; ethical
   premises, 233; sense, 151
Externality, 67-68
Evaluation, 225
Evaluative process, 223
Evaluative questions, 146
Evidence, 97
Evolution, 40, 41
Evolutionary process, 38

Facts, 122, 123, 165
Fanon, Franz, 261
Fame and success, 124-125
Fatalism, 51
Federal aid, 275

Federal government, 6
Feuerbach, Ludwig Andreas, 25
Finiteness, 43
Finitude, 44
Flagstaff, 310
Flanders, Ned A., 110-111
Flew, Antony, 98
Foreign wars, 314-315
Formal curriculum, 122
Franklin, Benjamin, 210
Freedom: choice, 172; human, 51;
   inquiry, 189, 193; price, 292; struggle
   for, 328; term, 29
Freedoms, 254
Free universities, 171
Free will, 49
French Resistance, 86
French Socialists, 26
Freud, Sigmund, 11, 22, 55
Freudianism, 11-16
Fromm, Erich, 233
Function-dysfunctional model, 138

Gage, N. L., 94
Galileo, 178, 181, 184, 189
Galloway, Charles M., 113
Gandhi, 328
Gautama, 33
Gay-Lussac's Law, 186
Genet, Jean, 54
Geogenesis, 38
Geosphere, 38
Getzels, Jacob W., 216
German universities, 211
Germany, 246
Gilman, Daniel Coit, 246, 247
Goals, 111, 187
God, 32, 35-38, 54
Goethe, 128
Gossip, retreats from self, 49
Governor, 209
Grading system, 64
Graduate education, 211, 246
Graduate schools, 243, 293
Gravitation, Law of, 182
Great Society, 315
Greece, 6
Greek dramas, 52
Greeks, 112
Green, T. H., 316
Green, Thomas F., 96
Guevera, Che, 261

Habits, 153
Hall, Edward T., 112, 330

Hartland-Swann, John, 159
Harvard, 246
Hauser, Phillip M., 330
Hegel, Georg W. F., 25
Hegelian idealism, 246
Heidegger, Martin, 47, 48, 49
Heisenberg, Werner, 185
Henry, Jules, 79-80
Hershey, Lewis B., 258
High-brow, 245
Higher education: basic function, 251;
    humanistic roles, 265-268; role
    conflict, 242; socialization, 252;
    success, 124
Hilgard, Ernest R., 92
Hinduism, 32
Homeostasis, 21
Honor program, 172
Hopi Indians, 79
Human affairs, 189-196
Human betterment, 137
Humaness, 324-328
Humanism, new, 208
Humanistic psychology, 20-23
Humanities: origin, 207-213;
    reinterpreting, 213-216
Human nature, 4-7, 10
Humiliation, 74-75, 86
Hungary, 29
Huxley, T. H., 228, 231
Hypothetical imperatives, 82

I, response to attitudes of others, 72
I.B.M., 65
Ibsen, Henrik, 54
Id, 12, 14
Ideal: continuous progress, 70; relative,
    129-132; utility, 249
Idealism, 243
Identity: defined, 81; self-knowledge,
    167; sense of, 74, 168; shaped, 68
I-It, subject-object relationship, 84
Illusory happiness, 28
Illusory perception, 148
Impartiality, 150
Indeterminacy principle, 185
India, 256
Indian philosophy, 32
Indians, 80
Individualization, 45, 71
Indivisible person, 81
Indoctrination, 95, 97-100
Inductive method, 18
Industrial age, 231
Industrialization, 231

Industrial Revolution, 37
Infantile, 14
Infantile sexuality, 13
Influence, teacher, 109-111
Informal educational opportunity, 214
Information, autobiographical, 166, 167
Inner-city schools, 78
Inner motivations, 165
Inner self, 19
Inquiry, 153, 189, 193
Institutional goals, 277
Instrumental questions, 146
Intellectual independence, 136
Intellectualist bias, 162
Intention in teaching, 101-102
Interaction Analysis, 110
Inventions, technological, 253
Iron Curtain, 29
Issues, normative, 82-88
Italian Renaissance, 208
Italy, 256
I-Thou, mutual relation, 84, 138, 139

Jainism, 32
James, William, 211
Japan, 33
Jaspers, Carl, 47, 52
Jesus, 36, 44
Johns Hopkins, 246, 247
Johnson administration, 315
Jourard, Sidney, 71
Judaic-Christian ethic, 30
Judaic-Christian preconceptions, 34
Judaism, 32
Jung, Carl, 14
Justice, 29

Kalamazoo Case, 124
Kant, Immanuel, 43, 82-84, 137, 138
Karman, 33
Kepler, Johannes, 184
Kepler's laws, 186
Kerner Report, 299, 318
Kerr, Clark, 65
Kierkegaard, Sören, 47
Kinesthetic elements, 17
King, Martin Luther, Jr., 257
Knowing: forms of, 158; process,
    156, 157
Knowledge: certainty, 152, 153, 154;
    explosion, 245; misleading notion,
    157; new, 231; optimal structuring,
    102-103; preserving, 251; relevant,
    170-175; reliable, 147; undesirable,
    162

Korea, 33, 256
Kozol, Jonathan, 75
Krishna, 32

Labor, 23
Land-grant colleges, 246
Land-grant movement, 249
Language, 108
Languages, study of, 243
Latin America, 23, 256
Latin grammar school, 210
Laws, 181-189
Leaders of culture, 129
League for Industrial Democracy, 262
Learned behavior, 9
Learning: breadth, 243; broad, 245;
    predispositions to, 102; process, 158;
    psychological guide, 246; sequence
    required for, 102, 104; theories, 92
Leavis, F. R., 227
Left Hegelians, 25
Leibniz, Gottfried, 51, 52, 81, 128
Leveling process, 290
Liberal culture: conceptions of higher
    education, 242; ideal, 242-245,
    249, 250
Liberalism, 318
Liberals, teaching staff, 78
Liberty, 292
Life-affirming spirit, 57
Life goals, 165
Life-negating view, 56-57
Life science, 199
Life-style, 252
Literary humanists, 230
Literary men, 244, 245
Literary model, 236
Literature, 226
Locke, John, 80, 244, 315
Lock-step system, 171
Logical positivists, 191
Logic of Teaching, 106-109
Love, defined by Teilhard, 41
Low-brow, 245

MacIntyre, Alasdair, 265-266
Majority population, 133
Malcolm X, 77
Malraux, André, 86-87, 128
Man, treatment of, 15
Manipulated individual, 75
Manpower, 250, 251
Man's Fate, 87
Man's future, perils to, 309-319
Man's Hope, 86

Manual, 87
Mao Tse-tung, 261
Marcel, Gabriel, 47
Marcuse, Herbert, 261, 273
Marx, Karl, 23-30, 55, 64
Marxists, 263, 264
Maslow, Abraham, 216
Masochism, 12
Mass media, 70, 245
Materialistic values, 174
Mathematical operations, 184
McLuhan, Marshall, 70
Me, attitudes adopted, 72
Mead, George Herbert, 71, 73, 167
Means, 232
Measurement, 181-189
Measuring procedures, 184
Medicare, 290
Medievalists, 8
Medieval society, 26
Megalopolis, 313
Memory, 17
Memory, encyclopedic, 122-124
Mendel, Arthur P., 30
Merit, 294, 296
Meritocracy, 321-324
Meritocratic system, 258
Merton, Robert K., 73
Messianic revolt, 54
Methodological questions, 146
Meux, Milton, 106-109
Mexican Americans, 29
Michigan, 77
Michigan State University, 259
Michigan Supreme Court, 124
Middle Ages, 6
Middle-brow, 245
Middle class youth, 244
Mill, John Stuart, 18, 316, 317
Military-industrial complex, 172, 174
Mind, solidity of, 243
M. I. T., 259, 260
Mode of production, 26
Modernism, 212
Monads, 81
Monolog, 106
Montaigne, 130
Moonlighting, 64
Moore, Alexander, 77
Moore, G. E., 51
Moral anxiety, 44
Moral competencies, 138
Morals, shaping, 252
Moral standards, 13
Motivation, 20

Moves, pedagogical, 108
Multiversity, 65
Mumford, Lewis, 212
My self, nature of, 81

N.A.A.C.P., 78
Narcissistic individuals, 14
National Defense Education Act, 251
National goals, 251
Naturalism, 54
Naturalistic religions, 32
Naturalistic world, 43
Nature, teleological view, 40
Nature of man, 49
Natural sciences, 6
Nausea, 50
Navajo Indians, 112
Nazi Germany, 131, 139
Negro children, 78
Negroes, 29, 77, 112
Neurosis, 44
Neurotic behavior, 14
Newark, 257
New Deal, 317
Newfield, Jack, 261
New Left, 242, 248, 257, 262
New Testament, 35
Newton, 182, 184
Newtonian theory, 186
New York City, 275, 284, 304
Nietzsche, Friedrich, 35-37, 42, 45, 71,
    169, 224
Nirvana, 34
Noblesse oblige, 289
Nondemocratic societies, 132, 134
Nonverbal behavior, 111-114
Noogenesis, 38
Noosphere, 42
Normality, 22
Normative dimension, 223-225
Normative issues, 82-88
Nothing, existentialist term, 50
Nuclear weapons, 194
Nuremburg trial, 131, 139

Objectivity, 150
Obsessional individuals, 14
Observed data, identifying, 18
Office of Education, 300
Omega, 38, 41
O'Neill, Eugene, 54
Ontic anxiety, 44
Ontological perspective, 326
Ontological position, 328
Open admissions, 258

Operant behavior, 19
Opportunity: concept of equal
    educational, 285-296; educational,
    297; equality, 294
Organisms: characteristic, 187, 188;
    living, 188
Oriental Americans, 29
Original sin, 53
Orthodoxy, departure from, 46
Other selves, identity, 81
Otto, 43
Overpopulation, 312-314
Overurbanization, 313-314

Paine, Thomas, 244
Paleontologist, 38
Pansophia, 130
Participation, 45, 71, 134
Participatory democracy, 262
Pass-fail system, 172
Pathological anxiety, 44
Pavlov, Ivan, 19
Periclean Athens, 53
Permissive school, 9
Perry, Ralph Barton, 210, 212, 213
Person: concept, 80-82; educated, 137;
    rational being, 83; theory of, 81
Personal factors, 7
Personal knowledge, 174, 175
Personal understanding, 169
Pesticides, 195
Petrach, 208
Ph.D. degrees, 246, 247
Phenomenon of Man, 38
Philosophical factors, 7
Philosophy of science, 201
Phlogiston theory, 97
Physical science, 199
Physiological needs of man, 7
Piel, Gerald, 194
Pinter, Harold, 54
Pirandello, Luigi, 54
Planck, Max, 185, 187
Planning, inadequate, 318-319
Plato, 210, 244, 321
Playwrights revolt, 54
Polarity of being, 45
Political factors, 7
Political liberties, 54
Political philosophy, 316-318
Political system, 285-287
Pollution, 8, 310-311
Port Huron Statement, 262
Portugal, 256
Positivism, 18, 190

Postindustrial society, 124, 324
Posttechnological: age, 319; society, 134
Pragmatism, 250
Prejudice, 79
Price, Derek, 231
Private foundations, 6
Private learning industries, 301
Problems, approaches to, 136
Productivity, 319
Professional programs, 249
Progressive Labor Party (PLP), 263, 264
Proletariat, 26
Proof, 233
Provincialism, 128
Prussian absolutism, 26
Psychism, 40
Psychoanalysis, 11, 14
Psychogenesis, 38
Psychology: humanistic, 20-23; third
    force in, 20
Psychoneurosis, 14
Psychosphere, 40
Ptolemaic system, 189
Public service, 250
Public verification, 149
Publish or perish doctrine, 247
Pure science, 192
Puritanism, 312, 315
Puritans, 8

Quantification, 67
Quantum theory, 187
Quintilian, 130, 209
Quotas, 64

Racism, white, 299
Racists, teaching staff, 78
Radicalism, New, 261
Radicalization, 262, 264
Rama, 32
Ramparts, 259
Rational beings, 83
Rational inquiry, 266
Reacting moves, 108
Reading, 127
Realities of the Urban Classroom, 77
Reality, 243
Reason, use of, 70
Reciprocating episodes, 107
Reductionism, 17
Reflex, 19
Reformation, 37
Reichenback, Hans, 149
Reid, Thomas, 80, 81
Reinforcement, 19, 102, 105

Relative, historically and culturally, 138
Relevance, 149, 175
Relevancy, 172
Reliability, 144
Religion, 28, 32, 42
Religious orthodoxy, 54
Religious training, 245
Renaissance, 37, 126, 127, 130, 184,
    190, 228
Renaissance humanism, 210, 211
Renaissance ideals, 208
Repression, 13
Republic, 321
Republican parties, 264
Research: conceptions of, 242; function,
    246; role, 245-248; secret, 172
Respondent, behavior, 19
Responding moves, 108
Response, 19
Responsibility, 49
Restrictive school, 9
Retarded children, 132
Ricardo, David, 26
Riesman, David R., 89
Riot Commission Report, 257
RNA, 188
Robinson, John A. T., 35
Robot relationship, 75
Role playing, 71, 73
Roman ideal, 130
Ruskin, John, 227
Ryle, Gilbert, 158, 159

Sadism, 12
Sahara, 86
San Francisco State College, 261
Sartre, Jean-Paul, 47, 48, 49, 50
Savio, Mario, 255
SDS, 263, 264
Schaff, Adam, 28-29
Scheffler, Israel, 156
Schleirmacher, Friedrich, 43
Scholarly publication, 247
Schweitzer, Albert, 128
Science: human affairs, 189-196; pure,
    192; role, 192-196; search for
    evidence, 247; use, 70
Sciences and the humanities, 225-236
Scientific approach, 16
Scientific community, 180, 232
Scientific culture, 227
Scientific research, 246
Scientific socialism, 30
Scientism, 180, 191
Scientists, 232, 233

Scotia, New York, 310
Secondary education, 210
Secret research, 172
Secularism, 54
Self-concept, 72, 81, 167
Self-encapsulization, 126
Self-understanding, 162
Self-knowledge: developing, 164-170;
    impediments, 170; importance of,
    160-164; types, 165
Sense statements, 151
Sensitive awareness, 153
Sensory observation, 18
Sequence, learning, 102, 104
Serenity, 243
Service, vocational, 249
Services, universities, 253
Shakespeare, 42, 53
Shaman, 56
Shaw, Bernard, 42, 54
Siddharta, 33
Skills, 100, 153
Skinner, B. F., 18-20
Slave relationship, 75
Smith, B. Othanel, 106-109
SNCC, 257
Snow, C. P., 226, 227
Social criticism, 266
Social factors, 7
Social institutions, 76
Socialism, 27
Socialistic humanism, 28-29
Socialists, 26
Socialization, 95, 252, 279
Social justice, 30
Social relations, depersonalization, 68
Social revolt, 54
Social roles, 9
Social sciences, 6, 207
Social scientists, 266
Social Security, 290
Society, contemporary, 192, 204
Sociology, father of, 190
Soliciting moves, 108
Solidity of mind, 243
Sontag, Susan, 235
Sophocles, 52
Southeast Asia, 86
South Korea, 256
South Vietnam, 256
Soviet Union, 309
Spain, 256
Spanish Civil War, 86
Specialist, 125
Spiritual anxiety, 44

Stability, group's, 278
Standards, 223, 225
Stereotyped thinking, 128
Stereotyping, 67
Stimuli, 19
Stimulus-response model, 16
Strawson, P. F., 81-82
Strindberg, Johan A., 54
Structuralism, 16
Structuring move, 108
Student: alienated, 65; culture, 261, 262;
    I.B.M. number, 65; movements,
    255-265
Student militance, 260-265
Students, college, 199
Students, radicalizing effect, 260
Students, working class, 250
Students for a Democratic Society (SDS),
    262
Students' personal concerns, curriculum,
    66
Study and work analogy, 64
Success and fame, 124-125
Suicide rates, national, 73
Superconsciousness, 41
Super ego, 12, 14
Supernaturalism, 32, 43, 54
Supreme Court, 300
Surplus value, 27
Synthetic statements, 148
Systems, Bureaucratic Educational,
    283-285

Talent, specialized, 124
Tampa, 257
Taxation, progressive, 290
Teacher, authority figure, 98
Teacher influence, 109-111
Teacher preparation, 107
Teacher talk, 110
Teachers, humanistic qualities, 79
Teachers' nonverbal behavior, 113
Teachers' tasks, 95
Teaching: empirical studies, 105-114;
    intention in, 101-102; logic, 106-109
Teaching and indoctrination, 97-100
Teaching process, 92
Teaching staff, 78
Technical knowledge, 249
Teilhard de Chardin, Pierre, 38-42
Teleological view, 40
Tensions, 136
Tenth Amendment, 276
Tests, admission, 259
Thantos, 11

Theists, existentialists, 47
Theatre, modern, 53
Theories, relation of laws, 186
Theory, 181-189
Theory of instruction, 94
Thorndike, Edward L., 19, 211
Thus Spake Zarathustra, 224
Tibet, 33
Tillich, Paul, 35, 43-47, 71, 73, 89, 138
Tocqueville, Alexis de, 288-289
Traditional theological notion, 45
Tragedy, classical, 53
Transcendent Deity, 30, 32, 35
Trauma, 74
Treaty of London, 139
Truth, 97, 231
Truths: absolute, 56; Buddhist, 34
Turkey, 256

UNESCO, 311
Union Theological Seminary, 43
Unitary sensibility, 236
United Nations, 311
United Nations Declaration of Human
    Rights, 131, 139
United States, 311
Universal education, 211, 286
Universal law, 181
Universal man, 126
Universal Wisdom, 130
Universities: function, 251;
    multipurpose, 242
University, role conflict, 242-255
University of Chicago, 43
University roles, 251-255
Upanishads, 33
Urban values, 252
Urbanization, 54
Utility: conceptions, 242; function, 267;
    ideal, 249, 250; role, 248-251
Utopianism, 29

Vahanian, Gabriel, 36, 62
Van Gogh, Vincent, 224
Values, 328: cross-cultural, 138-139;
    democratic, 286; man creates, 50;
    students', 261
Value system, 52
Vedic tradition, 33

Verbal behavior, 112
Verification, public, 149
Verification Principle, 190
Victorian attitudes, 14
Victorians, 8
Vietnam, 256, 261, 262, 315
Vietnam war, 258, 259, 260
Vocationalism, 249
Vocational preparation, 245, 249
Vocational service, 249
Vocational training, 267

Walnut Trees of Altenburg, 87
Warfare, 172
Warfare state, 256
Watson, John B., 16-18
Weber, Max, 283
Welfare, 290
Weltanschauung, 52
West, religions of, 32
Western culture, 8, 74
West Germany, 256
Whitehead, Alfred North, 212
White racism, 257
Whole man, development, 243
Whyte, William H., 70
Williams, Tennesse, 54
Will power, 19
Wilson, John, 99
Within, consciousness, 39
Wittgenstein, Ludwig, 108
Women, emancipation, 312
Woozley, A. D., 154-155, 177
Work, 319
Work, man's, 24
Working class students, 250
World government, 309-311
World of work, 320
World war, second, 47, 65, 86, 257
World wars, 54

Young Americans for Freedom (YAF),
    264
Young Democrats, 264
Young Republicans, 264
Youth problems, 65

Zen, 261
Zuni Indians, 79

DATE DUE

DEMCO 38-296